"Will A[_____] [_____]
Take the Place
of Grass?"

"There is an increasing number of injuries on all three forms of artificial turf as compared to natural grass. . . . Five stadiums with the highest major injury rates, and 10 of the 12 most dangerous, each have synthetic turf surfaces. On the other hand, the four lowest in major injury rates, and 10 of the 11 least dangerous, all have natural grass. . . ."

More on this controversy,
and others, in

**The Pocket Book of PRO FOOTBALL
1977**

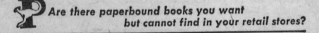

The Pocket Book of
PRO FOOTBALL 1977

Edited by Herbert M. Furlow
illustrated

A KANGAROO BOOK
PUBLISHED BY POCKET BOOKS NEW YORK

THE POCKET BOOK OF PRO FOOTBALL

POCKET BOOK edition published August, 1977

This original POCKET BOOK edition is printed from brand-new
plates made from newly set, clear, easy-to-read type.
POCKET BOOK editions are published by
POCKET BOOKS,
a Simon & Schuster Division of
GULF & WESTERN CORPORATION
1230 Avenue of the Americas,
New York, N.Y. 10020.
Trademarks registered in the United States
and other countries.

ISBN: 0-671-81344-7.
Published by POCKET BOOKS, New York.

Printed in the U.S.A.

Acknowledgments

The writing in *The Pocket Book of Pro Football 1977* is by Norman MacLean and myself. Special thanks go again this year to the National Football League's public-relations office in New York City and to all 28 of the NFL's club publicity directors. A word of appreciation also to Don R. Smith, Director of the Professional Football Hall of Fame in Canton, Ohio, who supplied research material for an expanded Hall of Fame section in this POCKET BOOK.

—Herbert M. Furlow, Editor

New York City
1977

Contents

THE 1977 NFL COLLEGE DRAFT

SUPER FEATURE

NFL 1976 STATISTICS

LET'S LOOK AT THE RECORDS

OFFICIATING IN THE NFL

1977
NATIONAL FOOTBALL LEAGUE
TELEVISION SCHEDULE

REGULAR SEASON

Sept. 19	San Francisco at Pittsburgh (night)	ABC
Sept. 26	New England at Cleveland (night)	ABC
Oct. 3	Oakland at Kansas City (night)	ABC
Oct. 10	Los Angeles at Chicago (night)	ABC
Oct. 17	Cincinnati at Pittsburgh (night)	ABC
Oct. 24	Minnesota at Los Angeles (night)	ABC
Oct. 31	N.Y. Giants at St. Louis (night)	ABC
Nov. 7	Washington at Baltimore (night)	ABC
Nov. 14	St. Louis at Dallas (night)	ABC
Nov. 21	Green Bay at Washington (night)	ABC
⌠Nov. 24	Chicago at Detroit	CBS
⌡Nov. 24	Miami at St. Louis	NBC
Nov. 28	Buffalo at Oakland (night)	ABC
Dec. 5	Baltimore at Miami (night)	ABC
⌠Dec. 10	Pittsburgh at Cincinnati	NBC
⌡Dec. 10	Washington at St. Louis	CBS
Dec. 12	Dallas at San Francisco (night)	ABC
⌠Dec. 17	Los Angeles at Washington	CBS
⟨Dec. 17	Buffalo at Miami	NBC
⌡Dec. 17	Minnesota at Detroit (night)	ABC

TV DOUBLEHEADER GAMES

(The following games will be seen on Sunday in many areas as parts of television "doubleheaders.")

Sept. 18	Dallas at Minnesota	CBS
Sept. 25	Oakland at Pittsburgh	NBC
Oct. 2	St. Louis at Washington	CBS
Oct. 9	Dallas at St. Louis	CBS
Oct. 16	Denver at Oakland	NBC
Oct. 16	Washington at Dallas	CBS
Oct. 23	Baltimore at New England	NBC
Oct. 30	Pittsburgh at Baltimore	NBC
Nov. 6	St. Louis at Minnesota	CBS
Nov. 13	Cincinnati at Minnesota	NBC
Nov. 20	Dallas at Pittsburgh	CBS
Nov. 27	Dallas at Washington	CBS
Dec. 4	Oakland at Los Angeles	NBC
Dec. 11	Minnesota at Oakland	CBS
Dec. 18	New England at Baltimore	NBC

POSTSEASON CHAMPIONSHIP GAMES

Dec. 24	AFC Divisional Playoffs	NBC
Dec. 26	NFC Divisional Playoffs	CBS
⌠Jan. 1	AFC Championship Game	NBC
⌡Jan. 1	NFC Championship Game	CBS
Jan. 15	Super Bowl XII at the Louisiana Superdome, New Orleans	CBS
Jan. 23	AFC–NFC Pro Bowl at Tampa (night)	ABC

1

LOOKING TOWARD SUPER BOWL XII

The Oakland Raiders, after huffing and puffing for years and years, finally made it, and there's every reason to believe they can do it again. Moreover, history indicates that any other club that desires to win the Super Bowl (and which one doesn't), will have to beat the Raiders first. The records show that the eventual winners of Super Bowls III, IV, V, VIII, IX, and X all defeated the Raiders in the playoffs before they copped the big prize. So it would seem that getting past Oakland is the first order of business.

The Steelers haven't retired yet, and they're eminently capable of storming back and taking it all. But the Raiders now have that intangible something called "momentum" and something even more important—the confidence that goes with being a Super Bowl winner. Cincinnati won't be satisfied with being a mere contender forever, and the Bengals could choose this as the year to break out of whatever keeps them from having a playoff role. The New England Patriots have already served notice that, henceforth, they'll have to be reckoned with—as they had to be last season when the Raiders barely got by them, 24–21.

The varied fortunes of the Los Angeles Rams bid fair to turn this season, with a Super Bowl berth in the offing. But Dallas is just as strong as, if not stronger than, Los Angeles, and the Minnesota Vikings cannot be left out of Super Bowl speculation for the foreseeable future, at least. St. Louis, Chicago, and San Francisco threaten to disrupt any forecast that dares ignore their claims as contenders.

Keep your season tickets or your TV sets handy. It's going to be another NFL spectacular.

NATIONAL FOOTBALL LEAGUE

1977 PREDICTIONS

American Conference

Eastern Division

1. NEW ENGLAND PATRIOTS	Ready to run for all the Beans
2. BALTIMORE COLTS	Bert Jones & Company should do well, even without Joe Thomas running the operation
3. MIAMI DOLPHINS	Don Shula's club will have to struggle to finish this high if defense isn't strengthened
4. BUFFALO BILLS	O. J. is back, but the Bills may need more time with Ringo before yelling Bingo
5. NEW YORK JETS	The coaching musical chairs continues as the Joe Namath era comes to an end

Central Division

1. CINCINNATI BENGALS	Doors do open if you knock long enough
2. PITTSBURGH STEELERS	Still a solid threat to rivet themselves to the top
3. CLEVELAND BROWNS	Forrest Gregg is bringing the Browns along, and they could become troublemakers
4. HOUSTON OILERS	They'll be trying to regain lost momentum

Western Division

1. OAKLAND RAIDERS	Will it be as hard to stay there as it was to get there?
2. SAN DIEGO CHARGERS	Steady improvement keeps the Chargers on the upgrade
3. DENVER BRONCOS	Quarterbacking still an unsettling factor
4. KANSAS CITY CHIEFS	Wiggin will again try to bring things up to date in Kansas City
5. SEATTLE SEAHAWKS	First season in their new permanent home, the AFC West

Wild Card Playoff Team: Pittsburgh Steelers
Super Bowl XII: Oakland Raiders

National Conference

Eastern Division

1. DALLAS COWBOYS	It just doesn't seem logical any other way
2. ST. LOUIS CARDINALS	A victory-oriented club, and they just might take off like rockets instead of redbirds
3. WASHINGTON REDSKINS	Whoever leads, they'll be pushing and shoving to get at them . . .
4. PHILADELPHIA EAGLES	Even William Penn would get a tryout at quarterback
5. NEW YORK GIANTS	The best pro football team in New Jersey

Central Division

1. MINNESOTA VIKINGS	Now it's Minnesota's turn to take the "almost-but-not-quite" role vacated by Oakland
2. CHICAGO BEARS	Which way? Walter Payton knows his directions and they're . . . up
3. DETROIT LIONS	Tommy Hudspeth wants a new model in Carville
4. GREEN BAY PACKERS	No resurgence in view . . . yet
5. TAMPA BAY BUCCANEERS	Whoever thought a team from Tampa Bay would **ever** play in Minnesota?

Western Division

1. LOS ANGELES RAMS	Right back, but will they find it duck soup in the Super Bowl?
2. SAN FRANCISCO 49ERS	They'll mount the main challenge to L.A.
3. NEW ORLEANS SAINTS	Way, **way** down yonder in New Orleans
4. ATLANTA FALCONS	Still trying to join the Contenders Club

Wild Card Playoff Team: St. Louis Cardinals
Super Bowl XII: Los Angeles Rams

AMERICAN
FOOTBALL
CONFERENCE

The National Football League has six new coaches going into the 1977 season, and the American Conference has exactly half of them. Barring the miraculous, however, there seems little chance that Jim Ringo at Buffalo, Tommy Hudspeth in Detroit, or Walt Michaels of the New York Jets will be able to disrupt the AFC leaders. And again, it appears that Oakland will lead the way, closely pushed by Cincinnati, Pittsburgh, New England, and Baltimore, with Cleveland and perhaps San Diego straining to break into the upper echelons.

Ken Stabler has assumed the classic quarterbacking role of Super Bowl winners, much in the manner of his predecessors—Bart Starr of Green Bay, Joe Namath of the New York Jets, Len Dawson of Kansas City, Johnny Unitas of Baltimore, Roger Staubach of Dallas, Bob Griese of Miami, and Terry Bradshaw of Pittsburgh. As such, Stabler will be a difficult advantage for Oakland's opposition to overcome, because the Raider quarterback is surely going to get better before he gets worse and levels off on that plateau that all up-and-coming signal-callers reach sooner or later. Oakland's challenge in the AFC West could come from either San Diego or Denver; the Chargers especially have been displaying a growing tendency to upset the apple cart whenever one pulls into their path.

Look for the Bengals to give the Steelers another down-to-the-wire, tough battle for the lead in the AFC

Central. Both clubs wound up 10–4 last season, with Pittsburgh getting the nod as division winner under the NFL's end-of-season tie-breaking rules. If Coach Bill Johnson can give the Bengal defense a stiffer stance, Cincinnati will be very tough to handle regardless of which unit is on the field. The Steelers, meanwhile, will be playing their usual brand of first-class pro football, but the opposing teams *will* have the psychological advantage of being underdogs—a role consistent winners cannot assume.

Some expert observers will tell you that Cleveland was last season's most improved team; Forrest Gregg brought the Browns from a 3–11 record in 1975 to 9–5 in 1976. It was impressive, and could provide the momentum to keep the Browns rolling into the new campaign with a virtue called determination. As for Houston, Coach Bum Phillips faces the task of getting the Oilers back onto the track they were following so well a couple of seasons ago.

Anyone who saw the New England Patriots play last season is convinced that Chuck Fairbanks is now ready to make his pitch for the Big Top. The Patriots are not only talented, they're young, and pro football thrives on that kind of combination. Baltimore will battle the Patriots all over the place, and could retain its hold on the AFC East title, but it'll be a rhubarb. Don Shula's Dolphins face extensive defensive problems, brought on by a long series of injuries, and O. J. Simpson is ready to help Buffalo get back on the road with Jim Ringo running things. Walt Michaels takes over as the New York Jets, once again, start on the long road back.

NEW ENGLAND PATRIOTS

Head Coach: Chuck Fairbanks
5th Year   Record: 26–30

1976 RECORD (11–3) (capital letters indicate home games)			1977 SCHEDULE (capital letters indicate home games)	
13	BALTIMORE	27	KANSAS CITY	Sept. 18
30	MIAMI	14	Cleveland (night, TV)	Sept. 26
30	Pittsburgh	27	N.Y. Jets	Oct. 2
48	OAKLAND	17	SEATTLE	Oct. 9
10	Detroit	30	San Diego	Oct. 16
41	N.Y. JETS	27	BALTIMORE	Oct. 23
26	BUFFALO	22	N.Y. JETS	Oct. 30
3	Miami	10	BUFFALO	Nov. 6
20	Buffalo	10	Miami	Nov. 13
21	Baltimore	14	Buffalo	Nov. 20
38	N.Y. Jets	24	PHILADELPHIA	Nov. 27
38	DENVER	14	Atlanta	Dec. 4
27	NEW ORLEANS	6	MIAMI	Dec. 11
31	Tampa Bay	14	Baltimore	Dec. 18
	Playoffs			
21	Oakland	24		

When it comes to choosing likely-looking rookies, Coach Chuck Fairbanks has very nearly set himself in a class by himself. Last year, for instance, he became known as a master trader by sending Jim Plunkett off to San Francisco in an exchange that enabled Fairbanks to have *three* first-round draft selections. And how did the former Oklahoma coach utilize these blue-ribbon choices? Consider:

• As choice No. 5 (in the first round), he selected Mike Haynes, the Arizona State All-America cornerback.
• No. 12 in the first round was Pete Brock, the All-America center from Colorado.

• And No. 21 was Tim Fox, another All-America defensive back, this time from Purdue.

Taken together, these three virtually turned New England around, giving the Patriots an 11–3 season and sending them into the playoffs via the wild-card route. And you'll find Patriot partisans who'll still argue that Oakland's Raiders were riding a wave of good luck when they knocked off New England 24–21 in the AFC divisional playoffs. But for the crazy bounce of a football, they insist, their Patriots would have been in the Super Bowl.

Fox and Haynes, as most informed football fans know, went on to make the all-rookie teams as they provided the Patriots with a badly needed defensive secondary that would work. Brock made the team as center (and part-time tight end) while becoming part of an offensive line that demonstrated considerable improvement over the 1975 model. Whether Fairbanks' choice of 1977 draftees will prove as notable remains, of course, to be seen. But the Patriots had five selections in the first three rounds, including first-round choices Raymond Clayborn, a defensive back from Texas, and Stanley Morgan, a wide receiver lately of the Tennessee Vols.

Quarterbacking was another strong factor in the New England surge from a 3–11 record in 1975 to a startling reversal of the numbers in 1976. Here, Fairbanks put everything in the hands of a second-year man, Steve Grogan, who had been a fifth-round draft choice out of Kansas State. Could Grogan possibly step into Plunkett's shoes? The answer became a resounding affirmative as Grogan demonstrated a remarkable quickness and, even more importantly, a leadership ability the Patriots had lumbered disastrously along without for some time.

Grogan threw for 18 touchdown passes, and actually *ran* for another 12 TDs.

Near the start of the 1976 season, after a discouraging 27–13 loss to Baltimore, the Patriots held a meeting at the suggestion of veteran tackle Tom Neville. Only players attended, and they told themselves that, as a team, they were as good as any club in the American Conference East. It was a collective ego trip, and accomplished wonders. In three successive weekends, the Patriots whipped the Dolphins and the world-champion Pittsburgh Steelers, and trounced the Oakland Raiders by a whopping 48–17 margin.

While the defensive secondary and Steve Grogan's quarterbacking provided a vital new impetus, the offensive and defensive lines joined in the resurgence as well. The offensive linemen tore out holes that sent the running backs on their way to nearly 3,000 yards. Sam (Bam) Cunningham fell just short of 1,000 yards, while Don Calhoun ran for 721 yards as a backup fullback playing for less than half the season.

Coach Fairbanks, for the first time since he left Norman, Oklahoma, where his Sooner football teams ranked among the nation's best, is finally beginning to feel at home—that is, at home with a winner.

"As I look forward to the 1977 season," he says, "if I had to select the one factor most important to this ball club, it would be this: For the first time in a long time, the Patriots have enjoyed success, and they are now a confident and talented young team. I believe this taste of success will be a driving force for everyone involved with the club to keep the Patriots at the top level of pro football in 1977."

If momentum alone can carry the Patriots to the heights, they might just cut a wide swath through the AFC East—and, who knows? If the flip of a coin or the bounce of a football should ordain it, even the Oakland

Raiders might find New England vigor too much to repel. And some schedule experts say New England has the NFL's "easiest" opposition. Of the 14 opposing teams, only three had winning records in 1976. The consolidated won-lost records of those 14 clubs last season was 74–122.

OFFENSE

Quarterbacks	Ht.	Wt.	Age	Exp.	College
Grogan, Steve	6-4	200	24	3	Kansas State
Owen, Tom	6-1	194	24	4	Wichita

The word is that Grogan and Owen are pretty well set as the Patriot QBs, barring the sudden appearance of a miracle man. Grogan's 48-percent completions record in 1976 wasn't all that good, but he apparently has ability to move the team.

Running Backs	Ht.	Wt.	Age	Exp.	College
Calhoun, Don	6-0	198	25	4	Kansas State
Cunningham, Sam	6-3	224	27	5	Southern California
Forte, Ike	6-0	196	23	2	Arkansas
Johnson, Andy	6-0	204	24	4	Georgia
Phillips, Jess	6-1	208	30	10	Michigan State
Ivory, Horace	5-11	198	22	R	Oklahoma

None of these is a superstar, but taken together they're a formidable lot overland. Cunningham knocked at the 1,000-Yard Club's door last season with 824 yards (4.8 average) while Calhoun picked up steam in his third NFL year (721 yards for a 5.6 average). Johnson was another consistent ground-gainer (699 yards)—and Steve Grogan ranked among the top ball-carrying QBs in the league. Ivory is a second-round draft choice from a good college team.

Receivers	Ht.	Wt.	Age	Exp.	College
Briscoe, Marlin (W)	5-11	180	32	10	Nebraska–Omaha
Burks, Steve (W)	6-5	211	24	3	Arkansas State
Stingley, Darryl (W)	6-0	195	25	5	Purdue
Vataha, Randy (W)	5-10	170	28	7	Stanford
Harris, Joe Dale (W)	6-3	194	23	1	Alabama
Chandler, Al (T)	6-3	229	26	4	Oklahoma
Francis, Russ (T)	6-6	240	24	3	Oregon

Morgan, Stanley (W)	5-11	174	22	R	Tennessee
Hasselbeck, Don (T)	6-7	245	22	R	Colorado

W=wide receiver   T=tight end

The group was fairly proficient at catching Grogan's passes whenever he decided not to run. Running backs Johnson and Cunningham led with 56 receptions between them, which says something about New England's pass-run attack. Francis caught 26 to make himself an early Foxboro favorite. Smallish Randy Vataha can still haul 'em in. Harris was on injured reserve in 1976. Hasselbeck adds height to the pass receiving corps, and Morgan can run after catches.

Interior Linemen	Ht.	Wt.	Age	Exp.	College
Adams, Sam (G)	6-3	252	28	6	Prairie View
Hannah, John (G)	6-2	265	26	5	Alabama
Sturt, Fred (G)	6-4	255	26	3	Bowling Green
Corbett, Steve (G)	6-4	248	26	3	Boston College
Gray, Leon (T)	6-3	256	26	5	Jackson State
McKay, Bob (T)	6-5	265	29	8	Texas
Neville, Tom (T)	6-4	253	34	12	Mississippi State
Jordan, Shelby (T)	6-7	260	25	3	Washington (Mo.)
Brock, Pete (C)	6-5	260	23	2	Colorado
Lenkaitis, Len (C)	6-4	250	31	10	Penn State

T=tackle   G=guard   C=center

The only new face here is Fred Sturt's. He has belonged to St. Louis and Washington (played seven games) before coming to New England as a free agent. This offensive line can and does move. It made the Patriots fourth in AFC total offensive yards in 1976 with an average of 335.3 yards per game. In rushing yardage alone the Patriots ranked second in the AFC, averaging 211.2 yards per game. Little wonder there are few new faces among this still very young aggregation.

Kickers	Ht.	Wt.	Age	Exp.	College
Smith, John (Pk)	6-0	185	28	4	Southampton
Patrick, Mike (P)	6-0	213	24	3	Mississippi State

Pk=placekicker   P=punter

John Smith, the pride of Southampton, England, kicked well enough in 1976 to lead the club in scoring. While not perfect, 42 of 46 points-after was good, and seven of his 15 FGs were from 40 yards or more out—one was from 49 yards. Patrick's 40.1 punting mark put him among the NFL's top ten. Not much to complain about here.

DEFENSE

Front Linemen	Ht.	Wt.	Age	Exp.	College
Adams, Julius (E)	6-4	260	29	7	Texas Southern
Lunsford, Mel (E)	6-3	250	27	5	Central State (Ohio)
McGee, Tony (E)	6-4	245	28	7	Bishop
Boyd, Greg (E)	6-6	265	23	1	San Diego State
Hanneman, Craig (E)	6-4	245	28	5	Oregon State
Bishop, Richard (T)	6-1	275	24	2	Louisville
Hamilton, Ray (T)	6-1	245	26	5	Oklahoma
Tipton, Dave (T)	6-2	255	25	3	Western Illinois
Cusick, Pete (T)	6-1	255	24	2	Ohio State
Moore, Arthur (T)	6-5	253	26	4	Tulsa

E=end   T=tackle

If the Patriots' offensive line rolled up impressive statistics in 1976, then the same can be said for the defensive troops. They permitted the opposition a total of 4,022 yards, or 287.3 per game, which made them sixth in the AFC. Against the rush, they ranked fourth, allowing 131.9 yards per game, and against the pass they were among the best. Boyd and Cusick were on the injury list, and their return should make the unit even stronger. None of this crowd has reached his thirtieth birthday; averaging 4.4 pro years each, they're a bit green while still being mean.

Linebackers	Ht.	Wt.	Age	Exp.	College
Hunt, Sam (M)	6-1	240	25	4	S. F. Austin
Nelson, Steve (M)	6-2	230	26	4	North Dakota State
Thomas, Donnie (M)	6-2	245	24	2	Indiana
Romaniszyn, Jim (M)	6-1	220	26	4	Edinboro State
Barnes, Pete (O)	6-1	240	32	11	Southern U.
King, Steve (O)	6-4	230	26	4	North Dakota State
Webster, George (O)	6-4	230	32	11	Michigan State
Zabel, Steve (O)	6-4	230	29	8	Oklahoma
Shoate, Rod (O)	6-1	218	24	2	Oklahoma

O=outside   M=middle

This unit has undergone some changes, but not many. Hunt, Nelson, Zabel, and Barnes were LBs in the 3–4 defense at season's end in 1976. Did they improve in pass defense over 1975? A good question, for the Patriots ranked sixth in AFC pass defense both years. Shoate and Romaniszyn are coming off injuries. And that's 11-year pro George Webster, now available for duty at Foxboro.

Cornerbacks	Ht.	Wt.	Age	Exp.	College
Germany, Willie	6-0	192	28	5	Morgan State
Haynes, Mike	6-3	195	23	2	Arizona State

Howard, Bob	6-2	177	31	11	San Diego State
Sanders, John	6-1	178	26	3	South Dakota
Clayborn, Raymond	6-1	183	22	R	Texas
Brown, Sidney	6-1	185	22	R	Oklahoma

Haynes became one of the few rookies to play in the Pro Bowl. His eight interceptions in 1976 wasn't tops in the NFL, but it was third best. Howard continues to perform well as he enters his eleventh pro year. Sanders was on injured reserve last season. Germany comes to Foxboro from Houston. Clayborn was a premier punt and KO returner in college, and Brown is an Oklahoman. This is a good outfit.

Safeties	Ht.	Wt.	Age	Exp.	College
Conn, Dick	6-0	180	26	4	Georgia
Fox, Tim	5-11	186	24	2	Ohio State
McCray, Prentice	6-1	187	26	4	Arizona State
Beaudoin, Doug	6-1	200	23	1	Minnesota

The Patriots had two All-America rookies in their 1976 secondary; one was Mike Haynes of Arizona State, and the other was Tim Fox, the erstwhile Ohio State flash. Both made their mark and then some. McCray, also an Arizona State product, intercepted five passes last season to wind up second only to Haynes on the club. He and Fox are the safeties, with Conn and the injured Beaudoin as the backups. Here, the Patriots are young and fully alert.

Note: A complete listing of New England's 1977 college draft selections can be found on page 254.

DEFENSIVE UNIT 3-4 DEFENSE

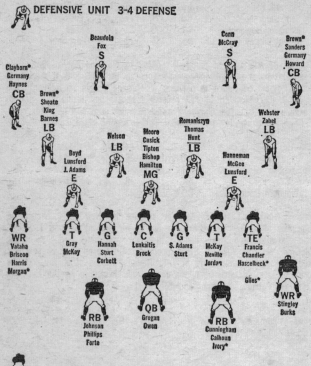

Beaudoin
Fox
S

Conn
McCray
S

Brown*
Sanders
Germany
Howard
CB

Clayborn*
Germany
Haynes
CB

Brown*
Shoate
King
Barnes
LB

Webster
Zabel
LB

Romaniszyn
Thomas
Hunt
LB

Nelson
LB

Moore
Cusick
Tipton
Bishop
Hamilton
MG

Boyd
Lunsford
J. Adams
E

Hanneman
McGee
Lunsford
E

WR
Vataha
Briscoe
Harris
Morgan*

T
Gray
McKay

G
Hannah
Sturt
Corbett

C
Lenkaitis
Brock

G
S. Adams
Sturt

T
McKay
Neville
Jordan

TE
Francis
Chandler
Hasselbeck*

Giles*

WR
Stingley
Burks

RB
Johnson
Phillips
Forte

QB
Grogan
Owen

RB
Cunningham
Calhoun
Ivory*

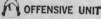

OFFENSIVE UNIT

1976 PATRIOTS STATISTICS

	Patriots	Opps.
Total Points Scored	376	236
Total First Downs	260	258
Third-Down Efficiency	76—192	90—209
Yards Rushing—First Downs	2957—150	1847—102
Passes Attempted—Completions	309—146	437—229
Yards Passing—First Downs	1737—95	2170—134
QB Sacked—Yards Lost	21—173	48—434
Interceptions—Return Average	23—22.0	20—19.0
Punts—Average Yards	67—40.1	75—38.8
Punt Returns—Return Average	48—13.1	37—7.8
Kickoff Returns—Return Average	46—23.6	71—22.0
Fumbles—Ball Lost	28—16	37—27
Penalties—Yards	102—918	88—764

STATISTICAL LEADERS

Scoring	TDs	Rush.	Pass.	Ret.	PATs	FGs	Total
Smith	0	0	0	0	42—46	15—25	87
Grogan	13	12	0	1	0	0	78
Johnson	10	6	4	0	0	0	60
Stingley	4	0	4	0	0	0	24
Cunningham	3	3	0	0	0	0	18
Francis	3	0	3	0	0	0	18
Chandler	3	0	3	0	0	0	18
Forte	2	1	1	0	0	0	12
Haynes	2	0	0	2	0	0	12
McCray	2	0	0	2	0	0	12

Rushing	Atts.	Yds.	Avg.	Longest	TDs
Cunningham	172	824	4.8	24	3
Calhoun	129	721	5.6	54	1
Johnson	169	699	4.1	69 (TD)	6
Grogan	60	397	6.6	41 (TD)	12
Phillips	24	164	6.8	46	1
Forte	25	100	4.0	26	1

Passing	Atts.	Com.	Yds.	Pct.	Int.	Longest	TDs
Grogan	302	145	1903	48.0	20	58 (TD)	18

Receiving	No.	Yds.	Avg.	Longest	TDs
Johnson	29	343	11.8	53	4
Cunningham	27	299	11.1	41	0
Francis	26	367	14.1	38 (TD)	3
Stingley	17	370	21.8	58 (TD)	4
Calhoun	12	56	4.7	12	0
Vataha	11	192	17.5	44	1

Interceptions	No.	Yds.	Avg.	Longest	TDs
Haynes	8	90	11.3	28	0
McCray	5	182	36.4	63 (TD)	2
Fox	3	67	22.3	29	0
Howard	3	28	9.3	15	0
Hunt	2	106	53.0	68 (TD)	1
Nelson	2	32	16.0	34	0

Punting	No.	Yds.	Avg.	Longest	Inside 20	Blocked
Patrick	67	2688	40.1	52	12	0

Punt Returns	No.	FCs	Yds.	Avg.	Longest	TDs
Haynes	45	0	608	13.5	89 (TD)	2

Kickoff Returns	No.	Yds.	Avg.	Longest	TDs
Phillips	14	397	28.4	71	0
Feacher	10	240	24.0	46	0
Calhoun	9	183	20.3	33	0

BALTIMORE COLTS

Head Coach: Ted Marchibroda

3rd Year   **Record:** 21–7

1976 RECORD (11–3) (capital letters indicate home games)			1977 SCHEDULE (capital letters indicate home games)	
27	New England	13	Seattle	Sept. 18
28	CINCINNATI	27	N.Y. Jets	Sept. 25
27	Dallas	30	BUFFALO	Oct. 2
42	TAMPA BAY	17	MIAMI	Oct. 9
28	MIAMI	14	Kansas City	Oct. 16
31	Buffalo	13	New England	Oct. 23
20	N.Y. Jets	0	PITTSBURGH	Oct. 30
38	HOUSTON	14	WASHINGTON (night, TV)	Nov. 7
37	San Diego	21	Buffalo	Nov. 13
14	NEW ENGLAND	21	N.Y. JETS	Nov. 20
17	Miami	16	Denver	Nov. 27
33	N.Y. JETS	16	Miami (night, TV)	Dec. 5
17	St. Louis	24	DETROIT	Dec. 11
58	BUFFALO	20	NEW ENGLAND	Dec. 18
	Playoffs			
14	PITTSBURGH	40		

It was another banner season in Baltimore, but in the end, something was lacking. The Colts stormed into the playoffs for the second straight year only to collapse before the Pittsburgh Steelers, just as they had done the year before. In fact, if it happens again, the Colts may replace Oakland as the NFL's reigning "we-almost-made-it" club, and those Baltimore fans won't like that classification one bit. Baltimore, we must remember, is one of the winningest sports towns around.

Ted Marchibroda enters his third year as head coach with a solid 21–7 record. And he's aware of what the club needs to gain more than a mere peep into the playoff doorway. Says he: "Our first priority will be improvement of defense. We need secondary and line-backer help. There's a strong possibility that we'll play

Sanders Shiver [a second-year man] at middle line-backer. On offense, Ron Lee will probably move to full-back. But overall, we need depth that will improve our special teams."

Aside from the coaching outlook and the need for a beefed-up defense, the big question in Baltimore still centers on the departed general manager, Joe Thomas, who now has the same job in San Francisco. (He was fired by the Colt front office.) Thomas was given the lion's share of the credit for bringing the Colts back from the abyss three years ago, but the managerial conflicts grew and grew until the Baltimore front office became a battleground rivaled only by an NFL weekend itself. In the final play, it was Thomas who had to go. Succeeding him as general manager is Dick Szymanski, a long-time player and personnel man with the Colts.

Forgetting the defensive shortcomings for a moment, a look at some of the offensive accomplishments brightens the picture for any loyal Colt fan (and they are legion, both in and out of Baltimore; in the South, the Colts were regional favorites long before Miami, New Orleans, and Atlanta put pro football teams into the field). The contemporary Baltimore offense is an impressive one to behold. In 1976, the following club records were set:

- Total offense, 5,236 yards (old record—5,008, in 1967)
- Rushing yardage, 2,309 yards (old record—2,217, in 1975)
- Most first downs, 301 (old record—80, in 1975)
- Most points in one game, 58 vs. Buffalo on Dec. 12, 1976 (old record—56 vs. Los Angeles in 1956, and vs. Green Bay in 1958)
- Most individual rushing yards in one season,

1,200, by Lydell Mitchell (old record—1,193, also by Mitchell, in 1975)

• Most individual attempts rushing in one season, 289, by Lydell Mitchell (which ties Mitchell's former record, set in 1975)

• Best pass reception average yardage in one season, 25.9, by Roger Carr (old record—25.6, by Jimmy Orr, in 1968)

• Highest pass completion percentage in one season, 60.4, by Bert Jones (old record—59.0, also by Jones, in 1975)

• Most points scored by a kicker in one season, 109, by Toni Linhart (old record—106, by Lou Michaels, in 1967); the Colts' individual scoring record is held by Lenny Moore—120 points in 1967

Among the more notable members of the Charging Colts returning for the new campaign are no fewer than *six* Pro Bowlers, a group chosen to play in the event last January in Seattle. This select six includes, as might be expected, the stellar passing duet of Bert Jones and Roger Carr, two guys who were collegians at Louisiana and have already proven almost as valuable to the Colts as the Louisiana Purchase was to the United States. And they'd probably bring about as much on the NFL open market.

Baltimore's All-Pros also include defensive end John Dutton, running back Lydell Mitchell, tackle George Kunz, and the premier kicker Toni Linhart. As the new season gets underway, all the fans' eyes will be on the star-studded Baltimore offense once again, but Marchibroda's eyes will be on something else—the unit that takes the field after the fourth down. And that defense has taken on some added strength with the addition of cornerback Norm Thompson in a deal with St. Louis.

OFFENSE

Quarterbacks	Ht.	Wt.	Age	Exp.	College
Jones, Bert	6-3	212	25	5	Louisiana State
Troup, Bill	6-5	220	26	4	South Carolina
Kirkland, Mike	6-1	187	23	2	Arkansas

The Colts haven't been easy to handle for at least two seasons now, and the reason is Bert Jones (if you're willing to purge the memory of the general manager from recent Baltimore history). Jones is doing a remarkable job in Baltimore—the biggest city, by the way, below the Mason-Dixon Line. If he hadn't thrown one interception (the ball was tipped by intended receiver Glenn Doughty) in the season's final game against Buffalo, Jones would have been the 1976 NFL passing champion with a 103.8 rating to Ken Stabler's 103.7. As it was, Jones finished with 102.6, second to Stabler. Jones's backup, Bill Troup, threw only 18 times last season, completing eight, but he might show more under steadier fire. And so might second-year man Mike Kirkland.

Running Backs	Ht.	Wt.	Age	Exp.	College
Mitchell, Lydell	5-11	195	28	6	Penn State
McCauley, Don	6-1	216	28	7	North Carolina
Stevens, Howard	5-5	165	27	5	Louisville
Leaks, Roosevelt	5-10	219	24	3	Texas
Lee, Ron	6-4	222	24	2	West Virginia

Lydell Mitchell swept for 1,200 yards in 1976, showing that he's in his prime entering his sixth year as a pro. Mitchell is only one of several Joe Paterno (Penn State) protégés who're making their marks indelibly on the NFL record books. The Colts are a strong rushing outfit—they finished fourth in AFC overland yardage in 1976. In addition to Mitchell's 1,200, many more yards were contributed (with less ball-toting) by McCauley, Leaks, Ron Lee, and QB Jones himself (214). At season's end, the depth chart showed Mitchell and Leaks with the starting RB assignments. It'll probably remain that way.

Receivers	Ht.	Wt.	Age	Exp.	College
Carr, Roger (W)	6-3	193	25	4	Louisiana Tech
Thompson, Ricky (W)	6-0	170	23	2	Baylor
Doughty, Glenn (W)	6-1	202	26	6	Michigan
Johnson, Marshall (W)	6-1	190	24	3	Houston
Scott, Freddie (W)	6-2	170	25	4	Amherst
Chester, Raymond (T)	6-4	236	29	8	Morgan State
Kennedy, Jimmie (T)	6-3	233	25	3	Colorado State
Burke, Randy (W)	6-1	189	22	R	Kentucky

W=wide receiver   T=tight end

If NFL individual pass receiving statistics were based upon the number of yards amassed instead of on the number of passes caught, Roger Carr would have finished 1976 ranking second in the entire NFL. As it was, he didn't even make the top ten, although he caught 43 for 1,112 yards and his average yards per catch record (25.9) was the best in the league. It goes to prove that when Carr catches one, he's apt to be quite a distance down the field looking over his shoulder for a Bert Jones special. The Colt pass receiving corps is superb. Doughty gives Jones a better-than-average alternate target, and so does Chester. Mitchell and McCauley also specialize in coming out of the backfield as receivers—and doing it well. Rookie Burke is speedy, like other things from Kentucky.

Interior Linemen	Ht.	Wt.	Age	Exp.	College
Taylor, David (T)	6-5	257	27	5	Catawba
Van Duyne, Bob (T)	6-4	245	25	4	Idaho
Pratt, Robert (G)	6-4	248	26	4	North Carolina
Huff, Ken (G)	6-4	260	24	3	North Carolina
Collett, Elmer (G)	6-5	246	32	11	San Francisco State
Kunz, George (T)	6-6	266	30	9	Notre Dame
Mendenhall, Ken (C)	6-3	249	29	7	Oklahoma
Blue, Forrest (C)	6-5	261	31	10	Auburn

T=tackle   G=guard   C=center

One of the best, if not the best, offensive lines in the NFL. The 1976 statistics speak for themselves. Baltimore's offense, rushing and passing, totaled 5,236 yards—an average of 374 yards per game. Both marks were tops in the NFL. Best in the NFL also were the passing offense marks—2,933 net yards for an average of 209.5 per game. The Colts ranked no worse than fourth in AFC rushing. It all adds up to a tremendous show of ability by the eight stalwarts listed above.

Kickers	Ht.	Wt.	Age	Exp.	College
Lee, David (P)	6-5	221	33	12	Louisiana Tech
Linhart, Toni (Pk)	5-11	181	35	5	Austria Tech

Pk=placekicker   P=punter

In addition to being the NFL's leading point scorer (109 in 1976), Toni Linhart is also an exceptional soccer player and a champion skier. He can do a lot of things with his feet, to be sure. The 35-year-old Austrian was mighty nigh perfect on points-after—49 out of 50—and 20 FGs out of 27 attempts is a fine average in anybody's league (even though he connected for only one out of six from 40 yards out). David Lee's punting was good enough to place him tenth in the NFL with a 39.7 average. QB Mike Kirkland is also a punter, should the need arise.

DEFENSE

Front Linemen	Ht.	Wt.	Age	Exp.	College
Cook, Fred (E)	6-4	247	25	4	S. Mississippi
Fernandes, Ron (E)	6-4	239	26	3	Eastern Michigan
Barnes, Mike (T)	6-6	260	26	5	Miami (Fla.)
Novak, Ken (T)	6-2	275	23	2	Purdue
Ehrmann, Joe (T)	6-4	254	28	5	Syracuse
Wells, Angelo (T)	6-3	250	23	1	Morgan State
Dutton, John (E)	6-7	268	26	4	Nebraska
Ozdowski, Mike (E)	6-5	240	22	R	Virginia

E=end   T=tackle

Marchibroda would like to make his defensives a little stronger, especially against the pass. But in the QB sacking department the Colts led the AFC in 1976, nailing the QB 57 times for a total yardage loss of 465. Overall, Baltimore finished tenth against the pass, fifth against the rush, and seventh in total defense in 1976. This unit has been criticized before. It's a young unit, and maybe the answer lies in the experience column.

Linebackers	Ht.	Wt.	Age	Exp.	College
MacLeod, Tom (O)	6-3	228	26	5	Minnesota
Luce, Derrel (O)	6-3	224	24	3	Baylor
Dalton, Stephen (O)	6-4	246	24	1	William & Mary
Cheyunski, Jim (M)	6-1	220	31	10	Syracuse
Shiver, Sanders (M)	6-2	221	22	2	Carson–Newman
Simonini, Ed (M)	6-0	220	23	2	Texas A&M
White, Stan (O)	6-1	220	27	6	Ohio State
Dickel, Dan (O)	6-4	230	26	4	Iowa
Keating, Brian (O)	6-2	229	25	2	Ottawa (Canada)

O=outside   M=middle

The Colt linebacking hasn't really been up to par since Mike Curtis left for Seattle in the expansion draft. Cheyunski, the ten-year vet, continues to lead, and MacLeod's absence due to injury in preseason 1976 was a big setback last year. Luce showed great promise as MacLeod's backup. A lot depends on how the young ones—Dalton, Shiver, Simonini, Dickel, and Keating—develop.

Cornerbacks	Ht.	Wt.	Age	Exp.	College
Mumphord, Lloyd	5-10	176	30	9	Texas Southern
Nettles, Doug	6-0	178	26	4	Vanderbilt
Munsey, Nelson	6-1	198	29	6	Wyoming
Oldham, Ray	6-0	190	26	5	Middle Tennessee
Thompson, Norm	6-1	180	32	7	Utah

This quartet could stand improvement. Mumphord has the experience, but he needs support. Nettles was out all last season injured. Munsey played eight games before being placed on the injured reserve. Oldham is a fair backup at both corner and safety. Thompson is St. Louis's loss and Baltimore's gain.

Safeties	Ht.	Wt.	Age	Exp.	College
Wallace, Jackie	6-3	197	26	4	Arizona
Salter, Bryant	6-5	196	27	7	Pittsburgh
Hall, Randy	6-3	185	25	3	Idaho
Baylor, Tim	6-6	191	23	2	Morgan State
Laird, Bruce	6-1	198	27	6	American International

Wallace intercepted five passes in 1976 to lead the Colts in interceptions for the year. Salter was brought in late last season to replace Spencer Thomas. As in the cornerback department, the safeties could stand the injection of new talent. (New England's success with secondary rookies can be cited as an example.)

Note: A complete listing of Baltimore's 1977 college draft selections can be found on page 248.

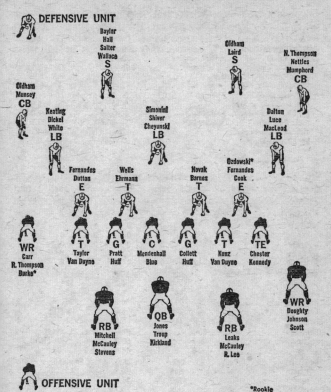

DEFENSIVE UNIT

Baylor
Hall
Salter
Wallace
S

Oldham
Laird
S

N. Thompson
Nettles
Mumphord
CB

Oldham
Munsey
CB

Keating
Dickel
White
LB

Simonini
Shiver
Cheyunski
LB

Dalton
Luce
MacLeod
LB

Fernandes
Dutton
E

Wells
Ehrmann
T

Novak
Barnes
T

Ozdowski*
Fernandes
Cook
E

WR
Carr
R. Thompson
Burke*

Taylor
Van Duyne
T

Pratt
Huff
G

Mendenhall
Blue
C

Collett
Huff
G

Kunz
Van Duyne
T

Chester
Kennedy
TE

RB
Mitchell
McCauley
Stevens

QB
Jones
Troup
Kirkland

RB
Leaks
McCauley
R. Lee

WR
Doughty
Johnson
Scott

OFFENSIVE UNIT

*Rookie

1976 COLTS STATISTICS

	Colts	Opps.
Total Points Scored	417*	246
Total First Downs	301	229
Third-Down Efficiency	109—200	70—184
Yards Rushing—First Downs	2309—133	1844—83
Passes Attempted—Completions	361—215	372—192
Yards Passing—First Downs	2927—144	2343—126
QB Sacked—Yards Lost	31—294	57—465
Interceptions—Return Average	15—14.1	10—14.6
Punts—Average Yards	59—39.7	79—36.9
Punt Returns—Return Average	40—7.9	33—7.0
Kickoff Returns—Return Average	51—20.6	77—22.3
Fumbles—Ball Lost	25—18	32—21
Penalties—Yards	92—786	88—781

*Includes one safety

STATISTICAL LEADERS

Scoring	TDs	Rush.	Pass.	Ret.	PATs	FGs	Total
Linhart	0	0	0	0	49—51	20—27	109
Carr	11	0	11	0	0	0	66
McCauley	11	9	2	0	0	0	66
Mitchell	8	5	3	0	0	0	48
Leaks	7	7	0	0	0	0	42
Doughty	5	0	5	0	0	0	30
Chester	3	0	3	0	0	0	18
Jones	2	2	0	0	0	0	12

Rushing	Atts.	Yds.	Avg.	Longest	TDs
Mitchell	289	1200	4.2	43	5
Leaks	118	445	3.8	42	7
McCauley	69	227	3.3	16	9
Lee, Ron	41	220	5.4	69 (TD)	1
Jones	38	214	5.6	17	2

Passing	Atts.	Com.	Yds.	Pct.	Int.	Longest	TDs
Jones	343	207	3104	60.3	9	79 (TD)	24
Troup	18	8	117	44.4	1	32	0

Receiving	No.	Yds.	Avg.	Longest	TDs
Mitchell	60	555	9.3	40 (TD)	3
Carr	43	1112	25.9	79 (TD)	11
Doughty	40	628	15.7	41	5
McCauley	34	347	10.2	44	2
Chester	24	467	19.5	40	3

Interceptions	No.	Yds.	Avg.	Longest	TDs
Wallace	5	105	21.0	41	0
White	3	26	8.7	15	0
Oldham	2	40	20.0	33	0
Luce	2	7	3.5	7	0

Punting	No.	Yds.	Avg.	Longest	Inside 20	Blocked
Lee, David	59	2342	39.7	56	21	0

Punt Returns	No.	FCs	Yds.	Avg.	Longest	TDs
Stevens	39	9	315	8.1	44	0

Kickoff Returns	No.	Yds.	Avg.	Longest	TDs
Stevens	30	710	23.7	83	0
Laird	7	143	20.4	25	0
Wallace	3	61	20.3	23	0
Kennedy	4	64	16.0	23	0

MIAMI DOLPHINS

Head Coach: Don Shula

8th Year   **Record:** 73–24–1

1976 RECORD (6–8) (capital letters indicate home games)		1977 SCHEDULE (capital letters indicate home games)	
30	Buffalo	21	Buffalo	Sept. 18
14	New England	30	San Francisco	Sept. 25
16	N.Y. JETS	0	HOUSTON	Oct. 2
28	LOS ANGELES	31	Baltimore	Oct. 9
14	Baltimore	28	N.Y. JETS	Oct. 16
17	KANSAS CITY (in OT)	20	SEATTLE	Oct. 23
23	Tampa Bay	20	SAN DIEGO	Oct. 30
10	NEW ENGLAND	3	N.Y. Jets	Nov. 6
27	N.Y. Jets	7	NEW ENGLAND	Nov. 13
3	Pittsburgh	14	Cincinnati	Nov. 20
16	BALTIMORE	17	St. Louis (TV)	Nov. 24
13	Cleveland	17	BALTIMORE (night, TV)	Dec. 5
45	BUFFALO	27	New England	Dec. 11
7	MINNESOTA	29	BUFFALO (TV)	Dec. 17

The Dolphins ended their 1976 season in the hospital
—a statement that can almost be taken literally. As they
went down to defeat in the finale with Minnesota, 29–7,
strong safety Charlie Babb tore the ligaments in his left
knee and became the *ninth* Dolphin to undergo knee
surgery during the all-too-long 6–8 season.

It isn't difficult to sympathize with Coach Don Shula,
mainly because he's never been an excuse-maker or an
"Alibi Al." As one of the NFL's outstanding coaches,
he's well aware of the fortunes of the game, and that the
ball bounces away from you just about as many times
as it bounces toward you.

But the injury list was grim. Even before the regular
season got underway, safety Dick Anderson and linebacker Mike Kolen were victims—while they were still
recovering from injuries sustained the year before. Then

two of the club's young and promising linebackers, Earnest Rhone and Kim Bokamper, came down with knee troubles. And as the season wore wearily along, linebacker Andy Selfridge, cornerback Tim Foley, safety Barry Hill, and wide receiver Howard Twilley joined the stretcher parade.

And knees weren't the only items of body structure that ran into trouble. Receiver Nat Moore broke his leg in the ninth game, guard Bob Kuechenberg complained of bone chips in an ankle before game No. 10 was over, linebacker Bob Matheson pulled a calf muscle early in the season and missed three games completely, and fullback Norm Bulaich's shoulder became separated in game No. 6. All of these fallen warriors were top-drawer personnel, a pretty rough fact of life and one that makes you wonder how the Dolphins managed to win even six games in 1976.

But what of the future, and, more specifically, the 1977 season? It doesn't take a brilliant prognosticator to figure the Dolphins will be out of the playoffs. With so many key players racked with injury, Shula would have to beat almost insurmountable odds to plug the gaps with good capable talent. And without such an achievement, the Miami season bids fair to again be a disaster defensively, just as it was in 1976.

The offense still has Bob Griese, one of the league's premier signal-callers, but even on the attack unit, injuries are taking their toll. The pass receiving unit progressed markedly with Duriel Harris, and Freddie Solomon, after recovering from kidney surgery, went on to pull in 27 passes for 453 yards in the second half of the season.

But Miami needs massive help at offensive tackle, along the defensive line, and in the defensive secondary. "I hate to be unrealistic about what needs to be done,"

Shula characteristically says. "We played defense in that final game against Minnesota just like we had all year— just a step away. I don't feel good about it, and it's been a long off season. We need help, young help, but if we can trade for veteran help, we'll trade."

The Dolphins' All-Pro guard, Larry Little, believes one reason Miami failed to come up with a winning season in 1976 is that many players on opposing teams were "settling old scores." Says Little, "I couldn't blame them for coming at us the way they did. For several years they'd heard how Miami did it this way or that way, until they must have gotten sick of hearing it. And I'd do the same thing myself. I'd point for Miami if I played on another team."

Even reliable and brainy Bob Griese had his bad moments during the unhappy season, and one miscall cost Miami a victory in the Cleveland game. The Browns were leading 17–13. The Dolphins had moved to Cleveland's three-yard line, and it was first down with 25 seconds left on the clock. Perhaps unaware of exactly what he was doing, Griese proceeded to call a running play that consumed the entire 25 seconds, and the game was over with the score still 17–13 in favor of Cleveland.

What should Griese have done? Everybody agrees that, with the Dolphins four points behind, he should have thrown a pass into the end zone. A TD would win, and an incompletion would stop the clock. You either score or halt the watch, as Griese reminded himself afterwards in remorse.

But what if the Dolphins had scored a touchdown on that final running play? Ah, that's different! Griese would have been hailed as a genius who'd caught the Browns flat-footed by running the ball when, obviously, they'd expected him to pass.

OFFENSE

Quarterbacks	Ht.	Wt.	Age	Exp.	College
Griese, Bob	6-1	195	32	11	Purdue
Strock, Don	6-5	216	26	4	Virginia Tech

Griese enters his eleventh season as a pro still hoping that he can lead the Dolphins back to their former glory despite the absence of "those three"—Csonka, Warfield, and Kiick—otherwise known as the "Wandering Three." (After WFL hitches, Csonka wound up with the Giants, Warfield back home in Cleveland, and Kiick out west again in Denver.) Few remember that back in 1966, Steve Spurrier (Florida) won the Heisman Trophy and Griese (Purdue) came in second in the balloting by sports writers around the country. Last season, they were both playing pro ball in Florida, but Tampa Bay cast Spurrier adrift after a 0–14 year. At 43, Earl Morrall has finally retired after 21 pro seasons, although for a while he seemed intent on upstaging George Blanda. Strock got in a little throwing time in 1976, enough to keep his arm limber for moments when Griese sits one out.

Running Backs	Ht.	Wt.	Age	Exp.	College
Malone, Benny	5-10	193	25	4	Arizona State
Davis, Gary	5-10	202	23	2	Calif. Polytechnic
Heath, Clayton	5-11	190	26	2	Wake Forest
Bulaich, Norm	6-1	220	30	8	Texas Christian
Nottingham, Don	5-10	210	28	7	Kent State
Winfrey, Stan	5-11	223	24	3	Arkansas State

This once proud unit doesn't give Griese's air-ground attack the one-two punch it used to have. Malone, still new at the pro game, ran for 797 yards in 1976, good for tenth individual ranking among AFC rushers, but that's about it. Bulaich still gets yardage (but not in big chunks), and so does Nottingham when he gets playing time. Shula may give his ace receiver, Nat Moore, a chance at running back. Moore was one of the nation's top RBs while he was at Florida U.

Receivers	Ht.	Wt.	Age	Exp.	College
Moore, Nat (W)	5-9½	180	25	4	Florida
Harris, Duriel (W)	5-11	175	23	2	New Mexico State
Smith, Barry (W)	6-1	190	26	5	Florida State
Solomon, Freddie (W)	5-11	181	24	3	Tampa
Twilley, Howard (W)	5-10	185	33	12	Tulsa
Holmes, Mike (W)	6-2	193	27	4	Texas Southern
Tillman, André (T)	6-4	230	24	3	Texas Tech
Mandich, Jim (T)	6-2	224	29	8	Michigan

McCreary, Loaird (T)	6-5	227	24	2	Tennessee State
Williams, Chandler (W)	6-0	180	25	2	Lincoln (Mo.)

W=wide receiver   T=tight end

Moore is a deep threat, and comes closest of any of this group to making the Miami fans forget about Warfield. Solomon is coming on, and will contribute much to a Miami comeback if it happens. Twilley and Mandich continue to provide both experience and depth. Harris, in his rookie year, did all right, leading in kickoff returns (with 17 for a 32.9 average) and catching 22 passes (averaging 16.9 yards per grab). A good year for this group could put the Dolphins up there.

Interior Linemen	Ht.	Wt.	Age	Exp.	College
Kuechenberg, Bob (G)	6-2	252	29	8	Notre Dame
Newman, Ed (G)	6-2	245	26	5	Duke
Mitchell, Melvin (G)	6-2½	260	24	2	Tennessee State
Langer, Jim (C)	6-2	253	28	8	South Dakota State
Little, Larry (G)	6-1	265	31	11	Bethune–Cookman
Young, Randy (C)	6-5	250	23	2	Iowa State
Moore, Wayne (T)	6-6	265	32	8	Lamar Tech
Drougas, Tom (T)	6-4	255	27	6	Oregon
Pesuit, Wally (T)	6-4½	250	23	2	Kentucky
Carlton, Darryl (T)	6-6	260	24	3	Tampa
Watson, Mike (T)	6-6	265	22	R	Miami (Ohio)

T=tackle   G=guard   C=center

Miami's offense, it might be said, sputtered in 1976. Overall, the Dolphins ranked ninth in AFC total offense, averaging 313.3 yards per game. They were slightly more effective against the pass than against the rush. Shula looks for changes here—and hopes for improvements. The word is that he's not entirely satisfied with Carlton's performance in or out of the game at tackle. Jim Langer and Larry Little are All-Pros and play that way. Mitchell came through his rookie year well and is a mighty tower on backup. Pesuit played one game with Atlanta. Moore's knees are shaky. Kuechenberg still keeps the enemy at bay at left guard. Things could be worse, but Shula likes it better.

Kickers	Ht.	Wt.	Age	Exp.	College
Yepremian, Garo (Pk)	5-8	175	33	11	(none)
Seiple, Larry (P)	6-0	214	32	11	Kentucky
Cody, Earl (P, Pk)	5-10	200	22	1	Eastern Kentucky

Pk=placekicker   P=punter

Veteran punter Seiple can double as a wide receiver now and then, but he spends most of his time punting (for a 38.2 yard average in 1976). Yepremian still gets points on the board. He was nearly perfect with 29 out of 31 PATs in 1976, and he made good 16 of 22 FGs (not counting one that was blocked). Five of those FGs came from 40 yards or more out, one from 53 yards. Cody is a free agent who can kick both ways.

DEFENSE

Front Linemen	Ht.	Wt.	Age	Exp.	College
Den Herder, Vern (E)	6-6	252	28	7	Central (Iowa)
Andrews, John (E)	6-6	251	25	3	Morgan State
Heinz, Bob (T)	6-6	265	30	10	Pacific (Calif.)
Crowder, Randy (T)	6-2	236	24	4	Penn State
Fernandez, Manny (T)	6-2	250	31	10	Utah
Reese, Don (T)	6-6	255	25	4	Jackson State
Stanfill, Bill (E)	6-5	252	30	9	Georgia
Duhe, A. J. (T)	6-4	248	22	R	Louisiana State
Baumhower, Bob (T)	6-3	241	22	R	Alabama

E=end   T=tackle

Ah! says the doctor, here lies the trouble! The Miami defense, if the official 1976 league statistics can be taken as gospel, simply didn't exist. The Dolphin defensive unit ranked twenty-sixth, repeat, twenty-sixth in the entire NFL with an average total yardage yield of 362.9 yards per game. Only Kansas City and Seattle gave up more. Miami's defense against the rush was much worse than average in 1976, but it was rock bottom against the pass, permitting an average of 190.7 aerial yards per game—that made Miami twenty-eighth in the NFL. There were some problems with injuries, and Stanfill's neck may keep him from playing end in his former style. Reese hasn't progressed as well as was hoped, and, for some reason, Crowder's performance last season didn't measure up to the year before. This unit managed to sack the opposing QB only 20 times. Rookies Duhe and Baumhower may take over sooner than expected.

Linebackers	Ht.	Wt.	Age	Exp.	College
Matheson, Bob (O)	6-4	235	32	11	Duke
Bokamper, Kim (O)	6-5	235	23	2	San Jose State
Chambers, Rusty (O)	6-1	220	24	3	Tulane
Towle, Steve (M)	6-2	233	23	3	Kansas
Kolen, Mike (M)	6-2	222	29	8	Auburn
Rhone, Earnest (O)	6-2	212	23	3	Henderson State
Gordon, Larry (O)	6-4	222	23	2	Arizona State
Selfridge, Andy (O)	6-3	220	28	6	Virginia
Bertuca, Tony (M)	6-2	225	28	3	Chico State

O=outside   M=middle

At season's end, Towle, Gordon, and Matheson were the front-line 'backers in this group. Kolen and Rhone were sidelined all season with injuries. Bertuca was last active with Baltimore in 1975. Bokamper made the team his rookie year. Matheson, the 11-year vet among these, intercepted two passes in 1976, a thing no other Dolphin could do any better. Much help is needed here.

Cornerbacks	Ht.	Wt.	Age	Exp.	College
White, Jeris	5-11	180	24	4	Hawaii
Foley, Tim	6-0	194	29	8	Purdue
Bachman, Ted	6-0	190	25	2	New Mexico State
Johnson, Curtis	6-1	196	29	8	Toledo
Williams, Felix	6-2	185	23	R	Florida A&M

While opposing quarterbacks were taking it easy against the Miami rush, they were also getting away with mayhem in the pass completion department. The Dolphin secondary succeeded in intercepting only 11 passes all season. Like the rest of Miami's defensive corps, the defensive backs had their troubles with injuries. Foley's ability to play is still a matter of conjecture at this season's opening.

Safeties	Ht.	Wt.	Age	Exp.	College
Babb, Charlie	6-0	190	27	6	Memphis State
Roberson, Vern	6-2	196	25	1	Grambling
Anderson, Dick	6-2	196	31	10	Colorado
Hill, Barry	6-3	185	24	3	Iowa State
Ellis, Ken	5-11	190	30	8	Southern U.

Help is needed here, as it is elsewhere in the secondary. All three of the veterans—Babb, Anderson, and Hill—have disabilities that are keeping them from performing at the 100-percent level. Roberson signed as a free agent after leading the Canadian league in interceptions in 1975. Somewhere out there in college football land, there's talent. The problem is to find it, and then get there firstest with the mostest.

Note: A complete listing of Miami's 1977 college draft selections can be found on page 253.

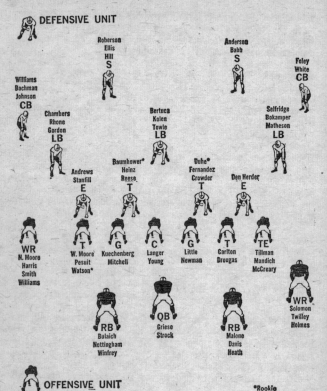

DEFENSIVE UNIT

Roberson
Ellis
Hill
S

Anderson
Babb
S

Foley
White
CB

Williams
Bachman
Johnson
CB

Chambers
Rhone
Gordon
LB

Bertuca
Kolen
Towle
LB

Selfridge
Bokamper
Matheson
LB

Andrews
Stanfill
E

Baumhower*
Heinz
Reese
T

Duhe*
Fernandez
Crowder
T

Den Herder
E

WR
N. Moore
Harris
Smith
Williams

T
W. Moore
Pesuit
Watson*

G
Kuechenberg
Mitchell

C
Langer
Young

G
Little
Newman

T
Carlton
Drougas

TE
Tillman
Mandich
McCreary

RB
Bulaich
Nottingham
Winfrey

QB
Griese
Strock

RB
Malone
Davis
Heath

WR
Solomon
Twilley
Holmes

OFFENSIVE UNIT

*Rookie

1976 DOLPHINS STATISTICS

	Dolphins	Opps.
Total Points Scored	263	264
Total First Downs	267	268
Third-Down Efficiency	77—191	91—199
Yards Rushing—First Downs	2118—122	2411—125
Passes Attempted—Completions	346—193	347—195
Yards Passing—First Downs	2268—125	2670—131
QB Sacked—Yards Lost	37—336	20—193
Interceptions—Return Average	11—13.1	15—8.5
Punts—Average Yards	62—38.2	63—41.1
Punt Returns—Return Average	35—11.9	34—8.0
Kickoff Returns—Return Average	55—24.5	57—21.6
Fumbles—Ball Lost	14—8	31—18
Penalties—Yards	70—582	94—716

STATISTICAL LEADERS

Scoring	TDs	Rush.	Pass.	Ret.	PATs	FGs	Total
Yepremian	0	0	0	0	29—31	16—23	77
Bulaich	4	4	0	0	0	0	24
Malone	4	4	0	0	0	0	24
Mandich	4	0	4	0	0	0	24
Moore, Nat	4	0	4	0	0	0	24
Solomon	4	1	2	1	0	0	24
Nottingham	3	3	0	0	0	0	18

Rushing	Atts.	Yds.	Avg.	Longest	TDs
Malone	186	797	4.3	31	4
Bulaich	122	540	4.4	35	4
Winfrey	52	205	3.9	13	1
Nottingham	63	185	2.9	13	3
Davis	31	160	5.2	57	1
Griese	23	108	4.7	26	0

Passing	Atts.	Com.	Yds.	Pct.	Int.	Longest	TDs
Griese	272	162	2097	59.6	12	47 (TD)	11
Strock	47	21	359	44.7	2	53 (TD)	3
Morrall	26	10	148	38.5	1	67 (TD)	1

Receiving	No.	Yds.	Avg.	Longest	TDs
Moore, Nat	33	625	18.9	67 (TD)	4
Bulaich	28	151	5.4	25	0
Solomon	27	453	16.8	53 (TD)	2
Harris	22	372	16.9	44	1
Mandich	22	260	11.8	31	4
Twilley	14	214	15.3	39	1
Tillman	13	130	10.0	16	1

Interceptions	No.	Yds.	Avg.	Longest	TDs
Ellis	2	40	20.0	40	0
Matheson	2	34	17.0	34	0
Babb	2	20	10.0	20	0
White	2	4	2.0	4	0

Punting	No.	Yds.	Avg.	Longest	Inside 20	Blocked
Seiple	62	2366	38.2	56	14	0

Punt Returns	No.	FCs	Yds.	Avg.	Longest	TDs
Solomon	13	0	205	15.8	79 (TD)	1
Moore, Nat	8	3	72	9.0	23	0
Harris	9	0	79	8.8	16	0

Kickoff Returns	No.	Yds.	Avg.	Longest	TDs
Harris	17	559	32.9	69	0
Davis	26	617	23.7	47	0
Nottingham	6	107	17.8	21	0

BUFFALO BILLS

Head Coach: Jim Ringo
(took over after fifth game in 1976)

2nd Year

Record: 0–9

1976 RECORD (2–12) (capital letters indicate home games)		1977 SCHEDULE (capital letters indicate home games)	
21	MIAMI 30	MIAMI	Sept. 18
3	HOUSTON 13	Denver	Sept. 25
14	Tampa Bay 9	Baltimore	Oct. 2
50	KANSAS CITY 17	N.Y. JETS	Oct. 9
14	N.Y. Jets 17	ATLANTA	Oct. 16
13	BALTIMORE 31	CLEVELAND	Oct. 23
22	NEW ENGLAND 26	Seattle	Oct. 30
14	N.Y. JETS 19	New England	Nov. 6
10	New England 20	BALTIMORE	Nov. 13
10	Dallas 17	NEW ENGLAND	Nov. 20
13	SAN DIEGO 34	Oakland (night, TV)	Nov. 28
14	Detroit 27	WASHINGTON	Dec. 4
27	Miami 45	N.Y. Jets	Dec. 11
20	Baltimore 58	Miami (TV)	Dec. 17

As one Buffalo fan expressed it, the best thing that can be said for the 1976 season is that it finally ended.

The problems began early, with O. J. Simpson's indecision on whether to play or not to play keeping matters a bit off balance for everyone, players and fans alike. Then, even before training camp opened, talented receiver Ahmad Rashad left the club after playing out his option. The Bills should have kept him, according to the best hindsight opinion available. The pass reception unit took another body blow when J. D. Hill was traded away, and this was followed by the departure of three top-flight defensive ends—Walt Patulski, Earl Edwards, and Pat Toomay. This trio left variously via the expansion draft and the trade route.

Coach Lou Saban hadn't counted on O. J. Simpson's

demand that he be traded, preferably to a West Coast club. With so much talent already leaving Buffalo, Saban suddenly found himself confronted with a situation bordering on disaster. O. J. finally returned, after holding out for a three-year contract said to be worth $2.5 million, but the whole hassle created a certain amount of dissension in the club. At one point running back Jim Braxton threatened to stage a one-man strike and refuse to play the first game against Miami.

Braxton relented and went on to play after all, but perhaps he should have stuck by his threat. Buffalo lost to the Dolphins, 30–21, and Braxton banged up his knee so badly he was sidelined for the rest of the season.

Although the Bills won a couple and lost a couple as the season opened, Lou Saban found the situation too much for his conception of the game and resigned as head coach after game No. 5. Offensive line coach Jim Ringo took over and presided over the loss of the next nine games, ending a miserable season made more miserable by highly regarded quarterback Joe Ferguson's shelving because of a back injury. When Ferguson left the scene, the Bills' debacle was complete. Only O. J. Simpson's brilliant dash for a league-leading 1,503 yards and the work of rookie linebacker Dan Jilek managed to keep Buffalo fans from losing interest in a club that, only the season before, had roused the entire city with its bid for a playoff berth.

But the main question is: What next?

Coach Ringo looks at things realistically enough. "Frustration," he says, "is difficult to finesse or forget. Even though the Bills lost [the record was 2–12] in 1976, it's to their credit that they never *accepted* losing. The distinction is important, and can turn last year's agony into this year's anticipation."

And what about the defense?

Ringo says, "Problems continue to plague our defensive unit. Offense alone cannot put us into a contending position. The obvious assignment: better defensive play, and soon. Last season, tackle Mike Kadish wound up as the only holdover starter [from 1975] on a completely restructured defensive line. We imported Sherman White from Cincinnati and started free agent Marty Smith alongside him at tackle. Rookies Ben Williams and Ken Jones shared the left end spot. Now, with Jones headed back to the offensive line where he played in college, the already slender defensive front wall is further thinned out. But we hope defensive end Tody Smith, picked up late last season from Houston on waivers, will establish his presence."

Ringo joined the Bills as offensive line coach in 1972. He was given a great deal of the credit when, in 1973, the Bills rushed for an NFL record 3,088 yards. The 43-year-old former Green Bay Packer served as an assistant coach with the Chicago Bears from 1969 through 1971 after completing a 15-year playing career in the NFL.

OFFENSE

Quarterbacks	Ht.	Wt.	Age	Exp.	College
Ferguson, Joe	6-1	184	27	5	Arkansas
Marangi, Gary	6-2	203	26	4	Boston College
Wyche, Sam	6-4	220	32	7	Furman

Ferguson missed half the 1976 season with back problems, just one of the reversals that beset the Bills last year. Marangi moved in, but a 35.3 completion percentage didn't measure up—Ferguson completes 50 percent. Wyche is the backup's backup. If Ferguson doesn't recoup, quarterbacking will again hamper the Bills.

Running Backs	Ht.	Wt.	Age	Exp.	College
Simpson, O.J.	6-1	212	30	9	Southern California
Hooks, Roland	6-0	197	24	2	N.C. State
Braxton, Jim	6-1	242	28	7	West Virginia
Kinney, Jeff	6-2	215	28	6	Nebraska

Brown, Curtis	5-10	190	22	R	Missouri
Powell, Darnell	6-0	197	23	2	Tennessee—
					Chattanooga

The late word from O. J. is that he now has hopes of playing for
two more seasons (presumably this one and next) before pursuing a
career in other fields. He has already made six movies. Braxton's
knee is on the mend; he missed 13 games last year because of it.
When they're together, he and O. J. provide the NFL's most devastating
one-two running attack. Hooks, Powell, and Kinney are good replace-
ments. Rookie Brown is good at KO returns too.

Receivers	Ht.	Wt.	Age	Exp.	College
Holland, John (W)	5-11	195	25	4	Tennessee State
Bell, Eddie (W)	5-10	160	29	8	Idaho State
Holliday, Ron (W)	5-11	180	29	2	Pittsburgh
Edwards, Emmett (W)	6-1	187	25	3	Kansas
Seymour, Paul (T)	6-5	246	27	5	Michigan
Gant, Reuben (T)	6-4	230	25	4	Oklahoma State
Coleman, Fred (T)	6-4	240	24	2	Northeast Louisiana
Chandler, Bob (W)	6-1	180	28	7	Southern California
Kimbrough, John (W)	6-0	170	22	R	St. Cloud State

W=wide receiver   T=tight end

The big man here is Chandler, whose 61 receptions for 824 yards
made him second among NFL receivers in 1976. The next nearest teammate had only 22, and he was—guess who? O. J. Simpson, who rolls
up yardage more ways than one. Seymour and Holland snared 31 jointly.
This unit could use another Chandler-type receiver. Newcomer is Eddie
Bell, formerly with the Jets and Chargers. Kimbrough comes with great
credentials from college division circles.

Interior Linemen	Ht.	Wt.	Age	Exp.	College
Foley, Dave (T)	6-5	247	30	8	Ohio State
Jones, Ken (T, G)	6-5	252	25	2	Arkansas State
McKenzie, Reggie (G)	6-4	244	27	6	Michigan
Adams, Bill (G)	6-3	246	27	5	Holy Cross
Montler, Mike (C)	6-4	245	33	9	Colorado
Parker, Willie (C)	6-3	252	29	6	North Texas State
Patton, Bob (C)	6-1	240	23	2	Delaware
DeLamielleure, Joe (G)	6-3	248	26	5	Michigan State
Wilcox, Will (G)	6-3	243	24	2	Texas
Green, Donnie (T)	6-7	252	29	7	Purdue
Devlin, Joe (T)	6-5	270	23	2	Iowa
Dunstan, Bill (T)	6-4	250	28	5	Utah State

T=tackle   G=guard   C=center

The offensive line had both good and bad notices in 1976. The Buffalo rushing game averaged 183.3 yards per game, third best in the entire NFL. Foley, McKenzie, Montler, DeLamielleure, Green & Company did their job well and return to do it again. In the passing area, Buffalo quarterbacks were sacked 33 times—not too bad, but not too good, either. An improved passing game could make this unit one of the very best.

Kickers	Ht.	Wt.	Age	Exp.	College
Bateman, Marv (P)	6-4	214	27	6	Utah
Jakowenko, George (Pk)	5-9	180	29	3	Syracuse

Pk=placekicker   P=punter

In 1976 O. J. Simpson led the league in rushing, Chandler almost led in pass receptions, and Bateman led in punting, with a 42.8 yard average on 86 boots. Jakowenko is a good placekicker; he got 21 of 24 PATs and 12 of 17 FGs in 1976.

DEFENSE

Front Linemen	Ht.	Wt.	Age	Exp.	College
Williams, Ben (E)	6-2	258	23	2	Mississippi
Kadish, Mike (T)	6-5	270	27	5	Notre Dame
Lloyd, Jeff (T)	6-6	255	23	2	West Texas State
Smith, Marty (T)	6-3	250	24	2	Louisville
White, Sherman (E)	6-5	250	29	6	California
Dokes, Phil (T)	6-5	260	22	R	Oklahoma State

E=end   T=tackle

An area for continued improvement. The defensive unit has ranked low among NFL clubs for at least two seasons, proving ineffective generally against both the pass and the rush. Kadish is a blue-chipper at tackle, and in his college career Dokes made 87 solo tackles and recovered nine fumbles. But help is needed here if Jim Ringo is to move the Bills up.

Linebackers	Ht.	Wt.	Age	Exp.	College
Skorupan, John (O)	6-2	225	26	5	Penn State
Ruud, Tom (O)	6-3	223	24	3	Nebraska
Johnson, Mark (O)	6-2	236	24	3	Missouri
Krakau, Merv (M)	6-2	233	26	5	Iowa State
Nelson, Bob (M)	6-4	232	24	3	Nebraska
Jilek, Dan (O)	6-2	212	24	2	Michigan
Cornell, Bo (O)	6-1	222	28	7	Washington

O=outside   M=middle

Skorupan, one of a long line of Penn State linebackers, leads this group. Jilek was one of the better rookies of 1976. Beyond those two, the Bills have a way to go before this unit is tip-top.

Cornerbacks	Ht.	Wt.	Age	Exp.	College
Harrison, Dwight	6-2	186	29	7	Texas A&I
Moody, Keith	5-11	171	24	2	Syracuse
Clark, Mario	6-2	184	23	2	Oregon
Brooks, Cliff	6-1	190	28	5	Tennessee State
James, Bobby	6-1	184	30	8	Fisk

Harrison plays his right cornerback with skill, and Clark proved he was cast properly as Buffalo's only first-round draftee of 1976. James, a former All-Pro, wants to play again, but an injured leg has sidelined him for two seasons now. Another defense area that needs help. Moody caught eyes as a rookie.

Safeties	Ht.	Wt.	Age	Exp.	College
Jones, Doug	6-2	205	27	4	California State
Green, Van	6-1	197	26	5	Shaw
Greene, Tony	5-10	170	28	7	Maryland
Freeman, Steve	5-11	185	24	3	Mississippi

Tony Greene is the best of these. Jones's year wasn't up to expectations. Van Green is coming off injury; he missed seven games in 1976.

Note: A complete listing of Buffalo's 1977 college draft selections can be found on page 248.

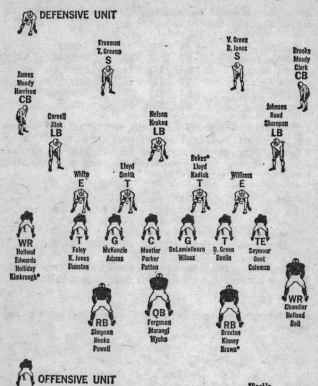

DEFENSIVE UNIT

Freeman
T. Greene
S

V. Green
D. Jones
S

James
Moody
Harrison
CB

Brooks
Moody
Clark
CB

Cornell
Jilek
LB

Nelson
Krakau
LB

Johnson
Ruud
Skorupan
LB

White
E

Lloyd
Smith
T

Dokes*
Lloyd
Kadish
T

Williams
E

WR
Holland
Edwards
Holliday
Kimbrough*

Foley
K. Jones
Dunstan
T

McKenzie
Adams
G

Montler
Parker
Patton
C

DeLamielleure
Wilcox
G

D. Green
Devlin
T

Seymour
Gant
Coleman
TE

RB
Simpson
Hooks
Powell

QB
Ferguson
Marangi
Wyche

RB
Braxton
Kinney
Brown*

WR
Chandler
Holland
Bell

OFFENSIVE UNIT

*Rookie

1976 BILLS STATISTICS

	Bills	Opps.
Total Points Scored	245	363
Total First Downs	250	262
Third-Down Efficiency	81—216	71—187
Yards Rushing—First Downs	2566—135	2476—128
Passes Attempted—Completions	383—156	337—163
Yards Passing—First Downs	1838—102	2254—110
QB Sacked—Yards Lost	33—246	30—221
Interceptions—Return Average	19—15.4	17—14.5
Punts—Average Yards	87—42.3	72—38.5
Punt Returns—Return Average	33—6.7	46—19.1
Kickoff Returns—Return Average	75—21.3	48—25.1
Fumbles—Ball Lost	44—26	37—23
Penalties—Yards	91—797	92—704

STATISTICAL LEADERS

Scoring	TDs	Rush.	Pass.	Ret.	PATs	FGs	Total
Chandler	10	0	10	0	0	0	60
Jakowenko	0	0	0	0	21—24	12—17	57
Simpson	9	8	1	0	0	0	54
Gant	3	0	3	0	0	0	18
Holland	3	0	2	1	0	0	18
Marangi	2	2	0	0	0	0	12

Rushing	Atts.	Yds.	Avg.	Longest	TDs
Simpson	290	1503	5.2	75 (TD)	8
Kinney	116	475	4.1	22	1
Marangi	39	230	5.9	21	2
Hooks	25	116	4.6	24	0
Ferguson	18	81	4.5	19	0
Washington	22	65	3.0	10	0
Ray	24	56	2.3	7	0

Passing	Atts.	Com.	Yds.	Pct.	Int.	Longest	TDs
Ferguson	151	74	1086	49.0	1	58 (TD)	9
Marangi	232	82	998	35.3	16	39	7

Receiving	No.	Yds.	Avg.	Longest	TDs
Chandler	61	824	13.5	58 (TD)	10
Simpson	22	259	11.8	43	1
Seymour	16	169	10.6	22	0
Holland	15	299	19.9	58 (TD)	2
Kinney	14	78	5.6	15	0
Gant	12	263	21.9	39	3
Hooks	6	72	12.0	28	0

Interceptions	No.	Yds.	Avg.	Longest	TDs
Greene	5	135	27.0	101 (TD)	1
Moody	3	63	21.0	44	0
Jones, Doug	3	5	1.7	5	0
Jilek	2	33	16.5	28	0
Clark	2	21	10.5	21	0

Punting	No.	Yds.	Avg.	Longest	Inside 20	Blocked
Bateman	86	3678	42.8	78	16	1

Punt Returns	No.	FCs	Yds.	Avg.	Longest	TDs
Moody	16	8	166	10.4	67 (TD)	1
Hooks	11	3	45	4.1	12	0

Kickoff Returns	No.	Yds.	Avg.	Longest	TDs
Moody	26	605	23.3	41	0
Hooks	23	521	22.7	79	0
Powell	4	101	25.3	26	0
Holmes	4	90	22.5	26	0

NEW YORK JETS

Head Coach: Walt Michaels
1st Year

1976 RECORD (3–11)		1977 SCHEDULE	
(capital letters indicate home games)		(capital letters indicate home games)	
17 Cleveland	38	Houston	Sept. 18
3 Denver	46	BALTIMORE	Sept. 25
0 Miami	16	NEW ENGLAND	Oct. 2
6 San Francisco	17	Buffalo	Oct. 9
17 BUFFALO	14	Miami	Oct. 16
7 New England	41	OAKLAND	Oct. 23
0 BALTIMORE	20	New England	Oct. 30
19 Buffalo	14	MIAMI	Nov. 6
7 MIAMI	27	SEATTLE	Nov. 13
34 TAMPA BAY	0	Baltimore	Nov. 20
24 NEW ENGLAND	38	PITTSBURGH	Nov. 27
16 Baltimore	33	New Orleans	Dec. 4
16 WASHINGTON	37	BUFFALO	Dec. 11
3 CINCINNATI	42	Philadelphia	Dec. 18

Just after the close of last season, Paul Zimmerman of the *New York Post* wrote an open letter to the Jets' new coach:

Dear Coach Michaels: Here's how you turn the Jets around. Get a pass-rushing defensive end. Get a pass-rushing defensive tackle. Get another pass-rushing defensive tackle. Put them all together with Larry Pillers and let the other guys try to fight for their jobs. That's how you turn the Jets around.

What Zimmerman wrote makes sense when you consider the pass-rushing achievements of the Jets last season. They got to the opposing quarterbacks just 16 times, the NFL low for 1976. And they almost tied the NFL record set four years ago by the New England Patriots,

44

who succeeded in sacking the opposing QBs just 15 times. But Michaels, a former linebacker of note himself, has more than just the pass-blitzing department to think about. The entire defensive unit needs more than, perhaps, can be provided in one season alone.

Aside from the end of Joe Namath's legendary career as a Jet quarterback, the biggest offensive news of 1976 (among the Jets) was a running back whose name is, appropriately, Gaines—Clark Gaines, that is. He's the hero of a very unusual story.

A total of 68 runing backs were chosen during the 1976 NFL collegiate draft in New York. Gaines, a six-foot, 198-pound speedster from Wake Forest, wasn't among those who were selected by the 28 NFL clubs. But the Jets were alert in this instance at least, and signed Gaines as a free agent. And what happened? Gaines ran for 724 yards to lead all NFL rookie rushers and became the Jets' Most Valuable Player. (Who needs the draft?)

On the defensive unit, there were also some shining moments for the rookies, even though such instances were few. The first-year linebacking trio of Greg Buttle, Bob Martin, and Larry Keller highlighted an otherwise unimpressive performance by the defense as a whole. The front line, too, had first-year standouts in Larry Pillers, an eleventh-round pick from Alcorn State, and Larry Faulk, a seventh-round choice from Kent State. And, turning again to the offense, veteran tackle Winston Hill extended his consecutive-games-played streak to 195. He now faces his fifteenth NFL season.

The most momentous development for the Jets, however, is the departure of Joe Namath, and what that will mean to the club's offensive style. Thirty-three-year-old Joe, as every fan knows, has gimpy knees—knees that have definitely seen better days. The opposition knew the way to get the Jets was to get Joe, and they did.

Unlike most successful modern quarterbacks, Namath has little or no mobility. He takes the ball from the center, fades back, uncorks his arm in a long or a short pass —and that's it. If anything interferes with that procedure, like onrushing defensive end types, then it's just a part of the game. Joe is a lot of things, but a scrambler he is not.

There's some question as to whether Richard Todd, Namath's protégé in his closing days with the Jets, can step into the breach. The Jets may need more than Todd is able to provide. And the new quarterback, whoever he is, may be much more mobile than Namath, necessitating changes in an offensive line that, for years, has been used to protecting a drop-back-no-scramble passer.

The announcement that Namath was being put on waivers by the Jets brought back a flood of memories. Joe's problems came into focus during a preseason game with the Detroit Lions back in 1971. The contest was played one Saturday night in Tampa. Joe had just thrown a pass that was intercepted by Detroit linebacker Mike Lucci—and Lucci was running for a touchdown with only Namath standing in the way. Namath was ready, but Detroit's Paul Naumoff, another linebacker, blocked him out of the play—and Joe came up holding his left knee and its torn ligaments. He had missed most of the previous season with a broken wrist; now he was facing his fourth knee operation.

Five years later, and it was a long time, a sad-eyed Joe was waving good-bye to New York—for he had just become a waiver himself.

OFFENSE

Quarterbacks	Ht.	Wt.	Age	Exp.	College
Todd, Richard	6-2	205	23	2	Alabama
Joachim, Steve	6-3	215	25	2	Temple

Now that Joe has been let out to sunnier pastures, fellow Alabama U. quarterback Richard Todd seems the likely successor—or does he? Todd's performance as Joe's stand-in hasn't been all that impressive, and Michaels may have to rethink the entire situation. Joachim is an untried second-year rookie who now may get a chance to show his stuff.

Running Backs	Ht.	Wt.	Age	Exp.	College
Giammona, Louie	5-9	180	24	2	Utah State
Davis, Steve	6-1	218	27	6	Delaware State
Gresham, Bob	5-11	195	29	7	West Virginia
Gaines, Clark	6-1	195	23	2	Wake Forest
Marinaro, Ed	6-2	207	27	6	Cornell
Stevenson, Irvin	6-2	225	24	2	Delaware State

See how they run! This group has lots of ball-carrying ability, light and fast as they are. Giammona (and wide receiver Lou Piccone) earned their jobs as "quick returners" on punts and kickoffs. Gresham carried only 30 times in 1976 for a 3.1 yard average. Marinaro ran two straight 100-yard games, tying a club record, but then hurt his foot and had to stop for a while. Taking Marinaro's place was rookie free agent Clark Gaines who, at season's end, wound up leading the Jet rushers with 724 yards (and a 4.6 average). He led in pass receptions as well, with 41. Davis didn't slough off, either; he racked up 418 yards in 94 attempts.

Receivers	Ht.	Wt.	Age	Exp.	College
Barkum, Jerome (W)	6-4	212	27	6	Jackson State
Piccone, Lou (W)	5-9	175	28	4	West Liberty
Satterwhite, Howard (W)	5-11	185	24	2	Sam Houston
Caster, Richard (T)	6-5	228	28	8	Jackson State
Osborne, Richard (T)	6-4	230	24	2	Texas A&M
Pawlewicz, Rick (T)	6-2	210	24	2	William & Mary
Knight, David (W)	6-1	175	26	5	William & Mary
Buckey, Don (W)	6-0	177	23	1	N.C. State
Walker, Wesley (W)	5-11	172	22	R	California

W=wide receiver   T=tight end

Barkum, one of the best, was hampered with a severely pulled muscle all last year, and Caster carried much of the receiving load. But Caster had to struggle with double-teaming defense all season. If both of these speedsters are in good shape, the Jets' passing game will get a big boost. In 1976 Knight came along fast, then slowed down, but he has potential. Satterwhite got attention as a rookie, catching seven for 110 yards. Buckey gets another chance this year. Rookie Walker holds NCAA career marks of 25.7 yards per pass catch.

Interior Linemen	Ht.	Wt.	Age	Exp.	College
Woods, Robert (T)	6-3	255	27	5	Tennessee State
Hill, Winston (T)	6-4	280	36	15	Texas Southern
Roman, John (G, T)	6-4	247	25	2	Idaho State
Rasmussen, Randy (G)	6-2	267	32	11	Kearney State
Austin, Darrell (C)	6-4	250	25	3	South Carolina
Fields, Joe (C)	6-2	240	23	3	Widener
Puetz, Gary (G)	6-3	265	25	5	Valparaiso
Krevis, Al (T)	6-6	263	25	3	Boston College
King, Steve (T)	6-5	245	24	2	Michigan
Shukri, Dave (T, C)	6-5	270	22	R	Penn State
Powell, Marvin (T)	6-5	274	22	R	Southern California

T=tackle   G=guard   C=center

The Jets' offensive unit finished way down the list in 1976. Overall, the club could gain only 252.1 yards per game, so they came out ranking twenty-fifth among the NFL's 28 teams. The rushing and passing offenses were equally ineffective. Jet QBs were sacked 45 times. Hill has played many games since joining the Jets in 1963. He's now 36 and retirement beckons. Rasmussen has put in a lot of time too, but he's still one of the best guards around. Austin was bothered last season with a recurring neck injury. Michaels is already blueprinting the offensive line to make room for Powell, the USC All-America tackle. He plans to move Puetz to guard to open up the right side for Powell. Austin would become the first-line center.

Kickers	Ht.	Wt.	Age	Exp.	College
Carrell, Duane (P)	5-10	185	28	4	Florida State
Leahy, Pat (Pk)	6-0	200	27	4	St. Louis U.

Pk=placekicker   P=punter

Quarterback Todd has also been known to punt a few, but Carrell's 39.7 average was good enough to place him among the league's top ten punters last season. Oddly, Leahy did better at kicking FGs, getting 16 of 20, than he did at PATs, of which he made only 11 of 16. One of those FGs was a 47-yarder.

DEFENSE

Front Linemen	Ht.	Wt.	Age	Exp.	College
Pillers, Lawrence (E)	6-3	250	25	2	Alcorn State
Newsome, Billy (E)	6-5	252	29	8	Grambling
Wasick, Dave (E)	6-0	245	24	2	San Jose State
Barzilauskas, Carl (T)	6-6	280	26	4	Indiana
Faulk, Larry (T)	6-3	260	23	2	Kent State
Neal, Richard (E)	6-3	260	29	9	Southern U.
Lomas, Mark (E)	6-4	250	29	7	Northern Arizona
Sanders, Clarence (E)	6-4	230	25	2	Cincinnati
Marshall, Tank (E)	6-5	255	22	R	Texas A&M

E=end   T=tackle

The Jets finished 1976 ranked twenty-fifth in league total offense, and they achieved the same distinction on defense, allowing an overall average of 351.1 yards per game. The passing defense was somewhat more impressive than defense against the rush, but not much. On the pass rush, the Jets sacked quarterbacks only occasionally. Opposing passers, it would seem, practically had time to rewrite playbooks if they so desired. Michaels could spend all his time working here. Marshall is reputed to resemble his nickname.

Linebackers	Ht.	Wt.	Age	Exp.	College
Buttle, Greg (O)	6-3	227	23	2	Penn State
Hennigan, Mike (O)	6-2	230	26	5	Tennessee Tech
Ebersole, John (M)	6-3	227	28	8	Penn State
Coleman, Don (O)	6-2	222	25	4	Michigan
Poole, Steve (M)	6-1	232	25	2	Tennessee
Russ, Carl (M)	6-2	227	24	3	Michigan
Martin, Bob (O)	6-1	217	24	2	Nebraska
Keller, Larry, (O)	6-2	220	24	2	Houston

O=outside   M=middle

Michaels was a four-time All-Pro linebacker in his playing days with the Browns, so he should know whereof he speaks. And he says Buttle is a future All-Pro. It figures—Buttle is a linebacker out of Penn State, where they have the patent on good ones. In fact, Michaels is strong here, since three of his second-year LBs have come through their rookie seasons in style; the other two are Martin and Keller. Keller was especially impressive in the two Jet victories over Buffalo, intercepting a pass that led to a TD, blocking a punt for six points, recovering two fumbles, and causing a fumble that set up a field goal. As for Buttle, Michaels declares: "When he hits people, he buries them."

Cornerbacks	Ht.	Wt.	Age	Exp.	College
Suggs, Shafer	6-2	195	23	2	Ball State
Sowells, Rich	6-0	181	28	7	Alcorn State
Marvaso, Tommy	6-1	191	24	2	Cincinnati
Taylor, Ed	6-0	170	24	3	Memphis State

The Jets' secondary was a disaster area at season's end. Taylor sustained both knee and ankle sprains in late-season contests, and Suggs was hobbled by an ankle that sidelined him the last two games. In addition, safety Phil Wise's severe knee sprain kept him out of the last two contests, forcing a general shuffling of linebacker and secondary personnel in order to field a defensive unit. In fact, at one point only three men were available for the defensive secondary—safety Burgess Owens, corner Rich Sowells, and swing man Tommy Marvaso. General Manager Al Ward got on the telephone trying to find a fourth . . . and not for bridge.

Safeties	Ht.	Wt.	Age	Exp.	College
Wise, Phil	6-0	190	28	7	Nebraska
Schroy, Ken	6-1	191	25	2	Maryland
Owens, Burgess	6-2	200	26	5	Miami (Fla.)

The Jets intercepted only 11 passes in 1976, and the opposition QBs successfully completed 55 percent of their throws. Injuries hampered both the cornerbacks and safeties as the season ground to a close. There's work to be done here.

Note: A complete listing of the New York Jets' 1977 college draft selections can be found on page 256.

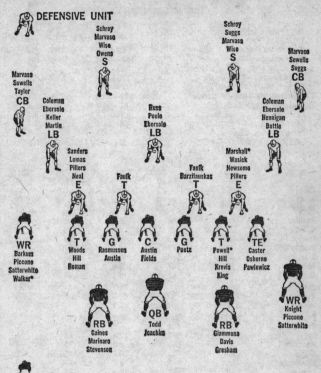

DEFENSIVE UNIT

Schroy
Marvaso
Wise
Owens
S

Schroy
Suggs
Marvaso
Wise
S

Marvaso
Sowells
Suggs
CB

Marvaso
Sowells
Taylor
CB

Coleman
Ebersole
Keller
Martin
LB

Russ
Poole
Ebersole
LB

Coleman
Ebersole
Hennigan
Buttle
LB

Sanders
Lomas
Pillers
Neal
E

Faulk
T

Faulk
Barzilauskas
T

Marshall*
Wasick
Newsome
Pillers
E

WR
Barkum
Piccone
Satterwhite
Walker*

T
Woods
Hill
Roman

G
Rasmussen
Austin

C
Austin
Fields

G
Puetz

T
Powell*
Hill
Krevis
King

TE
Caster
Osborne
Pawlewicz

WR
Knight
Piccone
Satterwhite

RB
Gaines
Marinaro
Stevenson

QB
Todd
Joachim

RB
Giammona
Davis
Gresham

OFFENSIVE UNIT

*Rookie

1976 JETS STATISTICS

	Jets	Opps.
Total Points Scored	169	383
Total First Downs	220	277
Third-Down Efficiency	69—188	102—214
Yards Rushing—First Downs	1924—104	2592—135
Passes Attempted—Completions	393—180	374—204
Yards Passing—First Downs	1606—93	2324—127
QB Sacked—Yards Lost	45—383	16—144
Interceptions—Return Average	11—13.3	28—15.4
Punts—Average Yards	81—39.7	65—41.1
Punt Returns—Return Average	40—7.2	55—8.3
Kickoff Returns—Return Average	73—21.9	39—23.1
Fumbles—Ball Lost	44—25	36—21
Penalties—Yards	71—627	84—796

STATISTICAL LEADERS

Scoring	TDs	Rush.	Pass.	Ret.	PATs	FGs	Total
Leahy	0	0	0	0	16—20	11—16	49
Gaines	5	3	2	0	0	0	30
Davis	3	3	0	0	0	0	18
Knight	2	0	2	0	0	0	12

Rushing	Atts.	Yds.	Avg.	Longest	TDs
Gaines	157	724	4.6	33	3
Davis	94	418	4.4	26	3
Marinaro	77	312	4.1	17	2
Giammona	39	150	3.8	35	1
Todd	28	107	3.8	22	1
Gresham	30	92	3.1	24	0

Passing	Atts.	Com.	Yds.	Pct.	Int.	Longest	TDs
Namath	230	114	1090	49.6	16	35	4
Todd	162	65	870	40.1	12	44 (TD)	3

Receiving	No.	Yds.	Avg.	Longest	TDs
Gaines	41	400	9.8	27	2
Caster	31	391	12.6	41	1
Marinaro	21	168	8.0	35	0
Knight	20	403	20.2	44 (TD)	2
Giammona	15	145	9.7	28	0
Piccone	12	147	12.3	23	0
Gresham	11	66	6.0	13	0

Interceptions	No.	Yds.	Avg.	Longest	TDs
Sowells	2	46	23.0	27	0
Taylor	2	22	11.0	22	0
Buttle	2	20	10.0	14	0
Martin	2	15	7.5	15	0

Punting	No.	Yds.	Avg.	Longest	Inside 20	Blocked
Carrell	81	3218	39.7	72	13	0

Punt Returns	No.	FCs	Yds.	Avg.	Longest	TDs
Piccone	21	0	173	8.2	60 (TD)	1
Giammona	12	1	117	9.8	25	0

Kickoff Returns	No.	Yds.	Avg.	Longest	TDs
Giammona	23	527	22.9	34	0
Piccone	31	699	22.5	58	0
Denson	6	129	21.5	29	0
Jackson	10	207	20.7	30	0

CINCINNATI BENGALS

Head Coach: Bill Johnson

2nd Year   **Record:** 10–4

1976 RECORD (10–4) (capital letters indicate home games)		1977 SCHEDULE (capital letters indicate home games)	
17	DENVER	7	CLEVELAND	Sept. 18
27	Baltimore	28	SEATTLE	Sept. 25
28	GREEN BAY	7	San Diego	Oct. 2
45	Cleveland	24	vs. Green Bay at Milwaukee	Oct. 9
21	TAMPA BAY	0	Pittsburgh (night, TV)	Oct. 17
6	Pittsburgh	23	DENVER	Oct. 23
27	Houston	7	HOUSTON	Oct. 30
21	CLEVELAND	6	Cleveland	Nov. 6
20	LOS ANGELES	12	Minnesota	Nov. 13
31	HOUSTON	27	MIAMI	Nov. 20
27	Kansas City	24	N.Y. GIANTS	Nov. 27
3	PITTSBURGH	7	Kansas City	Dec. 4
35	Oakland	20	PITTSBURGH (TV)	Dec. 10
42	N.Y. Jets	3	Houston	Dec. 18

The near-miss Bengals are beginning to feel like the Oakland Raiders used to. General manager Paul Brown and coach Bill Johnson posted a 10–4 record, which wasn't enough. The Bengals were 9–2 going into a final three-game stretch against Pittsburgh, Oakland, and the Jets. All they needed was a win over the Steelers, but they blew it. And, still, all they needed was two straight over the Jets and Oakland. But Oakland bombed them, exposing the poor pass defense, and it was all over—again.

The Bengals are a good team, and they could be a great one. In 1976 they lost to the Baltimore Colts 28–27 on a key fumble by Ken Riley after a turn-around interception by that cornerback. Against the Steelers, with Cincinnati winning 3–0, Boobie Clark lost the ball on his own 24 and Pittsburgh took it in for the key 7–3 win.

Defensive end Coy Bacon led the NFL in sacks last year with 26, making the deal with San Diego look very good. Riley led the AFC with nine interceptions, although the NFL coaches figured that Lamar Parrish, who always draws the best receivers, was the All-Pro. Archie Griffin, the two-time Heisman winner, started every game and finished with 625 yards—only 49 yards fewer than the combined first-year totals of Greg Pruitt, Otis Armstrong, and Lydell Mitchell, other small running backs, in their first NFL seasons.

Quarterback Ken Anderson wasn't the virtuoso of the previous season, but he did throw 19 TD passes. He can put it up as well as anyone and is a proven leader.

Middle linebacker Jim Leclair finally got out of the shadow of Bill Bergey, but despite Leclair's success, the Bengal coaching hierarchy had to be disappointed with the showing of its offensive line. Boobie Clark led the rushing attack with only 671 yards. Because of the less-than-sensational running attack, the Bengals had to depend on Anderson via the air lanes—and the other teams knew it.

Johnson would like the front four to do better, although Bacon was a veritable virtuoso of violence last year. The Steeler and Colt linemen muscled the Bengal trenchmen when it counted, however, and this, in part, proved to be the difference between winning and coming in second.

Although Brown sneaked an early edition of the expansion Bengals into the AFC playoffs with 8–6 one year, Cincinnati still doesn't believe it can win the big ones against Pittsburgh and Oakland. This is part of the problem. They desperately need to develop their offensive line to help out Griffin and Clark. Rocky Bleier isn't exactly O. J. Simpson, but he ground out 1,000-

plus yards for Pittsburgh; meanwhile, the more talented Griffin was not able to do the same with the Bengals.

Cincinnati could beat Pittsburgh and win the AFC Central this year, and they could wind up third behind archrival Cleveland, a fate that Brown would consider worse than death. It may be up to an improved rushing attack and more judicious play-calling by the coaching staff, who live on Ken Anderson's arm at present. If either Anderson or wide receiver Isaac Curtis gets hurt, the long-range Cincy attack will bog down. But the bomb is not the road to the Super Bowl, and the Bengals must diversify their attack and go overland more if they hope to unseat Pittsburgh in the division and Oakland in the playoffs.

In any event, look for Cincinnati to unwind an even more determined effort to grab the big NFL prizes. Bill Johnson, in his first year, proved that he is a fit successor for Paul Brown, the great pro coach who has already become a legend out there in the Midwestern football lands.

OFFENSE

Quarterbacks	Ht.	Wt.	Age	Exp.	College
Anderson, Ken	6-6	211	28	7	Augustana (Ill.)
Reaves, John	6-3½	202	27	6	Florida

Anderson, the leader in 1975, dropped out of the top ten in NFL passing last year, but still is one of the best arms in the NFL. He dropped to 53.0 percent, 19 TDs, and 14 interceptions in 1976. He is still just about the best in the NFL, with the possible exceptions of Ken Stabler and Bert Jones. Backup John Reaves did his thing and won his game when Ken Anderson was hurt, and he's better than previously rated; he had unhappy experiences with the Philadelphia Eagles.

Running Backs	Ht.	Wt.	Age	Exp.	College
Griffin, Archie	5-9	191	23	2	Ohio State
Elliott, Lenvil	5-11	207	26	5	Northeast Missouri

Shelby, Willie	5-10	190	24	2	Alabama
Clark, Boobie	6-2	245	27	5	Bethune—Cookman
Davis, Tony	5-10	210	24	2	Nebraska
Fritts, Stan	6-2	215	25	3	N.C. State
Johnson, Pete	6-0	245	22	R	Ohio State
Voight, Mike	6-0	204	22	R	North Carolina

Clark led in 1976 with 671 yards, Archie Griffin was next, and then came Lenvil Elliott with 276. The Bengals were fifth from last in running the ball in the AFC. Griffin should get better as he picks up NFL savvy. Clark could bust for 1,000 yards if he's totally healthy. These are "musts" for the Bengals to challenge again. Griffin still has to prove he can be a dominant runner. Johnson was the all-time top scorer at Ohio State, no mean achievement.

Receivers	Ht.	Wt.	Age	Exp.	College
McDaniel, John (W)	6-1	194	26	4	Lincoln (Mo.)
Brooks, Billy (W)	6-4	215	24	2	Oklahoma
Trumpy, Bob (T)	6-6	231	32	10	Utah
Curtis, Isaac (W)	6-1	195	27	5	San Diego State
McInally, Pat (W)	6-5	200	24	2	Harvard
Cobb, Mike (T)	6-5	243	22	R	Michigan State

W=wide receiver   T=tight end

Curtis was scintillating in 1976, with long-range gallops after catching 41 passes. He racked up 766 yards and six TDs. Clark came out of the backfield for 23 catches, Elliott for 22. Trumpy caught 21, often in key situations, and scored seven TDs. Brooks disappointed and might not make it this year. McDaniel, pressed into service, set a one-game Cincinnati record and will get more playing time. Cobb was an All Big Ten pass catcher.

Interior Linemen	Ht.	Wt.	Age	Exp.	College
Mayes, Rufus (T)	6-5	268	30	9	Ohio State
Bujnoch, Glenn (G, T)	6-5	260	24	2	Texas A&M
Shinners, John (G)	6-2	259	30	9	Xavier
Fairchild, Greg (G)	6-4	258	23	2	Tulsa
Lapham, Dave (G)	6-4	258	25	4	Syracuse
Johnson, Bob (C)	6-5	255	31	10	Tennessee
Holland, Vernon (T)	6-5	272	29	7	Tennessee State
Hunt, Ron (T)	6-6	274	22	2	Oregon

T=tackle   G=guard   C=center

The regulars are Mayes, Shinners, Johnson, Lapham, and Holland. Holland and Johnson are pretty good, but the Bengals don't have a pulling guard to lead Griffin on his sweeps. Lapham may get a shot at a regular job this year.

Kickers	Ht.	Wt.	Age	Exp.	College
McInally, Pat (P)	6-5	200	24	2	Harvard
Bahr, Chris (Pk)	5-9	170	24	2	Penn State

Pk=placekicker   P=punter

Pat McInally, who also plays wide receiver, is the Bengal punter. He kicked 76 for a 39.5 average in 1976, and one of those was a 60-yarder. Bahr also earned his keep. The former Penn State bull's-eye specialist placekicked 39 of 42 PATs and 14 FGs out of 27 tries. Two of those FGs came from 50 yards or more out, while three were good from 40-plus yards. Good kicking all around.

DEFENSE

Front Linemen	Ht.	Wt.	Age	Exp.	College
Burley, Gary (E)	6-3	262	25	2	Pittsburgh
Johnson, Ken (E)	6-6	262	30	7	Indiana
Brown, Bob (T)	6-5	280	37	13	Arkansas AM&N
Kollar, Bill (T)	6-4	256	25	4	Montana
Carpenter, Ron (T)	6-5	265	29	8	N.C. State
Bacon, Coy (E)	6-4	270	35	10	Jackson State
Edwards, Eddie (T)	6-5	250	22	R	Miami (Fla.)
Whitley, Wilson (T)	6-3	268	22	R	Houston

E=end   T=tackle

Bacon sacked the quarterback 26 times in 1976 to top the NFL, but he sometimes got fooled by the run. Brown, Carpenter, and Burley are not impregnable. The Bengals were seventh against the rush last year, which is too low for a genuine contender; they allowed 1,912 rushing yards. Kollar may get more time this fall, but Brown must consider revamping his front four—1976 was their second bad year in a row. First-year men Edwards and Whitley are first-round draft choices.

Linebackers	Ht.	Wt.	Age	Exp.	College
Harris, Bo (O)	6-3	228	24	3	Louisiana State
Devlin, Chris (O)	6-2	228	24	3	Penn State
LeClair, Jim (M)	6-3	237	27	6	North Dakota
Cameron, Glenn (M)	6-1	230	24	3	Florida
Williams, Reggie (O)	6-1	230	23	2	Dartmouth
Kuhn, Ken (O)	6-1	233	23	1	Ohio State

O=outside   M=middle

The legend of Bill Bergey has ceased to haunt Cincinnati, and Jim LeClair is now the MLB in full possession. Williams and Harris became regular last year but still have much to learn. Cameron backs up LeClair in the middle. Kuhn was on injured reserve in 1976.

Cornerbacks	Ht.	Wt.	Age	Exp.	College
Parrish, Lemar	5-10	180	30	8	Lincoln (Mo.)
Morgan, Melvin	5-11	175	24	2	Mississippi Valley
Riley, Ken	5-11	183	30	9	Florida A&M
Perry, Scott	6-0	185	23	2	Williams

Riley had nine interceptions in 1976, helping the Bengals lead the AFC with 26. Parrish had three and went to the Pro Bowl. Scott and Morgan are in the wings with long waits ahead of them.

Safeties	Ht.	Wt.	Age	Exp.	College
Casanova, Tom	6-2	194	27	6	Louisiana State
Cobb, Marvin	6-0	185	24	3	Southern California

Casanova made the All-AFC squad last year and scored twice on interception runbacks and once on a fumble return. He plucked off five passes; Marvin Cobb grabbed three. A solid group that had Cincy topping the NFL in pass defense—they allowed only 1,758 yards last season.

Note: A complete listing of Cincinnati's 1977 college draft selections can be found on page 249.

DEFENSIVE UNIT

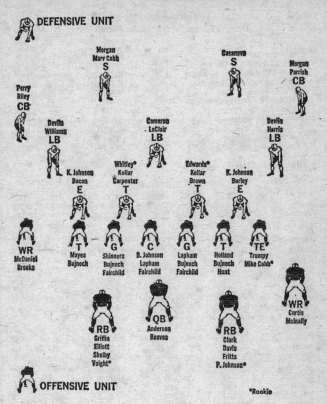

Morgan
Marv Cobb
S

Casanova
S

Morgan
Parrish
CB

Perry
Riley
CB

Devlin
Williams
LB

Cameron
LeClair
LB

Devlin
Harris
LB

K. Johnson
Bacon
E

Whitley*
Kollar
Carpenter
T

Edwards*
Kollar
Brown
T

K. Johnson
Burley
E

WR
McDaniel
Brooks

Mayes
Bujnoch
T

Shinners
Bujnoch
Fairchild
G

B. Johnson
Lapham
Fairchild
C

Lapham
Bujnoch
Fairchild
G

Holland
Bujnoch
Hunt
T

Trumpy
Mike Cobb*
TE

WR
Curtis
McInally

RB
Griffin
Elliott
Shelby
Voight*

QB
Anderson
Reaves

RB
Clark
Davis
Fritts
P. Johnson*

OFFENSIVE UNIT

*Rookie

1976 BENGALS STATISTICS

	Bengals	Opps.
Total Points Scored	335*	210
Total First Downs	238	234
Third-Down Efficiency	71—186	61—201
Yards Rushing—First Downs	2109—114	1919—116
Passes Attempted—Completions	370—187	364—177
Yards Passing—First Downs	2191—110	1758—103
QB Sacked—Yards Lost	37—252	46—444
Interceptions—Return Average	26—12.7	15—6.8
Punts—Average Yards	76—39.5	86—38.1
Punt Returns—Return Average	54—6.4	41—7.9
Kickoff Returns—Return Average	49—21.1	66—24.5
Fumbles—Ball Lost	38—20	34—15
Penalties—Yards	79—700	90—768

*Includes one safety

STATISTICAL LEADERS

Scoring	TDs	Rush.	Pass.	Ret.	PATs	FGs	Total
Bahr	0	0	0	0	39—42	14—27	81
Clark	8	7	1	0	0	0	48
Trumpy	7	0	7	0	0	0	42
Curtis	6	0	6	0	0	0	36
Casanova	3	0	0	3	0	0	18
Elliott	3	0	3	0	0	0	18
Griffin	3	3	0	0	0	0	18
Fritts	3	3	0	0	0	0	18

Rushing	Atts.	Yds.	Avg.	Longest	TDs
Clark	151	671	4.4	24	7
Griffin	138	625	4.5	77 (TD)	3
Elliott	69	276	4.0	24	0
Fritts	47	200	4.3	13	3
Davis	36	178	4.9	16	1

Passing	Atts.	Com.	Yds.	Pct.	Int.	Longest	TDs
Anderson	338	179	2367	53.0	14	85 (TD)	19
Reaves	22	8	76	36.4	1	19	2

Receiving	No.	Yds.	Avg.	Longest	TDs
Curtis	41	166	18.7	85 (TD)	6
Clark	23	158	6.9	19	1
Elliott	22	188	8.5	29 (TD)	3
Trumpy	21	323	15.4	48 (TD)	7
Myers	17	267	15.7	63	1
Brooks	16	191	12.0	25	0
Griffin	16	138	8.6	23	0

Interceptions	No.	Yds.	Avg.	Longest	TDs
Riley	9	141	15.7	53 (TD)	1
Casanova	5	109	21.8	33 (TD)	2
Cobb	3	55	18.3	28	0

Punting	No.	Yds.	Avg.	Longest	Inside 20	Blocked
McInally	76	2999	39.5	61	12	0

Punt Returns	No.	FCs	Yds.	Avg.	Longest	TDs
Shelby	21	4	162	7.7	30	0
Parrish	20	2	122	6.1	32	0

Kickoff Returns	No.	Yds.	Avg.	Longest	TDs
Shelby	30	761	25.4	97 (TD)	1
Elliott	5	98	19.6	22	0
Griffin	3	56	18.7	23	0
Parrish	3	62	20.7	28	0

PITTSBURGH STEELERS

Head Coach: Chuck Noll

9th Year   **Record: 65–46–1**

1976 RECORD (10–4) (capital letters indicate home games)		1977 SCHEDULE (capital letters indicate home games)	
28	Oakland	31	SAN FRANCISCO (night, TV)	Sept. 19
31	CLEVELAND	14	OAKLAND	Sept. 25
27	NEW ENGLAND	30	Cleveland	Oct. 2
6	Miami	17	Houston	Oct. 9
16	Cleveland	18	CINCINNATI (night, TV)	Oct. 17
23	CINCINNATI	6	HOUSTON	Oct. 23
27	N.Y. Giants	0	Baltimore	Oct. 30
23	SAN DIEGO	0	Denver	Nov. 6
45	Kansas City	0	CLEVELAND	Nov. 13
14	MIAMI	3	DALLAS	Nov. 20
32	HOUSTON	16	N.Y. Jets	Nov. 27
7	Cincinnati	3	SEATTLE	Dec. 4
42	TAMPA BAY	0	Cincinnati (TV)	Dec. 10
21	Houston	0	San Diego	Dec. 18
Playoffs				
40	Baltimore	14		
7	Oakland	24		

The Steelers were disappointed last year—but their failure to win a third Super Bowl in a row may work in coach Chuck Noll's favor this time around. The Steelers will be more coachable, and it's hard to conceive of a team with as much talent as Pittsburgh making the early mistakes that put them behind the eight ball after five weeks of the schedule.

The Steelers have talent at every position. Quarterback Terry Bradshaw doesn't figure to get hurt twice as he was in 1976, and even if he does, sophomore Mike Kruczek has proven he can run a ball-control game and win. Bradshaw threw the ball only 92 times last year for an under-par 47.9 percent. Kruczek, under orders, dumped it off 85 times for a whopping 60 percent; he never hit for a TD pass, but made up for it by handing off to Franco Harris, who rambled for 14 TDs and 1,128 yards. Terrific Terry had ten TD passes.

Lynn Swann, the Super Bowl hero of 1975, doesn't figure to be hurt again, either—and that's a plus. He led the Steelers last year with only 28 receptions, which shows you how sluggish the Pittsburgh attack had become. Noll plans to put the ball up more often in 1977, and he will fit Frank Lewis and John Stallworth into his game plan. He also intends to dump off to Rocky Bleier, the superb blocking back, when it's third and clutch. Bleier rushed for 1,036 yards in 1976.

The once totally impregnable Steeler defense was still awesome last year, and it produced the great comeback from the early 1–4 record to the final 10–4. The front four became a front five due to Mean Joe Greene's pinched nerve, which has slowly improved. Along with Greene, Ernie Holmes (finally cleared of a drug rap), Dwight White, L. C. Greenwood, and Steve Furness can stop the run and harass the quarterback.

The Steelers led the AFC in rushing defense, were second in passing defense, and were first overall in 1976. Their linebackers, led by the mad dog Jack Lambert who always seems zeroed in on the ball, are tops. The secondary, led by Mel Blount and J. T. Thomas at the corners and featuring Glen Edwards and Mike Wagner as the safeties, is also hard to beat.

Placekicker Roy Gerela was hampered by a groin pull in the stretch—and this hurt. He should be all right when the bell rings, however.

Punter Bobby Walden is a pro who is best under pressure, but his age (39) is against him.

Noll's task in 1976 was to put fear into the Steelers, who figured they were a living legend and couldn't be beat. After their 1–4 start, they needed twelve straight to make the Super Bowl again and fell two short. *Sic transit gloria.*

The motivation will be there for the Steelers to hold off the challenge of both Cincinnati and Cleveland in the toughest of all divisions, the AFC Central, and to make their way back to the Super Bowl. Can they do it? Yes.

Will they do it? Much is up to Terry Bradshaw—and even more, perhaps, to Swann. Lynn, at top operating speed, gives the Steelers the threat of the long bomb. Their two 1,000-yard runners were the product of too much three-yards-and-a-cloud-of-dust type attack.

Of course, the Steelers' rushing attack was the best in the AFC with 2,971 yards, but their passing fell short—only 1,666 yards—and placed them third from the bottom in the conference.

Noll matured as a coach last year, showing that he didn't panic in adversity, and he may have learned from losing. It will all come down to mental attitude—if the Steelers want it more than the Bengals they will win the AFC Central; if not, the dynasty will have died aborning.

OFFENSE

Quarterbacks	Ht.	Wt.	Age	Exp.	College
Bradshaw, Terry	6-3	210	29	8	Louisiana Tech
Kruczek, Mike	6-0	196	24	2	Boston College
Graff, Neil	6-3	200	27	4	Wisconsin

Bradshaw is numero uno—and may be even better with a year of partial watching. He knows the job is his, and the Pittsburgh offensive linemen believe in him. Kruczek has earned his backup spot, but don't bet that the more experienced Graff might not get a shot in an emergency. Bradshaw can pull the ball down and run with it; Kruczek really cannot, and he sticks in the pocket. Graff has failed with the Patriots and others, but experience can be a factor in surviving.

Running Backs	Ht.	Wt.	Age	Exp.	College
Bleier, Rocky	5-11	210	31	9	Notre Dame
Fuqua, John	5-11	200	30	9	Morgan State
Deloplaine, Jack	5-10	205	23	2	Salem
Collier, Mike	5-11	200	24	2	Morgan State

Harris, Franco	6-2	230	27	6	Penn State
Harrison, Reggie	5-11	220	27	4	Cincinnati
Thornton, Sidney	5-11	233	22	R	N.W. Louisiana

How many teams boast two 1,000-yard running backs of the caliber of Harris and Bleier? Al Davis was right—Harris' presence is the difference when Oakland plays Pittsburgh. With Franco hurt the Raiders won rather easily. Harris carried the Steelers in mid-year when Bradshaw and Swann were hors de combat, and he should be ready for another good year. Bleier is still underrated, but his blocking and pass catching make him almost as valuable as superstud Franco. Dapper Frenchy Fuqua would start on some teams. Reggie Harrison slammed for 235 yards in 54 shots last year. Deloplaine is the breakaway hope. Thornton has good rushing credentials from Creole State.

Receivers	Ht.	Wt.	Age	Exp.	College
Lewis, Frank (W)	6-1	196	30	7	Grambling
Stallworth, John (W)	6-2	185	25	4	Alabama A&M
Garrett, Reggie (W)	6-1	175	27	3	Eastern Michigan
Leak, Curtis (W)	5-11	180	23	1	Johnson C. Smith
Brown, Larry (T)	6-4	230	28	7	Kansas
Grossman, Randy (T)	6-1	215	24	4	Temple
Cunningham, Bennie (T)	6-4	255	23	2	Clemson
Swann, Lynn (W)	6-0	180	25	4	Southern California
Bell, Theo (W)	5-11½	180	24	2	Arizona
Pough, Ernie (W)	6-1	174	25	2	Texas Southern
Smith, Jim (W)	6-4	198	22	R	Michigan

W=wide receiver   T=tight end

Lynn Swann is the game breaker, and he played hurt in 1976. He can fly and split the seams of a zone. Swann's 28 receptions were down from his 49 of the year before. After that it was Bleier coming out of the backfield with 24 and Harris with 23. The Steelers need to go to Swann and Frank Lewis (17) more often, and they need to remember that they have tight ends—Grossman and Cunningham. All-America Jim Smith can run, catch, and return anything.

Interior Linemen	Ht.	Wt.	Age	Exp.	College
Kolb, Jon (T)	6-3	262	30	9	Oklahoma State
Pinney, Ray (C, T)	6-4	240	23	2	Washington
Mullins, Gerry (T, G)	6-3	240	28	7	Southern California
Davis, Sam (G)	6-1	250	33	11	Allen U.
Clack, Jim (G, C)	6-3	250	30	7	Wake Forest
Webster, Mike (C)	6-1	245	25	4	Wisconsin
Files, Jim (C)	6-2	246	24	2	McNeese State
Gravelle, Gordon (T)	6-5	255	28	6	Brigham Young

T=tackle   G=guard   C=center

Center Ray Mansfield has retired; he finished as the backup (after 12 big seasons) to Mike Webster. Messrs. Gravelle, Kolb, Davis, Clack, and Mullins are underrated but do almost as much as O. J. Simpson's more renowned linemen. Clack is a super sub.

Kickers	Ht.	Wt.	Age	Exp.	College
Walden, Bobby (P)	6-1	197	39	14	Georgia
Gerela, Roy (Pk)	5-10	190	29	9	New Mexico State

Pk=placekicker   P=punter

Roy Gerela had a sub-par, injury-filled 1976, and made only 14 of 26 FG tries. He'll bounce back. Bobby Walden was out of the top ten with a 39.2 average last year. His age could be a factor, and the Steelers are looking for a Ray Guy. QB Bradshaw can also punt on occasion.

DEFENSE

Front Linemen	Ht.	Wt.	Age	Exp.	College
Greenwood, L. C. (E)	6-6	246	31	8	Arkansas AM&N
Banaszak, John (E)	6-4	232	27	3	Eastern Michigan
Greene, Joe (T)	6-4	275	31	9	North Texas State
Furness, Steve (T, E)	6-4	255	27	6	Rhode Island
Dunn, Gary (T)	6-3	240	24	2	Miami (Fla.)
Holmes, Ernie (T)	6-3	260	29	6	Texas Southern
White, Dwight (E)	6-4	255	28	7	East Texas State
Beasley, Tom (T)	6-5	237	22	R	Virginia Tech

E=end   T=tackle

Steeler opponents were held to a measly 1,457 yards in 1976—and Mean Joe Greene is well again. The front four is the main stem of the big D that won both Super Bowls. Ernie Holmes should be better; Steve Furness is underrated; Greenwood and White are intimidators. Pittsburgh doesn't sack the quarterback as much as · some teams, but they play it more conservatively and cut off the run.

Linebackers	Ht.	Wt.	Age	Exp.	College
Ham, Jack (O)	6-1	225	29	7	Penn State
Kellum, Marv (O)	6-2	225	25	4	Wichita State
Lambert, Jack (M)	6-4	220	25	4	Kent State
Humphrey, Al (O)	6-3	225	24	2	Tulsa
Toews, Loren (O)	6-3	222	26	5	California
Cole, Robin (O)	6-2	226	22	R	New Mexico

O=outside   M=middle

Andy Russell has retired, leaving Toews the heir apparent. He did well when Russell was out with a broken finger last year. Lambert is still a tiger in the middle, Ham is very good, and Kellum's itching to play. A solid group. Cole is good if he can make it with these dudes.

Cornerbacks	Ht.	Wt.	Age	Exp.	College
Thomas, J. T.	6-2	196	26	5	Florida State
Allen, Jimmy	6-2	194	25	4	UCLA
Sexton, Brent	6-1	190	24	2	Elon
Blount, Mel	6-3	200	29	8	Southern U.

Thomas and Blount are All-Pros, and Blount was MVP of the Pro Bowl last year. Blount tied for the Pittsburgh lead with six interceptions in 1976. Allen wants Blount's job, but . . .

Safeties	Ht.	Wt.	Age	Exp.	College
Wagner, Mike	6-1	210	29	7	Western Illinois
Shell, Donnie	5-11	195	25	4	S.C. State
Gaines, Wentford	6-0	185	24	2	Cincinnati
Hooker, Allen	5-11	175	23	2	Texas Christian
Edwards, Glen	6-0	185	30	7	Florida A&M

Edwards had six interceptions in 1976, to tie with Mel Blount for the top spot. Wagner is top-notch, while Shell is gaining experience and might do well if tried.

Note: A complete listing of Pittsburgh's 1977 college draft selections can be found on page 257.

DEFENSIVE UNIT

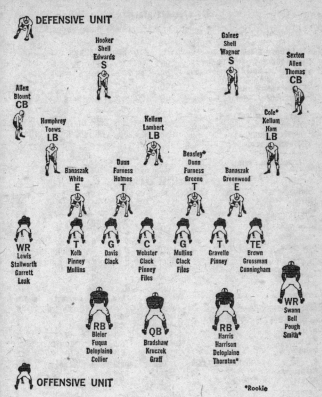

S
Hooker
Shell
Edwards

S
Gaines
Shell
Wagner

CB
Sexton
Allen
Thomas

CB
Allen
Blount

LB
Humphrey
Toews

LB
Kellum
Lambert

LB
Cole*
Kellum
Ham

E
Banaszak
White

T
Dunn
Furness
Holmes

T
Beasley*
Dunn
Furness
Greene

E
Banaszak
Greenwood

WR
Lewis
Stallworth
Garrett
Leak

T
Kolb
Pinney
Mullins

G
Davis
Clack

C
Webster
Clack
Pinney
Files

G
Mullins
Clack
Files

T
Gravelle
Pinney

TE
Brown
Grossman
Cunningham

WR
Swann
Bell
Pough
Smith*

RB
Bleier
Fuqua
Deloplaine
Collier

QB
Bradshaw
Kruczek
Graff

RB
Harris
Harrison
Deloplaine
Thornton*

OFFENSIVE UNIT

*Rookie

1976 STEELERS STATISTICS

	Steelers	Opps.
Total Points Scored	342*	138
Total First Downs	271	182
Third-Down Efficiency	81—208	61—210
Yards Rushing—First Downs	2971—163	1457—69
Passes Attempted—Completions	277—143	373—158
Yards Passing—First Downs	1666—94	1865—96
QB Sacked—Yards Lost	27—269	41—313
Interceptions—Return Average	22—11.9	12—8.8
Punts—Average Yards	76—39.2	94—37.4
Punt Returns—Return Average	71—9.0	36—5.7
Kickoff Returns—Return Average	41—20.9	61—21.0
Fumbles—Ball Lost	40—19	42—24
Penalties—Yards	111—836	80—637

*Includes one safety

STATISTICAL LEADERS

Scoring	TDs	Rush.	Pass.	Ret.	PATs	FGs	Total
Harris	14	14	0	0	0	0	84
Gerela	0	0	0	0	40—43	14—26	82
Bleier	5	5	0	0	0	0	30
Harrison	4	4	0	0	0	0	24
Stallworth	3	1	2	0	0	0	18
Bradshaw	3	3	0	0	0	0	18
Swann	3	0	3	0	0	0	18
Lewis	2	1	1	0	0	0	12
Deloplaine	2	2	0	0	0	0	12
Kruczek	2	2	0	0	0	0	12

Rushing	Atts.	Yds.	Avg.	Longest	TDs
Harris	289	1128	3.9	30	14
Bleier	220	1036	4.7	28	5
Harrison	54	235	4.4	27	4
Bradshaw	31	219	7.1	17	3
Kruczek	18	106	5.9	22 (TD)	2
Deloplaine	17	91	5.4	19	2

Passing	Atts.	Com.	Yds.	Pct.	Int.	Longest	TDs
Bradshaw	192	92	1177	47.9	9	50	10
Kruczek	85	51	758	60.0	3	64	0

Receiving	No.	Yds.	Avg.	Longest	TDs
Swann	28	516	18.4	47	3
Bleier	24	294	12.3	32	0
Harris	23	151	6.6	39	0
Lewis	17	306	18.0	64	1
Grossman	15	181	12.1	35	1

Interceptions	No.	Yds.	Avg.	Longest	TDs
Edwards	6	95	15.8	55	0
Blount	6	75	12.5	28	0
Thomas	2	43	21.5	38	0

Punting	No.	Yds.	Avg.	Longest	Inside 20	Blocked
Walden	76	2982	39.2	58	22	0

Punt Returns	No.	FCs	Yds.	Avg.	Longest	TDs
Bell	39	2	390	10.0	35	0
Deloplaine	17	0	150	8.8	36	0
Fuqua	71	0	77	7.0	13	0

Kickoff Returns	No.	Yds.	Avg.	Longest	TDs
Deloplaine	17	385	22.6	39	0
Pough	18	369	20.5	29	0

CLEVELAND BROWNS

Head Coach: Forrest Gregg

3rd Year **Record:** 12–16

1976 RECORD (9–5) (capital letters indicate home games)		**1977 SCHEDULE** (capital letters indicate home games)	
38	N.Y. JETS	17	Cincinnati	Sept. 18
14	Pittsburgh	31	NEW ENGLAND (night, TV)	Sept. 26
13	Denver	44	PITTSBURGH	Oct. 2
24	CINCINNATI	45	OAKLAND	Oct. 9
18	PITTSBURGH	16	Houston	Oct. 16
20	Atlanta	17	Buffalo	Oct. 23
21	SAN DIEGO	17	KANSAS CITY	Oct. 30
6	Cincinnati	21	CINCINNATI	Nov. 6
21	Houston	7	Pittsburgh	Nov. 13
24	PHILADELPHIA	3	N.Y. Giants	Nov. 20
24	Tampa Bay	7	LOS ANGELES	Nov. 27
17	MIAMI	13	San Diego	Dec. 4
13	HOUSTON	10	HOUSTON	Dec. 11
14	Kansas City	39	Seattle	Dec. 18

Coach Forrest Gregg started 1976 needing surgery for a malignant growth on his leg and ended the year accepting kudos for turning the corner. Gregg reversed a 3–11 mark and brought it to 9–5, only a game in back of the Steelers' and Bengals' 10–4. He was picked as the NFL coach of the year by the Associated Press, and early in 1977 he was named to the Pro Football Hall of Fame.

Whether Cleveland's 1976 showing was a miracle not to be repeated—and therefore a mirage—will be determined by quarterback Brian Sipe, who started 12 games and proved himself a competent NFL passer. He gained the confidence of the team, especially of offensive linemen Tom DeLeone, Pete Adams, Bob Jackson, Barry Darrow, and Doug Dieken, who became one of the better young lines in the NFL.

Tiny Greg Pruitt had his second straight year as a 1,000-yard runner, helped by free agent fullback Cleo Miller, who blocked like a demon in 1976. When Pruitt was lost (he was in contention for the NFL lead when an ankle cut him down), Larry Poole took over and kept the attack functioning the last five games.

The Browns were sixth in the AFC on offense with a combined 4,542 yards; they finished fifth in rushing and sixth in passing. On defense they were fourth, surrendering 3,793 yards—only 1,761 via the rush, with 2,032 overhead.

The attack got better because Paul Warfield, the superb pass receiver, caught 38 passes and helped set up Reggie Rucker for 49 and Pruitt for 45. The opposition spent much of its time eyeballing Paul.

Thom Darden returned to his spot at free safety after a knee injury and led the team in interceptions. Clarence Scott returned to top form after suffering with a bad foot in 1975. Ron Bolton, obtained from New England, added savvy at the other corner.

Gerald Irons, who lost his linebacker spot with Oakland, helped greatly in 1976; he joined Bob Babich in the middle and Charlie Hall on the outside to give Cleveland solid linebacking. Jerry Sherk had another good year at one tackle, and Walter Johnson's play at the other belied his 13 years in the NFL.

The Browns played much of the season without their erstwhile No. 1 quarterback, Mike Phipps, who was hurt in the second half of the opening game. And they played five games without Pruitt. Now, Phipps has gone to Chicago in a trade.

Things could get better and they could get worse. But usually on a team coming off 3–11, everyone pulls together.

In other areas, Don Cockroft slipped a bit in his dual role as both placekicker and punter. Special teams win

more games than most think; can the Browns keep doing
the job in that area?

The problem for Gregg is that most of his key per-
·formers played at maximum in 1976, and he got a surprising season from Sipe when desperation loomed. Can
Brian really keep playing that well? (He was sixth in the
AFC last year, with 57.1 and 17 TDs.)

And finally, can the Browns' rushing attack, built
around a mini-fullback, Pruitt, continue to do the job?
These two offensive factors and the defense will show
whether the Browns and Gregg are genuine contenders
or were simply one-shot pretenders in 1976.

Schedules, like footballs, can take funny bounces,
and Cleveland's does this season. It would seem that
with the first four games being against Cincinnati, New
England, Pittsburgh, and Oakland, the Browns have the
toughest "start" in the NFL. Those four opponents won
44 games and lost but 12 last season.

OFFENSE

Quarterbacks	Ht.	Wt.	Age	Exp.	College
Sipe, Brian	6-1	190	28	4	Texas Southern
Mays, Dave	6-1	204	28	2	San Diego State

Was Sipe for real last year? Yes—but can he do it again, or will
he settle back to a lesser level? If he is that good the Browns have
a premier young passer. As for Mike Phipps, Cleveland had the best of
both worlds—they traded Paul Warfield to Miami for the draft rights to
Phipps way back when, and now Phipps has left for Chicago.

Running Backs	Ht.	Wt.	Age	Exp.	College
Pruitt, Greg	5-10	190	26	5	Oklahoma
Poole, Larry	6-0½	195	25	3	Kent State
Duncan, Brian	6-0	201	25	2	Southern Methodist
Miller, Cleo	5-11	202	25	4	Arkansas AM&N
Pruitt, Mike	6-0	214	23	2	Purdue

Greg Pruitt is exciting but unconvincing as a mini-power runner. Poole

is a good reserve and might even give Greg a run for his money.
Miller is a blocking back who got the job done in 1976. Mike Pruitt
hopes to play more this season. Cleveland is still looking to draft a
big back in the time-honored mold of Jimmy Brown and Leroy Kelly.

Receivers	Ht.	Wt.	Age	Exp.	College
Warfield, Paul (W)	6-0	188	35	13	Ohio State
Holden, Steve (W)	6-0½	194	26	5	Arizona State
Feacher, Ricky (W)	5-10	174	23	2	Mississippi Valley
Roan, Oscar (T)	6-6	214	26	3	Southern Methodist
Parris, Gary (T)	6-2	226	27	5	Florida State
Rucker, Reggie (W)	6-2	190	30	8	Boston University
Logan, Dave (W)	6-4	226	23	2	Colorado
Lefear, Billy (W)	5-11	197	27	6	Henderson State

W=wide receiver   T=tight end

Warfield may be slowing a bit in pure speed, but he knows how to get
loose—and he serves as a decoy, which gives Rucker room to operate.
Rucker caught 49 passes in 1976 for his second straight big year.
Greg Pruitt came out of the backfield for 45, missed five games, and
would have led except for his injury. Warfield had 38, Cleo Miller 16,
and tight end Roan 15. Lefear is coming off the injured reserve. Logan
may play QB too.

Interior Linemen	Ht.	Wt.	Age	Exp.	College
Dieken, Doug (T)	6-5	252	28	7	Illinois
Sheppard, Henry (T, G)	6-6	246	25	2	Southern Methodist
Adams, Pete (G)	6-4	260	26	3	Southern California
DeLeone, Tom (C)	6-2	248	27	6	Ohio State
Sullivan, Gerry (C, T)	6-4	250	25	4	Illinois
Jackson, Bob (G)	6-5	245	24	3	Duke
Dennis, Al (G)	6-4	250	26	3	Grambling
Darrow, Barry (T)	6-7	260	27	4	Montana
Kleber, Doug (T)	6-2	244	23	1	Illinois
Hutchison, Chuck (G)	6-3	250	29	7	Ohio State

T=tackle   G=guard   C=center

As a group, the Browns' interior linemen are one of the best young
lines in the NFL. Starters are Dieken, Adams, DeLeone, Jackson, and
Darrow. These guys came from nowhere last year and made the Browns'
attack click. More of same is a necessity.

Kickers	Ht.	Wt.	Age	Exp.	College
Cockroft, Don (P, Pk)	6-1	195	32	10	Adams State
Skladany, Tom (P)	6-0	192	22	R	Ohio State

Pk=placekicker   P=punter

Double-duty Don Cockroft missed the top ten in 1976 and had to settle for 38.9 as a punter; he should do better than that. As a placekicker he was 15 of 28 in FGs. Improvement is required if he's to hold both jobs. Skladany's college career punting average was 42.7 yards per boot.

DEFENSE

Front Linemen	Ht.	Wt.	Age	Exp.	College
Jones, Joe (E)	6-6	250	29	7	Tennessee State
St. Clair, Mike (E)	6-5	245	24	2	Grambling
Edwards, Earl (T, E)	6-7	256	31	9	Wichita State
Sherk, Jerry (T)	6-4½	250	29	8	Oklahoma State
Mitchell, Mack (E)	6-7½	245	25	3	Houston

E=end   T=tackle

Sherk was super again in 1976. Jones and Mitchell are the other starters, although Mitchell hasn't developed as well as was hoped. Edwards is an experienced reserve who doesn't hurt you when he plays. Tackle Walter Johnson was put on waivers after 12 NFL years.

Linebackers	Ht.	Wt.	Age	Exp.	College
Hall, Charlie (O)	6-3½	230	29	7	Houston
Graf, Dave (O)	6-2½	215	24	3	Penn State
Babich, Bob (M)	6-2	231	30	8	Miami (Ohio)
Ambrose, Dick (M)	6-0	235	24	3	Virginia
Irons, Gerald (O)	6-2	230	30	8	Maryland–E. Shore
Garlington, John (O)	6-1	221	31	10	Louisiana State
Jackson, Robert (O)	6-2	230	22	R	Texas A&M

O=outside   M=middle

They aren't household names, although Irons became pretty well known while he was with Oakland, but the Browns' linebackers are pretty good. Babich goes to the ball and Hall plays a tough outside. Ambrose can start if he's needed, and no one plays linebacker with the abandon of Hall. Jackson was a consensus All-America last season. He becomes the second Bob Jackson on the Cleveland roster.

Cornerbacks	Ht.	Wt.	Age	Exp.	College
Scott, Clarence	6-0	180	29	7	Kansas State
Bolton, Ron	6-2	170	27	6	Norfolk State
Peters, Tony	6-1½	192	24	3	Oklahoma

Bolton and Scott are the starters. Bolton did very well last year after coming from New England. Scott had four interceptions and Bolton three. The Browns overall had 21, a much better tally than in 1975; this was due to more aggressive play.

Safeties	Ht.	Wt.	Age	Exp.	College
Craven, Bill	5-10½	190	26	2	Harvard
Darden, Thom	6-2	193	27	5	Michigan
Brown, Terry	6-2	205	30	8	Oklahoma State

Darden returned after being on the injured list to star with a team-leading seven interceptions—only two in back of the AFC lead. Craven should be able to move into the other spot. The Browns improved from twenty-fourth against the pass in 1975 to fifth last year, part of the reason for the upward movement of the team.

Note: A complete listing of Cleveland's 1977 college draft selections can be found on page 249.

DEFENSIVE UNIT

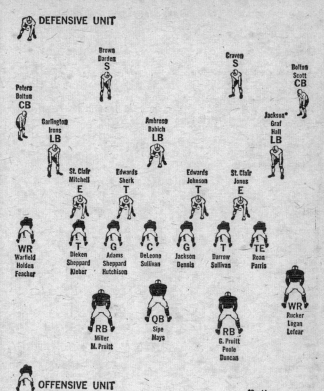

Brown
Darden
S

Craven
S

Bolton
Scott
CB

Peters
Bolton
CB

Garlington
Irons
LB

Ambrose
Babich
LB

Jackson*
Graf
Hall
LB

St. Clair
Mitchell
E

Edwards
Sherk
T

Edwards
Johnson
T

St. Clair
Jones
E

WR
Warfield
Holden
Feacher

T
Dieken
Sheppard
Kleber

G
Adams
Sheppard
Hutchison

C
DeLeone
Sullivan

G
Jackson
Dennis

T
Darrow
Sullivan

TE
Roan
Parris

RB
Miller
M. Pruitt

QB
Sipe
Mays

RB
G. Pruitt
Poole
Duncan

WR
Rucker
Logan
Lefear

OFFENSIVE UNIT

*Rookie

1976 BROWNS STATISTICS

	Browns	Opps.
Total Points Scored	267*	287
Total First Downs	260	244
Third-Down Efficiency	89—202	77—189
Yards Rushing—First Downs	2295—119	1761—109
Passes Attempted—Completions	373—209	392—225
Yards Passing—First Downs	2247—112	2032—111
QB Sacked—Yards Lost	19—152	32—321
Interceptions—Return Average	21—11.1	15—8.2
Punts—Average Yards	69—37.4	71—37.4
Punt Returns—Return Average	49—7.5	45—11.5
Kickoff Returns—Return Average	54—21.9	57—23.6
Fumbles—Ball Lost	45—22	24—11
Penalties—Yards	107—1037	89—711

*Includes one safety

STATISTICAL LEADERS

Scoring	TDs	Rush.	Pass.	Ret.	PATs	FGs	Total
Cockroft	0	0	0	0	27—30	15—28	72
Rucker	8	0	8	0	0	0	48
Warfield	6	0	6	0	0	0	36
Pruitt, Greg	5	4	1	0	0	0	30
Roan	4	0	4	0	0	0	24
Miller, Cleo	4	4	0	0	0	0	24

Rushing	Atts.	Yds.	Avg.	Longest	TDs
Pruitt, Greg	209	1000	4.8	64	4
Miller, Cleo	153	613	4.0	21	4
Poole	78	356	4.6	26	1
Pruitt, Mike	52	138	2.7	18	0
Sipe	18	71	3.9	17	0
Duncan	11	44	4.0	11	0

Passing	Atts.	Com.	Yds.	Pct.	Int.	Longest	TDs
Sipe	312	178	2113	57.1	14	52	17
Phipps	37	20	146	54.1	0	23 (TD)	3
Mays	20	9	101	45.0	1	21	0

Receiving	No.	Yds.	Avg.	Longest	TDs
Rucker	49	676	13.8	45	8
Pruitt, Greg	45	341	7.6	27	1
Warfield	38	613	16.1	37 (TD)	6
Miller, Cleo	16	145	9.1	38	0
Roan	15	174	11.6	23 (TD)	4
Poole	14	70	5.0	21	0

Interceptions	No.	Yds.	Avg.	Longest	TDs
Darden	7	73	10.4	21	0
Scott	4	11	2.8	5	0
Bolton	3	76	25.3	39	1
Babich	2	29	14.5	21	0

Punting	No.	Yds.	Avg.	Longest	Inside 20	Blocked
Cockroft	64	2487	38.9	51	9	3

Punt Returns	No.	FCs	Yds.	Avg.	Longest	TDs
Feacher	13	1	142	10.9	49	0
Holden	31	2	205	6.6	38	0

Kickoff Returns	No.	Yds.	Avg.	Longest	TDs
Holden	19	461	24.3	44	0
Duncan	6	145	24.2	27	0
Feacher	14	311	22.2	33	0
Pruitt, Mike	6	106	17.7	30	0

HOUSTON OILERS

Head Coach: O. A. (Bum) Phillips
3rd Year   Record: 15–13

1976 RECORD (5–9) (capital letters indicate home games)			1977 SCHEDULE (capital letters indicate home games)	
20	TAMPA BAY	0	N.Y. JETS	Sept. 18
13	Buffalo	3	Green Bay	Sept. 25
13	OAKLAND	14	Miami	Oct. 2
31	New Orleans	26	PITTSBURGH	Oct. 9
17	DENVER	3	CLEVELAND	Oct. 16
27	San Diego	30	Pittsburgh	Oct. 23
7	CINCINNATI	27	Cincinnati	Oct. 30
14	Baltimore	38	CHICAGO	Nov. 6
7	CLEVELAND	21	Oakland	Nov. 13
27	Cincinnati	31	Seattle	Nov. 20
16	Pittsburgh	32	KANSAS CITY	Nov. 27
20	ATLANTA	14	DENVER	Dec. 4
10	Cleveland	13	Cleveland	Dec. 11
0	PITTSBURGH	21	CINCINNATI	Dec. 18

The euphoria of 1975's 10–4 mark having been replaced by a crushing 5–9 in 1976, the Oilers face a season of question marks. Since the 10–4 mark came after two 1–13 seasons, it is being questioned as just one of those things. Houston got a great year out of Billy (White Shoes) Johnson two years back, and an adequate season from passer-punter Danny Pastorini. They also profited when Curley Culp made a remarkable comeback as the nose guard in the three-man rush line adopted by coach Bum Phillips. Last year it all turned to ashes, and Pastorini is so dissatisfied that he is demanding a trade despite having a year left on his contract.

In a sense, the Oilers went from rags to riches and back to rags. Now they hope to move back to about 8–6 or maybe 9–5, but realistically Phillips cannot hope to compete with Cincinnati or the Steelers. His meat is Cleveland, and right now the Browns have the edge.

Injuries decimated the Oilers last year. Billy J. was hurt during much of 1976, and his kick returns lost the magic of the previous campaign. The Oilers' rushing attack was only superior to Seattle's; Houston finished with 1,498 yards. Johnson had four kick-return TDs in 1975 but none last year, and he didn't get the Oilers field position as he had done before.

Pastorini had a bad year and announced he wanted to be traded; after he got hurt, John Hadl took over and moved the team better than Dan had. Pastorini threw only ten TD passes but did complete 54.0 percent of his tosses—a figure up from the horrendous 47.7 percent of the more successful 1975. Hadl, an ancient retread, is a fine backup on a contending team, but hardly the man Phillips wants to stake his future on. He did throw seven TD passes in only 113 attempts, though, and he helped the Oilers to something resembling offensive competitiveness.

The Oilers' vaunted defense, the steel around which the 10–4 season was built, came apart under the strain of injuries. Leading the AFC Central with a 4–1 record, Houston went into San Diego without safety Mike Weger and end Tody Smith. When the carnage was over, three more Oilers were out—free safety C. L. Whittington, offensive linebacker Ted Washington, and Washington's reserve, Duane Benson. The Chargers won with a late TD and the Oilers collapsed, losing seven of their last eight games.

Still, the Oilers' linebacking crew, led by Robert Brazile, continued to be super—which is a must in the 3–4 defense. Wide receiver Ken Burrough just missed on his second straight 1,000-yard season, but he's a constant threat to go all the way when Pastorini gets the ball to him.

The Houston defense still has Culp, Elvin Bethea, and Joe Owens up front, and they know the 3–4 pretty well now. A better running attack is a must; this will mean more help from Don Hardeman and Ronnie Coleman (who led the team last year with a mere 684 yards).

The Oilers' history shows poor selection of draft picks and eventual lack of depth as a result. When 1976 injuries piled up this destroyed the team. This year they have stockpiled draft choices. Their long-range future may lie in this draft; meanwhile, this *season* depends upon how much Phillips is able to convince Pastorini that his future lies in Houston. At last report, the coach was making some progress.

OFFENSE

Quarterbacks	Ht.	Wt.	Age	Exp.	College
Hadl, John	6-1	215	37	16	Kansas
Pastorini, Dan	6-3	205	28	7	Santa Clara
Foote, Jim	6-2	210	26	4	Delaware Valley
White, Alvin	6-3	218	24	2	Oregon State

In addition to his QB chores, Pastorini also does the punting, but only at a 36.7 pace. Don't bet against Hadl winding up as the Houston quarterback if Pastorini kicks up another fuss—and then watch the Oilers fill the air with passes. Hadl won with the old AFC San Diego Chargers, came close with the Rams, and messed up with the Packers. Pastorini is a young talent whose leadership qualities are suspect. Alvin White might be the Oiler quarterback of the future, and Foote has a chance to stick because of Hadl's age and Pastorini's wanting to leave.

Running Backs	Ht.	Wt.	Age	Exp.	College
Coleman, Ronnie	5-11	198	26	4	Alabama A&M
Dawkins, Joe	6-2	220	29	7	Arizona State
Rodgers, Willie	6-1	210	28	6	Kentucky State
Johnson, Al	6-0	200	27	6	Cincinnati
Willis, Fred	6-0	205	30	4	Boston College
Taylor, Altie	5-10	200	30	9	Utah State
Hardeman, Don	6-2	235	25	3	Texas A&I

Collert, Orlando	5-11	200	25	1	Middle Tennessee
Minor, Lincoln	6-2	220	26	2	New Mexico State
Wilson, Tim	6-3	225	22	R	Maryland
Carpenter, Rob	6-1	214	22	R	Miami (Ohio)

If ex-Detroit Lion Altie Taylor can stage a comeback, or Don Hardeman, once billed as the black Larry Csonka, can reach his potential, the Oilers' rushing attack might get better. It's up to Taylor and Hardeman to make Houston honest on the ground. Rodgers was on the injured list last season. Orlando Collert was previously listed on Houston's roster as Bobby Joe Easter. Wilson comes from a good Maryland team and Carpenter rated an honorable mention in the AP's All-America Mid-Am Conference.

Receivers	Ht.	Wt.	Age	Exp.	College
Burrough, Ken (W)	6-3	210	30	8	Texas Southern
Darby, Al (W)	6-5½	225	23	2	Florida
Barber, Mike (T)	6-3	235	24	1	Louisiana Tech
Alston, Mack (T)	6-3	230	30	8	Maryland State
Mialik, Larry (T)	6-2	230	27	6	Wisconsin
Sawyer, John (T)	6-2	230	24	3	S. Mississippi
Johnson, Billy (W)	5-9	170	25	4	Widener
Thomas, Earl (W)	6-2	215	29	7	Houston
Giles, Jimmy (W)	6-3	225	22	R	Alcorn State

W=wide receiver　　T=tight end

With no running attack Houston put the ball up in 1976, and it was usually caught by Burrough, who snagged 51 catches for 932 yards, or by "White Shoes" Johnson, who caught 47 for 495 yards. Johnson's kickoff return yardage dropped from 798 to 579 last season, and his punt returns dropped from 610 to 403. Coleman caught 40 passes and Fred Willis, coming out of the backfield, caught 32. Alston, the tight end, snagged only 19, but the Oilers don't go to him enough. Mialik and Barber spent 1976 on the injured reserve shelf. Giles played in the pro-player-producing Southwestern Athletic Conference.

Interior Linemen	Ht.	Wt.	Age	Exp.	College
Hunt, Kevin (T)	6-5	260	29	7	Doane
Sampson, Gregg (T)	6-6	270	27	6	Stanford
Simon, Bobby (G)	6-3	252	25	1	Grambling
Hayman, Conway (G)	6-3	262	28	5	Delaware
Harris, Larry (T)	6-3	274	25	1	Oklahoma State
Havig, Dennis (G)	6-2	256	28	7	Colorado
Mauck, Carl (C)	6-4	250	30	9	Southern Illinois
Lou, Ron (C)	6-2	242	26	5	Arizona State
Fisher, Ed (G)	6-3	250	28	4	Arizona State
Drungo, Elbert (T)	6-5	265	34	9	Tennessee State

Towns, Morris (T)	6-4	270	22	R	Missouri
Reihner, George (G)	6-5	250	22	R	Penn State

T=tackle   G=guard   C=center

It was the collapse of the interior line that caused Pastorini to pout last year. Regulars are Hunt, Hayman, Mauck, Fisher, and Drungo. Sampson is threatening Hunt. The boys need to get it together. Harris and Simon, if recovered from 1976 injuries, could help loads. Towns and Reihner received their share of All-America notices.

Kickers	Ht.	Wt.	Age	Exp.	College
Butler, Skip (P, Pk)	6-0	200	30	8	Texas—Arlington
Green, Mike (P)	6-4	195	23	1	Ohio

Pk=placekicker   P=punter

Pastorini is one of the punters. Butler was perfect for PATs last season, 24–24, and hit 16 out of 27 FGs. Linebacker Ted Thompson is also a backup placekicker. Green was drafted by Miami last season and averaged 38.0 yards on 15 preseason punts.

DEFENSE

Front Linemen	Ht.	Wt.	Age	Exp.	College
Owens, Joe (E)	6-3	255	31	8	Alcorn State
Burton, Albert (E)	6-5	270	25	2	Bethune—Cookman
Culp, Curley (MG)	6-1	265	31	10	Arizona State
Little, John (MG)	6-3	250	31	8	Oklahoma State
Gordon, Ted (E)	6-2	270	25	R	(none)
Bethea, Elvin (E)	6-2	255	31	10	North Carolina A&T

E=end   MG=middle guard

Owens is underrated, Culp is the heart of the 3–4, and Bethea is a monster rush liner. Little is a reserve. Phillips has dropped both Tody and Bubba Smith.

Linebackers	Ht.	Wt.	Age	Exp.	College
Washington, Ted (O)	6-1	245	29	5	Mississippi Valley
Benson, Duane (O)	6-2	225	32	11	Hamline
Kiner, Steve (M)	6-1	225	30	7	Tennessee
Stringer, Art (O)	6-1	223	23	1	Ball State
Rossovich, Tim (M)	6-4	240	31	9	Southern California
Bingham, Gregg (M)	6-1	230	26	5	Purdue
Thompson, Ted (M)	6-1	220	24	3	Southern Methodist
Brazile, Robert (O)	6-4	238	24	3	Jackson State

O=outside   M=middle

Brazile proved that his sophomore year was no jinx. He was even better than he was in his rookie season. Brazile is an All-Pro. Bingham, Kiner, and Washington are the other backers, and they aren't bad. Veteran backup Benson doesn't hurt you, but Kiner is solid, and there's fiery Rossovich in reserve. Stringer may be ready after sitting out 1976 hurt. One of the strong departments at Houston.

Cornerbacks	Ht.	Wt.	Age	Exp.	College
Stemrick, Greg	5-11	185	26	3	Colorado State
Alexander, Willie	6-3	195	28	7	Alcorn State
Moore, Zeke	6-3	195	34	11	Lincoln (Mo.)
Akili, Samaji Adi	6-2	192	25	4	N.M. Highlands

Houston intercepted only 11 passes all 1976, and it hurt. Alexander, Moore, and Stemrick, who finally got to start last year, are about even, though Moore may be losing step due to age. Samaji Adi Akili was previously listed on the Houston roster as Sam Williams.

Safeties	Ht.	Wt.	Age	Exp.	College
Atkins, Bob	6-3	210	31	10	Grambling
Weger, Mike	6-2	200	32	10	Bowling Green
Whittington, C. L.	6-1	200	25	4	Prairie View
Walker, Donnie	6-2	195	27	3	Central State (Ohio)
Reinfeldt, Mike	6-2	195	24	2	Wisconsin— Milwaukee

Whittington is first-class, and Atkins figures to edge out Reinfeldt eventually. Weger has plenty of experience and has been called good bench insurance.

Note: A complete listing of Houston's 1977 college draft selections can be found on page 252.

DEFENSIVE UNIT 3-4 DEFENSE

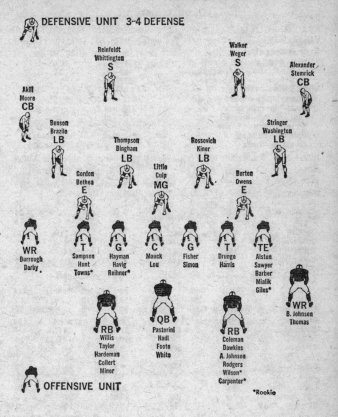

Reinfeldt
Whittington
S

Walker
Weger
S

Alexander
Stemrick
CB

Akill
Moore
CB

Benson
Brazile
LB

Stringer
Washington
LB

Thompson
Bingham
LB

Rossovich
Kiner
LB

Gordon
Bethea
E

Little
Culp
MG

Burton
Owens
E

WR
Burrough
Darby

T
Sampson
Hunt
Towns*

G
Hayman
Havig
Reihner*

C
Mauck
Lou

G
Fisher
Simon

T
Drungo
Harris

TE
Alston
Sawyer
Barber
Mialik
Giles*

WR
B. Johnson
Thomas

RB
Willis
Taylor
Hardeman
Collert
Minor

QB
Pastorini
Hadl
Foote
White

RB
Coleman
Dawkins
A. Johnson
Rodgers
Wilson*
Carpenter*

OFFENSIVE UNIT

*Rookie

1976 OILERS STATISTICS

	Oilers	Opps.
Total Points Scored	222	273
Total First-Downs	199	225
Third-Down Efficiency	65—210	79—221
Yards Rushing—First Downs	1498—71	2072—117
Passes Attempted—Completions	423—227	345—173
Yards Passing—First Downs	2072—110	1914—89
QB Sacked—Yards Lost	39—357	50—344
Interceptions—Return Average	11—16.0	19—10.3
Punts—Average Yards	100—35.3	95—39.1
Punt Returns—Return Average	49—10.1	60—11.1
Kickoff Returns—Return Average	59—20.7	53—21.4
Fumbles—Ball Lost	25—13	32—17
Penalties—Yards	100—802	107—935

STATISTICAL LEADERS

Scoring	TDs	Rush.	Pass.	Ret.	PATs	FGs	Total
Butler	0	0	0	0	24—25	16—26	72
Burrough	7	0	7	0	0	0	42
Coleman	6	2	3	1	0	0	36
Johnson, Billy	4	0	4	0	0	0	24
Willis	3	2	1	0	0	0	18

Rushing	Atts.	Yds.	Avg.	Longest	TDs
Coleman	171	684	4.0	39	2
Willis	148	542	3.7	44	2
Hardeman	32	114	3.6	21	1
Dawkins	31	61	2.0	7	1
Pastorini	11	45	4.1	11	0

Passing	Atts.	Com.	Yds.	Pct.	Int.	Longest	TDs
Pastorini	309	167	1795	54.0	10	67 (TD)	10
Hadl	113	60	634	53.1	8	69 (TD)	7

Receiving	No.	Yds.	Avg.	Longest	TDs
Burrough	51	932	18.3	69 (TD)	7
Johnson, Billy	47	495	10.5	40 (TD)	4
Coleman	40	247	6.2	19	3
Willis	32	255	8.0	42	1
Alston	19	174	9.2	29	1
Sawyer	18	208	11.6	53	1

Interceptions	No.	Yds.	Avg.	Longest	TDs
Whittington	5	103	20.6	50	0
Bingham	2	18	9.0	15	0

Punting	No.	Yds.	Avg.	Longest	Inside 20	Blocked
Pastorini	70	2571	36.7	74	12	0

Punt Returns	No.	FCs	Yds.	Avg.	Longest	TDs
Johnson, Billy	38	9	403	10.6	46	0
Coleman	7	2	91	13.0	69 (TD)	1

Kickoff Returns	No.	Yds.	Avg.	Longest	TDs
Johnson, Billy	26	579	22.3	53	0
Taylor	15	302	20.1	32	0
Johnson, Al	8	150	18.8	25	0
Hardeman	7	171	24.4	40	0

OAKLAND RAIDERS

Head Coach: John Madden

9th Year　　　　　　　　　　　**Record:** 83–22–7

1976 RECORD (13–1) (capital letters indicate home games)			1977 SCHEDULE (capital letters indicate home games)	
31	PITTSBURGH	28	SAN DIEGO	Sept. 18
24	Kansas City	21	Pittsburgh	Sept. 25
14	Houston	13	Kansas City (night, TV)	Oct. 3
17	New England	48	Cleveland	Oct. 9
27	San Diego	17	DENVER	Oct. 16
17	Denver	10	N.Y. Jets	Oct. 23
18	GREEN BAY	14	Denver	Oct. 30
19	DENVER	6	SEATTLE	Nov. 6
28	Chicago	27	HOUSTON	Nov. 13
21	KANSAS CITY	10	San Diego	Nov. 20
26	Philadelphia	7	BUFFALO (night, TV)	Nov. 28
49	TAMPA BAY	16	Los Angeles	Dec. 4
35	CINCINNATI	20	MINNESOTA	Dec. 11
24	SAN DIEGO	0	KANSAS CITY	Dec. 18
Playoffs				
24	NEW ENGLAND	21		
24	PITTSBURGH	7		
32	Minnesota	14		

What can the Raiders do for an encore? Win the Super Bowl again, but it will be harder than they think. Everything broke just right last year, with both Rocky Bleier and Franco Harris on the sidelines in the big playoff confrontation with Pittsburgh. The Raiders had something last year that was special. Supposedly blessed with a soft schedule, they won the big games against both Pittsburgh and Minnesota when the chips were down.

Ken Stabler led the NFL in passing with an amazing 66.7 percentage. He showed his smarts with ball control plus 27 TDs passing. In the playoffs, the Snake completed 41 of 67 passes for 501 yards and four TDs—and that with not a single interception.

Kenny probably has football's best pass receiving corps to throw to in Cliff Branch, Fred Biletnikoff, and tight end Dave Casper. Casper snagged 53 and ten TDs last season; Branch got the ball 46 times for 1,111 yards and 12 TDs, and Biletnikoff made 43 catches and seven TDs. Freddie was the star in the big game at the end. The Raiders finally saw one of their runners, Mark van Eeghen, crash the 1,000-yard barrier with 1,012— something that the injured Marv Hubbard usually failed at. Hubbard will be back, and that's a plus.

Oakland was third in the AFC in passing offense with 2,905 yards, and sixth in rushing with 2,285 yards. That's balance, but the real reason for the Raiders' success was the tremendous season the 3-4 defense put together after coach John Madden went to it in desperation because of injuries. What will happen to Dave Rowe, John Matuszak, and Otis Sistrunk when Horace Jones, Art Thoms, and Kelvin Korver get off the injured list is anyone's guess. Their return might destroy what had become a cohesive, all-for-one unit at the end of 1976. And then again, Madden has the option of going back to the standard front four, with just three linebackers.

That would put linebacker Willie Hall, super in 1976, on the bench instead of on the field with Phil Villapiano, Monte Johnson, and the Mad Stork, Ted Hendricks. But don't count on this switch, at least not early on.

There is still some pressure to return ancient George Blanda to the Raider roster; many feel he was cheated by a regulation out of the Super Bowl plaudits. When kicker Fred Steinfort was injured in midseason, Blanda's name came up, but an NFL regulation prohibits the signing of a player previously released by a team in preseason. Thus, enter Errol Mann, late of the Detroit Lions.

The Raiders are still supposed to lack enough rushing

to win the Super Bowl, according to some sources in Pittsburgh, but Clarence Davis rushed for over 500 yards last year, and Pete Banaszek knows where the end zone is—and notched 370 yards in 1976.

Punter Ray Guy is superb, and he may be the difference in close games. Whether Oakland improves its placekicking will probably be up to Steinfort, who wasn't seeing eye to eye with Al Davis when he left camp last summer.

Davis must be given credit for putting the Black and Silver together. He panicked to a degree after the 1975 loss, but things worked out. The word "dynasty" is a nasty word in the NFL—both the Green Bay Packers and the Miami Dolphins had two-year "dynasties," but they came a cropper in Year III. So did the invincible Pittsburgh Steelers. Can the Oakland Raiders make it two in a row—on their way to a dynasty?

Fans in California think so, and there is no reason the Raiders won't win the AFC West, but the playoffs could be another story. The Raiders, like most teams, are short of a good backup title-caliber quarterback. Mike Rae, from the Canadian league, got lucky last year, but he wouldn't hold up if he's needed for six games. Nevertheless, momentum and mental attitude mean a lot, so right now we pick the Raiders to repeat and take the Super Bowl again.

OFFENSE

Quarterbacks	Ht.	Wt.	Age	Exp.	College
Stabler, Ken	6-3	215	32	8	Alabama
Rae, Mike	6-1	190	26	2	Southern California
Humm, David	6-2	184	25	3	Nebraska
Blount, Jeb	6-3	205	23	1	Tulsa

Stabler was the best in the 1976 NFL passing stats with only 17 interceptions. Humm is a future, with Rae the incumbent backup. Everything is in good shape here. Blount missed his entire rookie season with injuries. The Raiders hope he'll be okay this year.

Running Backs	Ht.	Wt.	Age	Exp.	College
Davis, Clarence	5-10	195	28	7	Southern California
Garrett, Carl	5-10	205	30	9	N.M. Highlands
Ginn, Hubie	5-9	185	30	8	Florida A&M
van Eeghen, Mark	6-2	225	25	4	Colgate
Banaszak, Pete	6-0	210	33	12	Miami (Fla.)
Hubbard, Marv	6-1	235	31	8	Colgate
Moore, Manfred	6-0	200	27	4	Southern California
McKnight, Ted	6-2	198	22	R	Minnesota—Duluth

Davis was No. 2 to van Eeghen in 1976 with a surprising 516 yards in the balanced Oakland running game. Van Eeghen came of age with a 1,000-yard season. Add Hubbard to the starting contenders and Madden has a pleasant problem. Still, Garrett is only a scatback, good at kickoff returns, not a heavy-duty back. Ditto Hubie Ginn, the ex-Dolphin. Al Davis has Clarence, but no big stud fullback. In 1976, McKnight ran 1,482 yards for a 6.7 average and 22 TDs. That's impressive in any league.

Receivers	Ht.	Wt.	Age	Exp.	College
Branch, Cliff (W)	5-11	170	29	6	Colorado
Bradshaw, Morris (W)	6-1	195	25	4	Ohio State
Casper, Dave (T)	6-4	228	26	4	Notre Dame
Bankston, Warren (T)	6-4	235	30	9	Tulane
Biletnikoff, Fred (W)	6-1	190	34	13	Florida State
Siani, Mike (W)	6-2	195	27	6	Villanova

W=wide receiver   T=tight end

Branch is a track star in a football uniform who can outrun most defenders. Stabler went to Branch long and to Fred Biletnikoff and Dave Casper in the clutch, and won when he had to. Biletnikoff is getting old, but he still has the moves to get loose and stickum on his hands. Mike Siani would play regularly with most teams, but might play out his option.

Interior Linemen	Ht.	Wt.	Age	Exp.	College
Shell, Art (T)	6-5	265	31	10	Maryland—E. Shore
Lawrence, Henry (T)	6-4	273	26	4	Florida A&M
Sylvester, Steve (T)	6-4	262	24	3	Notre Dame
Upshaw, Gene (G)	6-5	255	32	11	Texas A&I
Medlin, Dan (G)	6-4	252	28	4	N.C. State
Dalby, Dave (C)	6-3	250	27	6	UCLA
Buehler, George (G)	6-2	270	30	9	Stanford
Vella, John (T)	6-4	260	27	6	Southern California

T=tackle   G=guard   C=center

The Raiders' offensive line has Shell, Upshaw, Dalby, Buehler, and Vella plus Dave Casper and WR Cliff Branch. They move people and should get the credit for the 2,285 yards, second best in the AFC, that the Black and Silver ran in 1976. Dalby took over from the legendary Jim Otto last year; Lawrence is still challenging for a regular job. Sylvester can play both tackle and center and is the utility man.

Kickers	Ht.	Wt.	Age	Exp.	College
Guy, Ray (P)	6-3	195	28	5	S. Mississippi
Mann, Errol (Pk)	6-0	205	36	10	North Dakota
Steinfort, Fred (Pk)	5-11	185	25	2	Boston College

Pk=placekicker   P=punter

Guy didn't win the punting title last year, but he's still the best in the NFL. In 1976 he was fourth, with 41.6. Mann was merely adequate when he took over in midseason; he made 8 of 21 overall between Detroit, where he started the season, and Oakland, where he ended it. Steinfort will get every opportunity to win back his job. He made four of eight in 1976.

DEFENSE

Front Linemen	Ht.	Wt.	Age	Exp.	College
Matuszak, John (E)	6-7	270	27	5	Tampa
Philyaw, Charles (E)	6-9	270	23	2	Texas Southern
Jones, Horace (E)	6-4	260	28	6	Louisville
Rowe, Dave (MG)	6-7	271	32	11	Penn State
Thoms, Art (MG)	6-5	250	31	8	Syracuse
McMath, Herb (MG)	6-4	245	23	2	Morningside
Korver, Kelvin (MG)	6-6	270	28	4	N.W. Louisiana
Sistrunk, Otis (E)	6-3	273	30	6	(none)

E=end   MG=middle guard   T=tackle

Wild Man John Matuszak flunked out everywhere but under Madden, who harnessed his raw talent. It says here he'll get into trouble again. Philyaw disappointed and was found wanting when used on the original four-man Raider line, but he may get another shot in this, his second year. Journeyman Dave Rowe did a super job last year and will at least make the roster. Sistrunk is high-grade. Jones, Thoms, and Korver were on injured reserve in 1976.

Linebackers	Ht.	Wt.	Age	Exp.	College
Villapiano, Phil (O)	6-2	225	28	7	Bowling Green
Hall, Willie (O)	6-2	225	28	5	Southern California
Johnson, Monte (M)	6-5	240	26	5	Nebraska
Bonness, Rik (M)	6-3	220	23	2	Nebraska
Tate, Franklin (O)	6-3	225	25	2	N.C. Central
Rice, Floyd (M)	6-3	225	28	7	Alcorn State
Hendricks, Ted (O)	6-7	220	30	9	Miami (Fla.)
Barnes, Rodrigo (O)	6-2	215	27	5	Rice

O=outside   M=middle

The four-man Oakland linebacking crew might be the best in the league. Hendricks is the best linebacker in the NFL, with reach, speed, and height as well as the smarts. Hall, a pickup, did exceptionally well last year. So did Monte Johnson, who led with four interceptions. Phil Villapiano is a household word now, and Barnes wouldn't hurt if he had to play. Tate was on the injured list last season.

Cornerbacks	Ht.	Wt.	Age	Exp.	College
Thomas, Skip	6-1	205	27	6	Southern California
Colzie, Neal	6-2	205	24	3	Ohio State
Brown, Willie	6-1	210	37	15	Grambling
Davis, Mike	6-3	199	22	R	Colorado

Colzie is the heir apparent to regular 15-year man Brown and the punt return man, but somehow in the big games it's still Brown. Skip Thomas is top drawer. Davis was a second-round draft choice, so he must have something.

Safeties	Ht.	Wt.	Age	Exp.	College
					Southern California
Atkinson, George	6-0	185	30	9	Morris Brown
Phillips, Charles	6-2	215	25	3	Ohio State
Tatum, Jack	5-11	206	29	7	College

Tatum has recovered from Franco Harris' immaculate reception of a few years ago and is a tough All-Pro. Atkinson is just tough—ask Lynn Swann. Phillips is a playing reserve who goes to the ball. Atkinson might have won the Super Bowl, at least as far as eliminating the Steelers was concerned, when he roughed up Swann in the 1976 NFL opener.

Note: A complete listing of Oakland's 1977 college draft selections can be found on page 256.

DEFENSIVE UNIT 3-4 DEFENSE

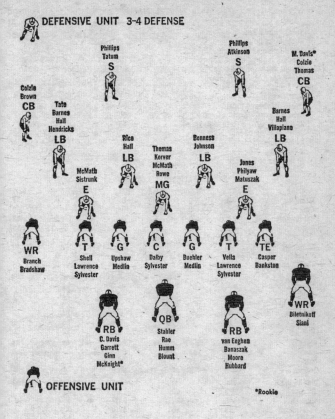

Phillips
Tatum
S

Phillips
Atkinson
S

M. Davis*
Colzie
Thomas
CB

Colzie
Brown
CB

Tate
Barnes
Hall
Hendricks
LB

Rice
Hall
LB

Thomas
Korver
McMath
Rowe
MG

Bonness
Johnson
LB

Barnes
Hall
Villapiano
LB

McMath
Sistrunk
E

Jones
Philyaw
Matuszak
E

WR
Branch
Bradshaw

T
Shell
Lawrence
Sylvester

G
Upshaw
Medlin

C
Dalby
Sylvester

G
Buehler
Medlin

T
Vella
Lawrence
Sylvester

TE
Casper
Bankston

WR
Biletnikoff
Siani

RB
C. Davis
Garrett
Ginn
McKnight*

QB
Stabler
Rae
Humm
Blount

RB
van Eeghen
Banaszak
Moore
Hubbard

OFFENSIVE UNIT

*Rookie

1976 RAIDERS STATISTICS

	Raiders	Opps.
Total Points Scored	350*	237
Total First Downs	303	261
Third-Down Efficiency	82—191	77—206
Yards Rushing—First Downs	2285—137	1903—98
Passes Attempted—Completions	361—232	389—197
Yards Passing—First Downs	2905—146	2476—138
QB Sacked—Yards Lost	28—290	46—370
Interceptions—Return Average	16—8.0	18—10.3
Punts—Average Yards	67—41.6	87—40.0
Punt Returns—Return Average	50—11.1	38—6.9
Kickoff Returns—Return Average	46—23.0	61—18.4
Fumbles—Ball Lost	21—10	27—9
Penalties—Yards	107—967	96—918

*Includes one safety

STATISTICAL LEADERS

Scoring	TDs	Rush.	Pass.	Ret.	PATs	FGs	Total
Branch	12	0	12	0	0	0	72
Casper	10	0	10	0	0	0	60
Biletnikoff	7	0	7	0	0	0	42
Mann	0	0	0	0	26—27	4—11	38
Banaszak	5	5	0	0	0	0	30
Steinfort	0	0	0	0	16—19	4—8	28
Davis	3	3	0	0	0	0	18
van Eeghen	3	3	0	0	0	0	18

Rushing	Atts.	Yds.	Avg.	Longest	TDs
van Eeghen	233	1012	4.3	21	3
Davis	114	516	4.5	31	3
Banaszak	114	370	3.2	15	5
Garrett	48	220	4.6	17	1
Ginn	10	53	5.3	16	0
Rae	10	37	3.7	12	1

Passing	Atts.	Com.	Yds.	Pct.	Int.	Longest	TDs
Stabler	291	194	2737	66.7	17	88 (TD)	27
Rae	65	35	417	53.8	1	37 (TD)	6
Humm	5	3	41	60.0	0	29	0

Receiving	No.	Yds.	Avg.	Longest	TDs
Casper	53	691	13.0	30 (TD)	10
Branch	46	1111	24.2	88 (TD)	12
Biletnikoff	43	551	12.8	32 (TD)	7
Davis	27	191	7.1	17	0
van Eeghen	17	173	10.2	21	0
Banaszak	15	74	4.9	20	0

Interceptions	No.	Yds.	Avg.	Longest	TDs
Johnson	4	40	10.0	22	0
Brown	3	25	8.3	22	0
Thomas	2	26	13.0	14	0

Punting	No.	Yds.	Avg.	Longest	Inside 20	Blocked
Guy	67	2785	41.6	66	13	0

Punt Returns	No.	FCs	Yds.	Avg.	Longest	TDs
Colzie	41	3	448	10.9	32	0
Moore	6	0	78	12.0	23	0

Kickoff Returns	No.	Yds.	Avg.	Longest	TDs
Jennings	16	417	26.1	55	0
Garrett	18	388	21.5	36	0
Colzie	6	115	19.2	26	0

SAN DIEGO CHARGERS

Head Coach: Tommy Prothro

4th Year   **Record: 13—29**

1976 RECORD (6—8) (capital letters indicate home games)			1977 SCHEDULE (capital letters indicate home games)	
30	Kansas City	16	Oakland	Sept. 18
23	Tampa Bay	0	Kansas City	Sept. 25
43	ST. LOUIS	24	CINCINNATI	Oct. 2
0	Denver	26	New Orleans	Oct. 9
17	OAKLAND	27	NEW ENGLAND	Oct. 16
30	HOUSTON	27	KANSAS CITY	Oct. 23
17	Cleveland	21	Miami	Oct. 30
0	Pittsburgh	23	Detroit	Nov. 6
21	BALTIMORE	37	DENVER	Nov. 13
0	DENVER	17	OAKLAND	Nov. 20
34	Buffalo	13	Seattle	Nov. 27
20	KANSAS CITY	23	CLEVELAND	Dec. 4
13	SAN FRANCISCO (In OT)	7	Denver	Dec. 11
0	Oakland	24	PITTSBURGH	Dec. 18

The San Diego Chargers haven't finished above .500 since 1969, but this may be the year. They have added Johnny Rodgers of Montreal Alouettes fame, picked up Chip Myers from the Cincinnati Bengals, and signed Max Coley of Denver as offensive coordinator. Coley replaces Bill Walsh, who left to coach Stanford.

Walsh was important. It was his offense that gave the Chargers early electricity and eventually a 6–8 record in 1976, which was a vast improvement over the previous messes.

Quarterback Dan Fouts, who came alive under Walsh, will be on his own in 1977. Fouts hit former Bengal Charley Joiner for half a hundred receptions in 1976, but there was no one opposite him on the other side of the field. Now head coach Tommy Prothro can choose between Rodgers and Chip Myers, a long-time

Cincinnati teammate of Joiner's. Gary Garrison, hurt in game No. 2 last year, will return in 1977, and that will help the attack.

Rickey Young ripped through for 802 yards in 1976, and former 1,000-yard runner Don Woods for 450. This isn't enough, though, and it will be up to Coley to change the scope of the attack. Diversification must give the runners a better chance because of the air game and the long-range striking power of Rodgers, Joiner, and Myers.

Prothro always has been an attack-minded coach, and there is still some doubt that he can mold a good enough defense to win big in the NFL. His defense was ninth in the AFC last year; the Chargers allowed 4,676 combined yards. While the trade of Coy Bacon to Cincinnati secured Joiner and truly helped both teams, Bacon was missed up front last year. Fred Dean, Louie Kelcher, Gary Johnson, and Leroy Jones weren't a replica of the Fearsome Foursome, although they improved to a degree against the run, allowing 2,048 yards. San Diego allowed 285 points last season and needs to drop that figure by about fifty.

The Chargers' pass defense isn't the best—and it frequently gets beat at the end of the game when the money is on the line. San Diego was seventh in interceptions last year with 20, but Prothro needs a safety and a corner to help cut down on the aerial TDs against his boys. They allowed 21 in 1976—the same figure as in 1975.

Better placekicking from Ray Wersching and the same from punter Jeff West might turn more than one game around. West had a 40.7 average last year, but wasn't too hot in the clutch.

The problem on attack is to revitalize the offensive line and pep up the morale in the backfield. High-priced Mercury Morris is unhappy and may get traded now that Rodgers is on the scene. In 1976 he had 50 carries, 256 yards, and a 5.1 average, which might prove his point. Joe Washington, the No. 1 draft of 1976, comes off two knee operations this year; Bo Mathews is also competing with running backs Woods and Young.

Look for San Diego to put even more points on the board in 1977 than they did last year. Their 248 in 1976 wasn't awful, and perhaps 300 with 225 against would give them second place ahead of Denver and a long-range shot at the wild card playoff berth.

The Chargers will live and die with their defense, as most teams do. If the front four can snap to it and get some help from the secondary and the linebacking crew, things might get better fast. Don Goode really isn't good enough, though, and Prothro is looking for an experienced middle backer to guide the crew.

As it stands now, San Diego in 1977 will be worth the raised price of their tickets because they'll still specialize in those frenetic, cliff-hanging, 30–28 games with the outcome in doubt to the last gun. But second place is their highest hope in the AFC West, and to make that they'll have to get hep on defense in order to muscle past Denver's admittedly stubborn big D.

OFFENSE

Quarterbacks	Ht.	Wt.	Age	Exp.	College
Fouts, Dan	6-3	204	26	5	Oregon
Longley, Clint	6-1	195	25	4	Abilene Christian
Jeffrey, Neal	6-1	180	24	2	Baylor

Dan Fouts, the former water boy of the San Francisco 49ers, made it as a regular last year and should be the Charger leader for ten years. Not so, says the Mad Bomber, Clint Longley, the former Dallas backup who threw only 24 times in 1976. Neal Jeffrey, more experienced than Longley, is also around.

Running Backs	Ht.	Wt.	Age	Exp.	College
Young, Rickey	6-2	193	24	3	Jackson State
Morris, Mercury	5-10	192	30	9	West Texas State
Woods, Don	6-1	210	26	4	New Mexico
Matthews, Bo	6-4	230	26	4	Colorado
Scarber, Sam	6-2	232	29	3	New Mexico
Washington, Joe	5-10	184	24	1	Oklahoma

A plethora of running backs awaits new offensive coach Max Coley, who might make better use of Mercury Morris except that he's inherited CFL star Johnny Rodgers, who wants to prove he's a running back, not a flanker, which is what they used him as most of the time in Montreal. Don Woods can bowl people over and will be hard to dislodge, and Rickey Young can ramble with the best. Bo Matthews and Sam Scarber are in the wings with top draft pick Joe Washington, who tore up a knee in camp last year.

Receivers	Ht.	Wt.	Age	Exp.	College
McDonald, Dwight (W)	6-2	187	26	3	San Diego State
Myers, Chip (W)	6-6	205	32	10	N.W. Oklahoma
Dorsey, Larry (W)	6-1	195	24	2	Tennessee State
Garrison, Gary (W)	6-1	194	33	12	San Diego State
Curran, Pat (T)	6-3	238	32	9	Lakeland
Joiner, Charlie (W)	5-11	185	30	9	Grambling
Owens, Artie (W)	5-10	170	24	2	West Virginia
Rodgers, Johnny (W)	5-10	178	25	R	Nebraska
Tuttle, John (W)	6-1	187	25	1	Kansas State

W=wide receiver   T=tight end

After having been drafted No. 1 by San Diego in 1973 and spending four years in the Canadian league, Heisman Trophy winner Johnny Rodgers finally makes it as a rookie in the NFL. McDonald was a 1976 disappointment. Dorsey, another flop in 1976, will get another shot this year. Curran, a former Ram, is a good tight end. Charley Joiner had 50 receptions and 1,056 yards for seven TDs in 1976; he'll do less this year because of the presence of Chip Myers and Rodgers. Veteran third-down clutch receiver Gary Garrison, back from an injury, should help. Tuttle sat out with an injury in 1976.

Interior Linemen	Ht.	Wt.	Age	Exp.	College
Shields, Billy (T)	6-7	260	24	3	Georgia Tech
Singleton, Ron (T)	6-7	245	24	2	Grambling
Wilkerson, Doug (G)	6-3	262	30	8	N.C. Central
Aiu, Charles (G)	6-2	248	23	2	Hawaii
Perretta, Ralph (C)	6-2	252	24	3	Purdue
Flanagan, Ed (C)	6-3	245	33	13	Purdue
Macek, Don (G)	6-3	253	23	2	Boston College

Washington, Russ (T)	6-7	285	31	10	Missouri
Rush, Bob (C)	6-5	255	22	R	Memphis State

T=tackle   G=guard   C=center

The regulars are Shields, Wilkerson, Perretta, Macek, and Russ Washington. Fouts gets along with his crew, but most of the line is still young and learning, and it gets beaten by the better front fours. Old pro Ed Flanagan is a solid backup. Rush had All-America mentions at college.

Kickers	Ht.	Wt.	Age	Exp.	College
West, Jeff (P)	6-3	220	24	3	Cincinnati
Wersching, Ray (Pk)	5-10	222	27	5	California

Pk=placekicker   P=punter

Ray Wersching kicked only four of eight field goals in 1977, which indicates that Coach Prothro doesn't really trust him. Jeff West was seventh in NFL punting. He is adequate.

DEFENSE

Front Linemen	Ht.	Wt.	Age	Exp.	College
Dean, Fred (E)	6-3	219	25	3	Louisiana Tech
Lee, John (E)	6-2	247	24	2	Nebraska
Kelcher, Louis (T)	6-5	282	24	3	Southern Methodist
DeJurnett, Charles (T)	6-4	270	25	2	San Jose State
Jones, Leroy (E)	6-8	245	27	2	Norfolk State
Johnson, Gary (T)	6-2	262	25	3	Grambling
Teerlinck, John (T)	6-5	245	26	3	Western Illinois

E=end   T=tackle

Dean, Kelcher, Johnson, and Jones may decide the Chargers' fate this year. DeJurnett is still trying to unseat a regular, and Prothro wants to try a couple of big ends in the Coy Bacon mold. Teerlinck is coming off injury.

Linebackers	Ht.	Wt.	Age	Exp.	College
Goode, Don (O)	6-2	225	26	4	Kansas
Middletown, Rick (O)	6-2	234	26	4	Ohio State
Graham, Tom (M)	6-2	235	27	6	Oregon
Horn, Bob (M)	6-3	235	23	2	Oregon State
Lowe, Woodrow (O)	6-0	227	23	2	Alabama
Preston, Ray (O)	6-0	223	23	2	Syracuse

O=outside   M=middle

Goode is questionable as a regular. Graham is adequate in the middle but he's not a leader, and Low is the best of the trio. Horn may challenge Graham. Help is needed here in the form of a take-charge Bill Bergey type.

Cornerbacks	Ht.	Wt.	Age	Exp.	College
Colbert, Danny	5-11	176	27	4	Tulsa
Tolbert, Jim	6-4	210	33	11	Lincoln (Mo.)
Williams, Mike	5-10	181	24	3	Louisiana State
King, Keith	6-5	215	22	R	Colorado State

Williams and Colbert held their starting spots and got a bit more savvy last year. They should improve, but veteran Tolbert may wind up playing. King is a good defender from the college Western Conference.

Safeties	Ht.	Wt.	Age	Exp.	College
Fuller, Mike	5-9	195	24	3	Auburn
Stringert, Hal	5-11	185	25	3	Hawaii
Fletcher, Chris	5-11	189	29	8	Temple

Fuller is a pretty fair punt return and kickoff man. He and Stringert are the regular safeties. They're average, but Prothro cannot win a division with them.

Note: A complete listing of San Diego's 1977 college draft selections can be found on page 258.

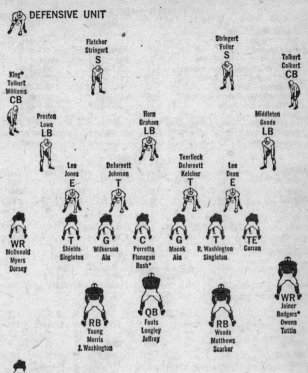

DEFENSIVE UNIT

Fletcher
Stringert
S

Stringert
Fuller
S

Tolbert
Colbert
CB

King*
Tolbert
Williams
CB

Preston
Lowe
LB

Horn
Graham
LB

Middleton
Goode
LB

Lee
Jones
E

DeJurnett
Johnson
T

Teerlinck
DeJurnett
Kelcher
T

Lee
Dean
E

WR
McDonald
Myers
Dorsey

T
Shields
Singleton

G
Wilkerson
Aiu

C
Perretta
Flanagan
Rush*

G
Macek
Aiu

T
R. Washington
Singleton

TE
Curran

RB
Young
Morris
J. Washington

QB
Fouts
Longley
Jeffrey

RB
Woods
Matthews
Scarber

WR
Joiner
Rodgers*
Owens
Tuttle

OFFENSIVE UNIT

*Rookie

1976 CHARGERS STATISTICS

	Chargers	Opps.
Total Points Scored	248	285
Total First Downs	256	259
Third-Down Efficiency	79—195	91—204
Yards Rushing—First Downs	2040—111	2048—113
Passes Attempted—Completions	388—223	386—219
Yards Passing—First Downs	2416—127	2628—132
QB Sacked—Yards Lost	46—271	23—194
Interceptions—Return Average	20—15.0	18—10.3
Punts—Average Yards	82—38.7	66—41.2
Punt Returns—Return Average	45—10.9	45—13.4
Kickoff Returns—Return Average	52—20.7	49—21.9
Fumbles—Ball Lost	28—13	24—11
Penalties—Yards	78—579	92—823

STATISTICAL LEADERS

Scoring	TDs	Rush.	Pass.	Ret.	PATs	FGs	Total
Joiner	7	0	7	0	0	0	42
Young	5	4	1	0	0	0	30
Fritsch	0	0	0	0	11—14	6—12	29
Wersching	0	0	0	0	14—16	4—8	26
McDonald	4	0	4	0	0	0	24
Woods	4	3	1	0	0	0	24
Matthews	4	3	0	1	0	0	24
Scarber	2	1	1	0	0	0	12
Morris	2	2	0	0	0	0	12

Rushing	Atts.	Yds.	Avg.	Longest	TDs
Young	162	802	5.0	46 (TD)	4
Woods	126	450	3.6	24	3
Morris	50	256	5.1	30	2
Scarber	61	236	3.9	14	1
Matthews	46	199	4.3	42 (TD)	3

Passing	Atts.	Com.	Yds.	Pct.	Int.	Longest	TDs
Fouts	359	208	2535	57.9	15	81 (TD)	14
Longley	24	12	130	50.0	3	28 (TD)	2

Receiving	No.	Yds.	Avg.	Longest	TDs
Joiner	50	1056	21.1	81 (TD)	7
Young	47	441	9.4	33	1
Woods	34	224	6.6	34	1
Curran	33	349	10.6	29	1
Scarber	14	96	6.9	13	1
Matthews	12	81	6.8	15	0
McDonald	11	161	14.6	44 (TD)	4

Interceptions	No.	Yds.	Avg.	Longest	TDs
Goode	6	82	13.7	27	0
Williams	4	76	19.0	35	0
Graham	3	55	18.3	25	0
Hayes	2	37	18.5	37 (TD)	1

Punting	No.	Yds.	Avg.	Longest	Inside 20	Blocked
West	38	1548	40.7	57	9	0
Hoopes	42	1628	38.8	57	8	2

Punt Returns	No.	FCs	Yds.	Avg.	Longest	TDs
Fuller	33	0	436	13.2	43	0
Bell	7	0	31	4.4	10	0
Williams	5	1	23	4.6	15	0

Kickoff Returns	No.	Yds.	Avg.	Longest	TDs
Owens	25	551	22.0	40	0
Fuller	20	420	21.0	47	0

DENVER BRONCOS

Head Coach: Red Miller

1st Year

1976 RECORD (9–5) (capital letters indicate home games)			1977 SCHEDULE (capital letters indicate home games)	
7	Cincinnati	17	ST. LOUIS	Sept. 18
46	N.Y. JETS	3	BUFFALO	Sept. 25
44	CLEVELAND	13	Seattle	Oct. 2
26	SAN DIEGO	0	KANSAS CITY	Oct. 9
3	Houston	17	Oakland	Oct. 16
10	OAKLAND	17	Cincinnati	Oct. 23
35	Kansas City	26	OAKLAND	Oct. 30
6	Oakland	19	PITTSBURGH	Nov. 6
48	TAMPA BAY	13	San Diego	Nov. 13
17	San Diego	0	Kansas City	Nov. 20
14	N.Y. GIANTS	13	BALTIMORE	Nov. 27
14	New England	38	Houston	Dec. 4
17	Kansas City	16	SAN DIEGO	Dec. 11
28	Chicago	14	Dallas	Dec. 18

They fired John Ralston because he didn't win the Super Bowl last year, but that doesn't mean his successor, Red Miller, will either. Ralston did pretty well with the tools he had, and maybe the win-starved Bronco fans just expected too much. Ralston had bought time by promising a Super Bowl team, and in the end it cost him his job.

Craig Morton is the new messiah in the Rockies, and it behooves Bronco fans to look at his records of failures, first with a championship Dallas team and later with the Giants, who were terrible. Sophomore quarterback Craig Penrose, or maybe even former WFL heaver Norris Weese, might be the answer down the road. And Steve Spurrier, who had the misfortune to quarterback Tampa Bay's 0–14 season last year, is now a member of this group.

The Broncs were 9–5 last year but out of the playoffs. They were fourth from the bottom on total offense, though they were a pretty solid third on total defense, surrendering just 3,734 yards. Thus, deficiencies on attack are the problem.

Otis Armstrong, the 5-10 scatback, came back from an injury for a 1,000-yard season in 1976, but runner-up Jon Keyworth had only 349 yards. Jim Kiick didn't play enough, even on third-down passes out of the backfield. Lonnie Perrin got barely a hundred yards, and Mike Franckowiak didn't show that much.

The Broncos need a big back to complement Armstrong's zigging and zagging, and unless they get one, they will still have to depend upon Morton's somewhat suspect air arm.

In the receiving department, Steve Ramsey put the ball up for Armstrong 39 times, the most of any Bronco. That's hardly game-breaking stuff, even though Armstrong can break a run any time he gets the ball. Morton is also prone to the dump-off, so things might not change that much. Moses Haven and Jack Dolbin are good clutch receivers, but a major part of the Broncos' attack last year was Rick Upchurch, who totaled more than 1,000 yards on combined punt and kickoff returns. He led the NFL in punt returns.

Denver had its best record ever last year—and still fired a tough coach in Ralston, who was of the old school.

Whether Morton and Armstrong—along with Key-worth, Moses, and Riley Odoms, the super tight end—can turn it around is a moot point. They *must* help the defense, which last year held opponents to only 206 points, second lowest in the AFC. Morton's record, his mental approach when things get tough, and his arm trouble make the trade of Steve Ramsey for Morton look like nothing more than a trade for the sake of showing the fans that something was being done.

In Denver, there isn't much hope of catching the Oakland Raiders for first place, but there is the hope that the Broncos might edge out New England, Baltimore, Cincinnati, or Pittsburgh for the wild card playoff spot. That's a tall order for a new coach putting in a new system.

Denver needs a big running fullback to make Armstrong more efficient—but then, who doesn't? Last year the Broncs depended too much on their special teams and defense to get needed points or field position. Miller wants some new offensive linemen to help open the holes, and he wants a cornerback to shore up the secondary. Still, that secondary and the linebackers had 24 interceptions last year—not bad, if you need the ball desperately for field position.

Whether Miller can stand up under the heavy pressure of the intense Denver fan interest is also something to consider. Denver is no longer a sleeping cow town in the Rockies. Its fans are sophisticated and used to winning because of the success of the basketball Nuggets.

It all may boil down to the offensive line and Morton. The same was true of the Giants the last two years and they flubbed the dub. If Denver can repeat the 9–5 of last year they'll be doing well. Look for them third in the AFC West.

Word is that although the Broncos still use the three-man defensive line, they may switch back to the orthodox four-man line if end Paul Smith and tackle Lyle Alzado are sufficiently recovered from injuries. The Broncos are usually a strong pass rushing team, but not so in 1976.

OFFENSE

Quarterbacks	Ht.	Wt.	Age	Exp.	College
Penrose, Craig	6-3	222	24	2	San Diego State
Weese, Norris	6-1	195	26	2	Mississippi
Morton, Craig	6-4	210	34	13	California
Spurrier, Steve	6-2	198	32	11	Florida

Morton is a tried veteran who did guide Dallas to the Super Bowl, but he has a bad arm and is getting on in age. In fact Morton, never too mobile, is Denver's prayer for 1977, but he was labeled a loser in both Dallas and with the Giants. Penrose has a big collegiate reputation and didn't do that badly when he took over for Steve Ramsey last year. He needs a bit more accuracy. Weese used to fill the air in the WFL, and if Morton blows it he might get the first shot. He rolled out for 142 yards on the ground in 1976. Spurrier, formerly of San Francisco and Tampa Bay, was signed on as a free agent.

Running Backs	Ht.	Wt.	Age	Exp.	College
Armstrong, Otis	5-10	196	27	4	Purdue
Kiick, Jim	5-11	215	31	8	Wyoming
Keyworth, Jon	6-3	230	27	4	Colorado
Perrin, Lonnie	6-1	222	25	2	Illinois
Franckowiak, Mike	6-3	220	24	3	Central Michigan
Jenkins, Darrell	6-2	235	1	25	San Jose State
Lynch, Fran	6-1	205	11	32	Hofstra
Lytle, Rob	6-1	195	22	R	Michigan

Scatback Armstrong came all the way back from his knee injury—1,008 yards says it all. Kiick was used sparingly and totaled only 114 yards in 1976. Keyworth was the No. 2 back; Perrin scrambled for 118 yards. Help needed here. Lynch was out with injuries in 1976. Jenkins was waived by the 49ers. Lytle was a consensus All-America at Michigan.

Receivers	Ht.	Wt.	Age	Exp.	College
Moses, Haven (W)	6-2	208	31	10	San Diego State
Dolbin, Jack (W)	5-10	180	29	3	Wake Forest
Odoms, Riley (T)	6-4	230	27	6	Houston
Brown, Boyd (T)	6-4	216	25	4	Alcorn State
Upchurch, Rick (W)	5-10	170	25	3	Minnesota
Schultz, John (W)	5-10	182	24	2	Maryland

W=wide receiver   T=tight end

Moses wasn't utilized properly in 1976—he caught only 25 passes, while Otis Armstrong came out of the backfield for 39 and tight end Riley Odoms caught 30. Keyworth snagged 22 short ones and so it went, with

Jack Dolbin catching 19. Morton doesn't have a history of throwing long, so talents like Moses and Dolbin may go to waste.

Interior Linemen	Ht.	Wt.	Age	Exp.	College
Bain, Bill (T)	6-4	270	25	3	Southern California
Hyde, Glenn (T)	6-3	250	26	4	Pittsburgh
Parrish, Scott (T)	6-6	265	24	2	Utah State
Glassic, Tom (G)	6-4	254	23	2	Virginia
Goodman, Harvey (G)	6-4	260	25	2	Colorado
DuLac, Bill (G)	6-4	260	26	4	Eastern Michigan
Howard, Paul (G)	6-3	260	27	5	Brigham Young
Maples, Bobby (C)	6-3	256	32	10	New Mexico
Olsen, Phil (C)	6-4	260	29	7	Utah State
Minor, Claudie (T)	6-4	280	26	4	San Diego State
Schindler, Steve (G)	6-3	260	22	R	Boston College
Brislin, Charles (G)	6-3	255	23	1	Mississippi State
Oliver, Al (T)	6-7	270	25	1	UCLA
Silvia, Dave (T)	6-4	245	26	1	Yankton

T=tackle   G=guard   C=center

Bain, Glassic, super center Maples, and Minor were the starters last year, but that may change as Miller works in new faces. It's already changed for guard Tommy Lyons, who was given his release. Glassic is a comer, and Olsen will get still another chance. Schindler is a promising rookie. Cohesion is needed—individual talent is there.

Kickers	Ht.	Wt.	Age	Exp.	College
Van Heusen, Bill (P)	6-1	200	31	10	Maryland
Turner, Jim (Pk)	6-2	205	36	14	Utah State
Faulk, Rich (P)	6-3	195	24	1	San Francisco State
Steele, Larry (P)	5-10	180	27	1	Santa Rosa

Pk=placekicker   P=punter

Backup QB Norris Weese does the punting along with Van Heusen, who can play wide receiver when he's asked. Turner finished tenth among the NFL's top kick-scoring leaders in 1976.

DEFENSE

Front Linemen	Ht.	Wt.	Age	Exp.	College
Chavous, Barney (E)	6-3	252	26	5	S.C. State
White, Jim (E)	6-4	250	29	5	Colorado State
Carter, Rubin (T)	6-0	256	25	3	Miami (Fla.)
Hammond, Wayne (T)	6-5	257	24	2	Montana State
Grant, John (T)	6-3	235	27	5	Southern California
Alzado, Lyle (E)	6-3	252	28	7	Yankton

Smith, Paul (E)	6-3	256	32	10	New Mexico
Imhof, Martin (E)	6-6	252	28	6	San Diego State
Cozens, Randy (E)	6-4	235	24	1	Pittsburgh
Manor, Brison (E)	6-4	248	25	1	Arkansas
Moore, Randy (T)	6-2	241	23	2	Arizona State
Smith, Charlie (E)	6-5	245	24	1	N.C. Central

E=end   T=tackle

White, Chavous, Carter, and Grant start, but wait until Alzado gets off the injured list. Actually, Smith, Alzado, White, and Chavous are the front four, with Carter backing up, but Denver has so much depth that everyone gets some playing time—and Denver usually shuts down the opposition. Paul Smith slipped last year and lost his starting spot. Cozens, Manor, Moore, and Charlie Smith are coming off the casualty list.

Linebackers	Ht.	Wt.	Age	Exp.	College
Rizzo, Joe (O)	6-1	220	27	4	Kings Point
Swenson, Bob (O)	6-3	220	24	3	California
Gradishar, Randy (M)	6-3	233	25	4	Ohio State
May, Ray (M)	6-1	230	32	11	Southern California
Turk, Godwin (M)	6-2	230	27	4	Southern U.
Baska, Rich (M)	6-3	225	25	2	UCLA
Jackson, Tom (O)	5-11	220	26	5	Louisville
Evans, Larry (O)	6-2	216	24	2	Mississippi College
Huddleston, John (M)	6-3	231	23	1	Utah

O=outside   M=middle

Gradishar is becoming a household name, and Swenson and Jackson aren't far behind in ability. Ray May returns from an injury in 1977 and could win a spot; at any rate, the linebacking situation is a plus. Jackson led Denver's pass interceptors with seven last year.

Cornerbacks	Ht.	Wt.	Age	Exp.	College
Wright, Louis	6-2	195	24	3	San Jose State
Jones, Calvin	5-7	169	26	5	Washington
Hardee, Billy	6-0	185	~23	2	Virginia Tech
Kelley, Vernie	5-11	190	24	1	Pacific (Calif.)

Miller might like a different cornerback. Wright and Jones are the incumbents. Hardee is hanging in there after his rookie year.

Safeties	Ht.	Wt.	Age	Exp.	College
Foley, Steve	5-11	181	24	2	Tulane
Jackson, Bernard	5-11	179	27	6	Washington State
Thompson, Bill	6-1	200	31	9	Maryland State
Potl, Randy	6-3	190	25	4	Stanford
Beaman, Bruce	5-10	173	27	1	Illinois

| Knoff, Kurt | 6-3 | 188 | 23 | 1 | Kansas |
| Pane, Chris | 5-11 | 180 | 24 | 2 | Chico State |

Thompson, perhaps, turned in the best performance among these in 1976. But overall good play in the clutch was lacking. Eleven-year-man John Rowser was given his walking papers.

Note: A complete listing of Denver's 1977 college draft selections can be found on page 250.

DEFENSIVE UNIT 3-4 DEFENSE

Pane
Poltl
S

Beaman
Knoff
Thompson
S

Kelley
Hardee
Wright
CB

B. Jackson
Jones
Foley
CB

Boothe
Evans
T. Jackson
LB

Baska
Gradishar
LB

Huddleston
Turk
Rizzo
LB

Swenson
LB

C. Smith
Imhof
Manor
Alzado
E

Moore
Hammond
Grant
Carter
MG

White
Cozens
P. Smith
Chavous
E

WR
Upchurch
Dolbin

T
Bain
Goodman
Oliver

G
Glassic
Hyde
Bristin
Schindler*

C
Olsen
Maples

G
Howard
Brannan

T
Minor
Parrish
Silvia

TE
Odoms
Brown

WR
Moses
Schultz
Van Heusen

RB
Armstrong
Kiick
Jenkins

QB
Penrose
Weese
Morton
Spurrier

RB
Keyworth
Perrin
Franckowiak
Lytle*

OFFENSIVE UNIT

*Rookie

1976 BRONCOS STATISTICS

	Broncos	Opps.
Total Points Scored	315	206
Total First Downs	239	222
Third-Down Efficiency	69—193	73—222
Yards Rushing—First Downs	1932—106	1709—90
Passes Attempted—Completions	353—168	391—214
Yards Passing—First Downs	2204—114	2013—104
QB Sacked—Yards Lost	48—306	33—253
Interceptions—Return Average	24—19.0	22—11.8
Punts—Average Yards	84—35.1	91—37.3
Punt Returns—Return Average	51—12.5	43—8.7
Kickoff Returns—Return Average	46—23.4	50—24.1
Fumbles—Ball Lost	23—12	23—13
Penalties—Yards	105—986	88—715

STATISTICAL LEADERS

Scoring	TDs	Rush.	Pass.	Ret.	PATs	FGs	Total
Turner	0	0	0	0	36—39	15—21	81
Moses	7	0	7	0	0	0	42
Armstrong	6	5	1	0	0	0	36
Upchurch	6	1	1	4	0	0	36
Odoms	5	2	3	0	0	0	30
Keyworth	4	3	1	0	0	0	24

Rushing	Atts.	Yds.	Avg.	Longest	TDs
Armstrong	247	1008	4.1	31	5
Keyworth	122	349	2.9	13	3
Weese	23	142	6.2	20	0
Perrin	37	118	3.2	14	2
Klick	31	114	3.7	19	1
Upchurch	6	71	11.8	25	1
Ramsey	13	51	3.9	15	0

Passing	Atts.	Com.	Yds.	Pct.	Int.	Longest	TDs
Ramsey	270	128	1931	47.4	13	71 (TD)	11
Weese	47	24	314	51.1	6	43	1

Receiving	No.	Yds.	Avg.	Longest	TDs
Armstrong	39	457	11.7	36 (TD)	1
Odoms	30	477	15.9	47	3
Moses	25	498	19.9	71 (TD)	7
Keyworth	22	201	9.1	31	1
Dolbin	19	354	18.6	40	1
Upchurch	12	340	28.3	59 (TD)	1

Interceptions	No.	Yds.	Avg.	Longest	TDs
Jackson	7	136	19.4	46 (TD)	1
Rowser	4	104	26.0	41 (TD)	2
Foley	4	95	23.8	34	0
Gradishar	3	44	14.7	31 (TD)	1
Swenson	2	26	13.0	26	0

Punting	No.	Yds.	Avg.	Longest	Inside 20	Blocked
Weese	52	1852	35.6	55	5	0
Van Heusen	31	1093	35.3	52	4	1

Punt Returns	No.	FCs	Yds.	Avg.	Longest	TDs
Upchurch	39	3	536	13.7	92 (TD)	4
Thompson	6	0	60	10.0	20	0
Foley	5	0	42	8.4	16	0

Kickoff Returns	No.	Yds.	Avg.	Longest	TDs
Perrin	14	391	27.9	43	0
Upchurch	22	514	23.4	64	0

KANSAS CITY CHIEFS

Head Coach: Paul Wiggin

3rd Year   **Record:** 10–18

1976 RECORD (5–9) (capital letters indicate home games)			**1977 SCHEDULE** (capital letters indicate home games)	
16	SAN DIEGO	30	New England	Sept. 18
21	OAKLAND	24	SAN DIEGO	Sept. 25
17	NEW ORLEANS	27	OAKLAND (night, TV)	Oct. 3
17	Buffalo	50	Denver	Oct. 9
33	Washington	30	BALTIMORE	Oct. 16
20	Miami (in OT)	17	San Diego	Oct. 23
26	DENVER	35	Cleveland	Oct. 30
28	Tampa Bay	19	GREEN BAY	Nov. 6
0	PITTSBURGH	45	Chicago	Nov. 13
10	Oakland	21	DENVER	Nov. 20
24	CINCINNATI	27	Houston	Nov. 27
23	San Diego	20	CINCINNATI	Dec. 4
16	Denver	17	SEATTLE	Dec. 11
39	CLEVELAND	14	Oakland	Dec. 18

On the surface, the Kansas City Chiefs made no significant progress in 1976—their second straight 5–9 season. Paul Wiggin, who started with a three-year pact, and therefore had a year to go, is now happily ensconced with a new three-year arrangement, which gives him time to get the Chiefs back on the warpath. He may *need* time.

Kansas City is still respectable and on a given day can beat anyone. Still, negative points remain—the most glaring is the fact that the Chiefs had the worst defense in the NFL last season, giving up an average of 383 yards per game. They ranked twenty-seventh against the rush and twenty-third against the pass. Things might even get worse, defensively speaking, in view of the fact that the three lone survivors of the 1969 Super Bowl winning Chiefs—linebackers Willie Lanier and Jim

Lynch and cornerback Emmitt Thomas—aren't getting any younger. Lanier and Lynch are seriously pondering retirement.

On attack, the Chiefs were pretty good last season. They finished seventh in the NFL, averaging 343 yards per game. Their passing attack—209 yards per game—was the most productive of yardage in the NFL. That's right, in the entire league, only a fraction less than Baltimore's.

Mike Livingston, long in the shadow of Lenny Dawson, has emerged as a genuine NFL quarterback. He was tenth in NFL passing stats last year, with 55.9 percent completions, 12 TDs, and only 13 interceptions (a figure he cut drastically compared to his previous half-season ratios).

Livingston has a young and exciting offensive line to work with; they really move people out. Matt Herkenhoff, Charlie Gentry, Tom Condon, Jim Nicholson, and super-stud tight end Walter White have come fast.

White is a potential All-Pro tight end, and Henry Marshall is a big-play wide receiver in the mold of the departed Otis Taylor.

One of the things Wiggin needs most is a stud running back. We seem to say that in almost every analysis, but it couldn't be more true of the Chiefs. Woody Green has been hurt for three years, MacArthur Lane is getting old, and versatile Ed Podolak is thinking about quitting.

The defensive situation is even worse, however. The defensive line shows little ability to rush the passer, and the linebackers are nearing the end. Only in the secondary, where youngsters Gary Barbaro and Tim Gray came alive, are there signs of youth and hope.

Before the Chiefs can hope for a playoff berth, Wiggin must somehow build his defense. The Steelers won their Super Bowls on defense, and so did the Raiders and the Dolphins. Kansas City's attack has changed drastically since the days of Dawson's conservative running approach and ball control; it runs up and down the field like crazy. But the defense gives more points than the attack can scare up.

The emergence of Livingston after six years as Dawson's caddy was essentially a surprise. Most NFL coaches rated Mike low; this was based on his ineffectual relief of Dawson over the years. But given his chance, and with no one looking over his shoulder, Livingston came through.

The pass-oriented attack had MacArthur Lane, an aging running back, actually win the NFL pass receiving title with 66 catches (good for 686 yards). Walter White and Larry Brunson caught 80 jointly. Henry Marshall catches them deep and is a long-range threat.

The rushing attack still lacks a big gun; Lane led last year with 542 yards. Wiggin nevertheless demonstrated that he could build an attack out of people who hadn't exactly burned up the NFL in the previous year. Podolak, hard-working as ever, was second with 371 yards, and Green had 322. Tommy Reamon, who led the WFL in ground-gaining in 1974, was given 103 chances to carry the ball and wound up with only 314 yards. He may get more time this year—at Chicago, where he was sent in exchange for a draft choice.

If the Chiefs can cut 100 points off the horrendous 376 they allowed in 1976, they could challenge Denver and San Diego for the runner-up spot in the AFC West. It's up to the defense, as usual.

OFFENSE

Quarterbacks	Ht.	Wt.	Age	Exp.	College
Livingston, Mike	6-4	212	32	10	Southern Methodist
Adams, Tony	6-0	198	27	3	Utah State
Nott, Mike	6-3	203	25	2	Santa Clara

Livingston proved his point last year. Tenth in the NFL, the leader of a versatile, high-scoring attack that produced 290 points, at 32 he has five productive years ahead. Adams, the former WFL bomb-thrower, may be underrated—he can put the ball up. Nott is not so bad, either,

Running Backs	Ht.	Wt.	Age	Exp.	College
Podolak, Ed	6-1	205	30	9	Iowa
Harrison, Glynn	5-11	191	23	2	Georgia
Green, Woody	6-1	205	26	4	Arizona State
Jennings, J. J.	6-1	220	24	2	Rutgers
Lane, MacArthur	6-1	220	34	10	Utah State
McNeil, Pat	5-9	208	23	1	Baylor
Margado, Arnold	6-0	210	25	1	Hawaii
Reed, Tony	5-11	200	22	R	Colorado

How long can Lane do the super job he did in 1976? That question bothers Wiggin. A big back, Lane might have a replacement in sight in J. J. Jennings, the one-time Rutgers and WFL hero. Veteran workhorse Podolak, who is slow but steady, might quit, but meanwhile he's still versatile and valuable. Green must prove he can play a full year without getting hurt. Margado comes as a free agent and Reed had good All-America mentions in college.

Receivers	Ht.	Wt.	Age	Exp.	College
Marshall, Henry (W)	6-2	205	23	1	Missouri
Pearson, Barry (W)	5-11	185	27	6	Northwestern
White, Walter (T)	6-3	218	26	3	Maryland
Masters, Billy (T)	6-5	240	33	11	Louisiana State
Brunson, Larry (W)	5-11	180	28	4	Colorado
McBee, Ike (W)	5-11	175	23	2	San Jose State
Williams, Lawrence (W)	5-10	173	24	3	Texas Tech

W=wide receiver   T=tight end

Marshall is a budding Otis Thomas, with speed and power. White is a super-stud young tight end; Masters, a vet, is the backup. MacArthur Lane, a running back, led the NFL in catches in 1976—it was the second year in a row that the Chiefs depended on the short pass to a back. (In 1975 Ed Podolak led the team in pass receiving.) In 1976 White was second with 47, Brunson proved he could play with 33, Marshall had 28, Masters had 18, and Podolak grabbed 13. Once a rusted, out-of-date nothing, the air arm came alive last season. Now Masters must recover from surgery for a slipped disc to get into action again.

Interior Linemen	Ht.	Wt.	Age	Exp.	College
Herkenhoff, Matt (T)	6-4	255	26	2	Minnesota
Getty, Charles (T)	6-4	260	25	4	Penn State
Walters, Rod (G)	6-3	258	23	2	Iowa
Beisler, Randy (G)	6-5	244	33	12	Indiana
Rudnay, Jack (C)	6-3	240	29	8	Northwestern
Ane, Charlie (C)	6-1	233	25	3	Michigan State
Olsen, Orrin (C)	6-1	245	24	2	Brigham Young
Condon, Tom (G)	6-3	240	25	4	Boston College
Nicholson, Jim (T)	6-6	275	27	4	Michigan State
Simmons, Bob (T)	6-4	260	23	1	Texas

T=tackle   G=guard   C=center

Regulars are Herkenhoff, Getty, Rudnay, Condon, Nicholson, and Walter White. This is pure youth, and if Wiggin can rebuild the defense as he did the attack line, Kansas City won't have to worry. Ane and Rudnay are from the Chiefs' glorious past. Beisler is also veteran insurance, but youth is having its fling and will get better with savvy and experience. Simmons was out with injury in 1976.

Kickers	Ht.	Wt.	Age	Exp.	College
Wilson, Jerrel (P)	6-2	222	36	15	S. Mississippi
Stenerud, Jan (Pk)	6-2	187	33	11	Montana State

Pk=placekicker   P=punter

Stenerud and Wilson are two of the finest in the NFL. They are getting older, true, but the Chiefs aren't really looking elsewhere yet. In 1976 Stenerud was 21 of 38 in FG attempts—Wiggin gave him a lot of work. Wilson had a 42.0 average, third in the league.

DEFENSE

Front Linemen	Ht.	Wt.	Age	Exp.	College
Paul, Whitney (E)	6-3	220	24	2	Colorado
Estes, Lawrence (E)	6-6	250	30	6	Alcorn State
Lohmeyer, John (E)	6-4	229	26	4	Emporia State
Maddox, Bob (T)	6-5	249	28	5	Frostburg State
Lee, Willie (T)	6-4½	249	27	2	Bethune—Cookman
Wolf, James (T)	6-3	250	25	3	Prairie View
Simons, Keith (T)	6-3	254	23	2	Minnesota
Young, Wilbur (E)	6-6	285	28	7	William Penn
Magrum, Bud (T)	6-4	255	28	1	Colorado

E=end   T=tackle

The ever-changing front four is a problem area. Regulars are Paul, Maddox, Wolf, and Young. Who, when, where? Estes, a former WFL type, Simons, Lee, and Lohmeyer are all hopefuls. Help, help. First-year man Magrum may provide some.

Linebackers	Ht.	Wt.	Age	Exp.	College
Andrews, Billy (O)	6-0	220	32	11	S.E. Louisiana
Werner, Clyde (O)	6-3	230	29	7	Washington
Viney, Rudy (O)	6-1	220	23	2	Pacific (Calif.)
Lanier, Willie (M)	6-1	245	32	11	Morgan State
Lynch, Jim (M)	6-1	225	32	11	Notre Dame
Elrod, Jimbo (M)	6-0	209	23	2	Oklahoma
Rozumek, Dave (O)	6-1½	212	23	2	New Hampshire
Howard, Thomas (O)	6-2	208	22	R	Texas Tech

O=outside   M=middle

If the Chiefs could turn back the clock on Lanier and Lynch, their linebacking corps would be in great shape. Even the third member of the trio, Andrews, is 32, so all three are in their final years—provided Wiggin can even talk Lanier and Lynch into playing. Clyde Werner may get a shot if Andrews fouls up. Rozumek is behind Lynch. Howard was a Kodak All-America, but what will the game films show?

Cornerbacks	Ht.	Wt.	Age	Exp.	College
Reardon, Kerry	5-11	180	28	7	Iowa
Collier, Tim	5-11	166	23	2	East Texas State
Thomas, Emmitt	6-2	192	34	12	Bishop
Green, Gary	5-11	184	22	R	Baylor

The Chiefs went to the ball pretty well in 1976 with 23 interceptions —that placed them tied for third in the AFC. Reardon led with five. Veteran corner Thomas is still pretty adequate, but time's afleeting. Collier is in the wings.

Safeties	Ht.	Wt.	Age	Exp.	College
Gray, Tim	6-1	200	24	3	Texas A&M
Taylor, Steve	6-3	204	23	2	Kansas
Barbaro, Gary	6-3½	198	23	2	Nicholls State
Bograkus, Steve	5-11	171	23	2	Central Michigan

Gray had four interceptions in 1976, and with Barbaro he gives the Chiefs some hope at safety. Both are young.

Note: A complete listing of Kansas City's 1977 college draft selections can be found on page 252.

DEFENSIVE UNIT

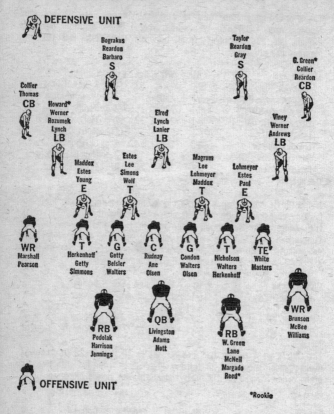

Bograkus
Reardon
Barbaro
S

Taylor
Reardon
Gray
S

G. Green*
Collier
Reardon
CB

Collier
Thomas
CB

Howard*
Werner
Rozumek
Lynch
LB

Elrod
Lynch
Lanier
LB

Viney
Werner
Andrews
LB

Maddox
Estes
Young
E

Estes
Lee
Simons
Wolf
T

Magrum
Lee
Lohmeyer
Maddox
T

Lohmeyer
Estes
Paul
E

WR
Marshall
Pearson

T
Herkenhoff
Getty
Simmons

G
Getty
Belsler
Walters

C
Rudnay
Ane
Olsen

G
Condon
Walters
Olsen

T
Nicholson
Walters
Herkenhoff

TE
White
Masters

WR
Brunson
McBee
Williams

RB
Podolak
Harrison
Jennings

QB
Livingston
Adams
Nott

RB
W. Green
Lane
McNeil
Margado
Reed*

OFFENSIVE UNIT

*Rookie

1976 CHIEFS STATISTICS

	Chiefs	Opps.
Total Points Scored	290*	376
Total First Downs	275	309
Third-Down Efficiency	79—210	78—184
Yards Rushing—First Downs	1873—104	2861—161
Passes Attempted—Completions	419—229	375—215
Yards Passing—First Downs	2929—151	2496—133
QB Sacked—Yards Lost	42—374	22—188
Interceptions—Return Average	23—7.0	17—14.6
Punts—Average Yards	67—41.7	63—39.7
Punt Returns—Return Average	34—12.6	39—9.6
Kickoff Returns—Return Average	64—24.0	55—23.0
Fumbles—Ball Lost	31—16	35—20
Penalties—Yards	97—789	88—762

*Includes one safety

STATISTICAL LEADERS

Scoring	TDs	Rush.	Pass.	Ret.	PATs	FGs	Total
Stenerud	0	0	0	0	27—33	21—38	90
White	7	0	7	0	0	0	42
Lane	6	5	1	0	0	0	36
Podolak	5	5	0	0	0	0	30
Reamon	5	4	1	0	0	0	30
Marshall	3	1	2	0	0	0	18
Masters	3	0	3	0	0	0	18

Rushing	Atts.	Yds.	Avg.	Longest	TDs
Lane	162	542	3.3	20	5
Podolak	88	371	4.2	22 (TD)	5
Green	73	322	4.4	27	1
Reamon	103	314	3.0	14	4
Livingston	31	89	2.9	19	2

Passing	Atts.	Com.	Yds.	Pct.	Int.	Longest	TDs
Livingston	338	189	2682	55.9	13	57	12
Adams	71	36	575	50.7	4	49 (TD)	3

Receiving	No.	Yds.	Avg.	Longest	TDs
Lane	66	686	10.4	44	1
White	47	808	17.2	41	7
Brunson	33	656	19.9	57	1
Marshall	28	443	15.8	31 (TD)	2
Masters	18	269	14.9	30	3
Podolak	13	156	12.0	23	0

Interceptions	No.	Yds.	Avg.	Longest	TDs
Reardon	5	26	5.2	22	0
Gray	4	19	4.8	11	0
Lanier	3	28	9.3	14	0
Barbaro	3	27	9.0	16	0
Thomas	2	30	15.0	29	0
Collier	2	10	5.0	10	0
Lynch	2	7	3.5	7	0

Punting	No.	Yds.	Avg.	Longest	Inside 20	Blocked
Wilson	65	2729	42.0	62	14	1

Punt Returns	No.	FCs	Yds.	Avg.	Longest	TDs
Brunson	31	0	387	12.5	48	0

Kickoff Returns	No.	Yds.	Avg.	Longest	TDs
William	25	688	27.5	64	0
Reamon	19	424	22.3	35	0
Harrison	13	278	21.4	35	0

SEATTLE SEAHAWKS

Head Coach: Jack Patera

2nd Year   Record: 2–12

1976 RECORD (2–12) (capital letters indicate home games)		1977 SCHEDULE (capital letters indicate home games)	
24	ST. LOUIS 30	BALTIMORE	Sept. 18
7	Washington 31	Cincinnati	Sept. 25
21	SAN FRANCISCO 37	DENVER	Oct. 2
13	DALLAS 28	New England	Oct. 9
20	Green Bay (at Milwaukee) 27	TAMPA BAY	Oct. 16
13	Tampa Bay 10	Miami	Oct. 23
14	DETROIT 41	BUFFALO	Oct. 30
6	Los Angeles 45	Oakland	Nov. 6
30	ATLANTA 13	N.Y. Jets	Nov. 13
21	Minnesota 27	HOUSTON	Nov. 20
27	NEW ORLEANS 51	SAN DIEGO	Nov. 27
16	N.Y. Giants 28	Pittsburgh	Dec. 4
7	CHICAGO 34	Kansas City	Dec. 11
10	Philadelphia 27	CLEVELAND	Dec. 18

The Seahawks won the Expansion Bowl over the Tampa Buccaneers, but what does that really mean down the road? Not much, and coach Jack Patera and general manager John Thompson know it.

As perhaps was expected in many quarters, Tony Dorsett won't be carrying the ball for Seattle, now or in the foreseeable future—if ever at all. Just before the draft began last May at the Hotel Roosevelt in New York, Seattle and Dallas announced a trade that gave the Cowboys the right to choose Dorsett as their No. 2 selection in the first round in exchange for a No. 14 choice in the first round plus three second-round choices. When all the smoke cleared away and all the wheeling and dealing was over, Dallas had Dorsett and Seattle had these: Duke Fergerson, a former Cowboy wide receiver; rookie tackle Tom Lynch from Boston College;

rookie linebacker Terry Beeson from Kansas; center Geoff Reece from the Los Angeles Rams; and Steve August, a rookie offensive guard from Tulsa U.

Quarterback Jim Zorn was the NFC offensive rookie of the year in 1976, but he played poorly in the final third of the season—and he must learn to stop forcing his passes. Those 27 interceptions last year kept the Seattle offense from sustaining many of its longer drives. Turnovers hurt.

The receiving isn't bad; last year rookie Steve Largent caught 54 footballs for 705 yards. And Sam McCullum is pretty fair, too. Receiving is a Seahawk strength.

The rushing is weak and not up to NFL standards, although Sherman Smith has made a place for himself in the league. He never was a running back before this year, but he bulldozed through for 537 yards in 1976 and came out of the backfield for many pass receptions. Not bad for a novice. Zorn and Don Testerman both gained 246 yards. Dorsett would be a wondrous help.

The offensive line, being experienced, was pretty good. It helped the all-rookie backfield. It is the team's strongest area, in fact. Tackles Nick Bebout and Norm Evans, the Dolphin original; guards Bob Penchion, Bob Newton, and John Demarie; and centers Fred Hoaglin and Art Keuhn did a good job, and should be okay in 1977.

The front four lacked quickness—Notre Dame rookie Steve Niehaus was almost the entire pass rush. Richard Harris helped in the later stages, and Bob Lurtsema tries. Carl Barasich and Dave Tipton are spare parts.

The linebacking crew was rated highly, but disappointed. Mike Curtis gets caught inside on sweeps and, with his bad knee, lacks the speed for much pursuit. Ken Geddes gave way to Sammy Green, and Ed Bradley kept getting beaten. Greg Collins is a future; Green has potential.

The secondary held up pretty well, with Eddie McMillan playing consistently. Dave Brown and Al Matthews played well at safety, and Rolly Woolsey and Ernie Jones shared the other corner. Not a problem spot.

The 1976 kicking game was fair, with placekicker John Leypoldt, an ex-Buffalo Bill, taking over in mid-year and doing well. Punter Rick Engles, a low draft, helped, but tailed off toward the end.

Defensively, the Seahawks gave up 386 yards and 30 points per game. Quarterbacks who had trouble putting points on the board against other opponents did so against Seattle. And the tackling was poor, very poor.

The offensive unit moved the ball—with great help from the veteran offensive line. Zorn can throw, and only his penchant for the key interception (and the unfortunate, costly fumbling at the wrong time) stopped Seattle from having a really great offensive team for a first-year outfit.

Can Seattle move up in the standings now that they've shifted to the AFC West? Perhaps, but, realistically, all the teams in that division are quite a bit better. Kansas City has defense problems, Denver an attack problem, San Diego a turnover situation that hasn't quite meshed. If one of them falls back to 2–12 or something like that, Seattle might surge to 4–10, but that isn't likely to happen.

Quarterback Zorn is the key, although a sleeper could be pass master Bill Munson, who talked himself off the Detroit Lions. With the protection the offensive line gives, Munson might take Zorn's job and lend maturity to the attack.

No matter—Seattle for last.

OFFENSE

Quarterbacks	Ht.	Wt.	Age	Exp.	College
Zorn, Jim	6-2	200	24	2	Calif. Poly—Pomona
Munson, Bill	6-2	205	36	14	Utah State
Myer, Steve	6-2	188	23	2	New Mexico

Zorn developed rapidly in the first two-thirds of the season. He played poorly after that and must overcome his rookie-type mistakes and penchant for throwing into crowds—the latter results in interceptions. His 27 errant tosses in 1976 were too many, but his 12 TDs weren't that bad. He needs to improve his 47.4 percentage and be more patient. Munson can pass with the best, and if given protection in the pocket might take over from Zorn. He came from the Detroit Lions.

Running Backs	Ht.	Wt.	Age	Exp.	College
Smith, Sherman	6-4	217	23	3	Miami (Ohio)
Nelson, Ralph	6-2	195	23	3	(none)
Ross, Oliver	6-0	210	28	5	Alabama A&M
Testerman, Don	6-2	230	25	2	Clemson
McKinnis, Hugh	6-1	219	29	5	Arizona State
Bates, Larry	6-1	218	23	1	Miami (Fla.)

Converted quarterback Smith did a job last year roared for 537 yards. Testerman is a big back with potential. McKinnis disappointed but can scamper. Nelson, Oliver, and Bates all will get chances unless Seattle signs a Tony Dorsett type.

Receivers	Ht.	Wt.	Age	Exp.	College
McCullum, Sam (W)	6-2	203	25	4	Montana State
Raible, Steve (W)	6-2	195	23	2	Georgia Tech
Howard, Ron (T)	6-4	225	26	4	Seattle U.
McMakin, John (T)	6-3	225	27	6	Clemson
Largent, Steve (W)	5-11	184	23	2	Tulsa
Waddell, Charles (T)	6-5	233	24	1	North Carolina
Walker, Ralph (W)	6-3	190	24	R	St. Mary's (Calif.)
Fergerson, Duke (W)	6-1	193	23	2	San Diego State

W=wide receiver   T=tight end

McCullum is a good wide receiver with average speed. He isn't Lynn Swann, but he'll do for now. McCullum caught 32 passes for 506 yards in 1976, but Largent and tight end Howard beat him with more catches. Sherman Smith came out of the backfield for 36 and 384. McMakin might challenge Howard this year, and Seattle has a pretty fair group of other wide receivers. The position is pretty well set up for an expansion group. Fergerson comes from Dallas in the Dorsett-draft deal.

Interior Linemen	Ht.	Wt.	Age	Exp.	College
Bebout, Nick (T)	6-5	260	26	5	Wyoming
Simonson, Dave (T)	6-6	248	25	4	Minnesota
Penchion, Ben (G)	6-6	252	28	6	Alcorn State
Coder, Ron (G)	6-3	250	23	2	Penn State
Hoaglin, Fred (C)	6-4	250	33	12	Pittsburgh
Kuehn, Art (C)	6-3	255	24	2	UCLA
Newton, Bob (G)	6-4	260	28	7	Nebraska
Demarie, John (G)	6-3	248	32	11	Louisiana State
Evans, Norm (T)	6-5	250	35	13	Texas Christian
Jolley, Gordon (T)	6-5	245	28	6	Utah
Reece, Geoff (C)	6-4	247	25	2	Washington State
August, Steve (G)	6-4	243	22	R	Tulsa
Lynch, Tom (T)	6-6	260	22	R	Boston College

T=tackle   G=guard   C=center

The class of the Seahawks is the interior line. Regulars are Bebout, Penchion, Hoaglin, Newton, and Evans. They open the holes and are backed ably by Kuehn and Demarie. A solid setup for a few years, with age the only minus factor. Reece, August, and Lynch are also on hand because of the Dorsett trade-away.

Kickers	Ht.	Wt.	Age	Exp.	College
Engles, Rick (P)	5-10	170	23	2	Tulsa
Leypoldt, John (Pk)	6-2	230	31	7	(none)
Sorenson, Rich (Pk)	6-1	190	23	1	Chico State

Pk=placekicker   P=punter

Engles punted 80 times for 38.3 in 1976. Seattle won't make the playoffs with him, but he isn't that bad. Leypoldt restored order after being cut by the Buffalo Bills, where he missed a key field goal. He was eight of 15 on FGs at Buffalo and Seattle. Sorenson is a high-rated rookie.

DEFENSE

Front Linemen	Ht.	Wt.	Age	Exp.	College
Tipton, Dave (E)	6-6	246	28	7	Stanford
Barisich, Carl (E, T)	6-4	255	26	5	Princeton
Chalmers, Mark (E)	6-5	255	25	1	Texas
Niehaus, Steve (T)	6-4	270	23	2	Notre Dame
Woods, Larry (T)	6-6	270	29	8	Tennessee State
Harris, Richard (T)	6-5	258	29	7	Grambling
Lurtsema, Bob (E)	6-6	250	35	11	Western Michigan
Fine, Tom (E)	6-5	245	24	1	Notre Dame
Simpson, Bob (E)	6-5	240	23	1	Colorado
Boyd, Dennis (E)	6-6	245	22	R	Oregon State

E=end   T=tackle

Tipton is an occasional starter along with Barisich. Neither hurt you that much, but they can be moved out and don't exert too much pressure on the passer. Chalmers, Fine, and Simpson are rookies who will get chances. Niehaus was the best pass rusher around in 1976 and will remain the leader of the front four. Harris came fast the second half of the season, and Lurtsema lent experience and fire, if not much skill. Boyd had All-America mentions in college.

Linebackers	Ht.	Wt.	Age	Exp.	College
Geddes, Ken (O)	6-3	235	30	7	Nebraska
Green, Sammy (O)	6-2	228	23	2	Florida
Dionas, Steve (O)	6-2	225	23	1	Montana
Bradley, Ed (M)	6-2	239	27	6	Wake Forest
Collins, Greg (M)	6-3	227	25	3	Notre Dame
Curtis, Mike (O)	6-2	232	34	13	Duke
Coffield, Randy (O)	6-3	215	24	2	Florida State
Hutcherson, Ken (O)	6-0	225	25	2	Livingston
Cronan, Pete (O)	6-2	238	22	R	Boston College
Beeson, Terry (O)	6-2	240	22	R	Kansas

O=outside   M=middle

Geddes disappointed last year. He was better with the Rams, where he was surrounded by talent. Green took Geddes' job and has the tools. Bradley suffered greatly in 1976 and may lose his spot. Collins could take over for Bradley. Curtis knows what to do but is over the hill. The others are inexperienced, but may get opportunities. Cronan comes off a good Boston College team.

Cornerbacks	Ht.	Wt.	Age	Exp.	College
McMillan, Eddie	6-0	190	26	5	Florida State
Jones, Ernie	6-3	180	24	2	Miami (Fla.)
Brown, Oreasor	6-0	190	24	R	Pacific (Calif.)
Woolsey, Rolly	6-1	182	24	3	Boise State

Seattle had 15 interceptions in 1976, not even half of Los Angeles' leading 32 in the NFC. McMillan played well along with Jones at one corner. Woolsey led with four interceptions. Brown is a future.

Safeties	Ht.	Wt.	Age	Exp.	College
Matthews, Al	5-11	190	30	8	Texas A&I
Blackwood, Lyle	6-0	190	26	5	Texas Christian
Dufek, Don	6-0	195	23	2	Michigan
Brown, Dave	6-1	190	24	3	Michigan

Matthews lent class to the safety spot. Brown had four interceptions. Blackwood has experience and Dufek is the young hope.

Note: A complete listing of Seattle's 1977 college draft selections can be found on page 259.

DEFENSIVE UNIT

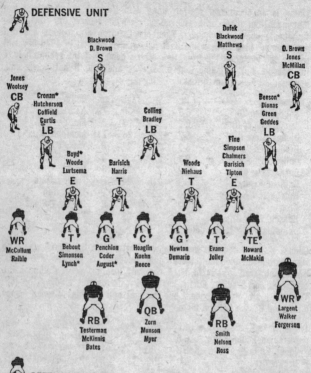

Blackwood
D. Brown
S

Dufek
Blackwood
Matthews
S

O. Brown
Jones
McMillan
CB

Jones
Woolsey
CB

Cronan*
Hutcherson
Coffield
Curtis
LB

Collins
Bradley
LB

Beeson*
Dionas
Green
Geddes
LB

Boyd*
Woods
Lurtsema
E

Barisich
Harris
T

Woods
Niehaus
T

Fine
Simpson
Chalmers
Barisich
Tipton
T   **E**

WR
McCullum
Raible

T
Bebout
Simonson
Lynch*

G
Penchion
Coder
August*

C
Hoaglin
Kuehn
Reece

G
Newton
Demarie

T
Evans
Jolley

TE
Howard
McMakin

WR
Largent
Walker
Fergerson

RB
Testerman
McKinnis
Bates

QB
Zorn
Munson
Myer

RB
Smith
Nelson
Ross

OFFENSIVE UNIT

*Rookie

1976 SEAHAWKS STATISTICS

	Seahawks	Opps.
Total Points Scored	229*	429
Total First Downs	237	323
Third-Down Efficiency	59—221	96—219
Yards Rushing—First Downs	1413—75	2881—166
Passes Attempted—Completions	480—229	367—223
Yards Passing—First Downs	2649—140	2524—136
QB Sacked—Yards Lost	28—225	27—246
Interceptions—Return Average	15—14.5	30—12.9
Punts—Average Yards	82—37.4	65—35.0
Punt Returns—Return Average	39—6.3	56—9.5
Kickoff Returns—Return Average	79—20.3	46—22.6
Fumbles—Ball Lost	30—18	23—13
Penalties—Yards	80—684	106—926

*Includes one safety

STATISTICAL LEADERS

Scoring	TDs	Rush.	Pass.	Ret.	PATs	FGs	Total
Leypoldt	0	0	0	0	19—22	8—12	43
Smith	5	4	1	0	0	0	30
Largent	4	0	4	0	0	0	24
McCullum	4	0	4	0	0	0	24
McKinnis	4	4	0	0	0	0	24
Zorn	4	4	0	0	0	0	24
McMakin	2	0	2	0	0	0	12
Raible	2	0	1	1	0	0	12
Testerman	2	1	1	0	0	0	12

Rushing	Atts.	Yds.	Avg.	Longest	TDs
Smith	119	537	4.5	53 (TD)	4
Zorn	52	246	4.7	19	4
Testerman	67	246	3.7	16	1
Nelson	52	173	3.3	25	1

Passing	Atts.	Com.	Yds.	Pct.	Int.	Longest	TDs
Zorn	439	208	2571	47.4	27	80 (TD)	12
Munson	37	20	295	54.1	3	44	1

Receiving	No.	Yds.	Avg.	Longest	TDs
Largent	54	705	13.1	45	4
Howard	37	422	11.4	30	0
Smith	36	384	10.7	45	1
McCullum	32	506	15.8	72 (TD)	4
Testerman	25	232	9.3	25	1
McKinnis	13	148	11.4	22	0

Interceptions	No.	Yds.	Avg.	Longest	TDs
Brown	4	70	17.5	33	0
Woolsey	4	19	4.8	13	0
Matthews	3	60	20.0	40 (TD)	1

Punting	No.	Yds.	Avg.	Longest	Inside 20	Blocked
Engles	80	3067	38.3	55	13	2

Punt Returns	No.	FCs	Yds.	Avg.	Longest	TDs
Blackwood	19	2	132	6.9	26	0
Brown	11	5	74	6.7	19	0
Largent	4	0	36	9.0	12	0

Kickoff Returns	No.	Yds.	Avg.	Longest	TDs
Ross	30	655	21.8	45	0
Bolton	15	280	18.7	30	0
Blackwood	10	230	23.0	45	0
Dufek	9	177	19.7	44	0

NATIONAL
FOOTBALL
CONFERENCE

The burning question in the National Football Conference is: Just how much better is the formerly upstart American Football Conference, modern offspring of the old American Football League? Oakland's crushing win over Minnesota in Super Bowl XI, coupled with the many previous Super disasters suffered by Minnesota, Dallas, et al., has just about stripped the once proud NFC of its ego. Its best teams are still Minnesota, Dallas, St. Louis, Washington, and Los Angeles, and some young whippersnappers are beginning to growl in San Francisco and Chicago. These, then, are the National Football Conference's top-drawer clubs.

Can the Rams, who have the best personnel in the NFC, finally win the playoffs with Pat Haden at quarterback? Or even with Joe Namath? Why don't the Rams win when they get to the playoffs? Will the reorganized 49ers make a real challenge, or will they fall back in a year of evaluation by Joe Thomas and his new partners? This group bought out the family of the late Tony Morabito, who had owned the San Francisco club since 1946. At any rate, the Rams seem to have a lock on the NFC West title—again.

In the Central division, can the surging Bears, led by Walter Payton—who has made Chicago fans almost forget Gale Sayers—put it to the Vikings, who seem to win from memory alone? Have the Purple People Eaters and Fran Tarkenton finally gotten old, or is vintage wine still better than anything the Bears can throw at Minnesota? How about the Detroit Lions, reorganized for the you-count-'emth time? If a personnel-coordinator type like Joe Thomas can do it, why can't Tommy Hudspeth make the Lions roar?

In the East, the New York Giants and Philadelphia Eagles don't really count—except to their fans, who are legion. The battle is between Tom Landry's Cowboys, Don Coryell's Cardinals, and George Allen's perennially ancient Washington Redskins. Landry has the bodies but is starting to worry about the condition of his quarterbacks. Roger Staubach has a bad hand and Danny White, the heir apparent, has knee trouble. Will the retirement of Lee Roy Jordan, only the second middle linebacker Dallas has ever had, disrupt the balance in a finely meshed machine?

The Cardinals were 10–4 last year but missed the playoffs. They will probably live or die on whether they can get their defense to put more pressure on the other guy's passer—something they just didn't seem able to do last year. Will Terry Metcalf continue to retrogress from his high standard of 1975? Is this natural, and, if so, what can Coryell do to take up the slack?

The Redskins will once more have to be reckoned with, but probably not in the Super Bowl. They will probably make the playoffs, as usual, but at whose expense? Joe Theismann is Allen's logical choice for quarterback, but 39-year-old Billy Kilmer has just signed up again, which means Allen will probably succumb to temptation and use him.

A warm note in the NFC Central is the permanent addition of Tampa Bay. Don't be surprised if Green Bay, at least, gets bumped off by the Buccaneers. The Pack is back in *bad* shape, with below-NFL-standard player personnel. Atlanta is starting over—again—much to the frustration of most Dixie fans, who can't understand how the Dolphins could do it so quickly while the Falcons falter so consistently. New Orleans hopes that quarterback Archie Manning's passing arm is healthy again; if it's not, the Saints will again be marching out of contention.

First places should go Dallas, Minnesota, and Los Angeles; the wild card will most likely be St. Louis.

DALLAS COWBOYS

Head Coach: Tom Landry

18th Year   **Record:** 137–93–6

1976 RECORD (11–3) (capital letters indicate home games)			1977 SCHEDULE (capital letters indicate home games)	
27	PHILADELPHIA	6	Minnesota	Sept. 18
24	New Orleans	6	N.Y. GIANTS	Sept. 25
30	BALTIMORE	27	TAMPA BAY	Oct. 2
28	Seattle	13	St. Louis	Oct. 9
24	N.Y. Giants	14	WASHINGTON	Oct. 16
17	St. Louis	21	Philadelphia	Oct. 23
31	CHICAGO	21	DETROIT	Oct. 30
20	Washington	7	N.Y. Giants	Nov. 6
9	N.Y. GIANTS	3	ST. LOUIS (night, TV)	Nov. 14
17	BUFFALO	10	Pittsburgh	Nov. 20
10	Atlanta	17	Washington	Nov. 27
19	ST. LOUIS	14	PHILADELPHIA	Dec. 4
26	Philadelphia	7	San Francisco (night, TV)	Dec. 12
14	WASHINGTON	27	DENVER	Dec. 18
	Playoffs			
12	LOS ANGELES	14		

For the sake of a running back, Dallas lost its berth in the Super Bowl and Calvin Hill, little used by George Allen and the Redskins, proved his point in the final game, when he helped the Skins to the play-offs over the almost inert bodies of his former team-mates.

Tom Landry's main priority was the addition of a big running back, something he got away without in 1975 —and something he appeared to have with the addition of Duane Thomas and Ron Johnson in preseason. Both of those worthies came up short and were re-leased. The loss of Hill to the WFL, and then to the Redskins, hurt more than anyone in Cowboyland cares to admit.

The acquisition of Heisman Trophy winner Tony

Dorsett in the recent NFL college draft undoubtedly provides the Cowboys with added hope that their running back problem may be on the way to being solved. If Dorsett, a record-breaking type as a collegian, isn't as big physically (five feet 11 inches and 192 pounds) as the Dallas brass would prefer, he may still be more than adequate with his speed and natural ability as a hard-to-catch ball carrier. Dorsett signed a reported $1.2 million five-year contract— the biggest money package ever for a Dallas player, and on terms similar to those concluded between Ricky Bell and the Tampa Bay Buccaneers.

Only twice during the 1976 season did a Dallas runner top the 100-yard mark in a game—Robert Newhouse against Seattle, and Scott Laidlaw against Philadelphia. Note the opposition. The Cowboys were twelfth in NFL ground offense in 1976, leaving us with a bromide: A team that cannot run must pass. A team that must pass sometimes can't.

The stolidness of the attack wasn't helped by the hand injury suffered by quarterback Roger Staubach; it just naturally hampered his throwing in the final games of 1976. Most likely everything will be fine, but you never know, and Roger the artful dodger is now 35. And All-Pro guard Blaine Nye, who leads the sweeps, may retire. Guards of his caliber aren't easily replaced.

When everyone is healthy, the pass catching situation seems to be a plus; there are clutch man Drew Pearson, Golden Richards the deep threat, and tight end Billy Joe DuPree.

The Big D in Dallas stands for the Cowboy defense, still excellent in the clutch, although the stats showed them only fifth in the NFC last year; they allowed 266.4 yards per game. In the matter of allowing fewest points against, Minnesota led the NFC with 176, Los Angeles and San Francisco each allowed 190, and

Dallas allowed 194. Only once in the last seven games did the other guys get more than twenty points.

Lee Roy Jordan has finally retired as the middle linebacker. Bob Breunig will switch into his natural middle backer position and MLB Randy White moves to the outside. They considered switching White to the front line, but if White had moved up front, who would he have replaced? Larry Cole? Bill Gregory? Jethro Pugh? None of these men would have appreciated less playing time. So it's an OLB post for Randy in 1977. The defensive secondary is pretty deep and should remain so—Mel Renfro is coming back for another season.

Danny White's knee hasn't responded, and his cartilage problem may need surgery. The Mad Bomber, Clint Longley, should have waited. White, who is Staubach's backup, also serves as the team's punter, and his kicking fell off with his bad knee.

Dallas stood pat last year; the same 43 people who suited up for the opener dressed for the playoff game against the Los Angeles Rams. This won't happen in 1977—Landry and personnel director Gil Brandt have vowed it. But they'd better come up with the big fullback or the attack will do them in again. Thirteen TDs from the attack as the season passed mid-schedule isn't enough, no matter how good the defense is.

Brandt usually finds someone from Nowhere University who becomes All-Pro for very little bread. He has done this quite a bit in the secondary—witness Charlie Waters, Cliff Harris, Benny Barnes, and, last year, Aaron Kyle. It hasn't worked with quite as much *élan* amongst the running backs.

The Dallas attack scored 296 points last season; the only folks to exceed the Cowpokes' total were Los Angeles with 351, St. Louis with 309, and Minnesota with 305. But the margin in the playoffs and the Super Bowl is frequently razor thin. Maybe Dorsett will provide the needed catalyst—if not in the short range, perhaps in the long.

OFFENSE

Quarterbacks	Ht.	Wt.	Age	Exp.	College
Staubach, Roger	6-3	197	35	9	Navy
White, Danny	6-2	180	25	2	Arizona State
Carano, Glenn	6-2	204	22	R	Nevada—Las Vegas

Staubach is still a premier, top-flight NFL passer. But his age makes him somewhat suspect. He was eighth in NFL individual passing last year with 56.4 percent, 2,715 yards, and 14 TDs. The jury's still out on whether he has passed his peak. Danny White is Staubach's heir apparent and a good kicker, too—when he's healthy. But he has a knee problem that might require surgery. White hit 13 of 20 and made two TDs in limited action last year. He filled the air when he was in the defunct WFL. Carano completed 53 percent of his passes—and 13 TDs—in 1976.

Running Backs	Ht.	Wt.	Age	Exp.	College
Pearson, Preston	6-1	208	32	11	Illinois
Dennison, Doug	6-0	208	26	4	Kutztown State
Young, Charles	6-1	220	25	4	N.C. State
Newhouse, Robert	5-10	205	27	6	Houston
Laidlaw, Scott	6-0	206	24	3	Stanford
Jensen, Jim	6-3	230	24	2	Iowa
Dorsett, Tony	5-11	192	22	R	Pittsburgh
Smith, John	5-11	186	23	1	Boise State

Dennison led Dallas last year with 542 yards. He has potential for better. Newhouse fell off to 450, more like his production when he backstopped Calvin Hill. He's too small to be a big ground gainer. Laidlaw, another hopeful, had 424 yards and one 100-yard game. Preston Pearson is a veteran who doesn't hurt you. Jensen is big but untested. Dorsett was the first NCAA collegian to rack up four 1,000-yard rushing seasons.

Receivers	Ht.	Wt.	Age	Exp.	College
Richards, Golden (W)	6-0	190	27	5	Hawaii
Johnson, Butch (W)	6-1	187	23	2	California—Riverside

DuPree, Billy Joe (T)	6-4	230	27	5	Michigan State
Saldi, Jay (T)	6-3	225	23	2	South Carolina
Howard, Percy (W)	6-4	210	25	3	Austin Peay
Pearson, Drew (W)	6-0	185	26	5	Tulsa
Hill, Tony (W)	6-2	180	22	R	Stanford

W=wide receiver   T=tight end

Drew Pearson, the man everyone fears, caught 58 for 806 yards to lead the NFC last year. He is a master. DuPree, a regular again with Jean Fugett gone to Washington, caught 42 for 680 yards. Richards, who has blinding speed and makes Pearson more effective, caught only 19 before getting hurt. Preston Pearson, out of the backfield on third down, latched onto 23; Laidlaw ditto for 38. Johnson is a future as a deep receiver. Saldi backs up DuPree. Howard was injured in 1976, but rates high with the Cowboys. He once caught a game-winning Super Bowl pass. Hill ranked seventh in NCAA pass receptions last year.

Interior Linemen	Ht.	Wt.	Age	Exp.	College
Neely, Ralph (T)	6-6	252	34	13	Oklahoma
Donovan, Pat (T)	6-4	250	24	3	Stanford
Scott, Herbert (G)	6-2	250	24	3	Virginia Union
Lawless, Burton (G)	6-4	250	24	3	Florida
Fitzgerald, John (C)	6-5	252	29	7	Boston College
Davis, Kyle (C)	6-4	245	25	3	Oklahoma
Eidson, Jim (C, G)	6-3	264	23	2	Mississippi State
Nye, Blaine (G)	6-4	255	31	10	Stanford
Rafferty, Tom (G, C)	6-3	250	23	2	Penn State
Wright, Rayfield (T)	6-6	255	32	11	Fort Valley State
Belcher, Val (G)	6-3	252	22	R	Houston

T=tackle   G=guard   C=center

Neely plays it year to year and probably will be back; Scott got better at guard; Fitzgerald is a superior center. Nye plans to quit, and the hope is that Rafferty can move in. Wright is getting on, but he's still super at tackle. Lawless may also get a shot at Nye's spot. Davis is top flight at center, and everyone hopes he's coming off the injured list; Belcher received plenty of All-America notice. The problem with the attack last year wasn't with the interior line—they did a super job in 1975 with a smallish backfield, but couldn't pull it off again in 1976.

Kickers	Ht.	Wt.	Age	Exp.	College
Herrera, Efren (Pk)	5-9	190	26	4	UCLA
White, Danny	6-2	180	25	2	Arizona State

Pk=placekicker   P=punter

While being groomed as Staubach's successor, Danny White also does the Cowboy punting. Herrera kicks effectively; he was 34 of 34 on PATs in 1976 and 18 of 23 FGs—that got him 88 points and sixth place among NFL kick scorers. White's punting fell off to 38.4 last year because of his knee problem.

DEFENSE

Front Linemen	Ht.	Wt.	Age	Exp.	College
Jones, Ed (E)	6-9	265	26	4	Tennessee State
Schaum, Greg (E)	6-4	246	23	2	Michigan State
Pugh, Jethro (T)	6-6	248	33	13	Elizabeth City
Gregory, Bill (T)	6-5	252	28	7	Wisconsin
Cole, Larry (T)	6-5	250	31	10	Hawaii
Martin, Harvey (E)	6-5	252	27	5	East Texas State

E=end   T=tackle

Too Tall Jones is still better at rushing the passer than at stopping the runner, but we'll choose him on our team. Pugh seems to get better all the time, while Cole is underrated. Martin is an All-Pro for years to come and is better than Too Tall, even if he gets less ink. Gregory is the first man on the sub board.

Linebackers	Ht.	Wt.	Age	Exp.	College
Breunig, Bob (M)	6-2	228	24	3	Arizona State
White, Randy (O)	6-4	240	24	3	Maryland
Hegman, Mike (O)	6-1	221	24	2	Tennessee State
Lewis, D. D. (O)	6-1	215	32	9	Mississippi State
Henderson, Thomas (O)	6-2	223	24	3	Langston

O=outside   M=middle

Breunig, a natural middle backer, will start now that Lee Roy Jordan has retired. Breunig played left linebacker last year, but has more smarts than big stud Randy White, who will move to the outside. This leaves D. D. Lewis on the other outside backer spot and opens the way for Henderson as the outside backup. Any changeover like this can cause some problems with cohesion and play analysis. Hegman may get additional playing time if anyone falters. Breunig, incidentally, becomes only the third Cowboy middle linebacker in the club's history. (The first was Jerry Tubbs, now a Cowboy assistant coach.)

Cornerbacks	Ht.	Wt.	Age	Exp.	College
Barnes, Benny	6-1	190	26	6	Stanford
Kyle, Aaron	5-10	181	23	2	Wyoming
Renfro, Mel	6-0	190	35	14	Oregon
Washington, Mark	5-11	186	29	8	Morgan State
Reece, Beasley	6-1	186	23	2	North Texas State

Barnes and veteran Renfro are the regulars, with Kyle champing at the bit. Washington is also a fine corner. He led Dallas with four interceptions in 1976, but as a team the Cowpokes didn't go to the ball often enough, intercepting only 16 times. Reece played wide receiver as a rookie but requested a change to defensive back—the position he played in college.

Safeties	Ht.	Wt.	Age	Exp.	College
Waters, Charlie	6-2	195	28	8	Clemson
Harris, Cliff	6-1	190	29	8	Ouachita
Hughes, Randy	6-4	210	24	3	Oklahoma

Waters is just about the finest safety in the NFL, but one who never seems to make All-Pro, for some reason. He just does the job. Harris is also solid, and Hughes is an experience-gathering backup.

Note: A complete listing of Dallas's 1977 college draft selections can be found on page 250.

DEFENSIVE UNIT

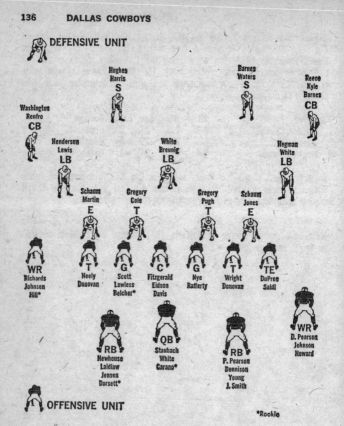

Hughes
Harris
S

Barnes
Waters
S

Reece
Kyle
Barnes
CB

Washington
Renfro
CB

Henderson
Lewis
LB

White
Breunig
LB

Hegman
White
LB

Schaum
Martin
E

Gregory
Cole
T

Gregory
Pugh
T

Schaum
Jones
E

WR
Richards
Johnson
Hill*

T
Neely
Donovan

G
Scott
Lawless
Belcher*

C
Fitzgerald
Eidson
Davis

G
Nye
Rafferty

T
Wright
Donovan

TE
DuPree
Saldi

RB
Newhouse
Laidlaw
Jensen
Dorsett*

QB
Staubach
White
Carano*

RB
P. Pearson
Dennison
Young
J. Smith

WR
D. Pearson
Johnson
Howard

OFFENSIVE UNIT

*Rookie

1976 COWBOYS STATISTICS

	Cowboys	Opps.
Total Points Scored	296*	194
Total First Downs	269	246
Third-Down Efficiency	98—220	81—213
Yards Rushing—First Downs	2147—111	1821—113
Passes Attempted—Completions	390—222	391—187
Yards Passing—First Downs	2737—140	1909—111
QB Sacked—Yards Lost	30—230	44—328
Interceptions—Return Average	16—8.3	13—11.9
Punts—Average Yards	72—38.0	92—40.0
Punt Returns—Return Average	45—11.0	28—9.0
Kickoff Returns—Return Average	42—24.5	62—20.6
Fumbles—Ball Lost	26—16	32—12
Penalties—Yards	94—761	71—643

* Includes two safeties

STATISTICAL LEADERS

Scoring	TDs	Rush.	Pass.	Ret.	PATs	FGs	Total
Herrera	0	0	0	0	34—34	18—23	88
Pearson, Drew	7	0	6	1	0	0	42
Dennison	6	6	0	0	0	0	26
Laidlaw	4	3	1	0	0	0	24
Pearson, Preston	3	1	2	0	0	0	18
Richards	3	0	3	0	0	0	18
Staubach	3	3	0	0	0	0	18
Newhouse	3	3	0	0	0	0	18
DuPree	2	0	2	0	0	0	12
Johnson	2	0	2	0	0	0	12

Rushing	Atts.	Yds.	Avg.	Longest	TDs
Dennison	153	542	3.5	14	6
Newhouse	116	450	3.9	24 (TD)	3
Laidlaw	94	424	4.5	28	3
Pearson, Preston	68	233	3.4	21	1
Young	48	208	4.3	24	0
Staubach	43	184	4.3	18	3

Passing	Atts.	Com.	Yds.	Pct.	Int.	Longest	TDs
Staubach	369	208	2715	56.4	11	53	14
White, Danny	20	13	213	65.0	2	56	2

Receiving	No.	Yds.	Avg.	Longest	TDs
Pearson, Drew	58	806	13.9	40 (TD)	6
DuPree	42	680	16.2	38 (TD)	2
Laidlaw	38	325	8.6	26	1
Pearson, Preston	23	316	13.7	30	2
Richards	19	414	21.8	56	3
Newhouse	15	86	5.7	16	0

Interceptions	No.	Yds.	Avg.	Longest	TDs
Washington	4	49	12.3	22	0
Harris	3	32	10.7	29	0
Renfro	3	23	7.7	23	0
Waters	3	6	2.0	5	0

Punting	No.	Yds.	Avg.	Longest	Inside 20	Blocked
White, Danny	70	2690	38.4	54	13	2

Punt Returns	No.	FCs	Yds.	Avg.	Longest	TDs
Johnson	45	11	489	10.9	55	0

Kickoff Returns	No.	Yds.	Avg.	Longest	TDs
Johnson	28	693	24.8	74	0
Jensen	13	313	24.1	35	0

ST. LOUIS CARDINALS

Head Coach: Don Coryell

5th Year　　　　　　　　　　**Record:** 35–20–1

1976 RECORD (10–4) (capital letters indicate home games)		
30	Seattle	24
29	GREEN BAY	0
24	San Diego	43
27	N.Y. GIANTS	21
33	PHILADELPHIA	14
21	DALLAS	17
10	Washington	20
23	SAN FRANCISCO (in OT)	20
17	Philadelphia	14
30	Los Angeles	28
10	WASHINGTON	16
14	Dallas	19
24	BALTIMORE	17
17	N.Y. Giants	14

1977 SCHEDULE (capital letters indicate home games)	
Denver	Sept. 18
CHICAGO	Sept. 25
Washington	Oct. 2
DALLAS	Oct. 9
Philadelphia	Oct. 16
NEW ORLEANS	Oct. 23
N.Y. GIANTS (night, TV)	Oct. 31
Minnesota	Nov. 6
Dallas (night, TV)	Nov. 14
PHILADELPHIA	Nov. 20
MIAMI (TV)	Nov. 24
N.Y. Giants	Dec. 4
WASHINGTON (TV)	Dec. 10
Tampa Bay	Dec. 18

How do you win ten games in the National Football League and not make the playoffs? Ask Don Coryell, coach of the cardiac Cardinals. He knows. The St. Louis Swifties did it in 1976 and hope they can avoid a similar disappointment this year.

"This team was our best," insists Coryell. "And the reason is simple. We overcame adversity better than any of the previous editions. We proved we were for real, even if we didn't get into the playoffs this time around."

The Big Red defeated three playoff teams—the Dallas Cowboys, the Los Angeles Rams, and the Baltimore Colts—which is no mean feat. But they lost twice to the ancient Redskins and wound up third in the NFC East—virtually a fate worse than death. The Cards staged an incredible rally to beat the Rams

30–28 and then blew one a week later to the Redskins, 16–10, when they could have skunked Washington and made the playoffs.

In 1976 the Big Red set record upon record. They established new club marks for total yards (5,136), first downs (307), rushing first downs (140), rushing attempts (580), and pass completion percentage (56.1).

The Cards also led the NFC in offense and led in fewest quarterback sacks in 1976. Eight of their ten wins came by seven points or less, though. They defeated the 49ers in overtime and the Rams in the final seven seconds, which certainly gives them the California championship.

"We missed on two plays during the 1976 season. Mel Gray dropped a TD pass in the end zone in the last minute of the 16–10 loss to Washington. Again, in the last minute against Dallas [St. Louis lost 14–19], Jim Hart's pass to J. V. Cain was still in the air when he was hit by both Charlie Waters and Cliff Harris. No penalty was called, and there went our season," says Coryell sadly.

The Cards did overcome injuries and problems. Terry Metcalf, Mr. Excitement, missed two games. During the year three starting defensive linemen and two linebackers were lost with injuries. Receivers Ike Harris and Gray missed a total of five games.

St. Louis has now been 10–4, 11–3, and 10–4—close but no cigar. Most feel the defense is still suspect. A star linebacker is wanted to take up the slack caused by the retirement of Larry Stallings. The Cardinals will also need another proven cornerback since they traded Norm Thompson to Baltimore for a third-round draft choice. Some new defensive secondary talent has been added, even though the only cornerback drafted was Greg Lee of Western Illinois in the twelfth round. A draft-choice trade brings six-year veteran safety Neal Craig to St. Louis from Cleveland, and a similar deal makes former Packer cornerback Perry Smith a Cardinal.

Jim Hart has proven that he can put points on the scoreboard. The Cards' 309 were second only to the Rams' 351 in the NFC last year. Terry Metcalf saw the light and agreed to run back kicks after pouting over this assignment earlier in the year. Jim Otis grinds out yardage in unspectacular style. Hart puts it up to Mel Gray, J. V. Cain, and Pat Tilley and gets results; he also finds ways to spring Metcalf into an open field, where he's the most exciting runner in the NFL.

Last year the Big Red defense was sixth in the NFC, allowing 4,089 yards overall. That put them just in back of Dallas, but it didn't really do the job in the clutch. And the passing defense was weak, allowing 2,110 yards (tenth in the NFC). Only 19 interceptions means they didn't go to the ball often enough in key situations.

St. Louis seems to have an edge on both Washington and Dallas as far as offense goes, but the 'Skins beat them when they have to, and so do the Cowpokes. Coryell recognizes this and is trying to do something about it.

Winning in the NFL isn't easy. If Hart should get hurt, the Cards would be in trouble—neither Bill Donckers nor Mike Wells is ready to take over. On the other hand, if Metcalf gets sidelined, they do have a change in Mel Gray.

Molding the defense so that the Big Red puts more pressure on the quarterback than it has in the past is a big part of Coryell's job. St. Louis needs more rush liners among the first 20 sack leaders in order to give the weak secondary a chance.

Whether the Cards win a couple more this year or lose a couple more and drop out of contention may be up to the defense—and also to Hart's ability to sustain a high-intensity attack. No one believed St. Louis was for real after their 10–4 in 1974, but they have proved they can continue to win the close ones very often.

The problem is that very often hasn't been often enough.

OFFENSE

Quarterbacks	Ht.	Wt.	Age	Exp.	College
Hart, Jim	6-1	210	33	12	Southern Illinois
Donckers, Bill	6-1	205	26	2	San Diego State
Wells, Mike	6-5	225	26	4	Illinois
Pisarkiewicz, Steve	6-2	205	22	R	Missouri

Hart is a top-notch quarterback who is, perhaps, the best at the two-minute drill. He was seventh in the league last year with 56.2 percent completions, 18 TDs, and only 13 interceptions. Donckers comes from coach Don Coryell's old school, San Diego State, and will get some training. Wells is a body the Giants rejected. In college, Pisarkiewicz was known as a tough, intense leader.

Running Backs	Ht.	Wt.	Age	Exp.	College
Metcalf, Terry	5-10	185	26	5	Long Beach State
Morris, Wayne	6-0	200	23	2	Southern Methodist
Latin, Jerry	5-10	190	24	3	Northern Illinois
Otis, Jim	6-0	225	29	8	Ohio State
Jones, Steve	6-0	200	26	5	Duke
Franklin, George	6-3	230	22	R	Texas A&I

Metcalf wasn't quite as good last year as he has been, but he's still a threat to go all the way every time he touches the ball. He rushed for 537 yards, caught 33 passes for 388, ran back 17 punts for 188, and ran back 16 kicks for 325 in 1976. That adds up to 1,438 yards—good, but not the super Metcalf. He did miss two games and was ably subbed by Morris, who may get more time this year. Latin is a solid reserve behind Morris and Metcalf. Otis is the grind-it-out tough guy who gets third-down yardage when it's needed. He slammed for 891 yards in 1976. Slow but steady. Jones did pretty well when he was used in place of Otis, and had more speed in picking up 451.

Receivers	Ht.	Wt.	Age	Exp.	College
Gray, Mel (W)	5-9	175	29	7	Missouri
Tilley, Pat (W)	5-10	175	24	2	Louisiana Tech
Cain, J. V. (T)	6-4	225	25	4	Colorado
Smith, Jackie (T)	6-4	230	37	15	N.W. Louisiana
Joyce, Terry (T)	6-6	230	23	2	Missouri Southern
Harris, Ike (W)	6-3	205	25	3	Iowa State
Hammond, Gary (W)	5-11	185	28	5	Southern Methodist
Baker, Mel (W)	6-0	190	27	4	Texas Southern

W=wide receiver   T=tight end

Harris was the pass receiving leader in 1976 with 52—a surprise, as most people think of Gray in this role. But Gray was hurt part of the year and only caught 36 (good for 686 and five TDs). Harris only caught one TD pass and needs to improve this stat. Cain came into his own with 26 catches for 400 yards and five TDs. Terry Metcalf carried the ball after 33 catches, and underrated Tilley, playing behind Gray, caught 26 for 407. Overall, the pass reception corps is in great shape.

Interior Linemen	Ht.	Wt.	Age	Exp.	College
Finnie, Roger (T)	6-3	250	32	9	Florida A&M
Oates, Brad (T)	6-6	270	24	2	Brigham Young
Young, Bob (G)	6-1	270	35	12	Howard Payne
Wortman, Keith (G)	6-2	250	27	6	Nebraska
Banks, Tom (C)	6-2	245	29	6	Auburn
Brahaney, Tom (C)	6-2	250	26	5	Oklahoma
Dobler, Conrad (G)	6-3	255	27	6	Wyoming
Dierdorf, Dan (T)	6-3	280	28	7	Michigan
Allison, Hank (G)	6-3	225	30	5	San Diego State

T=tackle   G=guard   C=center

Regulars are Finnie, Young, Banks, Dobler, and Dierdorf. They protect Hart and spring Terry Metcalf, but they're largely unheralded. Brahaney is an excellent backup center, and Wortman is the first reserve. Is Dobler really the meanest man in the NFL, or is it all a sham?

Kickers	Ht.	Wt.	Age	Exp.	College
Bakken, Jim (Pk)	6-0	200	37	16	Wisconsin
Joyce, Terry (P)	6-6	230	23	2	Missouri Southern
Hoopes, Mitch (P)	6-1	210	25	3	Arizona

Pk=placekicker   P=punter

Tight end Terry Joyce does the punting (in 1976 he had a 36.4 yard average). In 1977 Bakken enters his sixteenth year as a pro, and he's still ringing up both PATs and FGs. His 93 points ranked him third among NFL kick scorers in 1976. Hoopes has punted for both San Diego and Dallas.

DEFENSE

Front Linemen	Ht.	Wt.	Age	Exp.	College
Bell, Bob (E)	6-4	250	29	7	Cincinnati
Brooks, Leo (E)	6-6	240	30	8	Texas
Davis, Charlie (T)	6-2	265	26	4	Texas Christian
Okoniewski, Steve (T)	6-3	255	28	6	Montana
Dawson, Mike (T)	6-4	270	24	2	Arizona
Zook, John (E)	6-5	250	30	9	Kansas
Yankowski, Ron (E)	6-5	250	31	7	Kansas State
Patulski, Walt (E)	6-6	260	27	5	Notre Dame

E=end   T=tackle

Zook is the best of the front four. Bell is dissatisfied, but he signed a one-year contract anyway. Davis and Dawson could be better. Okoniewski is a journeyman. Patulski sat out 1976 with injuries. Help needed, or St. Louis could get the blues.

Linebackers	Ht.	Wt.	Age	Exp.	College
Beauchamp, Al (O)	6-2	235	33	10	Southern U.
Kearney, Tim (M)	6-2	230	27	6	Northern Michigan
Arneson, Mark (O)	6-2	220	28	6	Arizona
Gersbach, Carl (O)	6-1	230	30	8	West Chester
McGraw, Mike (O)	6-2	215	24	2	Wyoming
Neils, Steve (O)	6-2	215	26	4	Minnesota
White, Ray (M)	6-2	220	28	5	Syracuse
Allerman, Kurt (O)	6-3	221	22	R	Penn State

O=outside   M=middle

Larry Stallings has retired and Greg Hartle is gone too, leaving the linebacking crew thin. Kearney and Arneson are penciled in as the regulars, with steady Al Beauchamp the trial utility. Gersbach may give Kearney a tussle. McGraw has speed and is a good tackler. Allerman learned the linebacker's trade at Penn State. Enough said.

Cornerbacks	Ht.	Wt.	Age	Exp.	College
Crump, Dwayne	5-11	180	27	5	Fresno State
Wehrli, Roger	6-0	190	30	9	Missouri
Smith, Perry	6-1	195	25	5	Colorado State
Nelson, Lee	5-10	185	23	2	Florida State

Wehrli is almost a household name in Greater St. Louis. Norm Thompson was too but he was unhappy and left for Baltimore in a trade. This makes way for Crump, who can do the job. Former Packer Smith figures here, too.

Safeties	Ht.	Wt.	Age	Exp.	College
Reaves, Ken	6-3	210	33	12	Norfolk State

Duren, Clarence	6-1	190	27	5	California
Sensibaugh, Mike	5-11	190	28	7	Ohio State
Severson, Jeff	6-1	185	28	6	Long Beach State
Craig, Neal	6-1	190	29	7	Fisk

The Big Red gambles on the defense and came in tenth against the NFC pass last year with 19 interceptions. Sensibaugh led with four and proved a valuable acquisition (they got him from Kansas City). Reaves is experienced, but may be slowing down, which should give Duren an opening. Craig was acquired in a draft deal with Cleveland.

Note: A complete listing of St. Louis's 1977 college draft selections can be found on page 258.

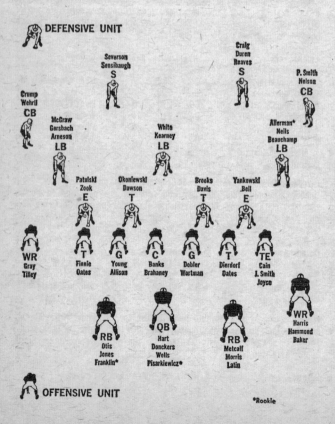

DEFENSIVE UNIT

Craig
Duren
Reaves
S

Severson
Sensibaugh
S

P. Smith
Nelson
CB

Crump
Wehrli
CB

McGraw
Gersbach
Arneson
LB

White
Kearney
LB

Allerman*
Neils
Beauchamp
LB

Patulski
Zook
E

Okoniewski
Dawson
T

Brooks
Davis
T

Yankowski
Bell
E

WR
Gray
Tilley

T
Finnie
Oates

G
Young
Allison

C
Banks
Brahaney

G
Dobler
Wortman

T
Dierdorf
Oates

TE
Cain
J. Smith
Joyce

RB
Otis
Jones
Franklin*

QB
Hart
Donckers
Wells
Pisarkiewicz*

RB
Metcalf
Morris
Latin

WR
Harris
Hammond
Baker

OFFENSIVE UNIT

*Rookie

1976 CARDINALS STATISTICS

	Cardinals	Opps.
Total Points Scored	309	267
Total First Downs	307	239
Third-Down Efficiency	96—208	78—196
Yards Rushing—First Downs	2301—140	1979—111
Passes Attempted—Completions	392—220	342—176
Yards Passing—First Downs	2835—142	2110—105
QB Sacked—Yards Lost	17—132	31—248
Interceptions—Return Average	19—12.8	13—10.3
Punts—Average Yards	66—35.3	71—38.8
Punt Returns—Return Average	36—9.7	33—9.2
Kickoff Returns—Return Average	54—20.4	66—24.6
Fumbles—Ball Lost	44—24	32—20
Penalties—Yards	84—683	83—698

STATISTICAL LEADERS

Scoring	TDs	Rush.	Pass.	Ret.	PATs	FGs	Total
Bakken	0	0	0	0	33—35	20—27	93
Jones	9	8	1	0	0	0	54
Metcalf	7	3	4	0	0	0	42
Gray	5	0	5	0	0	0	30
Cain	5	0	5	0	0	0	30
Morris	4	3	1	0	0	0	24
Otis	2	2	0	0	0	0	12

Rushing	Atts.	Yds.	Avg.	Longest	TDs
Otis	233	891	3.8	23	2
Metcalf	134	537	4.0	36	3
Jones	113	451	4.0	19	8
Morris	64	292	4.6	27	3
Latin	25	115	4.6	26	1

Passing	Atts.	Com.	Yds.	Pct.	Int.	Longest	TDs
Hart	388	218	2946	56.2	13	77 (TD)	18

Receiving	No.	Yds.	Avg.	Longest	TDs
Harris	52	782	15.0	40	1
Gray	36	686	19.1	77 (TD)	5
Metcalf	33	388	11.8	48 (TD)	4
Jones	29	152	5.2	15	1
Tilley	26	407	15.7	45	1
Cain	26	400	15.4	35	5

Interceptions	No.	Yds.	Avg.	Longest	TDs
Thompson	4	83	20.8	38	0
Sensibaugh	4	60	15.0	35 (TD)	1
Wehrli	4	31	7.8	26	0
Reaves	2	41	20.5	25	0
White	2	20	10.0	16	0

Punting	No.	Yds.	Avg.	Longest	Inside 20	Blocked
Joyce	64	2331	36.4	54	12	2

Punt Returns	No.	FCs	Yds.	Avg.	Longest	TDs
Metcalf	17	1	188	11.1	38	0
Tilley	15	0	146	9.7	17	0

Kickoff Returns	No.	Yds.	Avg.	Longest	TDs
Latin	16	357	22.3	39	0
Metcalf	16	325	20.3	33	0
Morris	9	181	20.1	34	0

WASHINGTON REDSKINS

Head Coach: George Allen

7th Year   **Record:** 58–25–1

1976 RECORD (10–4) (capital letters indicate home games)			1977 SCHEDULE (capital letters indicate home games)	
19	N.Y. GIANTS	17	N.Y. Giants	Sept. 18
31	SEATTLE	7	ATLANTA	Sept. 25
20	Philadelphia (in OT)	17	ST. LOUIS	Oct. 2
7	Chicago	33	Tampa Bay	Oct. 9
30	KANSAS CITY	33	Dallas	Oct. 16
20	DETROIT	7	N.Y. GIANTS	Oct. 23
20	ST. LOUIS	10	PHILADELPHIA	Oct. 30
7	DALLAS	20	Baltimore (night, TV)	Nov. 7
24	San Francisco	21	Philadelphia	Nov. 13
9	N.Y. Giants	12	GREEN BAY (night, TV)	Nov. 21
16	St. Louis	10	DALLAS	Nov. 27
24	PHILADELPHIA	0	Buffalo	Dec. 4
37	N.Y. Jets	16	St. Louis (TV)	Dec. 10
27	Dallas	14	LOS ANGELES (TV)	Dec. 17
	Playoffs			
20	Minnesota	35		

Calvin proved Washington wasn't over the Hill when he blasted through Dallas in the final game of 1976 and gave George Allen a playoff berth. It might have saved Mr. Ice Cream's job, even though he won't admit it. Allen had one year left on his $125,000 seven-year contract, but owner Edward Bennett Williams tore up the old pact and gave George another one with five years more, plus a raise of $25,000 annually.

Washington finished 10–4 as the NFC wild card; they had two wins over St. Louis, which was also 10–4. Then they bombed out in the playoffs to Minnesota, making themselves look old in the process.

Allen will have to make up his mind about his quarterback. Billy Kilmer is disenchanted with the

Washington media and is now living in New Orleans —a significant move. He blasted Allen in January, then took back what he said.

Kilmer and Joe Theismann were in and out of the lineup last year, with Kilmer 108 for 206 and 12 TDs and Theismann 79 for 163 and eight TDs. Kilmer's percentage was 52.4 and Joe was under the halfway mark with 48.5. Joe is the future answer, but "The future is now," to quote Allen in a much-quoted quote. Still, George wants to talk Billy out of retirement in case Joe gets hurt or flubs up.

Despite the constant change and continual stream of injuries to Kilmer, Washington posted 291 points last year, to make fifth in the NFC and put them right in the stream of things with other contenders. The Redskins were sixth in total offense with 4,096 yards. The split was fairly even, with 2,111 yards rushing and 1,985 passing.

The running game is a mini-problem despite the presence of big-name running backs like John Riggins, Larry Brown, Calvin Hill, and Mike Thomas (who ground out a 1,000-yard season for only $28,000). Thomas wants bread to compare with Riggins' and Hill's princely salaries. Riggins doesn't seem to care now that he has the money, and Hill wants playing time or he will quit and become a lawyer. Brown's knees are suspect, but he can still carry the mail.

The pass receiving is still pretty fair, but Roy Jefferson has been retired by Allen. Frank Grant is now the big gun of the aerial corps. Tight end Jean Fugett was a ten-strike last year and played very well. The offensive line did better than most think, and opened holes for Thomas' scampering. But Brown couldn't hit those holes fast enough, and Hill only carried 79 times.

The Washington defense, where most of the ancients

are in semiretirement, was seventh in 1976 with 4,122 yards surrendered overall. It was pretty good against the pass, but got burned on several runs.

Diron Talbert led Washington with 12½ sacks, which really isn't enough for the leader. The front four needs to put more pressure on the passer. Incumbents are Ron McDole, now entering his dotage; Dave Butz, coming into his own after a big deal with St. Louis two years back and ready for a decade in the Washington trenches; and Talbert and Dennis Johnson, with Bill Brundige backing them up. But Washington still needs a hard-charging defensive lineman.

Part of the sputtering attack that shone bright was the punt returning of Eddie Brown, who fell only nine yards short of an NFL record. Brown logged 646 yards. And he got 738 out of kickoff returns, taking up much of the slack and getting the Redskins into good field position.

Washington could use some help on the offensive line, and they need a spare cornerback in case Pat Fischer retires. Overall, Allen must realize that he is essentially a *pre*tender as far as the Super Bowl is concerned, and only a *con*tender for a playoff spot; the 'Skins have no real hope of surviving in the post-season games.

The answer has to come from Theismann; certainly it will not come from backup Brian Dowling or from Kilmer, who is injury-prone and 38. Theismann is 28 and is entering his third year with Washington after spending three in the Canadian league. It may be now or never for Joe, who reportedly doesn't get much help from Billy Kilmer in the matter of tutelage.

Theismann is a good athlete; he even ran back kick-offs in his early time with Washington. And he once threw a memorable TD from a fake field goal while serving as the holder. But he still tries to force his passes and throws into crowds. This eventually means interceptions and there's still some doubt whether he can move the club into the end zone in the clutch. It's really up to him, though, to make Washington something more than an "over-the-hill" gang.

OFFENSE

Quarterbacks	Ht.	Wt.	Age	Exp.	College
Kilmer, Billy	6-0	204	38	16	UCLA
Theismann, Joe	6-0	184	28	4	Notre Dame
Dowling, Brian	6-2	195	30	3	Yale

Kilmer is the incumbent quarterback, and he wants the job even if he hates both George Allen and the Washington media. He can get the job done and squeeze the team into the playoffs, but he isn't the future of the Redskins and can only get worse, or worse hurt. Theismann is the great white hope of the Washington fans and should make it in time, but maybe not this year. Dowling is a retread who never was.

Running Backs	Ht.	Wt.	Age	Exp.	College
Riggins, John	6-2	230	28	7	Kansas
Brown, Larry	5-11	195	30	9	Kansas State
Spencer, Willie	6-4	235	24	2	(none)
Thomas, Mike	5-11	190	24	3	Nevada–Las Vegas
Hill, Calvin	6-4	227	30	8	Yale
Brunet, Bob	6-1	205	31	8	Louisiana Tech
Moss, Eddie	6-0	215	28	5	S.E. Missouri

Riggins is an overrated one-time 1,000-yard runner who came from the Jets; he became a blocking back for Thomas, who gets only one tenth the money Riggins does. Brown, a great veteran, says he'll play another season although he's also signing with a Wall Street brokerage firm. Spencer can run through a brick wall and might win a job if he gets playing time. He was a WFL hero. Thomas is the best Redskin back, and bulled his way for 1,101 yards in 1976. Riggins had only 572. Hill saved the season in the final game against Dallas and should be played more so he can run more than 301 yards. Brunet is a steady reserve. Moss comes from St. Louis as a free agent.

Receivers	Ht.	Wt.	Age	Exp.	College
Grant, Frank (W)	5-11	181	27	5	Southern Colorado
Buggs, Danny (W)	6-2	185	24	3	West Virginia
Fugett, Jean (T)	6-4	226	26	6	Amherst

Smith, Jerry (T)	6-3	208	34	13	Arizona State
Larson, Bill (T)	6-4	230	24	2	Colorado State
Taylor, Charley (W)	6-3	210	35	14	Arizona State
Jones, Larry (W)	5-10	170	26	4	N.E. Missouri
Fryer, Brian (W)	6-1	185	24	2	Edmonton (Canada)
Clune, Don (W)	6-3	195	25	4	Pennsylvania

W=wide receiver   T=tight end

Grant is the big catch man—he made 50 for 818 yards and five TDs in 1976. Buggs is a gutsy reserve who won't make it. Mike Thomas ran for 28 catches and 290 yards in 1976, with Riggins latching onto 21 for 172. Fugett was super in the clutch, with 27 for 334 yards and six TDs. Smith is an honored reserve who finally lost his job to Fugett. Larson is a young man lost amongst veterans. Taylor and Jones are coming off 1976 injuries. Clune signed as a Seattle free agent.

Interior Linemen	Ht.	Wt.	Age	Exp.	College
Stokes, Tim (T)	6-5	252	27	4	Oregon
Kuziel, Bob (C)	6-5	255	27	3	Pittsburgh
Saul, Ron (G)	6-3	254	29	8	Michigan State
Nugent, Dan (G)	6-3	250	27	2	Auburn
Laaveg, Paul (G)	6-4	250	29	7	Iowa
Hauss, Len (C)	6-2	235	35	14	Iowa
Fritsch, Ted (C)	6-2	242	27	6	St. Norbert
Hermeling, Terry (G)	6-5	255	31	8	Nevada—Reno
Starke, George (T)	6-5	249	29	5	Columbia

T=tackle   G=guard   C=center

The interior line is populated by Stokes, Saul, Hauss, Hermeling, and Starke. Not bad, and not so good either. Hauss is too old and Kuziel might take over. And Hermeling might hand it all over to Nugent.

Kickers	Ht.	Wt.	Age	Exp.	College
Bragg, Mike (P)	5-11	186	31	10	Richmond
Moseley, Mark (Pk)	6-0	205	29	6	Stephen F. Austin

Pk=placekicker   P=punter

In 1976 Bragg kicked 90 times, which is too many, for 38.9 percent. Moseley led the NFC in scoring with 97 points, 22 of 34 field goals, and 31 of 32 extra points.

DEFENSE

Front Linemen	Ht.	Wt.	Age	Exp.	College
McDole, Ron (E))	6-4	265	38	17	Nebraska
Hickman, Dallas (E)	6-6	235	25	2	California
Lewis, Stan (E)	6-5	245	24	2	Wayne State (Neb.)

	Ht.	Wt.	Age	Exp.	College
Butz, Dave (T)	6-7	285	27	5	Purdue
Brundige, Bill (T)	6-5	270	29	8	Colorado
Lorch, Karl (T)	6-3	258	27	2	Southern California
Jackson, Joey (T)	6-4	255	27	3	New Mexico State
Talbert, Diron (T)	6-5	255	33	11	Texas
Johnson, Dennis (E)	6-4	260	26	4	Delaware
Manning, Roosevelt (E)	6-5	260	27	5	N.E. Oklahoma

E=end   T=tackle

McDole is too old and needs to be replaced. He plays on a reconstructed knee. Butz served his indoctrination period and is a star who'll get even better. Talbert is a tough pro despite his age. Johnson pushed aside Brundige last year, but Brundige is young enough to come back while serving as an excellent reserve. Lorch, Hickman, and Lewis are youths getting a rare look from Allen.

Linebackers	Ht.	Wt.	Age	Exp.	College
Dusek, Brad (O)	6-2	214	27	4	Texas A&M
Wysocki, Pete (O)	6-2	225	29	3	Western Michigan
McLinton, Harold (M)	6-2	135	30	9	Southern U.
Tillman, Rusty (M)	6-2	230	29	8	Northern Arizona
Hartle, Greg (M)	6-2	225	26	4	Newberry
Hanburger, Chris (O)	6-2	218	26	13	North Carolina
O'Dell, Stu (O)	6-1	220	26	4	Indiana
Cooper, Bert (O)	6-1	212	25	2	Florida State
Tate, John (O)	6-3	215	25	2	Jackson State

O=outside   M=middle

Dusek and Hanburger are solid, but McLinton is shaky in the middle. Tillman may get a trial behind McLinton. Wysocki does well when he gets to play. Hartle comes from St. Louis as a free agent. Cooper is a refugee from the Tampa Bay disaster area.

Cornerbacks	Ht.	Wt.	Age	Exp.	College
Fischer, Pat	5-9	170	37	17	Nebraska
Lavender, Joe	6-4	190	28	5	San Diego State
Williams, Gerard	6-1	184	25	2	Langston

Lavender from the Eagles and Fischer, a Redskin institution, are the incumbents, and Lavender is getting better all the time. Will Fischer continue to hang in there with his gritty tough play? Williams hopes he won't. In 1976 Lavender led Washington with eight interceptions; Fischer had five.

Safeties	Ht.	Wt.	Age	Exp.	College
Houston, Ken	6-3	198	33	11	Prairie View
Scott, Jake	6-0	188	32	8	Georgia
Owens, Brig	5-11	190	34	12	Cincinnati
Brown, Eddie	5-11	190	25	4	Tennessee

Scott, the ex-Miami hero, and Houston, the ex-Oiler, are the very competent regulars. Kickoff return man Brown hopes for playing time this year. Owens backs up both; he lost out to Scott.

Note: A complete listing of Washington's 1977 college draft selections can be found on page 260.

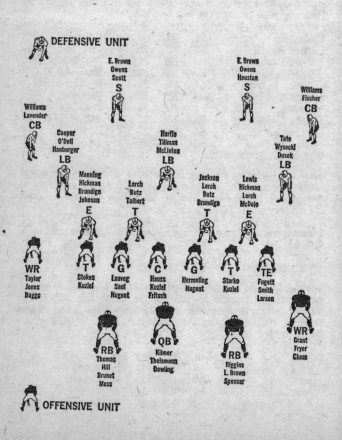

DEFENSIVE UNIT

E. Brown
Owens
Scott
S

E. Brown
Owens
Houston
S

Williams
Fischer
CB

Williams
Lavender
CB

Cooper
O'Dell
Hanburger
LB

Hartle
Tillman
McLinton
LB

Tate
Wysocki
Dusek
LB

Manning
Hickman
Brundige
Johnson
E

Lorch
Butz
Talbert
T

Jackson
Lorch
Butz
Brundige
T

Lewis
Hickman
Lorch
McDole
E

WR
Taylor
Jones
Buggs

T
Stokes
Kuziel

G
Laaveg
Saul
Nugent

C
Hauss
Kuziel
Fritsch

G
Hermeling
Nugent

T
Starke
Kuziel

TE
Fugett
Smith
Larson

RB
Thomas
Hill
Brunet
Moss

QB
Kilmer
Theismann
Dowling

RB
Riggins
L. Brown
Spencer

WR
Grant
Fryer
Clune

OFFENSIVE UNIT

1976 REDSKINS STATISTICS

	Redskins	Opps.
Total Points Scored	291*	217
Total First Downs	255	215
Third-Down Efficiency	65—206	62—219
Yards Rushing—First Downs	2111—114	2205—109
Passes Attempted—Completions	370—187	355—146
Yards Passing—First Downs	1985—122	1917—91
QB Sacked—Yards Lost	38—303	44—324
Interceptions—Return Average	26—7.3	20—7.5
Punts—Average Yards	90—38.9	93—38.9
Punt Returns—Return Average	52—13.2	44—7.3
Kickoff Returns—Return Average	50—21.3	63—16.2
Fumbles—Ball Lost	36—23	38—22
Penalties—Yards	90—868	95—818

* Includes one safety

STATISTICAL LEADERS

Scoring	TDs	Rush.	Pass.	Ret.	PATs	FGs	Total
Moseley	0	0	0	0	31—32	22—34	97
Thomas	9	5	4	0	0	0	54
Fugett	6	0	6	0	0	0	36
Grant	5	0	5	0	0	0	30
Riggins	4	3	1	0	0	0	24
Smith	2	0	2	0	0	0	12
Jefferson	2	0	2	0	0	0	12

Rushing	Atts.	Yds.	Avg.	Longest	TDs
Thomas	254	1101	4.3	28	5
Riggins	162	572	3.5	15	3
Hill	79	301	3.8	15	1
Theismann	17	97	5.7	22	1
Brown, Larry	20	56	2.8	11	0

Passing	Atts.	Com.	Yds.	Pct.	Int.	Longest	TDs
Kilmer	206	108	1252	52.4	10	53 (TD)	12
Theismann	163	79	1036	48.5	10	44	8

Receiving	No.	Yds.	Avg.	Longest	TDs
Grant	50	818	16.4	53 (TD)	5
Thomas	28	290	10.4	34	4
Jefferson	27	364	13.5	27	2
Fugett	27	334	12.4	33 (TD)	6
Riggins	21	172	8.2	18	1
Brown, Larry	17	98	5.8	15	0

Interceptions	No.	Yds.	Avg.	Longest	TDs
Lavender	8	77	9.6	28	0
Fischer	5	38	7.6	32	0
Houston	4	25	6.3	12	0
Scott	4	12	3.0	6	0

Punting	No.	Yds.	Avg.	Longest	Inside 20	Blocked
Bragg	90	3503	38.9	56	15	0

Punt Returns	No.	FCs	Yds.	Avg.	Longest	TDs
Brown, Eddie	48	8	646	13.5	71 (TD)	1
Scott	3	0	27	9.0	11	0

Kickoff Returns	No.	Yds.	Avg.	Longest	TDs
Brown, Eddie	30	738	24.6	67	0
Fryer	9	166	18.4	27	0
Brunet	4	85	21.3	24	0

PHILADELPHIA EAGLES

Head Coach: Dick Vermeil

2nd Year   **Record:** 4—10

1976 RECORD (4—10) (capital letters indicate home games)			1977 SCHEDULE (capital letters indicate home games)	
7	Dallas	27	TAMPA BAY	Sept. 18
20	N.Y. GIANTS	7	Los Angeles	Sept. 25
17	WASHINGTON (in OT)	20	Detroit	Oct. 2
14	Atlanta	13	N.Y. Giants	Oct. 9
14	St. Louis	33	ST. LOUIS	Oct. 16
13	Green Bay	28	DALLAS	Oct. 23
12	MINNESOTA	31	Washington	Oct. 30
10	N.Y. Giants	0	NEW ORLEANS	Nov. 6
14	ST. LOUIS	17	WASHINGTON	Nov. 13
3	Cleveland	24	St. Louis	Nov. 20
7	OAKLAND	26	New England	Nov. 27
0	Washington	24	Dallas	Dec. 4
7	DALLAS	26	N.Y. GIANTS	Dec. 11
27	Seattle	10	N.Y. JETS	Dec. 18

Last year was Dick Vermeil's first season as coach of the Eagles, and, thanks to the New York Giants and the NFL schedule maker, 1977 will be his second season at the helm of the hapless Philadelphians. The 1976 edition of the Eagles managed to win four games —half of them in their home-and-home rivalry with the Giants, and one each from Atlanta and Seattle.

The Eagles played Atlanta early when the Falcons were in an advanced state of disorganization and disorientation. And they played the Seahawks last, when the expansion club's weaknesses were totally exposed and exploitable.

What's going to happen this season is anybody's guess, but things don't look much rosier in the City of Brotherly Love than they did a year ago. Besides, the Giants figure to have a competitive ball club this time around, and the schedule might not be quite so co-operative.

Interestingly for what was far from the most attractive team in the league, the Eagles drew 393,003 fans to Veterans Stadium. This average of 56,143 spectators was treated to displays that included five defeats in seven games and a total of 104 of the Eagles' 165 points for the campaign. But by the time the season finale against Seattle rolled around, the attendance was only 37,949. This might be a harbinger of things to come, for if the attendance shrinks, Vermeil will surely vanish.

To compound the felony, the Eagles are bereft of their choices on the first two rounds of the draft this year. Vermeil is fond of saying that sometimes good ball players show up on the lower rounds of the draft. He points to running back Mike Hogan—a ninth-round selection by the Eagles in last year's draft and the 247th man chosen by NFL clubs—who turned out to be the team's top rusher in 1976; he gained 561 yards in 123 attempts. If you had no choices in the draft's top rounds, you'd probably agree with Vermeil. On the other hand, when a man leads your rushing attack with only 561 yards, you have a problem.

The Eagles got themselves into the draft-choice box when they made deals in successive seasons for quarterback Roman Gabriel from Los Angeles and linebacker Bill Bergey from Cincinnati. Gabriel turned out to be less than was hoped for and was supplanted by young Mike Boryla as the top Eagle pigskin pitcher. Boryla completed 123 of 246 passes for 1,247 yards and nine touchdowns last year, while Gabriel was only 46 for 92 and 476 yards, with two tallies. Not only that, but there is fierce animosity between the two. It nearly came to physical confrontation at a couple of points in 1975, and these guys won't coexist for long. The situation is fraught with peril for Eagles coaches. It may have been solved by the deal for ex-Ram passer Ron Jaworski, however.

Bergey, on the other hand, turned out to be a great choice. In fact, he is virtually a one-man defense in Philadelphia. The front four leaks like a sieve and things may get worse since starting end Blenda Gay died during the off-season, a victim of domestic strife.

There is a school of thought that says that the "un-retirement" of the 37-year-old Gabriel late last season helped the Eagles offensively. This is clearly not a point of view shared by Boryla. And, in fact, the offense was so inconsistent that whatever improvement it may have experienced under Gabriel's direction was hardly noticeable in a team that scored so few points.

In 1974 the Eagles were a respectable 7–7. Since then they have gone 4–10 two straight seasons, changed coaches, and mortgaged their future by dealing away more top draft choices. The front office has been sing-ing a song, asking for patience amongst the fans at the Vet, for several years now. The refrain is starting to wear a little thin. The Philadelphia followers have been remarkably patient for a long time. The Eagles last made the finals in the NFL playoffs in 1960. Just how much longer the fans are going to remain placid is an open question.

Even now, the prospects for improvement aren't good. If Hogan is healthy for the entire season, he might become an outstanding back. He had two 100-yard games last season and missed six games with an injured shoulder. But he has little support. And All-Pro tight end Charlie Young went to Los Angeles in the Jaworski trade and will be missed.

On defense, the secondary figures to be weak unless Vermeil can find a couple of experienced free agents. The offensive line needs help, too, but that might come in the draft. In any event, Philadelphia will probably be a sleeper at best in a few games this season, but the Eagles are hardly a serious threat for the playoffs.

OFFENSE

Quarterbacks	Ht.	Wt.	Age	Exp.	College
Gabriel, Roman	6-4	225	37	16	N.C. State
Boryla, Mike	6-3	200	26	4	Stanford
Jaworski, Ron	6-2	185	26	4	Youngstown State
Walton, John	6-2	210	30	2	Elizabeth City

Gabriel came out of retirement in mid-year 1976. His body is that of a 30-year-old, but he has an old man's knee. He's still better than Boryla, who had his shot last year. Jaworski is the likely Philadelphia starter for 1977; the Polish Rifle will open up via the air lanes. He rusted on the Rams' bench and demanded a trade. Walton is a backup. Boryla passed for 50 percent last year with only nine TDs. He didn't take the Eagles into the end zone enough.

Running Backs	Ht.	Wt.	Age	Exp.	College
Hampton, Dave	6-0	210	30	9	Wyoming
Sullivan, Tom	6-0	190	27	6	Miami (Fla.)
Lusk, Herb	6-0	190	24	2	Long Beach State
Olds, Bill	6-1	224	26	5	Nebraska
Hynoski, Henry	6-0	210	24	3	Temple
Malone, Art	6-0	216	29	8	Arizona State
Hogan, Mike	6-2	205	23	2	Tennessee—Chattanooga

Hampton ran for only 267 yards for the Eagles in 1976 after being a 1,000-yarder with Atlanta. He isn't too old; more playing time is the answer. Sullivan has potential but got only 399 yards in 99 cracks last year. Lusk was so-so. Olds is the former Baltimore Colt blocking back who gave Lydell Mitchell running room. He flunked in Seattle and is back for another shot. Hynoski has had playing time with Cleveland.

Receivers	Ht.	Wt.	Age	Exp.	College
Carmichael, Harold (W)	6-8	225	28	7	Southern U.
Papale, Vince (W)	6-2	195	31	2	St. Joseph's (Pa.)
Krepfle, Keith (T)	6-3	225	25	3	Iowa State
Smith, Charles (W)	6-1	185	27	4	Grambling
McAlister, James (W)	6-1	205	26	3	UCLA

W=wide receiver   T=tight end

Carmichael, a veritable jumping jack, led the Eagles with 42 catches last year. He is a class catcher. Papale became a special-team whiz after making the Eagles as a free agent. Rags-to-riches Vince used to pay his way into Eagle games at Franklin Field. He's a Philadelphia area football sandlotter whose fantasies came true. With Charlie Young traded in the Jaworski deal, Krepfle is the heir apparent—if he's good enough. Smith caught 27 passes last year and has good speed. As running backs, Messrs. Hogan, Sullivan, Lusk, and McAlister caught 54 passes, with Hampton chipping in another dozen in the balanced Philly aerial attack. The one worry is the loss of Young, a superior player who might be the best tight end in the NFC. McAlister is switching from running back to wide receiver.

Interior Linemen	Ht.	Wt.	Age	Exp.	College
Walters, Stan (T)	6-6	270	29	6	Syracuse
Nelson, Dennis (T)	6-5	260	31	8	Illinois State
Johnson, Kirk (T)	6-5	277	25	2	Howard Payne
Key, Wade (G)	6-5	245	31	8	Southwest Texas
Bleamer, Jeff (G)	6-4	253	24	3	Penn State
Smelser, Dennis (G)	6-3	256	24	2	Texas A&M
Morriss, Guy (C)	6-4	255	26	5	Texas Christian
Franks, Dennis (C)	6-1	236	24	3	Michigan
Sisemore, Jerry (G)	6-4	260	26	5	Texas
George, Ed (T)	6-4	270	31	3	Wake Forest
Luken, Tom (G)	6-3	253	27	6	Purdue
Niland, John (G)	6-3	250	33	12	Iowa

T=tackle   G=guard   C=center

Walters, Key, Morriss, Sisemore, and George are the starters. But they don't really get the job done. The Eagles traveled only 2,080 yards overland in 1976—eighth in the NFC. Ed George, down from Canada, disappointed; and only Key had a good year. Help is vital.

Kickers	Ht.	Wt.	Age	Exp.	College
Jones, Spike (P)	6-2	195	30	8	Georgia
Muhlmann, Horst (Pk)	6-2	219	37	9	(none)
Bitterlich, Don (Pk)	5-7	166	23	2	Temple

Pk=placekicker   P=punter

West German native and resident Muhlmann may not return. He was 11 of 16 in FGs but is losing accuracy and getting old at the same time. Bitterlich blew the job at Seattle, so how much help will he be? Punter Spike Jones got lots of work last year—94 punts—but his 36.6 average was hardly good enough to help the Eagles better their usually poor field position.

DEFENSE

Front Linemen	Ht.	Wt.	Age	Exp.	College
Hairston, Carl (T, E)	6-3	245	25	2	Maryland—E. Shore
Sistrunk, Manny (T)	6-5	275	30	8	Arkansas AM&N
Lazetich, Pete (T)	6-3	245	27	5	Stanford
Wynn, Will (E)	6-4	245	28	5	Tennessee State

E=end   T=tackle

The 1976 Eagle front four was a distillation of much mix and fuss. Bill Dunstan was traded to Buffalo after losing his job to Sistrunk, who helped quite a bit. Look for another year of shuffling and another year with too many opponents' yards through the line. Last year Philadelphia surrendered 2,053 rushing yards; this made them seventh in the NFC, but better than highly rated Minnesota in eighth place. More personnel needed badly.

Linebackers	Ht.	Wt.	Age	Exp.	College
LeMaster, Frank (O)	6-2	231	25	4	Kentucky
Ehlers, Tom (O)	6-2	218	25	3	Kentucky
Bergey, Bill (M)	6-3	245	32	9	Arkansas State
Tautolo, Terry (M)	6-2	235	23	2	UCLA
Bunting, John (O)	6-1	220	27	6	North Carolina
Mahalic, Drew (O)	6-4	225	24	3	Notre Dame
Halverson, Dean (O)	6-2	230	31	9	Washington

O=outside   M=middle

Bergey is an All-Pro. Bunting and LeMaster aren't too far back. They have to be good if they're to contain runners pouring through the line. A strong spot.

Cornerbacks	Ht.	Wt.	Age	Exp.	College
Outlaw, John	5-10	180	31	9	Jackson State
Campbell, Tommy	6-0	188	28	2	Iowa State
Scales, Hurles	6-1	200	27	3	North Texas State
Clark, Al	6-0	185	29	7	Eastern Michigan
Shy, Melvin	6-1	195	24	2	Tennessee State

The 1976 Eagles finished tied for last in NFC pass interceptions—they got only nine. That hurts. Outlaw and Clark are the incumbent corners. Shy and Campbell will get long looks here because Vermeil isn't satisfied with his secondary.

Safeties	Ht.	Wt.	Age	Exp.	College
Logan, Randy	6-1	195	26	5	Michigan
Parker, Artimus	6-4	200	25	4	Southern California
Burke, Mark	6-1	180	23	2	West Virginia
Bradley, Bill	5-11	190	30	9	Texas

Philadelphia's pass defense was dead last in the NFC; the Eagles yielded 2,550 yards, although they allowed only 17 pass TDs. Bradley "led" with two interceptions, a figure matched by linebacker Bergey and cornerman Outlaw. Bradley and Logan are regulars with an excellent reserve, Parker, in the wings.

Note: A complete listing of Philadelphia's 1977 college draft selections can be found on page 257.

DEFENSIVE UNIT

Parker
Bradley
S

Burke
Parker
Logan
S

Shy
Campbell
Clark
CB

Scales
Campbell
Outlaw
CB

Halverson
Mahalic
Bunting
LB

Tautolo
Bergey
LB

Ehlers
LeMaster
LB

Wynn
E

Lazetich
T

Sistrunk
T

Hairston
E

WR
Carmichael
Papale

Walters
Nelson
Johnson
T

Key
Bleamer
Smelser
G

Morriss
Franks
C

Sisemore
Bleamer
Luken
Niland
G

George
Nelson
T

Krepfle
TE

RB
Hogan
Malone
Olds
Hynoski

QB
Gabriel
Boryla
Jaworski

RB
Sullivan
Hampton
Lusk

WR
Smith
Papale
McAlister

OFFENSIVE UNIT

1976 EAGLES STATISTICS

	Eagles	Opps.
Total Points Scored	165	286
Total First Downs	220	262
Third-Down Efficiency	71—220	95—227
Yards Rushing—First Downs	2080—109	2050—113
Passes Attempted—Completions	369—182	404—237
Yards Passing—First Downs	1492—91	2550—129
QB Sacked—Yards Lost	43—352	19—138
Interceptions—Return Average	9—21.7	18—10.5
Punts—Average Yards	97—35.5	86—37.9
Punt Returns—Return Average	41—10.4	53—7.6
Kickoff Returns—Return Average	58—19.8	44—20.5
Fumbles—Ball Lost	33—14	31—15
Penalties—Yards	91—722	105—927

STATISTICAL LEADERS

Scoring	TDs	Rush.	Pass.	Ret.	PATs	FGs	Total
Muhlmann	0	0	0	0	18—19	11—16	51
Carmichael	5	0	5	0	0	0	30
Smith, Charles	5	1	4	0	0	0	30
Sullivan	3	2	1	0	0	0	18
Boryla	2	2	0	0	0	0	12

Rushing	Atts.	Yds.	Avg.	Longest	TDs
Hogan	123	561	4.6	32	0
Sullivan	99	399	4.0	26	2
Hampton	71	267	3.8	59	1
McAlister	68	265	3.9	20	0
Lusk	61	254	4.2	22	0
Boryla	29	166	5.7	22	2
Olds	36	120	3.3	8	1

Passing	Atts.	Com.	Yds.	Pct.	Int.	Longest	TDs
Boryla	246	123	1247	50.0	14	48 (TD)	9
Gabriel	92	46	476	50.0	2	34	2
Walton	28	12	125	42.9	3	33	0

Receiving	No.	Yds.	Avg.	Longest	TDs
Carmichael	42	503	12.0	24	5
Young	30	374	12.5	29	0
Smith, Charles	27	412	15.3	48 (TD)	4
Hogan	15	89	5.9	18	0
Sullivan	14	116	8.3	21 (TD)	1
Lusk	13	119	9.2	42	0
McAlister	12	72	6.0	25	0

Interceptions	No.	Yds.	Avg.	Longest	TDs
Bradley	2	63	31.5	52	0
Bergey	2	48	24.0	37	0
Outlaw	2	19	9.5	19	0

Punting	No.	Yds.	Avg.	Longest	Inside 20	Blocked
Jones	94	3345	36.6	57	23	3

Punt Returns	No.	FCs	Yds.	Avg.	Longest	TDs
Marshall	27	9	290	10.7	29	0
Bradley	9	5	64	7.1	23	0
Clark	4	0	57	14.3	24	0

Kickoff Returns	No.	Yds.	Avg.	Longest	TDs
Marshall	30	651	21.7	41	0
McAlister	9	172	19.1	28	0
Lusk	7	155	22.1	27	0
Sullivan	5	108	21.6	26	0
Hampton	3	46	15.3	23	0

NEW YORK GIANTS

Head Coach: John McVay
(took over in midseason of 1976)
2nd Year　　　　　　　　　　**Record: 3–4**

1976 RECORD (3–11) (capital letters indicate home games)		**1977 SCHEDULE** (capital letters indicate home games)	
17	Washington	19	WASHINGTON	Sept. 18
7	Philadelphia	20	Dallas	Sept. 25
10	Los Angeles	24	Atlanta	Oct. 2
21	St. Louis	27	PHILADELPHIA	Oct. 9
14	DALLAS	24	SAN FRANCISCO	Oct. 16
7	Minnesota	24	Washington	Oct. 23
0	PITTSBURGH	27	St. Louis (night, TV)	Oct. 31
0	PHILADELPHIA	10	DALLAS	Nov. 6
3	Dallas	9	Tampa Bay	Nov. 13
12	WASHINGTON	9	CLEVELAND	Nov. 20
13	Denver	14	Cincinnati	Nov. 27
28	SEATTLE	16	ST. LOUIS	Dec. 4
24	DETROIT	10	Philadelphia	Dec. 11
14	ST. LOUIS	17	CHICAGO	Dec. 18

If Steve Ramsey wasn't the answer with the defensively strong Denver Broncos, why should he be the messiah who will lead the Giants from the wilderness of defeat and discord they have wandered in for lo! so many years? The Giants were 3–11 last year, which breaks down to 0–7 under Bill Arnsparger and 3–4 under new head man John McVay.

Once more revamping, the Jints will do things like throwing all the offensive linemen into a hopper and letting the best five play. John Hicks may try tackle instead of guard, Ron Mikolajczyk will be switched to tackle for a time, and guard Al Simpson, a disappointment in the past, will get a shot at tackle.

Ramsey may be penciled in as the starting quarterback in place of Craig Morton, for whom he was traded. Whether Ramsey is the answer is moot. The trade was mostly made to clear the air and relieve the Giant players of Morton, who wasn't liked.

Norm Snead has retired, leaving untried Jerry Golsteyn as the dark horse unless McVay can steal a quarterback from someone. Dennis Shaw, late of the Bills and Cardinals and a man experienced at running a ball-control attack, will also get more than a mere glance and could be the man.

The Giants' defense, which played far better than the record would indicate, allowed 4,191 yards in 1976 to finish ninth overall in the NFC. Three rookies played very well—Troy Archer, middle linebacker Harry Carson, and cornerback Willie Bryant. They will start this year for sure. The Giants want a large-sized tackle next to Archer and are trying to spring Carl Barzilauskas from the Jets. John Mendenhall is a solid pro. And the draft provided Gary Jeter, the USC All-America defensive tackle.

In other developments, strong side safety Robert Giblin, who missed the season with an injury, will try his hand as a weak-side linebacker. As a strong safety, he can't beat out Clyde Powers. As a weak safety he isn't as good as Jim Stienke. But Pat Hughes has been traded, and so Giblin might stick to linebacker.

The top priority has to be to improve the lousy, dull offense that Morton tried to palm off on Meadowlands patrons. They booed him all the way to Denver and continued to buy more tickets (76,000 per game) than fans of any other team in the NFL, but that can slow down if things don't get better.

McVay hired assistant coach Bob Gibson away from the Detroit Lions to serve as offensive coordinator. It was Gibson who supervised the renaissance of the Lions and Greg Landry.

Last year the Jint attack was fourth from last in the

NFC, with a combined 3,696 yards and a meager 170 points—only five more than the Eagles, who were last in that department, got. Retooling the attack means checking out Larry Csonka's surgical knee. It means the same with tackle Tom Mullen, who got hurt in the same game that messed up Zonk. Can Gordon Bell, a quick, smallish scatback, oust Doug Kotar from his starting halfback spot? Should smallish Ray Rhodes quit as a wide receiver and become a cornerback?

Overall, the Giants claim that a fleet wide receiver who can take a bomb all the way is their prime need. Maybe so, but it says here that both the offensive and defensive lines, and the corners, need help. The front four has been hurt by the retirement of defensive end Dave Gallagher, obtained from the Chicago Bears for a third-round draft. Gallagher was used sparingly, despite good work when he did perform, and he reacted accordingly.

Anytime a team revamps—and, in effect, runs open house at almost every position—it takes a certain amount of time to gain cohesion and a feeling of togetherness. The Giants, especially on the attack, were very much apart from each other last year. Owner Wellington Mara is becoming tired of losing and only gave McVay a two-year contract. If the team gets off to a poor start this year, look for more fur to fly even before the regular season opens. Winning in preseason will become important in establishing a winning attitude.

Kotar did pretty well with 731 yards last year, but Csonka disappointed with only 569—but Zonk got hurt, too. It wasn't quite like having the Miami holes opened by Larry Little and Norm Evans. And that's where chaos in the offensive line hurts. Doug Van Horn and Tom Mullen are left from the old guard.

Semi-new are Mike Gibbons, Simpson, Karl Chandler, and Mikolajczyk.

When McVay was imported from Memphis of the WFL, he brought with him a cadre of offensive linemen from both the Memphis Southmen and the Birmingham Americans. But somehow these players didn't click as a unit. They might be tried again, but not all WFL types make it in the NFL. Another question is: What happens to John Hicks, the combative guard who drew too many holding penalties in 1976?

Most NFL coaches like the Giants' defense, but shudder when the attack is mentioned. That should be McVay's first area of change—and the change will be one loyal Giant fans will appreciate the most.

OFFENSE

Quarterbacks	Ht.	Wt.	Age	Exp.	College
Ramsey, Steve	6-2	205	29	8	North Texas State
Shaw, Dennis	6-3	210	30	8	San Diego State
Golsteyn, Jerry	6-4	210	23	1	Northern Illinois

Ramsey had mediocre stats with the Broncos and could be the main reason John Ralston was fired. He's only 29, so the Giants gain comparative youth over old man Morton, but Steve had a poor 47.4 and only 11 TDs with Denver. He'll have to do better. Shaw failed at Buffalo and couldn't unseat Jim Hart with the Cards, but he's at the right age and has game experience. Personal problems bothered him in the past. He will stick. Golsteyn is the future hope of the Jersey Jints.

Running Backs	Ht.	Wt.	Age	Exp.	College
Kotar, Doug	5-11	205	26	4	Kentucky
Bell, Gordon	5-9	180	24	2	Michigan
Hammond, Bob	5-10	170	25	2	Morgan State
Csonka, Larry	6-2	237	30	9	Syracuse
White, Marsh	6-2	220	24	3	Arkansas
Watkins, Larry	6-2	230	31	9	Alcorn State
James, Po	6-1	202	28	6	New Mexico State

Kotar is too small, say some, but he outran Csonka last year. Csonka must prove that his knee is all right and that he can scamper without a great attack line in front of him. Bell did a job when he got the chance; he gained 233 yards last year. White is the heir apparent if Zonk can't make it. Watkins is a journeyman reserve.

Receivers	Ht.	Wt.	Age	Exp.	College
Robinson, Jimmy (W)	5-9	170	24	2	Georgia Tech
Wallace, Roger (W)	5-11	180	25	2	Bowling Green
Tucker, Bob (T)	6-3	230	32	8	Bloomsburg State
Shirk, Gary (T)	6-1	220	27	2	Morehead State
Gillette, Walker (W)	6-5	200	30	8	Richmond
Marshall, Ed (W)	6-5	200	30	3	Cameron State
Zimmerman, Don (W)	6-3	195	28	5	Northeast Louisiana
Rhodes, Ray (W)	5-11	185	27	4	Tulsa
Tullis, Walt (W)	6-0	170	22	1	Delaware State
Perkins, Johnny (W)	6-2	208	22	R	Abilene Christian
Gardner, Ron (W)	6-2	186	25	1	Windsor (Canada)
Fuhrman, Mike (T)	6-4	210	25	1	Memphis State

W=wide receiver   T=tight end

Tucker led the Giants in 1976 with 42 receptions, but he still was overlooked in the early going by both coach Arnsparger and quarterback Morton. He is top flight and would be hard to replace if hurt. Running back Kotar caught 36 passes in 1976, Gordon Bell 25. Robinson surprised with 18 and Rhodes proved too small; he got only 16. Morton's favorite receiver, Walker Gillette, may not make the team, especially when his 1976 report card of 16 catches for 263 yards and two TDs is analyzed. Zimmerman is a newcomer with five years of NFL experience.

Interior Linemen	Ht.	Wt.	Age	Exp.	College
Mullen, Tom (T)	6-3	245	25	4	S.W. Missouri
Gibbons, Mike (T)	6-4	262	26	2	S.W. Oklahoma
Ellenbogen, Bill (T)	6-5	255	27	2	Virginia Tech
Simpson, Al (G)	6-5	255	26	3	Colorado State
Mikolajczyk, Ron (G)	6-3	275	27	2	Tampa
Chandler, Karl (C)	6-5	250	25	4	Princeton
Hill, Ralph (C)	6-1	245	28	2	Florida A&M
Hicks, John (G)	6-2	258	26	4	Ohio State
Van Horn, Doug (T)	6-3	245	33	11	Ohio State
Leavitt, Dick (T)	6-4	280	23	2	Bowdoin

T=tackle   G=guard   C=center

Mullen's knee must be repaired if he is to challenge for his regular spot again. Simpson has all the potential in the world, but hasn't been entirely coachable. Mikolajczyk was caught holding too often in 1976, as was Hicks. Chandler is a dependable center and is backed by WFL type Hill. Van Horn most likely will go. He survived both the Red Webster and Bill Arnsparger eras. How much can a man take?

Kickers	Ht.	Wt.	Age	Exp.	College
Jennings, Dave (P)	6-4	205	25	4	St. Lawrence
Danelo, Joe (Pk)	5-9	166	24	3	Washington State

Pk=placekicker   P=punter

Jennings is one of the NFL's best kickers; certainly he's the best Giant punter since Ed Chandler. Danelo is spotty, inconsistent, and replaceable.

DEFENSE

Front Linemen	Ht.	Wt.	Age	Exp.	College
Martin, George (E)	6-4	245	24	3	Oregon
Dvorak, Rick (E, T)	6-4	245	25	4	Wichita State
Gregory, Jack (E)	6-5	255	32	11	Delta State
Mendenhall, John (T)	6-1	255	29	6	Grambling
Archer, Troy (T)	6-4	250	22	2	Colorado
Pietrzak, Jim (T)	6-5	260	24	4	Eastern Michigan
Bibbs, Ezil (T)	6-4	260	25	1	Grambling
Gallagher, Dave (T)	6-4	256	25	4	Michigan
Jeter, Gary (T)	6-3	247	22	R	Southern California

E=end   T=tackle

Martin, Mendenhall, Archer, and Dvorak don't make too bad a front four if all goes well. Mendenhall must accept the fate of remaining a Giant, and Archer must continue to improve. The return of Dave Gallagher from the retired list would help.

Linebackers	Ht.	Wt.	Age	Exp.	College
Van Pelt, Brad (O)	6-5	235	26	5	Michigan State
Lloyd, Dan (O)	6-2	225	24	2	Washington
Carson, Harry (M)	6-2	228	24	2	S.C. State
Kelley, Brian (O)	6-3	222	26	5	California Lutheran
Schmit, Bob (O)	6-1	220	26	3	Nebraska
Hughes, Pat (O)	6-2	225	30	8	Boston University
Giblin, Robert (O)	6-2	210	25	3	Houston
Sheats, Eddie (O)	6-2	225	26	2	Kansas
Cousino, Brad (M)	6-0	215	24	3	Miami (Ohio)

O=outside   M=middle

Van Pelt was just about the best Giant last year, and he'll be back this season after wavering as a free agent. Carson reminded oldtimers of a young Sam Huff, and Brian Kelley was better than expected. Former safety Giblin will try his hand at LB this year.

Cornerbacks	Ht.	Wt.	Age	Exp.	College
Bryant, Bill	5-11	195	26	2	Grambling
Ford, Charlie	6-3	195	26	7	Houston
Stuckey, Henry	6-1	175	28	5	Missouri
Colbert, Rondy	5-9	165	23	3	Lamar
Brooks, Bobby	6-1	195	26	4	Bishop
Rome, Pete	6-0	190	23	1	Miami (Ohio)

Bryant is a regular. Ford, Stuckey, and Colbert are experienced backups. The Giants intercepted only 12 passes in 1976; Stienke, Van Pelt, and Volk managed to steal two each.

Safeties	Ht.	Wt.	Age	Exp.	College
Powers, Clyde	6-1	195	26	4	Oklahoma
Volk, Rick	6-1	195	32	10	Michigan
Mallory, Larry	5-11	185	25	2	Tennessee State
Stienke, Jim	5-11	182	27	5	Southwest Texas

Volk proved he is still a top NFL safety after he joined the Giants. He and Powers give the club strength in the deep secondary. Stienke also plays corner on occasion.

Note: A complete listing of the New York Giants' 1977 college draft selections can be found on page 255.

DEFENSIVE UNIT

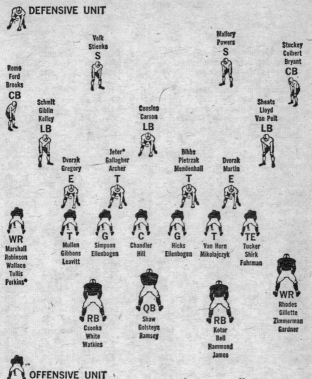

Volk
Stienke
S

Mallory
Powers
S

Stuckey
Colbert
Bryant
CB

Rome
Ford
Brooks
CB

Schmit
Giblin
Kelley
LB

Cousino
Carson
LB

Sheats
Lloyd
Van Pelt
LB

Dvorak
Gregory
E

Jeter*
Gallagher
Archer
T

Bibbs
Pietrzak
Mendenhall
T

Dvorak
Martin
E

WR
Marshall
Robinson
Wallace
Tullis
Perkins*

Mullen
Gibbons
Leavitt
T

Simpson
Ellenbogen
G

Chandler
Hill
C

Hicks
Ellenbogen
G

Van Horn
Mikolajczyk
T

Tucker
Shirk
Fuhrman
TE

RB
Csonka
White
Watkins

QB
Shaw
Golsteyn
Ramsey

RB
Kotar
Bell
Hammond
James

WR
Rhodes
Gillette
Zimmerman
Gardner

OFFENSIVE UNIT

*Rookie

1976 GIANTS STATISTICS

	Giants	Opps.
Total Points Scored	170	250
Total First Downs	216	251
Third-Down Efficiency	88—227	79—212
Yards Rushing—First Downs	1904—98	2203—120
Passes Attempted—Completions	326—175	330—189
Yards Passing—First Downs	1792—97	1988—119
QB Sacked—Yards Lost	44—312	31—242
Interceptions—Return Average	12—5.2	24—10.0
Punts—Average Yards	77—39.7	78—37.0
Punt Returns—Return Average	41—4.8	45—11.1
Kickoff Returns—Return Average	53—19.7	39—18.6
Fumbles—Ball Lost	27—12	32—15
Penalties—Yards	86—734	104—835

STATISTICAL LEADERS

Scoring	TDs	Rush.	Pass.	Ret.	PATs	FGs	Total
Danelo	0	0	0	0	20—21	8—21	44
Csonka	4	4	0	0	0	0	24
Kotar	3	3	0	0	0	0	18
Marshall	3	0	3	0	0	0	18
Bell	2	2	0	0	0	0	12
Gillette	2	0	2	0	0	0	12

Rushing	Atts.	Yds.	Avg.	Longest	TDs
Kotar	185	731	4.0	24	3
Csonka	160	569	3.6	13	4
Bell	67	233	3.5	26	2
White	69	223	3.2	29	1
Watkins	26	96	3.7	13	1
Morton	15	48	3.2	10	0

Passing	Atts.	Com.	Yds.	Pct.	Int.	Longest	TDs
Morton	284	153	1865	53.9	20	63 (TD)	9
Snead	42	22	239	52.4	4	31	0

Receiving	No.	Yds.	Avg.	Longest	TDs
Tucker	42	498	11.9	39	1
Kotar	36	319	8.9	30	0
Bell	25	198	7.9	20	0
Robinson	18	249	13.8	30 (TD)	1
Rhodes	16	305	19.1	63 (TD)	1
Gillette	16	263	16.4	62 (TD)	2

Interceptions	No.	Yds.	Avg.	Longest	TDs
Volk	2	14	7.0	11	0
Van Pelt	2	13	6.5	7	0

Punting	No.	Yds.	Avg.	Longest	Inside 20	Blocked
Jennings	74	3054	41.3	61	11	3

Punt Returns	No.	FCs	Yds.	Avg.	Longest	TDs
Robinson	24	7	106	4.4	22	0
Colbert	13	0	72	5.5	15	0

Kickoff Returns	No.	Yds.	Avg.	Longest	TDs
Robinson	20	444	22.2	32	0
Bell	18	352	19.6	37	0
Shirk	6	109	18.2	27	0

MINNESOTA VIKINGS

Head Coach: Bud Grant

11th Year   **Record:** 98–38–4

1976 RECORD (11–2–1) (capital letters indicate home games)		
40	New Orleans	9
10	LOS ANGELES (In OT)	10
10	Detroit	9
17	PITTSBURGH	6
20	CHICAGO	19
24	N.Y. GIANTS	7
31	Philadelphia	12
13	Chicago	14
31	DETROIT	23
27	SEATTLE	21
17	Green Bay (at Milwaukee)	10
16	San Francisco	20
20	GREEN BAY	9
29	Miami	7
Playoffs		
35	WASHINGTON	20
24	LOS ANGELES	13
14	Oakland	32

1977 SCHEDULE (capital letters indicate home games)	
DALLAS	Sept. 18
Tampa Bay (night)	Sept. 24
GREEN BAY	Oct. 2
DETROIT	Oct. 9
CHICAGO	Oct. 16
Los Angeles (night, TV)	Oct. 24
Atlanta	Oct. 30
ST. LOUIS	Nov. 6
CINCINNATI	Nov. 13
Chicago	Nov. 20
Green Bay	Nov. 27
SAN FRANCISCO	Dec. 4
Oakland	Dec. 11
Detroit (night, TV)	Dec. 17

The Minnesota Vikings' faults were revealed by the noneffort in the Super Bowl, but that doesn't mean that this defense-oriented team isn't the class of the NFC Central. There is no sign of panic in Minneapolis, St. Paul, or Bloomington. Bud Grant hasn't quit in disgust, and he hasn't threatened to trade most of the regulars.

If Grant had listened to the bleatings of the fans, most of his better players would have been elsewhere long ago, and Minnesota wouldn't have made three more trips to the Super Bowl—no matter how frustrating those trips may have been.

Still, Minnesota does have things to worry about. If Grant isn't going to shake up the cast, it might do some shaking of its own. Fran Tarkenton, beset by a bad knee and marital problems, although he's highly successful in television, indicated that he just might not play; then he changed his mind. If he *doesn't* play, Bob Lee, who once gave Atlanta a taste of winning, would be the No. 1 quarterback. But Tarkenton is on record as saying he expects to play for two more years.

The main Minnesota offensive weapon, all-purpose back Chuck Foreman, also indicated that if certain of his salary demands weren't met, he might play elsewhere. He has two years to run on his contract, but that doesn't seem to mean much these days. He threatens to quit unless his $100,000 stipend is doubled.

The success of the Vikings up until their Super failures is hard to analyze. And those who say the AFC is superior to the NFC really can't mean it to the degree the Minnesota team makes it look in Super Bowl play.

Age is creeping up on Minnesota, especially on the fabulous Purple People Eaters, but still they limited opponents to 3,671 yards in 1976—fourth best in the NFC and even better than the fabled Dallas defense. Only San Francisco, Detroit, and Los Angeles were better.

Carl Eller, Doug Sutherland—who isn't old at all—Alan Page, and Jim Marshall are a proud unit, even if Page was steam-rollered in the Super Bowl by his friend Gene Upshaw. Eller is 35, Sutherland only 29, Page 32, and Marshall 40. Mark Mullaney is the heir apparent in Marshall's case, but don't completely count the 18-year vet out.

A year ago the Vikings were worried over the loss to Atlanta of John Gilliam, the highly regarded wide receiver. They did pretty well, replacing him with Ahmad Rashad and Sammy White. Rashad was second to Chuck Foreman in club receptions—he got 53. White garnered 51 passes for 906 yards and a whopping ten TDs.

The loss of Foreman, however, would deal a devastating blow to the sometimes conservative Minnesota attack. Despite the carping, Tarkenton drove his boys to an aggregate 4,858 yards last year, good for fourth place in the NFC overall. The rushing attack came up with only 2,003 yards. Viking passes produced the best total in the NFC—2,855 yards.

Foreman emerged from the backfield for the most receptions in 1976—55 for 567 yards and one TD. Rushing the ball he gained 1,155 yards and crossed the goal line 13 times. That spells essentiality. Foreman has been the difference between the Vikings' being also-rans and winning in the playoffs most years.

Winning the NFC Central is almost a formality for the Vikings, but last year they felt the hot breath of the eager young Chicago Bears on their necks. They beat the Bears 20–19 and then lost 14–13. It was that close between the two teams.

One of the biggest things Minnesota has going for it is the rapport between Tarkenton and Grant. They understand each other and appreciate each other's viewpoints.

For Minnesota to win the Super Bowl, they first will have to win their division, which might get tougher with Detroit trying to overcome that runner-up jinx. Even then, they still will have the Rams, Cardinals, and Cowboys to edge past in the playoffs.

Will the January 1977 debacle have a mental effect on this team—especially its older members? Tarkenton was bitterly disappointed, but has bounced back and wants another shot. Foreman is still young and so are White and Rashad, but what about the Purple People Eaters? Are they ready to enter retirement, or do they have one more season left? On the answers to those questions will hinge the Vikings' fate in 1977.

OFFENSE

Quarterbacks	Ht.	Wt.	Age	Exp.	College
Tarkenton, Fran	6-0	190	37	17	Georgia
Lee, Bob	6-2	195	32	9	Pacific (Calif.)
Berry, Bob	5-11	185	35	13	Oregon
Kramer, Tommy	6-2	190	22	R	Rice

Tarkenton continues to set NFL records almost every time he throws the ball. His sore knee, which hampered him in the playoffs last year, has improved, and he wants another crack at the Super Bowl. He was sixth overall last year, with 61.9 percent; he mixed a variety of passes for 17 TDs. Lee once was Atlanta's regular and could take over when and if Tark quits. Berry is a journeyman who has had his shot, but doesn't do badly when he's forced to play. Tarkenton says he won't teach Kramer how to play QB. From his college record, maybe Kramer already knows.

Running Backs	Ht.	Wt.	Age	Exp.	College
McClanahan, Brent	5-10	202	27	5	Arizona State
Foreman, Chuck	6-2	207	27	5	Miami (Fla.)
Miller, Robert	5-11	204	24	3	Kansas
Johnson, Sammy	6-1	226	25	4	North Carolina
Groce, Ron	6-2	211	23	2	Macalester
Kellar, Mark	6-0	225	25	2	Northern Illinois

The ground attack is 50 percent Chuck Foreman and 50 percent everyone else. McClanahan made that key Super Bowl fumble, but did 382 yards as the No. 2 rusher last year. Miller was good for 286 in rather infrequent attempts. Johnson doesn't work much; he backs up Foreman. Groce ran the ball three times in 1976, so who knows?

Receivers	Ht.	Wt.	Age	Exp.	College
Rashad, Ahmad (W)	6-2	200	28	5	Oregon
Willis, Leonard (W)	5-10	180	24	2	Ohio State
Voigt, Stu (T)	6-1	225	29	8	Wisconsin
Craig, Steve (T)	6-3	231	26	4	Northwestern
White, Sammy (W)	5-11	189	23	2	Grambling
Grim, Bob (W)	6-0	188	32	11	Oregon State

W=wide receiver   T=tight end

Rashad escaped from Seattle in time to go to the Super Bowl. If he remains interested, Minnesota has a fine deep receiver. Willis is rated high in skill, but he's short on stature. Voigt has developed into a superior tight end. Craig is the TE reserve. White is the fly man, the Homer Jones part of the Tarkenton bomb squad. Grim returned to his old home and is solid insurance if either Rashad or White gets hurt.

Interior Linemen	Ht.	Wt.	Age	Exp.	College
Riley, Steve (T)	6-5½	258	25	6	Southern California
Goodrum, Charles (G)	6-3	256	27	5	Florida A&M
Hamilton, Wes (G)	6-3	255	24	2	Tulsa
Tinglehoff, Mick (C)	6-2	240	37	16	Nebraska
Dumler, Doug (C)	6-3	245	27	5	Nebraska
White, Ed (G)	6-2½	270	30	9	California
Yary, Ron (T)	6-5½	255	31	10	Southern California
Buetow, Bart (T)	6-5½	250	27	4	Minnesota
Nessel, John (T)	6-6	270	25	1	Penn State
Anderson, Scott (C)	6-5	256	26	3	Missouri
Swilley, Dennis (G)	6-3	245	22	R	Texas A&M

T=tackle   G=guard   C=center

Riley, Goodrum, fabled vet Tinglehoff, White, and Yary are the regular linemen. Dumler may move in on Tinglehoff; it has to happen sometime. Hamilton is the reserve guard, and Buetow is trying for Yary's job. Not the best unit in the NFL, but still capable of moving people and doing the job.

Kickers	Ht.	Wt.	Age	Exp.	College
Clabo, Neil (P)	6-2	200	25	3	Tennessee
Cox, Fred (Pk)	5-10	200	39	15	Pittsburgh
Danmeier, Rick (Pk)	6-0	183	25	1	Sioux Falls

Pk=placekicker   P=punter

Clabo was only forced to punt 69 times last year and did rather poorly—he earned a 38.8 average—but he didn't have any blocked. Cox goes on forever, it seems. In 1976 he came in fifth in scoring with 19 FGs out of 31 kicks and 32 of 36 PATs.

DEFENSE

Front Linemen	Ht.	Wt.	Age	Exp.	College
Eller, Carl (E)	6-6	247	35	14	Minnesota
Mullaney, Mark (E)	6-6	242	24	3	Colorado State
Sutherland, Doug (T)	6-3	250	29	8	Wisconsin—Superior
White, James (T)	6-3½	263	24	2	Oklahoma State
Page, Alan (T)	6-4	245	32	11	Notre Dame
Marshall, Jim (E)	6-4	240	40	18	Ohio State

E=end   T=tackle

Eller is still a super pass rusher, and he defends well against the run. Mullaney wants Marshall's job. Sutherland was moved into the front four three years ago and has fitted in nicely. Page has at least five good years left. What is there to say about Jim Marshall that hasn't been said already?

Linebackers	Ht.	Wt.	Age	Exp.	College
Blair, Matt (O)	6-5	229	26	4	Iowa State
McNeill, Fred (O)	6-2	229	25	4	UCLA
Winston, Roy (O)	5-11	222	37	16	Louisiana State
Reese, Steve (O)	6-2	232	25	4	Louisville
Siemon, Jeff (M)	6-2½	237	27	6	Stanford
Martin, Amos (M)	6-3	228	28	6	Louisville
Hilgenberg, Wally (O)	6-3	229	35	14	Iowa

O=outside   M=middle

Blair, Siemon, and Hilgenberg are top drawer. Siemon just keeps getting better. Blair replaced Roy Winston two years ago and has done well. McNeill, who blocked Ray Guy's punt in the Super Bowl, would like Hilgenberg's job, but age is no problem at linebacker. Reese comes up from Tampa Bay.

Cornerbacks	Ht.	Wt.	Age	Exp.	College
Wright, Nate	5-11	180	30	9	San Diego State
Blahak, Joe	5-10	188	27	5	Nebraska
Bryant, Bobby	6-1	170	33	9	South Carolina
Allen, Nate	5-11	174	29	7	Texas Southern
Hannon, Tom	6-0	196	22	R	Michigan State

Minnesota was sixth in the NFC last year with 19 interceptions. Wright led with seven. He, along with starter Bryant and backup Hall, gives good protection. Allen would be a regular on some teams. Hannon is good at punt blocking, returning, and tackling.

Safeties	Ht.	Wt.	Age	Exp.	College
Wright, Jeff	5-11	190	28	7	Minnesota
Beamon, Autry	6-0½	190	24	3	East Texas State
Krause, Paul	6-3	200	35	14	Iowa
Hall, Windlan	5-11	175	27	6	Arizona State

Krause is getting on, but Beamon should be able to carry on if necessary. Wright shores up the secondary; that's his job. Hall can also play corner.

Note: A complete listing of Minnesota's 1977 college draft selections can be found on page 254.

DEFENSIVE UNIT

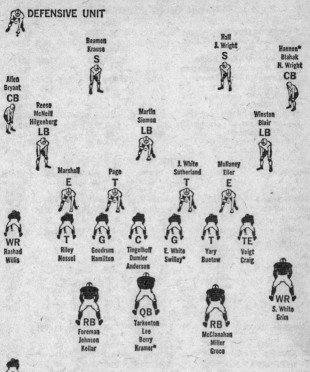

Beamon
Krause
S

Hall
J. Wright
S

Hannon*
Blahak
N. Wright
CB

Allen
Bryant
CB

Reese
McNeill
Hilgenberg
LB

Martin
Siemon
LB

Winston
Blair
LB

Marshall
E

Page
T

J. White
Sutherland
T

Mullaney
Eller
E

WR
Rashad
Willis

Riley
Nessel
T

Goodrum
Hamilton
G

Tingelhoff
Dumler
Anderson
C

E. White
Swilley*
G

Yary
Buetow
T

Voigt
Craig
TE

WR
S. White
Grim

RB
Foreman
Johnson
Kellar

QB
Tarkenton
Lee
Berry
Kramer*

RB
McClanahan
Miller
Groce

OFFENSIVE UNIT

*Rookie

1976 VIKINGS STATISTICS

	Vikings	Opps.
Total Points Scored	305	176
Total First Downs	294	207
Third-Down Efficiency	105—239	67—209
Yards Rushing—First Downs	2003—125	2102—103
Passes Attempted—Completions	442—270	323—158
Yards Passing—First Downs	2856—150	1575—91
QB Sacked—Yards Lost	31—262	45—320
Interceptions—Return Average	19—11.2	9—20.6
Punts—Average Yards	69—38.8	78—37.6
Punt Returns—Return Average	40—6.9	40—7.2
Kickoff Returns—Return Average	42—19.5	66—18.3
Fumbles—Ball Lost	34—20	24—15
Penalties—Yards	77—606	76—653

STATISTICAL LEADERS

Scoring	TDs	Rush.	Pass.	Ret.	PATs	FGs	Total
Cox	0	0	0	0	32—36	19—31	89
Foreman	14	13	1	0	0	0	84
White, Sammy	10	0	10	0	0	0	60
McClanahan	5	4	1	0	0	0	30
Rashad	3	0	3	0	0	0	18

Rushing	Atts.	Yds.	Avg.	Longest	TDs
Foreman	278	1155	4.2	46	13
McClanahan	130	382	2.9	19	4
Miller	67	286	4.3	36	0
Johnson	17	98	5.8	18	0
Tarkenton	27	45	1.7	20	1

Passing	Atts.	Com.	Yds.	Pct.	Int.	Longest	TDs
Tarkenton	412	255	2961	61.9	8	56 (TD)	17
Lee	30	15	156	50.0	2	21	0

Receiving	No.	Yds.	Avg.	Longest	TDs
Foreman	55	567	10.3	41 (TD)	1
Rashad	53	671	12.7	47	3
White, Sammy	51	906	17.8	56 (TD)	10
McClanahan	40	252	6.3	23	1
Voigt	28	303	10.8	44	1
Miller	23	181	7.9	19	1

Interceptions	No.	Yds.	Avg.	Longest	TDs
Wright, Nate	7	47	6.7	21	0
Allen	3	44	14.7	30	0
Krause	2	21	10.5	19	0
Bryant	2	30	15.0	25	0
Blair	2	25	12.5	20	0

Punting	No.	Yds.	Avg.	Longest	Inside 20	Blocked
Clabo	69	2678	38.8	55	5	0

Punt Returns	No.	FCs	Yds.	Avg.	Longest	TDs
Willis	30	10	207	6.9	29	0
Beamon	7	5	19	2.7	14	0
White, Sammy	3	1	45	15.0	31	0

Kickoff Returns	No.	Yds.	Avg.	Longest	TDs
Willis	24	552	23.0	57	0
White, Sammy	9	173	19.2	36	0
Miller	5	77	15.4	27	0

CHICAGO BEARS

Head Coach: Jack Pardee

3rd Year   **Record:** 11–17

1976 RECORD (7–7) (capital letters indicate home games)		1977 SCHEDULE (capital letters indicate home games)	
10	DETROIT	3	DETROIT	Sept. 18
19	San Francisco	12	St. Louis	Sept. 25
0	ATLANTA	10	NEW ORLEANS	Oct. 2
33	WASHINGTON	7	LOS ANGELES (night, TV)	Oct. 10
19	Minnesota	20	Minnesota	Oct. 16
12	Los Angeles	20	ATLANTA	Oct. 23
21	Dallas	31	Green Bay	Oct. 30
14	MINNESOTA	13	Houston	Nov. 6
27	OAKLAND	28	KANSAS CITY	Nov. 13
24	GREEN BAY	13	MINNESOTA	Nov. 20
10	Detroit	14	Detroit (TV)	Nov. 24
16	Green Bay	10	Tampa Bay	Dec. 4
34	Seattle	7	GREEN BAY	Dec. 11
14	DENVER	28	N.Y. Giants	Dec. 18

For many years, the Chicago Bears were a Windy City joke, with only Gale Sayers able to really excite the fans who gathered annually in ancient Soldier Field to watch the Bruins hibernate early on. Under owner–general manager, ofttimes coach, and original founder George "Papa Bear" Halas, the Bears were run in patriarchal fashion. This worked in the days when their main Western division protagonist was Green Bay, and the East was a battle between the Giants and the Redskins, but it meant nothing in modern pro football.

Two years ago, Halas sensed he wasn't in tune with the times and brought in Jim Finks, the one-time Minnesota Vikings' general manager. Finks named Jack Pardee (of WFL Florida Blazer fame) as coach, and set out to restore order.

When Sayers tore up his knee three different times a few years back, Chicago desperately searched for a replacement. For two years now they have billed running back Walter Payton as the new Sayers. He may eventually reach that stature, although he runs somewhat differently. Despite a problem in getting Payton around the corner on sweeps, he ran for 1,390 yards in 1976, much of it on his own.

At quarterback, Chicago went to young Bob Avellini, who was 2–2 in four starts in 1975 and started all 14 games last year for 7–7. That's not as much progress as Finks, a former quarterback, wanted, but as of now Avellini is still the starter. That could change with Mike Phipps now one of the Bears—he left Cleveland in a draft-choice deal. And former Falcon and Heisman winner Pat Sullivan is also now on the Chicago roster, looking for QB work.

Defense, at which Pardee excels in his coaching, was again Chicago's strength. Virtually the same players who gave up 379 points in 1975 cut that total to 216 last year. The Bears also led the NFL in the takeaway statistics with 19. Tackle Jim Osborne led with 15 sacks and the team had 49. Still, with Osborne, all-NFL Wally Chambers, and WFL type Ron Rydalch coming from the ends, that position scored only nine sacks.

The tight end situation is frustrating. Pardee handpicked his own man, former Florida Blazer star Greg Latta, but he has blocking shortcomings.

Linebacking is in pretty good hands, despite Dick Butkus' occasional snide remarks. Don Rives and Ross Brupbacher were solid, but Doug Buffone is plagued with a bad heel. The secondary surprised everyone last season, but there is no depth. Allan Ellis, Virgil Livers (who also returns kicks), Craig Clemons, and Doug Plant played without relief.

With Payton as the big runner, fullback Roland Harper appears set as No. 2, but injuries and the vicissitudes of NFL life might change that. The pass receiving corps isn't a show-stopper, although James Scott and Brian Baschnagel were coming fast at the end of the year.

The offensive line is young and fairly talented, although they need a pulling guard desperately, as mentioned. Lionel Antoine, Noah Jackson, Dean Neal, Jeff Seavy, and 1976 No. 1 draftee Dennis Lick got in theirs pretty often.

The resurgence of the Bears, who lost 20–19 to Minnesota and then beat the Vikings 14–13, has caused rising hopes for a challenge to the Purple People Eaters. This is possible if the Bears continue to improve, perhaps to 10–4, and Minnesota retrogresses. Right now, Francis Tarkenton, 37 and with a bad knee, can outplay Avellini seven days a week— and twice on Sunday if he's needed.

The Bears are exciting, challenging, and coming fast. They had a tough schedule in 1976, in one stretch playing Washington, Minnesota, Los Angeles, Dallas, Minnesota again, and Oakland, in that order. It gets easier this year, but first place might still be a bit too much for the Bruins to attain. Even so, this year's opposition clubs had an aggregate record of 85–108– 3 in 1976.

OFFENSE

Quarterbacks	Ht.	Wt.	Age	Exp.	College
Avellini, Bob	6-2	212	24	3	Maryland
Sullivan, Pat	5-11	201	27	6	Auburn
Phipps, Mike	6-3	205	29	8	Purdue

Avellini has courage, moxie, and drive, but his 43.5 percent completion average isn't NFL. Neither is only eight TDs. Carter, once the Bears' regular and also the Cincinnati starter, might get a shot if no one else makes it. Sullivan is just the right age if he is ever to become a first-stringer in the NFL. Phipps hopes his forward movement will resume in Chicago.

Running Backs	Ht.	Wt.	Age	Exp.	College
Harper, Roland	5-11½	205	24	3	Louisiana Tech
Adamle, Mike	5-9	197	48	7	Northwestern
Schreiber, Larry	6-0	204	30	7	Tennessee Tech
Payton, Walter	5-10½	204	23	3	Jackson State
Musso, Johnny	5-11	201	27	3	Alabama
Reamon, Tommy	5-10	192	24	2	Missouri
Earl, Robin	6-5	250	22	R	Washington

Harper works hard, and he logged 625 yards as numero duo to Walter Payton in 1976. Adamle is a kickoff return man and backup, a steady pro. Schreiber had a shot with the 49ers and flunked. Payton is the big man in Chicagoland, a slashing-type runner who can make yards on his own; he's just coming into maturity in his third year. Musso is bothered by bad knees. Reamon, acquired from Kansas City in a draft trade, was WFL rushing champion in 1974. He played for the Florida Blazers under coach Jack Pardee. Earl averaged five yards a carry rushing for Washington.

Receivers	Ht.	Wt.	Age	Exp.	College
Baschnagel, Brian (W)	6-0	193	23	2	Ohio State
Schubert, Steve (W)	5-10	184	26	4	Massachusetts
Rather, Bo (W)	6-1	186	27	5	Michigan State
Latta, Greg (T)	6-3	235	25	3	Morgan State
Bruer, Bob (T)	6-5	232	24	2	Mankato State
Kingsriter, Doug (T)	6-2	222	27	4	Minnesota
Scott, James (W)	6-1	193	25	2	Henderson J.C.
Burks, Randy (W)	5-10	172	24	2	S.E. Oklahoma
Shanklin, Ron (W)	6-1	187	29	8	North Texas State

W=wide receiver   T=tight end

Baschnagel worked out better than most expected he would. He caught 13 for 226 yards last year. The poor Chicago air game saw RB Harper

AMERICAN CONFERENCE ALL-PROS

Gene Upshaw
GUARD
Oakland Raiders

John Hannah
GUARD
New England Patriots

Mike Haynes
CORNERBACK
New England Patriots

Jack Lambert
LINEBACKER
Pittsburgh Steelers

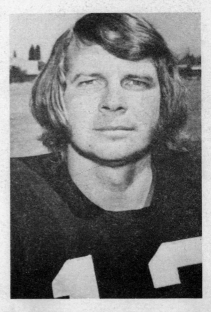

Ken Stabler
QUARTERBACK
Oakland Raiders

Lydell Mitchell
RUNNING BACK
Baltimore Colts

Ray Guy
PUNTER
Oakland Raiders

Curley Culp
DEFENSIVE TACKLE
Houston Oilers

Bert Jones
QUARTERBACK
Baltimore Colts

Mike Wagner
SAFETY
Pittsburgh Steelers

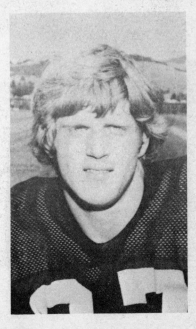

Dave Casper
TIGHT END
Oakland Raiders

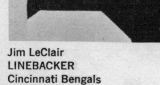

Jim LeClair
LINEBACKER
Cincinnati Bengals

Willie Lanier
LINEBACKER
Kansas City Chiefs

Roger Carr
WIDE RECEIVER
Baltimore Colts

Coy Bacon
DEFENSIVE END
Cincinnati Bengals

AFC ALL-PROS

Cliff Branch
WIDE RECEIVER
Oakland Raiders

Tom Casanova
SAFETY
Cincinnati Bengals

Greg Pruitt
RUNNING BACK
Cleveland Browns

Charley Joiner
WIDE RECEIVER
San Diego Chargers

Robert Brazile
LINEBACKER
Houston Oilers

NATIONAL CONFERENCE ALL-PROS

Monte Jackson
CORNERBACK
Los Angeles Rams

Ron Jessie
WIDE RECEIVER
Los Angeles Rams

Alan Page
DEFENSIVE TACKLE
Minnesota Vikings

Ron Yary
TACKLE
Minnesota Vikings

Jeff Siemon
LINEBACKER
Minnesota Vikings

Jim Bakken
KICKER
St. Louis Cardinals

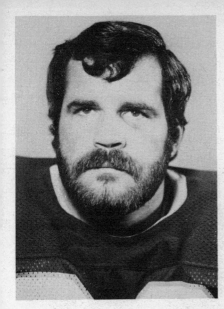

Bill Bergey
LINEBACKER
Philadelphia Eagles

Rich Saul
CENTER
Los Angeles Rams

Don Dierdorf
TACKLE
St. Louis Cardinals

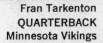

Fran Tarkenton
QUARTERBACK
Minnesota Vikings

Jack Youngblood
DEFENSIVE END
Los Angeles Rams

Brad Van Pelt
LINEBACKER
New York Giants

Blaine Nye
GUARD
Dallas Cowboys

Roger Staubach
QUARTERBACK
Dallas Cowboys

Walter Payton
RUNNING BACK
Chicago Bears

Harvey Martin
DEFENSIVE END
Dallas Cowboys

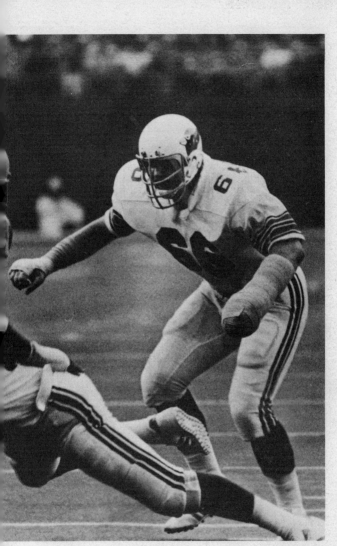

Conrad Dobler
GUARD
St. Louis Cardinals

Tommy Hart
DEFENSIVE END
San Francisco 49ers

Drew Pearson
WIDE RECEIVER
Dallas Cowboys

Billy Joe DuPree
TIGHT END
Dallas Cowboys

lead with 29 catches. Scott caught 26 for 512 yards and six TDs—not too bad. Latta had 18 for 254, which was about two weeks' work in the old WFL. Shanklin is top drawer but his wheels aren't, and the Bears hope for a recovery. Rather would rather catch the football.

Interior Linemen	Ht.	Wt.	Age	Exp.	College
Antoine, Lionel (T)	6-6	263	27	6	Southern Illinois
Jiggetts, Dan (T)	6-4	276	23	2	Harvard
Jackson, Noah (G)	6-2	273	26	3	Tampa
Sorey, Revie (G)	6-2	269	24	3	Illinois
Sevy, Jeff (G)	6-5	261	27	3	California
Neal, Dan (C)	6-4	250	28	5	Kentucky
Ward, John (C)	6-4	266	29	7	Oklahoma State
Peiffer, Dan (C)	6-3	254	26	3	S.E. Missouri
Lick, Dennis (T)	6-3	275	23	2	Wisconsin
Albrecht, Ted (T)	6-4	260	22	R	California

T=tackle   G=guard   C=center

Regulars are Antoine, Jackson, Neal, Sevy, and Lick. Antoine may give way to Jiggetts, and Sorey is challenging Sevy. A pulling guard would help here. Lick will improve even more this year than he did as a rookie. Albrecht may be just the type Payton likes to have up front.

Kickers	Ht.	Wt.	Age	Exp.	College
Parsons, Bob (P)	6-5	241	27	6	Penn State
Thomas, Bob (Pk)	5-10	174	25	3	Notre Dame

Pk=placekicker   P=punter

Parsons punted 99 times in 1976 for 37.6. Not bad, but not real good. Thomas was 12 of 25 on FGs; he's good in close, but erratic from past the 40. Parsons is also a tight end.

DEFENSE

Front Linemen	Ht.	Wt.	Age	Exp.	College
Hartenstine, Mike (E)	6-3	250	24	3	Penn State
Berry, Royce (E)	6-3	244	31	9	Houston
Meyers, Jerry (E)	6-4	255	23	2	Northern Illinois
Osborne, Jim (T)	6-3	251	28	6	Southern U.
Rydalch, Ron (T)	6-4	267	25	3	Utah
Hrivnak, Gary (E, T)	6-5	251	26	5	Purdue
Chambers, Wally (T)	6-6	250	26	5	Eastern Kentucky
Stillwell, Roger (E)	6-6	250	26	3	Stanford

E=end   T=tackle

Coach Pardee's pride and joy is the defense. The rush line has the great Chambers, Stillwell, Hartenstine, and Osborne. Stillwell is coming off surgery, but he is tough. Rydalch is a valued reserve. Berry does his part when he plays.

Linebackers	Ht.	Wt.	Age	Exp.	College
Brupbacher, Ross (O)	6-3	212	29	5	Texas A&M
Hicks, Tom (O)	6-4	235	25	2	Illinois
Buffone, Doug (O)	6-2	229	33	12	Louisville
Rives, Don (M)	6-2	226	26	4	Texas Tech
Muckensturm, Jerry (M)	6-4	226	24	2	Arkansas State
Bryant, Waymond (O)	6-3	239	25	4	Tennessee State
Malham, Mickey (O)	6-2	210	24	2	Arkansas State

O=outside   M=middle

Brupbacher is a solid outside linebacker. He had seven interceptions in 1976. Buffone is hoping to recover soon from two operations for Achilles tendon problems. Rives surprised with a hard-hitting performance as middle backer last year. Bryant plays if Buffone can't. The others are second-year men awaiting their opportunities.

Cornerbacks	Ht.	Wt.	Age	Exp.	College
Ellis, Allan	5-10	183	26	5	UCLA
Schmidt, Terry	6-0	178	25	4	Ball State
Livers, Virgil	5-8½	178	25	3	Western Kentucky
Spivey, Mike	6-0	196	22	R	Colorado

Last year Chicago tied Detroit for third in NFC interceptions with 24. Ellis stole six. Livers had three and is improving steadily. Schmidt is the backup.

Safeties	Ht.	Wt.	Age	Exp.	College
Plank, Doug	5-11½	203	24	3	Ohio State
Knox, Bill	5-9	195	26	4	Purdue
Fencik, Gary	6-1	188	23	2	Yale
Clemons, Craig	5-11	195	28	6	Iowa

Plank had four interceptions and was hard to beat in 1976. Clemons is pretty solid. Neither Knox nor Fencik is expected to get much time this year.

Note: A complete listing of Chicago's 1977 college draft selections can be found on page 248.

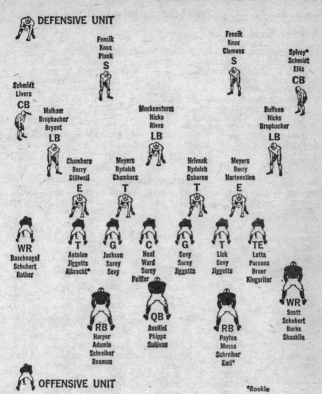

DEFENSIVE UNIT

Fencik
Knox
Plank
S

Fencik
Knox
Clemons
S

Spivey*
Schmidt
Ellis
CB

Schmidt
Livers
CB

Malham
Brupbacher
Bryant
LB

Muckensturm
Hicks
Rives
LB

Buffone
Hicks
Brupbacher
LB

Chambers
Berry
Stillwell
E

Meyers
Rydalch
Chambers
T

Hrivnak
Rydalch
Osborne
T

Meyers
Berry
Hartenstine
E

WR
Baschnagel
Schubert
Rather

T
Antoine
Jiggetts
Albrecht*

G
Jackson
Sorey
Sevy

C
Neal
Ward
Sorey
Peiffer

G
Sevy
Sorey
Jiggetts

T
Lick
Sevy
Jiggetts

TE
Latta
Parsons
Bruer
Kingsriter

WR
Scott
Schubert
Burks
Shanklin

RB
Harper
Adamle
Schreiber
Reamon

QB
Avellini
Phipps
Sullivan

RB
Payton
Musso
Schreiber
Earl*

OFFENSIVE UNIT

*Rookie

1976 BEARS STATISTICS

	Bears	Opps.
Total Points Scored	253*	216
Total First Downs	201	249
Third-Down Efficiency	70—212	80—222
Yards Rushing—First Downs	2363—115	1984—103
Passes Attempted—Completions	278—123	401—200
Yards Passing—First Downs	1480—67	2217—128
QB Sacked—Yards Lost	24—225	49—395
Interceptions—Return Average	24—9.0	15—14.2
Punts—Average Yards	100—37.3	85—36.3
Punt Returns—Return Average	43—6.3	44—7.9
Kickoff Returns—Return Average	51—21.3	54—17.9
Fumbles—Ball Lost	24—13	37—23
Penalties—Yards	114—984	87—699

* Includes two safeties

STATISTICAL LEADERS

Scoring	TDs	Rush.	Pass.	Ret.	PATs	FGs	Total
Payton	13	13	0	0	0	0	78
Thomas	0	0	0	0	27—30	12—25	63
Scott	6	0	6	0	0	0	36
Musso	4	4	0	0	0	0	26
Harper	3	2	1	0	0	0	18
Adamle	1	0	1	0	0	0	8

Rushing	Atts.	Yds.	Avg.	Longest	TDs
Payton	311	1390	4.5	60	13
Harper	147	625	4.3	28	2
Musso	57	200	3.5	11	4
Adamle	33	93	2.8	12	0
Avellini	18	58	3.2	15	1

Passing	Atts.	Com.	Yds.	Pct.	Int.	Longest	TDs
Avellini	271	118	1580	43.5	15	63 (TD)	8
Carter	5	3	77	60.0	0	55 (TD)	1
Parsons	2	2	48	100.0	0	25	0

Receiving	No.	Yds.	Avg.	Longest	TDs
Harper	29	291	10.0	39 (TD)	1
Scott	26	512	19.7	63 (TD)	6
Latta	18	254	14.1	58	0
Payton	15	149	9.9	34	0
Baschnagel	13	226	17.4	58	0

Interceptions	No.	Yds.	Avg.	Longest	TDs
Brupbacher	7	49	7.0	25	0
Ellis	6	47	7.8	22 (TD)	1
Plank	4	31	7.8	15	0
Livers	3	34	11.3	18	0
Bryant	2	6	3.0	3	0

Punting	No.	Yds.	Avg.	Longest	Inside 20	Blocked
Parsons	99	3726	37.6	62	20	1

Punt Returns	No.	FCs	Yds.	Avg.	Longest	TDs
Livers	28	0	205	7.3	51	0
Schubert	11	5	60	5.5	14	0

Kickoff Returns	No.	Yds.	Avg.	Longest	TDs
Baschnagel	29	754	26.0	48	0
Adamle	11	179	16.3	30	0
Harper	6	119	19.8	30	0

DETROIT LIONS

Head Coach: Tommy Hudspeth
(took over in midseason of 1976)

2nd Year   **Record: 5–5**

1976 RECORD (6–8) (capital letters indicate home games)			1977 SCHEDULE (capital letters indicate home games)	
3	Chicago	10	Chicago	Sept. 18
24	ATLANTA	10	NEW ORLEANS	Sept. 25
9	MINNESOTA	10	PHILADELPHIA	Oct. 2
14	Green Bay	24	Minnesota	Oct. 9
30	NEW ENGLAND	10	GREEN BAY	Oct. 16
7	Washington	20	San Francisco	Oct. 23
41	Seattle	14	Dallas	Oct. 30
27	GREEN BAY	6	SAN DIEGO	Nov. 6
23	Minnesota	31	Atlanta	Nov. 13
16	New Orleans	17	TAMPA BAY	Nov. 20
14	CHICAGO	10	CHICAGO (TV)	Nov. 24
27	BUFFALO	14	Green Bay	Dec. 4
10	N.Y. Giants	24	Baltimore	Dec. 11
17	LOS ANGELES	20	MINNESOTA (night, TV)	Dec. 17

Second place, their perennial spot, looked mighty good to the Detroit Lions when they came in third behind the Chicago Bears—and under .500–with only 6–8. Tommy Hudspeth, the personnel director turned coach, kept the coaching job by default when Swede Knox elected to remain with the Rams.

Hudspeth opened up a stodgy offense with the double wing and a double wide-receiver attack—and he witnessed the almost complete renaissance of quarterback Greg Landry. With Ed Hughes now the quarterback coach after years with Tom Landry at Dallas, the Cowboy shotgun may be used on third and long—which will save Landry's questionable knees. Landry had his best year in 1976 with a passing percentage of 57.7 and a No. 2 rating (behind James Harris) in the NFC. But owner William Clay Ford isn't one of his biggest boosters.

Detroit self-destructed against New Orleans and the New York Giants or they could have been 8–6 and second again. They were 1–6 on the road, which tells you something. Detroit lives on its defense, which was rated second in the NFC last year; the Lions surrendered only 3,587 yards overall. Jim Mitchell and Ken Sanders were standouts as Detroit survived the loss of three good tackles through surgery—Herb Orvis, Doug English, and Larry Hand. All return.

At linebacker, Charlie Weaver and Paul Naumoff had excellent years in 1976. The secondary has big-name bodies, but it gets beat at the wrong times too often. Charlie West has a bad knee and might pack it in. James Hunter, last year's No. 1 Lion draftee, might switch to corner from safety. Lem Barney and Levi Jackson did reasonably well last year, but here Dick Jauron's return after an injury may require some shuffling.

Offensively, the whole thing needs something different. Detroit did hang 262 points on the board in 1976 —not bad, but they didn't always get those points when they were needed. They lost to the Rams by three points and to the Vikings by the margin of a botched extra point. Dexter Bussey and Lawrence Gaines have 100-yard potential every game, but better reserve strength is needed.

J. D. Hill is back at wide receiver, which should help. He was lost in game No. 1 last year, leaving Ray Jarvis as the wide man. Jarvis was voted the MVP. Tight end Charlie Sanders is All-Pro, and rookie David Hill would start on some teams. The offensive line was spotty in 1976; Detroit came out fifth in rushing offense with 2,213 yards. Lynn Boden was inconsistent, while Rockne Freitas played well at tackle.

The Lions' statistics are better than their 6–8 won-lost record. When Rick Forzano was fired, he was in the midst of a player revolt and was 1–3. Hudspeth never made up those two games, but went 5–5. The .500 rut is where Detroit has been for over a decade; the Lions have never really been serious contenders.

With J. D. Hill, the Lions should have a deep threat if Landry's passing game remains constant. The offensive line opens holes pretty well, but last year they didn't really protect Landry, who still scrambles pretty well, even if gingerly, on those surgical knees. Detroit was sacked 67 times—a record.

Whether the relatively inexperienced Hudspeth, a front-office player evaluator, is the answer remains to be seen. Joe Thomas can judge pure playing talent but would never last as a coach. The cold-blooded approach turns off most men in the trenches. Hudspeth was rated warm and understanding by the Lion players, who really fired Forzano and forced a change to a softer boss.

In Detroit, nothing short of first place is good enough. The fans turn out in the three-year-old Pon Met, the domed stadium in Pontiac, Michigan, but the Lions are almost a comic strip in the newspapers.

Landry is 31 and must do the job or Hudspeth will turn to Joe Reed. Reed doesn't put it up that much, but runs a ball-control type of game—something some coaches want but most fans don't. Behind Landry and Reed is WFL reject Gary Danielson.

The Lions have a losing syndrome to overcome—most of it caused over the years by the presence of the awesome Minnesota Vikings in their division. When Minnesota clinches the division title every season, Detroit either starts its annual drive from the depths for second place and respectability, or lets down and slips out of second, as it finally did last year. There seems to be no answer, and, with Chicago coming of age, William Clay Ford's team may become No. 3 permanently.

OFFENSE

Quarterbacks	Ht.	Wt.	Age	Exp.	College
Landry, Greg	6-4	205	31	10	Massachusetts
Reed, Joe	6-1	195	29	6	Mississippi State
Danielson, Gary	6-2	195	26	2	Purdue

Landry has changed from a Fran Tarkenton-type scrambler to a good passing quarterback. Still, in 1976, he rushed for 234 yards to wind up fourth on the team, and passed for 17 TDs. Reed is the type of journeyman pro backup every team needs. Danielson is a hope, and that's all.

Running Backs	Ht.	Wt.	Age	Exp.	College
Bussey, Dexter	6-1	210	25	4	Texas—Arlington
Thompson, Bobby	5-11	195	30	3	Oklahoma
Hooks, Jim	5-11	225	26	4	Central State (Okla.)
Gaines, Lawrence	6-1	240	24	2	Wyoming
King, Horace	5-10	210	24	3	Georgia
Bolton, Andy	6-1	205	23	2	Fisk
Owens, Steve	6-2	215	30	7	Oklahoma
Kane, Rick	6-0	200	22	R	San Jose State

Bussey ground out 858 yards in 1976 and can go over 1,000 easily this year. Thompson is Bussey's relief. Hooks has potential if he overcomes his knee trouble. Gaines was a great rookie find; last year he got 659 yards, second only to Bussey. King can run over people whenever he gets to play. Bolton is a reserve at this point. Owens, the only Lion ever to rush 1,000 yards in a season, will try to make a comeback from the knee surgery that has plagued him for two years. He even went into retirement last year; now he wants to play again.

Receivers	Ht.	Wt.	Age	Exp.	College
Jarvis, Ray (W)	6-0	190	28	7	Norfolk State
Picard, Bob (W)	6-3	205	28	5	Eastern Washington
Hill, J. D. (W)	6-1	185	29	7	Arizona State
Sanders, Charlie (T)	6-4	230	31	10	Minnesota
Hill, David (T)	6-2	220	23	2	Texas A&I
Whyte, Dan (T)	6-2	225	23	1	Johnson C. Smith
Walton, Larry (W)	6-0	185	30	9	Arizona State
Thompson, Leonard (W)	5-10	190	25	3	Oklahoma State

W=wide receiver   T=tight end

Detroit and Washington were tied to lead the NFC last year with 20 TDs via the air, and part of the reason was surprise offensive MVP Ray Jarvis, who made 39 catches for 822 yards. And Sanders finally was used to better ends last year, with 35 for 545. Both men got five TDs. Bussey and Gaines carried the ball as pass receivers 28 and 23 times respectively. King did the same 21 times, and Walton worked in as the second wide man with 20. J. D. Hill's return helps the wide-receiver-based attack, making it a real scoring threat from every point on the field.

Interior Linemen	Ht.	Wt.	Age	Exp.	College
Hertwig, Craig (T)	6-8	270	25	3	Georgia
Yarborough, Jim (T)	6-5	265	31	9	Florida
Bolinger, Russ (G)	6-5	255	24	2	Long Beach State
Boden, Lynn (G)	6-5	270	24	3	South Dakota State
Morris, Jon (C)	6-4	250	35	14	Holy Cross
Markovich, Mark (C)	6-5	255	25	4	Penn State
Kowalkowski, Bob (G)	6-3	245	34	12	Virginia
Long, Ken (G)	6-3	265	24	2	Purdue
Freitas, Rockne (T)	6-6	275	32	10	Oregon State

T=tackle   G=guard   C=center

The regulars are Hertwig, Bolinger, Morris, Kowalkowski, and Freitas. Last year Hertwig pushed out Yarborough; Boden flunked, and Bolinger took his job for the most part. Markovich is the backup center, while Long is the swing man at guard. Check your program numbers—there may be some changes here.

Kickers	Ht.	Wt.	Age	Exp.	College
Weaver, Herman (P)	6-4	210	29	8	Tennessee
Ricardo, Benny (Pk)	5-10	175	23	2	San Diego State

Pk=placekicker   P=punter

Thunderfoot Weaver was not in the top ten last year, but he averaged 39.5. Ricardo may be the answer as the placekicker. He was ten of 14 on FGs after replacing Errol Mann, who wound up in the Super Bowl.

DEFENSE

Front Linemen	Ht.	Wt.	Age	Exp.	College
Sanders, Ken (E)	6-5	245	27	6	Howard Payne
Price, Ernest (E)	6-4	245	37	5	Texas A&I
Mitchell, Jim (T)	6-3	250	29	8	Virginia State
Orvis, Herb (T)	6-5	255	31	6	Colorado
Howard, Billy (E)	6-4	255	27	4	Alcorn State
English, Doug (T)	6-5	255	25	3	Texas
Woodcock, John (T)	6-3	240	23	2	Hawaii

Hand, Larry (T)	6-4	245	37	13	Appalachian State
Croft, Don (T)	6-4	255	28	6	Texas—El Paso

E=end   T=tackle

One of Detroit's strengths is the rush line, even if oldish Larry Hand is coming off a knee while playing out his option. So, in fact, are English and Orvis. Sanders and Mitchell are extra good, and Woodcock and Howard filled in for the injured stars last year. It will shake down with some of the older guys gone.

Linebackers	Ht.	Wt.	Age	Exp.	College
Naumoff, Paul (O)	6-1	215	32	11	Tennessee
Ten Napel, Garth (O)	6-1	210	23	2	Texas A&M
Laslavic, Jim (M)	6-2	240	26	5	Penn State
O'Neil, Ed (M)	6-3	235	25	4	Penn State
Weaver, Charlie (O)	6-2	225	28	7	Southern California

O=outside   M=middle

Naumoff is super good. Weaver is more than competent. Laslavic at times makes like Joe Schmidt in the middle. The reserves aren't really with it, so backup help is needed.

Cornerbacks	Ht.	Wt.	Age	Exp.	College
Barney, Lem	6-0	190	32	11	Jackson State
Jauron, Dick	6-0	190	27	5	Texas A&I
Williams, Walt	6-3	196	22	R	New Mexico State

The ball-snagging Lions finished third in NFC interceptions with 24 in 1976. Levi Johnson grabbed six to come in second only to James Hunter. Barney had only two but played more conservatively. The Lions have released veteran Ben Davis.

Safeties	Ht.	Wt.	Age	Exp.	College
West, Charlie	6-1	190	31	10	Texas—El Paso
Tyler, Maurice	6-1	190	27	5	Morgan State
Hunter, James	6-3	195	23	2	Grambling
Jauron, Dick	6-0	190	27	5	Yale

Hunter led the team with seven interceptions in 1976. West played well after Jauron got hurt, but Jauron should reclaim his spot. Tyler always makes the roster.

Note: A complete listing of Detroit's 1977 college draft selections can be found on page 251.

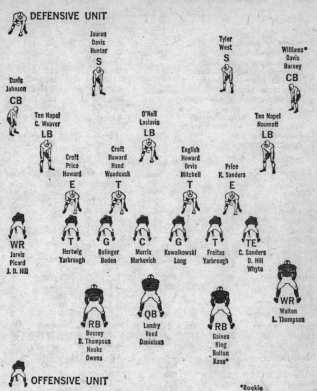

DEFENSIVE UNIT

Jauron
Davis
Hunter
S

Tyler
West
S

Williams*
Davis
Barney
CB

Davis
Johnson
CB

Ten Napel
C. Weaver
LB

O'Nell
Laslavic
LB

Ten Napel
Naumoff
LB

Croft
Price
Howard
E

Croft
Howard
Hand
Woodcock
T

English
Howard
Orvis
Mitchell
T

Price
K. Sanders
E

WR
Jarvis
Picard
J. D. Hill

Hertwig
Yarbrough
T

Bolinger
Boden
G

Morris
Markovich
C

Kowalkowski
Long
G

Freitas
Yarbrough
T

C. Sanders
D. Hill
Whyte
TE

RB
Bussey
B. Thompson
Hooks
Owens

QB
Landry
Reed
Danielson

RB
Gaines
King
Bolton
Kane*

WR
Walton
L. Thompson

OFFENSIVE UNIT

*Rookie

1976 LIONS STATISTICS

	Lions	Opps.
Total Points Scored	262	220
Total First Downs	259	191
Third-Down Efficiency	74—209	57—205
Yards Rushing—First Downs	2213—123	1901—94
Passes Attempted—Completions	356—201	313—137
Yards Passing—First Downs	2140—120	1686—76
QB Sacked—Yards Lost	67—490	28—218
Interceptions—Return Average	24—18.5	12—10.1
Punts—Average Yards	84—39.0	83—40.6
Punt Returns—Return Average	31—6.7	39—37.1
Kickoff Returns—Return Average	47—21.0	55—21.6
Fumbles—Ball Lost	38—21	27—15
Penalties—Yards	97—819	88—700

STATISTICAL LEADERS

Scoring	TDs	Rush.	Pass.	Ret.	PATs	FGs	Total
Ricardo	0	0	0	0	19—21	10—14	49
Sanders	5	0	5	0	0	0	30
Jarvis	5	0	5	0	0	0	30
Hill, David	5	0	5	0	0	0	30
Gaines	5	4	1	0	0	0	30
Mann	0	0	0	0	9—10	4—10	21
Bussey	3	3	0	0	0	0	18
Walton	3	0	3	0	0	0	18

Rushing	Atts.	Yds.	Avg.	Longest	TDs
Bussey	196	858	4.4	46	3
Gaines	155	659	4.3	26 (TD)	4
King	93	325	3.5	22	0
Landry	43	234	5.4	28	1
Reed	11	63	5.7	14	1
Thompson, Bobby	13	42	3.2	9	0

Passing	Atts.	Com.	Yds.	Pct.	Int.	Longest	TDs
Landry	291	168	2191	57.7	8	74 (TD)	17
Reed	62	32	425	51.6	3	57	3

Receiving	No.	Yds.	Avg.	Longest	TDs
Jarvis	39	822	21.1	74 (TD)	5
Sanders	35	545	15.6	36	5
Bussey	28	218	7.8	27	0
Gaines	23	130	5.7	24	1
King	21	163	7.8	19	0
Walton	20	293	14.7	28 (TD)	3
Hill, David	19	249	13.1	24 (TD)	5

Interceptions	No.	Yds.	Avg.	Longest	TDs
Hunter	7	120	17.1	39 (TD)	1
Johnson	6	206	34.3	76	1
Barney	2	62	31.0	26	1
Weaver, Charlie	2	24	12.0	19	0

Punting	No.	Yds.	Avg.	Longest	Inside 20	Blocked
Weaver, Herman	83	3280	39.5	69	15	1

Punt Returns	No.	FCs	Yds.	Avg.	Longest	TDs
Barney	23	22	191	8.3	30	0
West	3	2	9	3.0	4	0
Hunter	4	0	7	1.8	5	0

Kickoff Returns	No.	Yds.	Avg.	Longest	TDs
Hunter	14	375	26.8	84	0
Thompson, Bobby	22	431	19.6	59	0
Thompson, Leonard	5	86	17.2	32	0

GREEN BAY PACKERS

Head Coach: Bart Starr

3rd Year

Record: 9–19

1976 RECORD (5–9) (capital letters indicate home games)			1977 SCHEDULE (capital letters indicate home games)	
14	SAN FRANCISCO	26	New Orleans	Sept. 18
0	St. Louis	29	HOUSTON	Sept. 25
7	Cincinnati	28	Minnesota	Oct. 2
24	DETROIT	14	vs. Cincinnati at Milwaukee	Oct. 9
27	Seattle (at Milwaukee)	20	Detroit	Oct. 16
28	PHILADELPHIA	13	Tampa Bay	Oct. 23
14	Oakland	18	CHICAGO	Oct. 30
6	Detroit	27	Kansas City	Nov. 6
32	New Orleans (at Milwaukee)	27	vs. Los Angeles	
13	Chicago	24	at Milwaukee	Nov. 13
10	Minnesota (at Milwaukee)	17	Washington (night, TV)	Nov. 21
10	CHICAGO	16	MINNESOTA	Nov. 27
9	Minnesota	20	DETROIT	Dec. 4
24	Atlanta	20	Chicago	Dec. 11
			vs. San Francisco	
			at Milwaukee	Dec. 18

Bart Starr is finding that coaching and managing aren't nearly as easy as quarterbacking. At one time in his career, he was co-starter at Green Bay with a chap named Lamar McHan. Since McHan also punted, and Starr didn't fill the air like Sonny Jurgensen, there were those who thought Starr might not stick. Vince Lombardi decided otherwise, and slowly developed Bart into the consummate field general he became.

The present Green Bay general manager and coach doesn't have choices like that. He doesn't have the talent to make those kinds of picks.

Last year's 5–9 mark might even have been a mirage, achieved with all-out effort and a weak schedule (which gets tougher this year). Detroit is more than a single game better than Green Bay, and the Pack isn't, realistically, only two games back of the talented Chicago Bears.

What are Green Bay's biggest weaknesses? The receiving corps is poor. The offensive line is very shaky now that Gale Gillingham has definitely retired. The running back situation is deteriorating, and the defensive line is only average at best. Linebacker is unsettled. No Packer was selected for the Pro Bowl, which about sums it up.

Over the past five years Green Bay has traded away 13 draft picks and has only one man left on the roster to show for it. The John Hadl experiment at quarterback was the most damaging of all.

Starr had his contract extended for two more years, which he will need, and this season Green Bay finally does have a full quota of draft picks. Bart shook up the coaching staff last year after he accepted the resignations of offensive coordinator Paul Roach and offensive line coach Leon McLaughlin. Starr will handle the offense himself and Bill Curry will replace McLaughlin. Bob Lord was switched from special-teams coach to offensive backfield coach.

The retirement of Gillingham left the Packers' offensive line with Mark Koncar, Bruce Van Dyke, Larry McCarren, Mel Jackson, and Dick Himes as the regulars. Van Dyke and Himes almost retired, but finally decided to give it another go-round. Despite his bad knee, which caused him to quit, Gillingham was still Green Bay's most consistent lineman last year. Journeymen Bob Hyland and Dick Enderle, both former Giants, are the reserves, and help is needed.

The Green Bay backfield—where Starr, Paul Hornung, and Jim Taylor once roamed—now has Randy Johnson and Carlos Brown as quarterbacks. Johnson is better than people think, but he didn't cut it with the Falcons or the Giants, and was just a backup with

Washington. John Brockington has never regained his old 1,000-yard form, and he settled for 406 yards last year. Whether his problem is the offensive line or a falling-off of ability is hard to judge. Willard Harrell headed the club's rushers last year with 435 yards; Barty Smith was third (355) behind Brockington, and Erick Torkelson was fourth (289). That's pathetic.

The quarterback experiment with Lynn Dickey ended with a 47.3 completion percentage and only seven TDs passing; then Johnson was brought in to restore some order. Right now, for better or for worse, it's Randy.

Green Bay was next to last in the NFC in overall offense in 1976; the Pack gained just 3,452 yards, edging out only the disorganized Falcons, who had 3,103. On the defensive side, the Packers did fairly well, finishing eighth with 4,123 total yards allowed. Their pass defense was pretty good—fourth, with only 1,835 yards surrendered—but their rushing defense gave up 2,288 yards—fourth from last in the NFC.

Despite the good pass defense, Green Bay had only 11 interceptions, which means they seldom gambled. And it means the offense hardly ever got the benefit of a break with good field position.

What can Starr and the Packers Corporation do in long-range terms? Concentrate on draft picks and build the team. If Joe Thomas means almost instant success via the draft method, why can't Green Bay do something more modest, following the same precepts? It's up to player evaluation—and scouting, something that isn't Starr's fault. Maybe he ought to work out a trade with Dallas for Gil Brandt in exchange for, say, 40 draft choices.

OFFENSE

Quarterbacks	Ht.	Wt.	Age	Exp.	College
Johnson, Randy	6-3	205	33	11	Texas A&I
Brown, Carlos	6-3	210	25	3	Pacific (Calif.)
Dickey, Lynn	6-4	210	27	7	Kansas State

Retread Randy might fool some people if he feels the job is his. Brown has the arm, but not the head, at least not yet. The hope is that Bart can do the thinking and somebody can come along.

Running Backs	Ht.	Wt.	Age	Exp.	College
Torkelson, Eric	6-2	194	25	4	Connecticut
Harrell, Willard	5-8½	182	25	3	Pacific (Calif.)
Osborn, Dave	6-0	208	34	13	North Dakota
Brockington, John	6-1	225	29	7	Ohio State
Rambo, Dan	5-10	205	25	1	Carroll (Mont.)
Starch, Ken	5-11	219	23	2	Wisconsin
Smith, Barty	6-3½	240	25	4	Richmond
Middleton, Terdell	6-0	191	22	R	Memphis State

What running backs? Brockington has lost it and hopes to find it, but time is running out. Harrell is too small to be a big yardage man, and Osborn is a journeyman pickup from Minnesota. Torkelson is also too small to be the big bruiser Green Bay needs. Maybe Ken can put some Starch in the running attack. Middleton was drafted by St. Louis in the third round last May, then promptly sent to Green Bay in exchange for cornerback Perry Smith.

Receivers	Ht.	Wt.	Age	Exp.	College
Smith, Ollie (W)	6-3	200	28	4	Tennessee State
Odom, Steve (W)	5-8	174	25	4	Utah
McGeorge, Rich (T)	6-4	230	29	8	Elon
Askson, Burt (T)	6-2	225	32	5	Texas Southern
Payne, Ken (W)	6-1	185	27	4	Langston

W=wide receiver   T=tight end

Payne is the only top-flight receiver Green Bay has, and he gets double and triple teamed as a result. He led the club with 33 catches in 1976. McGeorge, a good tight end, caught 24, and Odom latched onto 23 last year. Askson is a WFL type who just asks to play.

Interior Linemen	Ht.	Wt.	Age	Exp.	College
Koncar, Mark (T)	6-4½	271	24	2	Colorado
Knutson, Steve (T)	6-3	254	26	3	Southern California
Van Dyke, Bruce (G)	6-2	255	33	12	Missouri
Jackson, Mel (G)	6-1	267	23	2	Southern California

Enderle, Dick (G)	6-2	250	30	9	Minnesota
McCarren, Larry (C)	6-3	248	26	5	Illinois
Hyland, Bob (C)	6-5	245	32	11	Boston College
Himes, Dick (T)	6-4	260	31	10	Ohio State
Scribner, Rick (G)	6-4	250	22	R	Idaho State

T=tackle   G=guard   C=center

Himes and Van Dyke are fairly solid performers. Jackson got playing time unexpectedly last year and did well enough. Enderle is a former Giant just hanging on. Hyland disappointed when he tried for McCarren's center spot. Koncar and Knutson handle one tackle berth and Himes holds down the other. But Fuzzy Thurstons they are not.

Kickers	Ht.	Wt.	Age	Exp.	College
Beverly, David (P)	6-2	180	27	4	Auburn
Marcol, Chester (Pk)	6-0	190	28	6	Hillsdale

Pk=placekicker   P=punter

Beverly is hardly a long-distance punter; last year he earned a 37.0 average for 83 punts. Marcol returned with ten of 19 FGs. He has done it in the past and the Packers hope he can decide a couple of close ones this season.

DEFENSE

Front Linemen	Ht.	Wt.	Age	Exp.	College
Williams, Clarence (E)	6-5	255	31	8	Prairie View
Barber, Bob (E)	6-3	240	26	2	Grambling
McCoy, M. P. (T)	6-5	275	29	8	Notre Dame
Roller, Dave (T)	6-1½	270	28	4	Kentucky
Pureifory, Dave (T)	6-1	255	28	6	Eastern Michigan
Roche, Alden (E)	6-4	255	32	8	Southern U.
Johnson, Ezra (E)	6-4	240	21	R	Morris Brown
Butler, Mike (E)	6-5	262	22	R	Kansas
Koch, Greg (T)	6-4	254	22	R	Arkansas

E=end   T=tackle

Williams, McCoy, Roller, and Roche make up the most able and strongest part of the Green Bay team. Barber and Pureifory know how to blunt an opposing offense when called upon as reserves. Depth, however, may be a problem here. Butler was a consensus All-America, and Johnson was named to several black All-Americas.

Linebackers	Ht.	Wt.	Age	Exp.	College
Weaver, Gary (O)	6-1	225	28	5	Fresno State
Toner, Tom (O)	6-3	235	27	5	Idaho State
Gueno, Jim (O)	6-2	220	23	2	Tulane

	Ht.	Wt.	Age	Exp.	College
Hansen, Don (M)	6-2	228	33	11	Illinois
Perko, Tom (M)	6-3	233	23	2	Pittsburgh
Acks, Ron (M)	6-2	225	33	10	Illinois
Carr, Fred (O)	6-5	240	31	10	Texas–El Paso

O=outside   M=middle

Weaver, Carr, and Hansen are the incumbents; Carr is the best. Perko is almost even with Hansen at MLB while Toner and Gueno are pushing Weaver—legally, that is. But this is still an unsettled area that needs attention.

Cornerbacks	Ht.	Wt.	Age	Exp.	College
Buchanon, Willie	6-0	190	27	6	San Diego State
McCoy, M. C.	5-11	183	24	2	Colorado

Buchanon is a regular, and McCoy waits in the wings. One of the better-manned positions, but more people are needed—good ones, of course.

Safeties	Ht.	Wt.	Age	Exp.	College
Luke, Steve	6-2	205	24	3	Ohio State
Hall, Charley	6-1	190	29	7	Pittsburgh
Wagner, Steve	6-2	208	23	2	Wisconsin
Gray, Johnnie	5-11	185	24	3	Fullerton State

Gray led the Pack with four interceptions in 1976, and Luke had two. They are the regular safeties. Hall is a capable swing man. Wagner is hoping for that break.

Note: A complete listing of Green Bay's 1977 college draft selections can be found on page 251.

DEFENSIVE UNIT

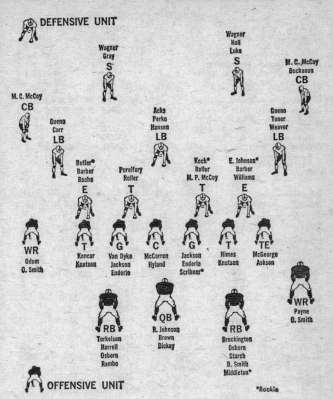

Wagner
Gray
S

Wagner
Hall
Luke
S

M. C. McCoy
Buchanon
CB

M. C. McCoy
CB

Gueno
Carr
LB

Acks
Perko
Hansen
LB

Gueno
Toner
Weaver
LB

Butler*
Barber
Roche
E

Purelfory
Roller
T

Koch*
Roller
M. P. McCoy
T

E. Johnson*
Barber
Williams
E

WR
Odom
O. Smith

T
Koncar
Knutson

G
Van Dyke
Jackson
Enderle

C
McCarren
Hyland

G
Jackson
Enderle
Scribner*

T
Himes
Knutson

TE
McGeorge
Askson

WR
Payne
O. Smith

RB
Torkelson
Harrell
Osborn
Rambo

QB
R. Johnson
Brown
Dickey

RB
Brockington
Osborn
Starch
B. Smith
Middleton*

OFFENSIVE UNIT

*Rookie

1976 PACKERS STATISTICS

	Packers	Opps.
Total Points Scored	218*	299
Total First Downs	210	262
Third-Down Efficiency	79—223	77—212
Yards Rushing—First Downs	1722—99	2288—132
Passes Attempted—Completions	357—164	354—196
Yards Passing—First Downs	1730—94	1835—107
QB Sacked—Yards Lost	41—375	43—357
Interceptions—Return Average	11—17.9	22—16.5
Punts—Average Yards	84—36.6	77—38.5
Punt Returns—Return Average	40—7.5	48—5.6
Kickoff Returns—Return Average	65—20.9	44—17.8
Fumbles—Ball Lost	37—23	27—15
Penalties—Yards	87—791	104—965

* Includes one safety

STATISTICAL LEADERS

Scoring	TDs	Rush.	Pass.	Ret.	PATs	FGs	Total
Marcol	0	0	0	0	24—27	10—19	54
Smith, Barty	5	5	0	0	0	0	30
Harrell	4	3	1	0	0	0	24
Payne	4	0	4	0	0	0	24
Odom	2	0	2	0	0	0	12
Torkelson	2	2	0	0	0	0	12
Brockington	2	2	0	0	0	0	12

Rushing	Atts.	Yds.	Avg.	Longest	TDs
Harrell	130	435	3.3	56	3
Brockington	117	406	3.5	29	2
Smith, Barty	97	355	3.7	16	5
Torkelson	88	289	3.3	15	2

Passing	Atts.	Com.	Yds.	Pct.	Int.	Longest	TDs
Dickey	243	115	1465	47.3	14	69 (TD)	7
Johnson	35	21	249	60.0	1	45	0
Brown	74	26	333	35.1	6	47	2

Receiving	No.	Yds.	Avg.	Longest	TDs
Payne	33	467	14.2	57 (TD)	4
McGeorge	24	278	11.6	28	1
Odom	23	456	19.8	66 (TD)	2
Smith, Ollie	20	364	18.2	47	1
Torkelson	19	140	7.4	31	0
Harrell	17	201	11.8	69 (TD)	1
Smith, Barty	11	88	8.0	35	0
Brockington	11	49	4.5	20	0

Interceptions	No.	Yds.	Avg.	Longest	TDs
Gray	4	101	25.3	67	1
Luke	2	30	15.0	15	0
Buchanon	2	28	14.0	22	0

Punting	No.	Yds.	Avg.	Longest	Inside 20	Blocked
Beverly	83	3074	37.0	60	14	1

Punt Returns	No.	FCs	Yds.	Avg.	Longest	TDs
Gray	37	7	307	8.3	27	0

Kickoff Returns	No.	Yds.	Avg.	Longest	TDs
McCoy, M. C.	18	457	25.4	65	0
Odom	29	610	21.0	88	0
Torkelson	6	123	20.5	29	0

TAMPA BAY BUCCANEERS

Head Coach: John McKay

2nd Year **Record:** 0–14

1976 RECORD (0–14) (capital letters indicate home games)		1977 SCHEDULE (capital letters indicate home games)	
0	Houston	20	Philadelphia	Sept. 18
0	SAN DIEGO	23	MINNESOTA (night)	Sept. 24
9	BUFFALO	14	Dallas	Oct. 2
17	Baltimore	42	WASHINGTON	Oct. 9
0	Cincinnati	21	Seattle	Oct. 16
10	Seattle	13	GREEN BAY	Oct. 23
20	MIAMI	23	San Francisco	Oct. 30
19	KANSAS CITY	28	Los Angeles	Nov. 6
13	Denver	48	N.Y. GIANTS	Nov. 13
0	N.Y. Jets	34	Detroit	Nov. 20
7	CLEVELAND	24	ATLANTA	Nov. 27
16	Oakland	49	CHICAGO	Dec. 4
0	Pittsburgh	42	New Orleans	Dec. 11
14	NEW ENGLAND	31	ST. LOUIS	Dec. 18

The Buccaneers became the first team in NFL history to lose their entire schedule, 14 games, in one season. And it didn't sit well with coach John McKay, who was used to winning big with Southern Cal.

Injuries and personnel changes played havoc with the Tampa Bay roster. Of the 39 offensive players who made the first preseason trip to Los Angeles, only 14 remained, or were able to play, by the season's finale. The defense decreased from 33 players to eight. Tampa Bay sold 38,500 season tickets, and now must worry whether building a team in a long, hard process will dim the enthusiasm of the Bay residents. But 1977 No. 1 NFL draftee Ricky Bell should draw plenty of fans to the games.

The Bucs were decimated by injuries last year, but

was that luck or a lack of conditioning? They had 17 players on the injured reserved list, an NFL high. The defense lost six starters to the injury total, and also lost middle guard Dave Pear for the final game. Lost for the season with knee injuries were Jim and Calvin Peterson, linebackers; cornerbacks Danny Reece and Mike Washington; and linemen Leroy and Dewey Selmon.

The offense was hit too, but not that hard; tackle Dave Reavis was out with knee surgery and running back Charlie Davis was sidelined in mid-year with a lame knee. Rookie quarterback Parnell Dickinson, who started once, had knee surgery too.

Seattle obviously did better than Tampa Bay in the expansion draft, and perhaps in the collegiate selections as well. Of the 20 college players picked by Tampa Bay, only four remained at the year's end. And the Bucs weren't the Pittsburgh Steelers with veterans at every position. The openings were there, but still, only defensive back Curtis Jordan, running back Jimmy DuBose, and offensive linemen Steve Young and Steve Wilson survived.

Early on this spring, McKay struck to deal with his quarterback problem, releasing veteran Steve Spurrier on waivers. The former Heisman Trophy winner started 12 of the games in the 1976 0–14 season. At the same time, quarterback Gary Huff, a pocket passer, was acquired from Chicago in a draft-choice trade. A winning QB is sought.

The addition of Anthony Davis, a hero with USC and with the Southern California Sun of the defunct WFL, is interesting, and you can be sure that he'll get to run back kicks and punts and handle the ball on at least every other play this year. He didn't see enough of that with Toronto in the Canadian loop, so the Bucs bought out his contract and signed him, gaining his NFL draft rights from the Jets.

"USC East," as the Bucs have been nicknamed (and don't think McKay doesn't resent it), thus will present all-USC starting runners, with 1976 rushing leader Louis Carter and runner-up Ed Williams in reserve. With former Oakland Raiders Harold Hart and Charlie Davis returning from the injured list and Bell on hand, running back shouldn't be a problem.

The receiving corps wasn't too bad in 1976; Morris Owens led the way. This year rookie George Ragsdale, the preseason whiz, will also come off the injured list. The Bucs do need mobile linebackers, offensive and defensive linemen, and that previously mentioned winning quarterback.

The physical condition of all the knee cases is critical. Will Lee Roy Selmon make it all the way back? McKay is still very high on him. If some of the knees don't hold up, the Tampa Bay defense could crumble, but only time can tell.

In order to get more NFL smarts into the situation, McKay hired Bill Nelson as the quarterback coach; he hopes Nelson can develop David Jaynes, Gary Huff, and Scott Gardner into tough quarterbacks. Willie Brown has moved from coaching receivers to coaching offensive backs, and Dick Voris has moved up from linebacker coach to personnel coordinator. Wayne Fontes continues with the secondary. Tom Bass is in charge of research after coaching the linebackers last year, and Phil Kreuger will assist with the linebackers.

It's obvious that McKay has reevaluated the prospects ahead for him and Tampa Bay. He desperately wants to win as many as four games and could be on the griddle if something positive doesn't happen with his all-USC running corps.

Tampa Bay has been switched to the NFC Central,

which means that the black-and-blue cold-belters from Minnesota, Chicago, Detroit, and Green Bay now have a warm-weather spot to vacation in. The Bucs hope to win some games on just that alone. Sand does have a way of getting into shoes.

OFFENSE

Quarterbacks	Ht.	Wt.	Age	Exp.	College
Dickinson, Parnell	6-2	185	24	2	Mississippi Valley
Gardner, Scott	6-2	200	24	1	Virginia
Jaynes, David	6-2	210	25	1	Kansas
Huff, Gary	6-1	198	26	5	Florida State

Steve Spurrier was sent packing in the spring of 1977. Huff came down from Chicago and has a chance to become McKay's man on the field. Parnell Dickinson is a future whom QB coach Bill Nelson will work with. Gardner is a hopeful. Jaynes still bounces from camp to camp after trying out with the Chiefs four years ago. Maybe Nelson can come up with a quarterback who can sell oranges.

Running Backs	Ht.	Wt.	Age	Exp.	College
Williams, Ed	6-1	245	26	4	Langston
DuBose, Jimmy	5-11	217	23	2	Florida
Carter, Louis	5-11	209	24	3	Maryland
Davis, Anthony	5-10	190	25	R	Southern California
Davis, Charlie	5-11	200	25	4	Colorado
McNeill, Rod	6-2	220	26	4	Southern California
Hart, Harold	6-0	211	24	3	Texas Southern
Bell, Ricky	6-2	218	22	R	Southern California

Williams ground out 324 yards in 1976. DuBose has recovered from an ankle and may get a shot, if for no other reason than his Florida background. Carter led Tampa Bay with 521 yards last year, and if Anthony Davis plays like he did in the Canadian league, he'll regain his spot. A.D. was all-everything in college and the WFL, but a big bust north of the border. Charlie Davis returns from the injury list. McNeill is still trying, and Hart is a good prospect who was injured after coming from Oakland. Bell may just ring that for Tampa Bay.

Receivers	Ht.	Wt.	Age	Exp.	College
McKay, John (W)	5-10	178	24	2	Southern California
Douglas, Freddie (W)	5-9	185	23	2	Arkansas
Ragsdale, George (W)	5-11	185	24	1	North Carolina A&T

Moore, Bob (T)	6-2	229	28	7	Stanford
Novak, Jack (T)	6-5	240	24	3	Wisconsin
Butler, Gary (T)	6-3	235	27	5	Rice
Owens, Morris (W)	6-0	190	24	3	Arizona State
Hagins, Isaac (W)	5-9	180	23	1	Southern U.
Haggerty, Steve (W)	5-10	173	25	1	Nevada–Las Vegas

W=wide receiver   T=tight end

The boom is on for Ragsdale, who also runs back kicks. We'll see. In 1976 John McKay, the coach's son, caught 20 passes for 302 yards and one TD, thereby earning his keep; he may be too slow to start in the long run, however. Moore is the incumbent tight end; he was second in club catching with 24 last year. Owens led the Bucs in receiving and should get better.

Interior Linemen	Ht.	Wt.	Age	Exp.	College
Young, Steve (T)	6-8	272	24	2	Colorado
Reavis, Dave (T)	6-5	250	27	2	Arkansas
Harper, Calvin (T)	6-5	275	25	1	Illinois State
Fest, Howard (G)	6-6	263	31	10	Texas
Ryczek, Dan (C)	6-3	250	27	5	Virginia
Gluchoski, Allen (C)	6-2	240	23	1	West Virginia
Wilson, Steve (G)	6-5	268	23	2	Georgia
Alward, Tom (G)	6-4	255	24	2	Nebraska
Johnson, Randy (G)	6-2	255	25	1	Georgia
Current, Mike (T)	6-4	270	32	11	Ohio State
Little, Everett (T)	6-4	265	25	2	Houston
Schaukowitch, Carl (G)	6-2	237	26	2	Penn State

T=tackle   G=guard   C=center

In 1976, Tampa Bay rushed next to last in the AFC (their previous residence), gaining only 1,503 yards. This means that incumbents Young, Fest, Ryczek, Wilson, and Current will be challenged, if at all possible. Reavis will get a look at either tackle or guard, and so will Alward and Little. Gluchoski bids to back up Ryczek. Schaukowitch was acquired from Denver on waivers. A three-year NFL veteran, he's also a Penn State engineering graduate who invents things. Perhaps he'll come up with an offensive machine that works for Tampa Bay.

Kickers	Ht.	Wt.	Age	Exp.	College
Green, Dave (P, Pk)	6-0	208	27	5	Ohio
Albert, Sergio (Pk)	6-3	195	25	3	U.S. International
Hunt, George (Pk)	6-1	215	28	6	Tennessee

Pk=placekicker   P=punter

Green did well with his kicks in 1976—when he had the opportunity. The Bucs didn't always get that close to the uprights. Albert once kicked for St. Louis in the tall shadow of Jim Bakken.

DEFENSE

Front Linemen	Ht.	Wt.	Age	Exp.	College
Rudolph, Council (E)	6-4	255	27	6	Kentucky State
Guy, Tim (E)	6-5	243	25	1	Oregon
Pear, Dave (T)	6-2	248	24	3	Washington
Bradley, Otha (T)	6-2	260	26	R	Southern California
Selmon, Lee Roy (E)	6-3	263	23	2	Oklahoma
Toomay, Pat (E)	6-6	244	29	8	Vanderbilt
Robinson, Glenn (E)	6-6	245	25	3	Oklahoma State
Hannah, Charles (E)	6-6	243	22	R	Alabama

E=end   T=tackle

At the end, Tampa Bay was using the 3–4 defense with Rudolph, Pear, and Leroy Selmon as the rush liners. Injury problems must be solved, or there'll be another year of yielding enough rushing yardage (2,560 in 1976) to rank third from last in conference ratings. Toomay could help if he wants to.

Linebackers	Ht.	Wt.	Age	Exp.	College
Peterson, Calvin (O)	6-3	215	25	4	UCLA
Maughan, Steve (O)	6-1	210	24	1	Utah State
Ball, Larry (M)	6-6	235	28	6	Louisville
Watson, Brad (M)	6-3	245	26	1	Western Kentucky
Pagac, Fred (M)	6-0	220	25	3	Ohio State
Wood, Richard (M)	6-2	215	24	3	Southern California
Lemon, Mike (M)	6-2	220	26	3	Kansas
Scavella, Steadman (M)	6-1	230	24	1	Miami (Fla.)
Peterson, Jim (O)	6-4	226	28	4	San Diego State
Gunn, Jimmy (O)	6-2	231	28	7	Southern California
Sims, Jimmy (O)	6-0	195	28	2	Southern California
Marion, Frank (O)	6-3	230	27	1	Florida A&M
Selmon, Dewey (M)	6-1	254	23	2	Oklahoma
Lewis, Dave (O)	6-4	230	22	R	Southern California

O=outside   M=middle

Calvin Peterson, Ball, Wood, and Jim Peterson are the four key men here. Many others will be tried, and perhaps Marion will surface— he was outstanding in the WFL. Maughan, out all last year, will present a good claim in 1977. The early depth chart shows Dewey Selmon at linebacker instead of tackle. He's coming off an injury.

Cornerbacks	Ht.	Wt.	Age	Exp.	College
Washington, Mike	6-3	190	25	2	Alabama
Jordan, Curtis	6-2	182	23	2	Texas Tech
Pierson, Reggie	5-11	185	24	2	Oklahoma State
Hogan, Floyd	5-11	180	24	1	Arkansas

Reece, Danny	5-11	190	22	2	Southern California
Word, Roscoe	5-11	170	25	4	Jackson State
Collier, Ozell	5-10	180	26	1	Colorado

Washington, Reece, and Word are the real pros amongst the corners. The Bucs intercepted only nine passes and were strafed via the air last year. Hogan will try to become one of the Heroes in 1977.

Safeties	Ht.	Wt.	Age	Exp.	College
Cotney, Mark	6-0	207	25	3	Cameron State
Arnold, Chris	6-2	200	25	2	Virginia State
Stone, Ken	6-1	180	27	5	Vanderbilt
Davis, Ricky	6-0	178	24	3	Alabama

Cotney is the strong side safety. Stone is the resident free safety, but he faces a challenge from Davis.

Note: A complete listing of Tampa Bay's 1977 college draft selections can be found on page 260.

DEFENSIVE UNIT 3-4 DEFENSE

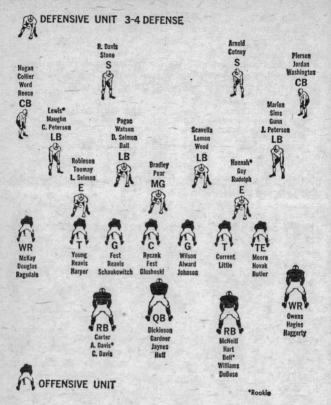

R. Davis
Stone
S

Arnold
Cotney
S

Hogan
Collier
Word
Reece
CB

Pierson
Jordan
Washington
CB

Lewis*
Maughn
C. Peterson
LB

Pagac
Watson
D. Selmon
Ball
LB

Scavella
Lemon
Wood
LB

Marion
Sims
Gunn
J. Peterson
LB

Robinson
Toomay
L. Selmon
E

Bradley
Pear
MG

Hannah*
Guy
Rudolph
E

WR
McKay
Douglas
Ragsdale

T
Young
Reavis
Harper

G
Fest
Reavis
Schaukowitch

C
Ryczek
Fest
Glushoski

G
Wilson
Alward
Johnson

T
Current
Little

TE
Moore
Novak
Butler

WR
Owens
Hagins
Haggerty

RB
Carter
A. Davis*
C. Davis

QB
Dickinson
Gardner
Jaynes
Huff

RB
McNeill
Hart
Bell*
Williams
DuBose

OFFENSIVE UNIT

*Rookie

1976 BUCCANEERS STATISTICS

	Buccaneers	Opps.
Total Points Scored	125	412
Total First Downs	191	283
Third-Down Efficiency	51—206	88—206
Yards Rushing—First Downs	1503—71	2560—136
Passes Attempted—Completions	376—181	321—180
Yards Passing—First Downs	1503—93	2241—124
QB Sacked—Yards Lost	50—423	24—171
Interceptions—Return Average	9—11.0	20—24.5
Punts—Average Yards	92—39.3	65—39.3
Punt Returns—Return Average	43—8.5	71—10.9
Kickoff Returns—Return Average	70—21.3	35—20.5
Fumbles—Ball Lost	30—17	33—19
Penalties—Yards	109—875	109—935

STATISTICAL LEADERS

Scoring	TDs	Rush.	Pass.	Ret.	PATs	FGs	Total
Owens	6	0	6	0	0	0	36
Green	0	0	0	0	11—14	8—14	35
Johnson	2	1	1	0	0	0	12
Williams	2	2	0	0	0	0	12

Rushing	Atts.	Yds.	Avg.	Longest	TDs
Carter	171	521	3.0	26	1
Williams	87	324	3.7	19	2
Johnson	47	166	3.5	27	1
McNeill	27	135	5.0	17	0
Davis, Charlie	41	107	2.6	13	1
Dickinson	13	103	7.9	46	0
DuBose	20	62	3.1	24	0
Spurrier	12	48	4.0	10	0

Passing	Atts.	Com.	Yds.	Pct.	Int.	Longest	TDs
Spurrier	311	156	1628	50.2	12	38	7
Dickinson	39	15	210	38.5	5	49	1
Hanratty	14	6	32	42.9	1	12	0

Receiving	No.	Yds.	Avg.	Longest	TDs
Owens	30	390	13.0	27 (TD)	6
Johnson	25	201	8.0	38	1
Moore, Bob	24	289	12.0	31	0
Williams	23	166	7.2	18	0
McKay	20	302	15.1	49	1
Carter	20	135	6.8	19	0

Interceptions	No.	Yds.	Avg.	Longest	TDs
Cotney	3	25	8.3	25	0
Stone	2	47	23.5	26	0
Jordan	2	10	5.0	10	0

Punting	No.	Yds.	Avg.	Longest	Inside 20	Blocked
Green	92	3619	39.3	56	12	0

Punt Returns	No.	FCs	Yds.	Avg.	Longest	TDs
Reece	20	0	143	7.2	30	0
Moore, Manfred	14	0	106	7.6	21	0
Douglas	4	0	78	19.5	32	0
Cotney	3	0	26	8.7	9	0

Kickoff Returns	No.	Yds.	Avg.	Longest	TDs
McNeill	17	384	22.6	43	0
Johnson	13	287	22.1	32	0
Carter	15	300	20.0	30	0
Douglas	7	167	23.9	29	0
Moore, Manfred	7	134	19.1	27	0

LOS ANGELES RAMS

Head Coach: Chuck Knox

5th Year

Record: 44–11–1

1976 RECORD (10–3–1) (capital letters indicate home games)				1977 SCHEDULE (capital letters indicate home games)	
30	Atlanta	14		Atlanta	Sept. 18
10	Minnesota (in OT)	10		PHILADELPHIA	Sept. 25
24	N.Y. GIANTS	10		SAN FRANCISCO	Oct. 2
31	Miami	28		Chicago (night, TV)	Oct. 10
0	SAN FRANCISCO	16		NEW ORLEANS	Oct. 16
20	CHICAGO	12		MINNESOTA (night, TV)	Oct. 24
16	New Orleans	10		New Orleans	Oct. 30
45	SEATTLE	6		TAMPA BAY	Nov. 6
12	Cincinnati	20		vs. Green Bay at Milwaukee	Nov. 13
28	ST. LOUIS	30		San Francisco	Nov. 20
23	San Francisco	3		Cleveland	Nov. 27
33	NEW ORLEANS	14		OAKLAND	Dec. 4
59	ATLANTA	0		ATLANTA	Dec. 11
20	Detroit	17		Washington (TV)	Dec. 17
	Playoffs				
14	Dallas	12			
13	Minnesota	24			

If Joe Willie Namath is to be the saviour who'll take the frustrated Rams to the Super Bowl, don't tell Pat Haden or James Harris, the incumbent L.A. quarterbacks. The acquaintance between ex-Jet Namath and Rams owner Carroll Rosenbloom, former owner of the Baltimore Colts, goes back to the 1969 Super Bowl, when Broadway Joe made whoopee on Saturday night and still had enough left on the ball to beat Rosenbloom's Colts on Super Sunday.

The Rams have now won the NFC West four years in a row and should win it again in 1977, with only token resistance from the San Francisco 49ers, but they fail at the only thing that really counts in California—the Big One. The run-happy Rams, with ball-control Harris and Haden running things, have all sorts of problems that Namath cannot change. Can

Joe make Harold Jackson, the premier wide receiver, happy by putting the ball up more often? Yes, he can, but he may not get the chance if coach Swede Knox has his way. Namath is most likely to play only when the Rams are playing catch-up. Then he'll read the defenses and fill the air with passes.

Right now, Haden is No. 1, and Knox wants James Harris to accept his role as No. 2 and be happy. That may not be possible, and if Harris insists on a trade, enter Namath.

The Rams scored the most NFC points in 1976 (351) and were tied with San Francisco for the runner-up spot for the fewest allowed (190). They limited the opposition to 3,656 yards overall, third in the conference, and their defense against the rush was tops (1,564 yards). Against the pass, the Rams allowed 2,092 yards, which landed them much further down in the ratings.

Haden is now accepted as the Rams' leader. He did a good job when he took over for the injured Harris in mid-year 1976; he passed for 57.1 percent and eight TDs. Harris, the statistical leader in the NFC, was 57.6 and also eight TDs. But the gut feeling is that Harris cannot win the big one, and that Haden, who doesn't have the arm James has, can.

The Rams' attack was first in the NFC in number of rushes (613) and yardage gained (2,528). It was led by Lawrence McCutcheon, who is glad he refused to shuffle off to Buffalo and make room for O. J. Simpson. John Cappelletti did well as the No. 2 back, and Los Angeles also has Jim Bertelsen, Rod Phillips, and specialist Cullen Bryant.

Despite the shuffling of quarterbacks, L.A. was fifth in NFC passing last year with 2,341 yards. Jackson led with 39 catches and 751 yards, and Ron Jessie was second with 34 and 779. All-NFC tight end

Charles Young, late of the Eagles, should make the attack even stronger, and he won't hurt the blocking either.

The Rams' defense is solid and the retirement of Merlin Olsen isn't likely to cause tremors on the playing field. Jack Youngblood, Mike Fanning, Larry Brooks, and Fred Dryer are the front four, with Jim Youngblood, Hacksaw Reynolds, and Isiah Robertson the linebackers. Dave Elmendorf leads a slick secondary.

Los Angeles is reportedly seeking a placekicker to succeed Tom Dempsey, whose failure at short range and astonishing success on long-distance kicks confuse and cause concern among the Rams' brass. Ex-CFL star Ian Sunter and Glen Walker are part of this derby. Rusty Jackson is the punter, but the Rams have had four punters in four years and another change wouldn't surprise anyone, although Jackson averaged 39.0 in 1976—not bad by NFL standards.

The Rams have suffered for a long time with the image of a club possessing overwhelming talent, but still unable to go all the way. In the pre-Rosenbloom era, the quarterback was Roman Gabriel, and in the early Rosenbloom–Knox days it was a combination of John Hadl and Gabriel, then Hadl and Harris, and now Haden–Harris. Will Namath–Haden–Harris finally achieve what the others couldn't?

The matter of pass protection is another crucial factor. The Rams work the sweeps very well, but don't really protect their passer. Ask Harris and Haden. Remember what San Francisco did to the Rams' front line in that national TV confrontation? Doug France, Tom Mack, Rich Saul, Dennis Harrah, and John Williams move people out, but don't always hold them out when the flow reverses. Namath must be protected, if he is to play—and so, for that matter, must Haden and Harris. Otherwise no quarterback can get the Rams to the Super Bowl.

OFFENSE

Quarterbacks	Ht.	Wt.	Age	Exp.	College
Haden, Pat	5-11	182	24	2	Southern California
Harris, James	6-4	210	30	8	Grambling
Namath, Joe	6-2	200	34	13	Alabama

Haden is a Rhodes scholar who is counted upon to "think" the Rams into the Super Bowl, if not in 1977, then eventually. His arm isn't a rifle, but he gets the job done and the troops believe in him. Harris has all the tools, including a good arm, and might still pull it off if he gets the chance under the right conditions. Weeb Ewbank, Namath's coach in the Jets' glory days, says Joe's knees are good and healthy.

Running Backs	Ht.	Wt.	Age	Exp.	College
McCutcheon, Lawrence	6-1	205	27	5	Colorado State
Bertelsen, Jim	5-11	205	27	6	Texas
Bryant, Cullen	6-1	235	26	5	Colorado
Scribner, Rob	6-0	200	26	5	UCLA
Cappelletti, John	6-1	217	25	4	Penn State
Phillips, Rod	6-0	220	25	3	Jackson State
Davis, Bradford	5-11	215	24	2	Louisiana State
Jodat, Jim	5-11	210	23	1	Carthage
Henson, John	6-1	228	24	1	Calif. Poly–SLO
Tyler, Wendell	5-10	188	22	R	UCLA
Waddy, Billy	5-11	184	22	R	Colorado

McCutcheon annually grinds out 1,000 yards, so why should 1977 be any different? Bertelsen is bouncing back from an injury and may challenge Cappelletti for the No. 2 running spot (which Bertelsen once owned). Bryant runs back punts and kicks with ease, and he can block with abandon in a regular spot if needed. Cappelletti proved his point last year and should do even better this time around. Phillips is another bruiser who fits into the run-oriented Rams' attack. Davis and the other rookies can only hope at present. Waddy can also play wide receiver. Tyler had a good record at UCLA.

Receivers	Ht.	Wt.	Age	Exp.	College
Jackson, Harold (W)	5-10	175	31	10	Jackson State
Scales, Dwight (W)	6-2	170	24	2	Grambling
Miller, Willie (W)	5-9	172	30	3	Colorado State
Nelson, Terry (T)	6-2	230	26	4	Arkansas AM&N

Jessie, Ron (W)	6-0	185	29	7	Kansas
Geredine, Tom (W)	6-2	189	27	4	N.E. Missouri
Gustafson, Ron (W)	6-1	185	24	1	North Dakota
Taylor, Jerrald (W)	6-2	187	25	1	Texas A&I
Young, Charles (T)	6-4	238	26	5	Southern California
Johns, Freeman (W)	6-1	175	23	1	Southern Methodist

W=wide receiver   T=tight end

Jackson is a premier wide receiver who wants to see the ball more, but he threatens to play out his option. Jessie is on a par with Jackson in ability and latched onto 34 passes last year to provide part of a double-barrelled deep aerial threat. Scales is the heir apparent if Jackson moves on. Geredine is behind Jessie, who can be temperamental. The addition of Young from the Eagles in the Jaworksi swap means that Klein will sometimes hit the bench.

Interior Linemen	Ht.	Wt.	Age	Exp.	College
France, Doug (T)	6-5	260	24	3	Ohio State
Slater, Jackie (T)	6-4	252	23	2	Jackson State
Mack, Tom (G)	6-3	250	34	12	Michigan
Horton, Greg (G)	6-4	245	26	2	Colorado
Saul, Rich (C)	6-3	250	29	8	Michigan State
Williams, John (G)	6-3	256	32	10	Minnesota
Harrah, Dennis (G)	6-5	257	24	3	Miami (Fla.)
Nuzum, Rick (C)	6-4	238	25	1	Kentucky
Fulton, Ed (G)	6-4	245	22	R	Maryland
Kahn, Mitch (C)	6-3	225	22	R	UCLA

T=tackle   G=guard   C=center

A solid group, recast with young men. France, Mack, Saul, Harrah, and Williams are the starters. Saul always has aches and pains, but he plays anyway. Pass protection is the offensive line's weakness on an otherwise blue-chip unit. Kahn and Fulton add nearly a quarter of a ton to the line.

Kickers	Ht.	Wt.	Age	Exp.	College
Jackson, Rusty (P)	6-2	190	27	2	Louisiana State
Dempsey, Tom (Pk)	6-1	260	30	9	Palomar J.C.
Walker, Glen (P, Pk)	6-2	220	25	1	Southern California
Sunter, Ian (Pk)	6-0	205	24	1	(none)

Pk=placekicker   P=punter

Jackson may be the 1977 punter and he may not, depending on a lot of things that can happen in camp and elsewhere. Dempsey is good on the long ones, inaccurate on the short ones. Figure that one out. Walker and Sunter will try to become regulars, or at least fairly active irregulars. Sunter set some placekicking records in the Canadian league.

DEFENSE

Front Linemen	Ht.	Wt.	Age	Exp.	College
Youngblood, Jack (E)	6-4	255	27	7	Florida
Jones, Cody (E)	6-5	240	26	4	San Jose State
Fanning, Mike (T)	6-6	260	24	3	Notre Dame
Brooks, Larry (T)	6-3	255	27	6	Virginia State
Dryer, Fred (E)	6-6	240	31	9	San Diego State
Cowlings, Al (E)	6-5	245	30	7	Southern California

E=end   T=tackle

The front four is very good, with Jack Youngblood getting better all the time, Fanning taking over and maturing, and Brooks likewise developing. Dryer has some weaknesses, but he does put pressure on the passer. Brooks and Youngblood know how to annoy the opposing passer, too. Retired Merlin Olsen may not be missed.

Linebackers	Ht.	Wt.	Age	Exp.	College
Youngblood, Jim (O)	6-3	239	27	5	Tennessee Tech
McLain, Kevin (O)	6-2	238	23	2	Colorado State
Kay, Rick (O)	6-4	235	28	4	Colorado
Rogers, Mel (O)	6-2	230	30	5	Florida A&M
Reynolds, Jack (M)	6-1	232	30	8	Tennessee
McCartney, Ron (O)	6-1	220	23	1	Tennessee
Ekern, Carl (M)	6-3	220	23	2	San Jose State
Robertson, Isiah (O)	6-3	225	28	7	Southern U.
Brudzinski, Bob (O)	6-4	224	22	R	Ohio State

O=outside   M=middle

Hacksaw Reynolds didn't make the Pro Bowl, but he's still super. Jim Youngblood is showing steady know-how, and Robertson is at a career peak. McLain may play more often as Youngblood shifts to middle occasionally, but Reynolds isn't likely to let that happen very often. Brudzinski was a consensus All-America.

Cornerbacks	Ht.	Wt.	Age	Exp.	College
Perry, Rod	5-9	170	24	3	Colorado
Thomas, Pat	5-9	180	23	2	Texas A&M
Jackson, Monte	5-11	189	24	3	San Diego State
Butler, Greg	5-10	175	24	1	Howard
Cromwell, Nolan	6-1	196	22	R	Kansas

The Rams led the NFL in interceptions in 1976 with 32, Jackson's ten being the best individual effort in the league. Perry garnered eight, and that should take care of the L.A. corners nicely. Cromwell turns defensive plays into offensive ones.

Safeties	Ht.	Wt.	Age	Exp.	College
Elmendorf, Dave	6-1	195	28	7	Texas
Simpson, Bill	6-1	180	26	4	Michigan State
Edwards, Oscar	6-0	187	22	R	UCLA

Elmendorf is a veteran strong safety who makes few mistakes. Simpson took over in 1976 and is consolidating his position. Cornerback Pat Thomas can also swing over to safety. Edwards signed on as a post-draft free agent (call it the mythical Round 13).

Note: A complete listing of Los Angeles's 1977 college draft selections can be found on page 253.

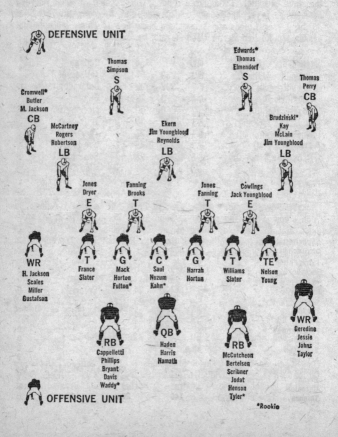

1976 RAMS STATISTICS

	Rams	Opps.
Total Points Scored	351	190
Total First Downs	265	213
Third-Down Efficiency	101—225	69—205
Yards Rushing—First Downs	2528—143	1564—79
Passes Attempted—Completions	315—171	397—199
Yards Passing—First Downs	2341—111	2092—118
QB Sacked—Yards Lost	32—288	45—395
Interceptions—Return Average	32—11.8	15—14.1
Punts—Average Yards	79—38.1	95—41.2
Punt Returns—Return Average	52—9.2	39—7.2
Kickoff Returns—Return Average	44—23.3	70—19.8
Fumbles—Ball Lost	29—21	31—16
Penalties—Yards	83—764	81—740

STATISTICAL LEADERS

Scoring	TDs	Rush.	Pass.	Ret.	PATs	FGs	Total
Dempsey	0	0	0	0	36—44	17—26	87
McCutcheon	11	9	2	0	0	0	66
Jessie	6	0	6	0	0	0	36
Jackson, Harold	5	0	5	0	0	0	30
Haden	4	4	0	0	0	0	24
Jackson, Monte	3	0	0	3	0	0	18
Bryant	3	2	0	1	0	0	18
Harris	2	2	0	0	0	0	12
Cappellettl	2	1	1	0	0	0	12
Bertelsen	2	2	0	0	0	0	12

Rushing	Atts.	Yds.	Avg.	Longest	TDs
McCutcheon	291	1168	4.0	40	9
Cappellettl	177	688	3.9	38	1
Phillips	34	206	6.1	33	1
Bertelsen	42	155	3.7	18	2
Haden	25	84	3.4	16	4
Harris	12	76	6.3	20	2

Passing	Atts.	Com.	Yds.	Pct.	Int.	Longest	TDs
Harris	158	91	1460	57.6	6	80 (TD)	8
Haden	105	60	896	57.1	4	65 (TD)	8
Jaworskl	52	20	273	38.5	5	42	1

Receiving	No.	Yds.	Avg.	Longest	TDs
Jackson, Harold	39	751	19.3	65 (TD)	5
Jessie	34	779	22.9	58 (TD)	6
Cappelletti	30	302	10.1	32 (TD)	1
McCutcheon	28	305	10.9	42	2

Interceptions	No.	Yds.	Avg.	Longest	TDs
Jackson, Monte	10	173	17.3	46 (TD)	3
Perry	8	79	9.9	43	0
Simpson	4	62	15.5	30	0
Robertson	4	28	7.0	14	0

Punting	No.	Yds.	Avg.	Longest	Inside 20	Blocked
Jackson, Rusty	77	3006	39.0	61	16	2

Punt Returns	No.	FCs	Yds.	Avg.	Longest	TDs
Bryant	29	2	321	11.1	25	0
Bertelsen	10	0	55	5.5	19	0
Scribner	8	1	54	6.8	20	0

Kickoff Returns	No.	Yds.	Avg.	Longest	TDs
Bryant	16	459	28.7	90 (TD)	1
Geredine	9	181	20.1	27	0
Thomas	7	140	20.0	30	0

SAN FRANCISCO 49ers

Head Coach: Ken Meyer

1st Year

1976 RECORD (8–6) (capital letters indicate home games)			1977 SCHEDULE (capital letters indicate home games)	
26	Green Bay	14	Pittsburgh (night, TV)	Sept. 19
12	CHICAGO	19	MIAMI	Sept. 25
37	Seattle	21	Los Angeles	Oct. 2
17	N.Y. JETS	6	ATLANTA	Oct. 9
16	Los Angeles	0	N.Y. Giants	Oct. 16
33	NEW ORLEANS	3	DETROIT	Oct. 23
15	ATLANTA	0	TAMPA BAY	Oct. 30
20	St. Louis (in OT)	23	Atlanta	Nov. 6
21	WASHINGTON	24	New Orleans	Nov. 13
16	Atlanta	21	LOS ANGELES	Nov. 20
3	LOS ANGELES	23	NEW ORLEANS	Nov. 27
20	MINNESOTA	16	Minnesota	Dec. 4
7	San Diego (in OT)	13	DALLAS (night, TV)	Dec. 12
27	New Orleans	7	vs. Green Bay at Milwaukee	Dec. 18

The Joe Thomas earthquake has hit the Bay Area and shaken Monte Clark loose from his job as the 'Niners coach. Thomas, who is generally credited with building the Minnesota Vikings, Miami Dolphins, and Baltimore Colts into powerhouses, is part of an ownership group that purchased the 49ers from the founding family of Tony Morabito. And there's a name that goes all the way back to the days of Frankie Albert and the old All-America Conference.

Clark had righted the ship, gotten San Francisco off to a 6–1 start, slipped a bit to 2–5 in the second part of 1976, and finished 8–6. San Francisco beat Los Angeles 16–0 on national TV, and later beat Super-Bowl-bound Minnesota. Jim Plunkett did his thing, which is sometimes good, and sometimes—well, just sometimes.

Taking over to succeed Clark is Ken Meyer, a former 49er assistant who for the past four years has served as offensive coordinator for the high-scoring Rams. He was also once a member of the New York Jets' staff under Weeb Ewbank. And now, Clark's legacy to Meyer is a quarterback problem.

Many feel that Plunkett, for whom the 49ers had traded away three draft picks and a reserve passer, failed last year. Plunkett, who was also controversial while he was with New England, didn't finish among the top ten NFL passers. He did reach 51.9 percent completions, which is better than the sub-50-percent seasons he's had in the past. He passed for 13 TDs and was intercepted 16 times—an old habit.

Rookie Scott Bull, an unknown really, may get a real look from Meyer. The 6-5, 211-pound Bull has a zest and enthusiasm that are contagious.

The offensive line, again a cause for concern in 1976—especially when Woody Peoples was hurt—did develop young Jean Barrett, who finally found a home at tackle. With Gene Washington, Jim Lash, and a healthy Willie McGee as the receivers, Plunkett (or whoever passes) should have no complaints. The running attack got great efforts last year from Wilbur Jackson and Delvin Williams, who broke the 1,000-yard barrier.

The defensive line is great; in 1976 Tommy Hart starred on national TV as the leader of the 'Niners sack pack. He eventually wound up with 16, fourth in the NFL. Veteran Cedrick Hardman and youngsters Cleveland Elam and Jimmy Webb are equally superb. Outside linebacker is also solid. Last year saw the development of a surprise in Dave Washington, and then the 49ers always have reliable Skip Vanderbundt. Willie Harper backs it up. Frank Nunley is getting older at middle backer and may need some relief.

In the secondary, someone is finally going to claim Jimmy Johnson's job. The 16-year cornerback has retired, but at the moment there are no obvious candidates to fill his very specialized shoes. Overall, the defense was the best in the NFC in 1976 and second only to the Steelers' Iron Curtain in the entire league. The 49ers led the loop in quarterback sacks with an astounding 61.

The injection of new financial strength—and Joe Thomas—into the Bay scene bodes well for San Francisco fans even though, at present, there is great resentment over the firing of Clark. After all, he was a *winning* coach, a type that isn't always easy to come by in the NFL.

Clark left because his original contract also gave him control over areas of draft, personnel changes, trades, and the like. These are the very areas in which Thomas excels, although his ruthless tactics turn off most fans (and many players and coaches who happen to get involved in his front-office operations). Thomas can judge a player as well as almost anyone in the game—and he can call the turn on a player who is near the end of the line. Witness his decision that linebacker Mike Curtis was nearing his finale with Baltimore. Curtis was made available to the Seattle expansion team, and had an uncharacteristically poor year in 1976.

In the past, Thomas was the man who traded away Johnny Unitas, a Colt institution, to San Diego—and watched as the Chargers wound up paying the over-aged Johnny U for nothing. Enter Bert Jones. Down the road, Joe Thomas will build the 'Niners until some day they can challenge Al Davis's Oakland Raiders—who recently, as Kipling might have said, have been coming up like thunder from across the Bay.

OFFENSE

Quarterbacks	Ht.	Wt.	Age	Exp.	College
Plunkett, Jim	6-2	219	30	7	Stanford
Bull, Scott	6-5	211	24	2	Arkansas
Domres, Marty	6-4	220	30	9	Columbia
Lawrence, Larry	6-1	208	28	3	Iowa
Hamilton, Steve	6-4	195	23	1	Emporia State

New front-office tycoon Joe Thomas is reported to dislike heavy-footed quarterbacks, and Jim Plunkett isn't the most agile in the NFL. But Plunkett is No. 1 until they take the job away from him, and it may take Thomas a year to get around to that. Bull is just that—a bull with hope and power. Domres is a journeyman backup who failed at San Diego and Baltimore. There are reports that his arm no longer has zip. Lawrence is a good reserve who might become better known.

Running Backs	Ht.	Wt.	Age	Exp.	College
Williams, Delvin	6-0	197	26	4	Kansas
Hofer, Paul	6-0	195	25	2	Mississippi
Johnson, Kermit	6-0	202	25	3	UCLA
Jackson, Wilbur	6-1	219	26	4	Alabama
Ferrell, Bob	6-0	206	25	2	UCLA
VanWagner, Jim	6-0	200	22	R	Michigan Tech

Williams ground out 1,203 yards and won at least two games all by himself in 1976. Johnson is a good future who may do as well as a regular if he gets the chance. Jackson, who runs over people rather than around them and away from them as Williams does, rambled for 792 yards in the balanced 'Niner attack last season. Hofer and Ferrell are experience-seeking reserves. VanWagner ranks fifth among NCAA career rushing leaders.

Receivers	Ht.	Wt.	Age	Exp.	College
Washington, Gene (W)	6-1	187	30	9	Stanford
Harrison, Kenny (W)	6-0	170	24	2	Southern Methodist
Lash, Jim (W)	6-2	199	26	5	Northwestern
McGee, Willie (W)	5-11	178	27	5	Alcorn State
Rivera, Steve (W)	5-11	184	23	2	California
Isabell, Leonard (W)	6-3	185	24	1	Tulsa
Lindsey, Terry (W)	6-0	190	25	1	Fullerton State
Mitchell, Tom (T)	6-4	226	33	11	Bucknell
Obradovich, Jim (T)	6-2	225	24	3	Southern California
Nemeth, Brian (T)	6-5	230	24	1	South Carolina
Boyd, Elmo (W)	6-0	190	22	R	Eastern Kentucky

W=wide receiver   T=tight end

Wilbur Jackson came out of the backfield to tie Washington for the most club catches last year—33. RB Delvin Williams also caught 27 and tight end Mitchell 20 as Plunkett went short more often than long. If Plunkett can stabilize his passing game, San Francisco can add the long threat and make their running attack even more potent. Lash is pretty good and backs up Washington. If McGee is healthy, look out! Lindsey would play regularly on some teams. Obradovich might push the aging Mitchell. Boyd was a good pass catcher in the fast little Ohio Valley conference.

Interior Linemen	Ht.	Wt.	Age	Exp.	College
Barrett, Jean (T)	6-6	248	26	5	Tulsa
Banaszek, Cas (T)	6-3	247	32	10	Northwestern
Lawson, Steve (G)	6-3	265	28	7	Kansas
Maurer, Andy (G)	6-3	265	29	8	Oregon
Taylor, John (G)	6-4	228	24	1	Pacific (Calif.)
Watson, John (C)	6-4	244	28	7	Oklahoma
Cross, Randy (C)	6-3	247	23	2	UCLA
Vertefeuille, Brian (C)	6-3	260	26	3	Idaho State
Peoples, Woody (G)	6-2	252	34	9	Grambling
Fahnhorst, Keith (T)	6-6	256	25	4	Minnesota
Douglas, Ceaser (T)	6-5	272	23	1	Illinois Wesleyan
Ayers, John (T)	6-5	238	24	1	West Texas State
Miller, Johnny (G)	6-1	241	23	1	Livingstone

T=tackle   G=guard   C=center

This unit had Barrett, Lawson, Watson, Maurer, and Fahnhorst as regulars at season's end in 1976. They aren't exactly household names. Peoples will reclaim one guard spot, probably from Maurer. Fahnhorst moved Banaszek aside last year, but that could reverse. Some of the other young ones may get chances in what is regarded as a 'Niner weak spot.

Kickers	Ht.	Wt.	Age	Exp.	College
Wittum, Tom (P)	6-1	191	27	5	Northern Illinois
Mike-Mayer, Steve (Pk)	6-0	179	30	3	Maryland

Pk=placekicker   P=punter

A breakdown in efficiency by Mike-Mayer cost the 49ers the loss of games to St. Louis and Washington—that happened after he had kicked ten FGs in succession. Overall, he wound up 16 for 28. Wittum finished sixth in the NFL punting ratings with a 40.8 average for 89 kicks. He does fine.

DEFENSE

Front Linemen	Ht.	Wt.	Age	Exp.	College
Hart, Tommy (E)	6-4	249	33	10	Morris Brown
Sandifer, Bill (E)	6-6	260	25	4	UCLA

Lewis, Reggie (E)	6-1	248	23	1	San Diego State
Webb, Jimmy (T)	6-4	247	25	3	Mississippi State
Cooke, Bill (T)	6-5	250	26	3	Massachusetts
Hardman, Cedrick (E)	6-4	244	29	8	North Texas State
Cline, Tony (E)	6-3	244	29	8	Miami (Fla.)
Elam, Cleveland (T)	6-4	252	25	3	Tennessee State
Galigher, Ed (T)	6-4	253	27	6	UCLA

E=end   T=tackle

Regular rush liners Hart, Hardman, Elam, and Webb will be hard to dislodge. They are the NFL's best at rushing the quarterback. Cline, formerly of the Raiders, was a waiver-list find who made good on the other side of the Bay. Galigher becomes a 49er through a draft trade with the Jets.

Linebackers	Ht.	Wt.	Age	Exp.	College
Vanderbundt, Skip (O)	6-3	222	31	9	Oregon State
Mitchell, Dale (O)	6-3	223	24	2	Southern California
Holmes, Ron (O)	6-1	220	24	1	Utah State
Nunley, Frank (M)	6-2	221	32	11	Michigan
Elia, Bruce (M)	6-1	217	24	3	Ohio State
Washington, Dave (O)	6-5	228	29	8	Alcorn State
Harper, Willie (O)	6-2	208	27	5	Nebraska

O=outside   M=middle

Nunley is being pushed by Elia, but most likely won't yield his job. Vanderbundt is superb and Washington did a great job last year on the outside when he was given a chance. Harper is the needed quick swing man.

Cornerbacks	Ht.	Wt.	Age	Exp.	College
Lewis, Eddie	6-0	177	24	2	Kansas
Leonard, Anthony	5-11	170	24	2	Virginia Union
Austin, Hise	6-4	197	27	3	Prairie View
Taylor, Bruce	6-0	186	29	8	Boston University
Oliver, Frank	6-1	190	25	2	Kentucky State

Despite great pressure on the quarterback, the 49er secondary came up with only nine interceptions in 1976. Cornerback Jimmy Johnson, after 16 years, has retired; Eddie Lewis will get an uncertain first shot. Taylor is the other regular, but Joe Thomas will shake up the situation just as though he were running the show himself. (What's that again?)

Safeties	Ht.	Wt.	Age	Exp.	College
Phillips, Mel	6-1	184	35	13	North Carolina A&T
Rhodes, Bruce	6-0	187	25	2	San Francisco State

| Williams, Jackie | 5-9 | 178 | 23 | 1 | Texas A&M |
| McGill, Ralph | 5-11 | 178 | 27 | 6 | Tulsa |

Safety Phillips is back in place, and so is McGill. Rhodes has potential and the time to shake it loose.

Note: A complete listing of San Francisco's 1977 college draft selections can be found on page 259.

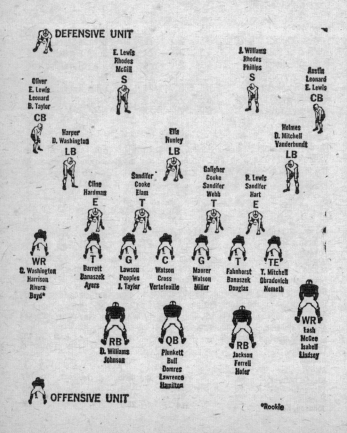

1976 49ers STATISTICS

	49ers	Opps.
Total Points Scored	270*	190
Total First Downs	242	218
Third-Down Efficiency	70—120	73—235
Yards Rushing—First Downs	2457—131	1784—94
Passes Attempted—Completions	306—155	374—180
Yards Passing—First Downs	1638—91	1776—102
QB Sacked—Yards Lost	34—325	61—573
Interceptions—Return Average	9—10.3	21—12.0
Punts—Average Yards	89—40.9	107—40.4
Punt Returns—Return Average	65—8.5	52—6.8
Kickoff Returns—Return Average	37—20.4	46—20.1
Fumbles—Ball Lost	30—13	37—16
Penalties—Yards	101—841	94—906

* Includes two safeties

STATISTICAL LEADERS

Scoring	TDs	Rush.	Pass.	Ret.	PATs	FGs	Total
Mike-Mayer	0	0	0	0	26—30	16—28	74
Williams	9	7	2	0	0	0	54
Washington, Gene	6	0	6	0	0	0	36
McGee	4	0	4	0	0	0	24
Bull	2	2	0	0	0	0	12
Jackson	2	1	1	0	0	0	12
Johnson, Sammy	2	2	0	0	0	0	12

Rushing	Atts.	Yds.	Avg.	Longest	TDs
Williams	248	1203	4.9	80 (TD)	7
Jackson	200	792	4.0	24	1
Johnson, Kermit	32	99	3.1	16	1
Plunkett	19	95	5.0	12	0
Hofer	18	74	4.1	17	0
Bull	15	66	4.4	18	2
Johnson, Sammy	24	52	2.2	12	2

Passing	Atts.	Com.	Yds.	Pct.	Int.	Longest	TDs
Plunkett	243	126	1592	51.9	16	85 (TD)	13
Bull	48	21	252	43.8	4	40	2
Domres	14	7	101	50.0	1	41	0

Receiving	No.	Yds.	Avg.	Longest	TDs
Washington, Gene	33	457	13.8	32	1
Jackson	33	324	9.9	55 (TD)	6
Williams	27	283	10.5	85 (TD)	2
Mitchell, Tom	20	240	12.0	27	1
McGee	13	269	20.7	52 (TD)	4

Interceptions	No.	Yds.	Avg.	Longest	TDs
Rhodes	3	42	14.0	30	0
Phillips	2	14	7.0	14	0
Vanderbundt	2	8	4.0	8	0

Punting	No.	Yds.	Avg.	Longest	Inside 20	Blocked
Wittum	89	3639	40.8	68	15	2

Punt Returns	No.	FCs	Yds.	Avg.	Longest	TDs
Leonard	35	5	293	8.4	60 (TD)	1
Rhodes	16	2	142	8.9	22	0
McGill	10	1	103	10.3	50 (TD)	1

Kickoff Returns	No.	Yds.	Avg.	Longest	TDs
Leonard	25	553	21.3	39	0
Hofer	5	91	18.2	23	0
Johnson, Kermit	4	114	28.5	40	0

NEW ORLEANS SAINTS

Head Coach: Hank Stram

2nd Year   Record: 4–10

1976 RECORD (4–10) (capital letters indicate home games)			1977 SCHEDULE (capital letters indicate home games)	
9	MINNESOTA	40	GREEN BAY	Sept. 18
6	DALLAS	24	Detroit	Sept. 25
27	Kansas City	17	Chicago	Oct. 2
26	HOUSTON	31	SAN DIEGO	Oct. 9
30	ATLANTA	0	Los Angeles	Oct. 16
3	San Francisco	33	St. Louis	Oct. 23
10	LOS ANGELES	16	LOS ANGELES	Oct. 30
20	Atlanta	23	Philadelphia	Nov. 6
27	Green Bay (at Milwaukee)	32	SAN FRANCISCO	Nov. 13
17	DETROIT	16	ATLANTA	Nov. 20
51	Seattle	27	San Francisco	Nov. 27
14	Los Angeles	33	N.Y. JETS	Dec. 4
6	New England	27	TAMPA BAY	Dec. 11
7	SAN FRANCISCO	27	Atlanta	Dec. 18

Hank Stram, we all are well aware, didn't win the Super Bowl last year with the Saints as he once did with the Kansas City Chiefs, but he did restore some sort of hope for the future. This was done without the services of Archie Manning, whose passing arm developed severe tendonitis that required surgery.

As a result, Bobby Scott and southpaw Bobby Douglass (believed by some to be the greatest running quarterback in history) finished up as the Saintly passers. They won twice as many games, exactly four, as the 1975 New Orleans pigskinners, but Stram was hardly satisfied. The offense improved mainly because of Chuck Muncie and Tony Galbreath, both rookie running backs. Neither gained 1,000 yards, but they were respectable as NFL rookies go. If the offense is to really take off and do the job required, Manning

228

will have to bounce back to super status and put more than 253 points on the board. That really wasn't bad, but a lot of the points came in "garbage time"—i.e., after the game's outcome was already decided.

The offensive line continues to be a juggler's paradise, just as it has been in previous regimes. This doesn't help the attack, no matter who's at quarterback.

Defensive progress will begin when the Saints acquire a pass rusher who can regularly crash into the other guys' backfield and disrupt things. (Pittsburgh has *four* such animals.) The Saints need a Jack Youngblood or a Coy Bacon or a Wally Chambers. Then the rest of the front line will be much more effective.

At present, there isn't even much chance for Stram to deal. On rating the top Saints, we come up with Muncie, Galbreath, defensive tackle Derland Moore, wide receiver Larry Burton, and defensive end Bob Pollard. Manning is untradeable because no one, not even Archie, knows if his arm can take the pressure of really throwing the football with something on it.

Stram may try to deal someone like Alvin Maxson, a reserve running back, offensive lineman Kurt Schumacher, or rush line end Steve Baumgartner. There is also the James-Harris-to-New-Orleans rumor to be dealt with if Manning's arm doesn't have its zip.

The entire history of the New Orleans franchise has been one of almost total frustration. Last year was no exception, but the high point for Stram was a personal one—the Saints beat his old team, the Chiefs, 27–17 for their first win.

New Orleans was fifth from the bottom in NFC total offense in 1976; the Saints moved only 3,758 yards. They were eighth in NFC passing—not bad, considering the constant switching around of personnel. Douglass all by himself once got 954 yards for the Chicago Bears. But between them, Douglass and Scott passed for only eight TDs in 1976—not enough to help keep the opposing defenses honest.

Stram doesn't have the linebackers to try the 3–4 defense that some of the poorer teams used successfully before they became player rich. Joe Federspiel is the best Saint backer, although the addition of Pat Hughes in a draft-choice trade with the Giants will help bolster the linebacking corps.

New Orleans just doesn't have top-flight personnel. Even Galbreath's 54 pass catches last year made him only seventh overall in the NFL; he scored only one touchdown, and, for all that huffing and puffing, gained a mere 420 yards. He was also the only receiver in the top ten who averaged less than nine yards a catch, his average being 7.8 yards. Most of Galbreath's receptions came on short dump-off passes that didn't cover much ground.

In order for Stram's regime to mean much, he must have a healthy Manning or acquire a type like James Harris or Jim Plunkett. Plunkett could actually show up in New Orleans; Joe Thomas doesn't really buy his act. (Stram and Joe are still on talking terms, and not all NFL general managers are.) The Saints need help from anywhere, but especially from Manning.

OFFENSE

Quarterbacks	Ht.	Wt.	Age	Exp.	College
Douglass, Bobby	6-4	228	29	9	Kansas
Scott, Bobby	6-1	197	28	6	Tennessee
Manning, Archie	6-3	200	28	7	Mississippi

If Manning is healthy the other guys are just average. Douglass didn't run last year, and when he passed it was still under 50 percent (in fact, it was 48.4). Scott surprised in a good, if not impressive, job with a 54.2 percent completion entry in the stats. Scott completed

103 passes on 190 throws. Douglass also made good 103 passes, but he did it on 213 throws.

Running Backs	Ht.	Wt.	Age	Exp.	College
Muncie, Chuck	6-3	220	24	2	California
Galbreath, Tony	6-0	220	23	2	Missouri
Strachan, Mike	6-0	200	24	3	Iowa State
Maxson, Alvin	5-11	201	26	4	Southern Methodist
Jones, Kim	6-4	243	24	2	Colorado State
McQuay, Leon	5-9	195	27	4	Tampa
Monroe, John	6-3	240	23	2	Bluefield State

Muncie wasn't everything he was advertised to be, and nobody is complaining to the FTC or even to Ralph Nader. He did gain 625 yards in 1976, and he managed to score twice. Galbreath took it in seven times via the ground and once overhead, and was the Saints' top running back pass catcher. Mike Strachan was used sparingly, which might have been a mistake. Maxson was big in 1975, not so big in 1976. McQuay could be a great breakaway runner if he'd take it easy. He didn't do very well running back kicks, but Stram will give him another shot this year.

Receivers	Ht.	Wt.	Age	Exp.	College
Burton, Larry (W)	6-1	193	25	3	Purdue
Owens, Tinker (W)	5-11	170	23	2	Oklahoma
Childs, Henry (T)	6-2	220	26	4	Kansas State
Seal, Paul (T)	6-4	223	25	4	Michigan
Thaxton, James (T)	6-2	230	28	4	Tennessee State
Herrmann, Don (W)	6-2	193	30	9	Waynesburg
Parker, Joel (W)	6-5	215	25	4	Florida

W=wide receiver   T=tight end

Galbreath grabbed 54 short ones last year and Herrmann caught 34 for 535 yards but never scored—a Saints' trademark, it seems. Muncie dropped his rushing role enough times to make 31 catches. Tight end Childs snagged 26; Burton pulled in 18. But the source of those passes, Manning's throwing arm, is the receiving corps' main hope.

Interior Linemen	Ht.	Wt.	Age	Exp.	College
Montgomery, Marv (T)	6-6	255	29	7	Southern California
Hart, Jeff (T)	6-5	252	24	3	Oregon State
Wickert, Tom (T)	6-4	252	25	4	Washington State
Stieve, Terry (G)	6-2	242	23	2	Wisconsin
Schumacher, Kurt (G)	6-3	246	24	3	Ohio State
Hill, John (C)	6-2	246	27	6	Lehigh
Gross, Lee (C)	6-3	235	24	3	Auburn
Zanders, Emanuel (G)	6-1	248	26	4	Jackson State

	Ht.	Wt.	Age	Exp.	
Morrison, Don (T)	6-5	250	27	7	Texas—Arlington
LeBel, Dave (T)	6-6	250	24	2	Clemson
McAleney, Ed (G)	6-3	243	24	2	Massachussetts

T=tackle   G=guard   C=center

The regulars up front are Montgomery, Stieve, Hill, Zanders, and Morrison. Odds are that only half will survive Stram's juggling as he tries to get consistency. Schumacher and Seal are the best reserves, but McAleney will also get some attention from the coaching brass.

Kickers	Ht.	Wt.	Age	Exp.	College
Szaro, Rich (Pk)	5-11	204	29	3	Harvard
Blanchard, Tom (P)	6-0	180	28	6	Oregon
Parsley, Cliff (P)	6-1	210	22	R	Oklahoma State

Pk=placekicker   P=punter

Rich Szaro did pretty well last year with 18 of 23 FGs. He will help. Blanchard retired last spring, then changed his mind and will punt again. Cliff Parsley's college career punting average was an impressive 42.7.

DEFENSE

Front Linemen	Ht.	Wt.	Age	Exp.	College
Dorris, Andy (E)	6-4	240	26	5	New Mexico State
Grooms, Elois (E)	6-4	250	24	3	Tennessee Tech
Pollard, Bob (E)	6-3	251	28	7	Weber State
Price, Elex (T)	6-3	253	27	5	Alcorn State
Winans, Jeff (T)	6-5	260	26	5	Southern California
Moore, Derland (T)	6-4	253	26	5	Oklahoma
Baumgartner, Steve (E)	6-7	255	26	5	Purdue
Ross, Louis (E)	6-7	276	30	4	S.C. State
DeBernardi, Fred (E)	6-6	250	28	2	Texas A&M
Moore, Maulty (T)	6-5	265	31	6	Bethune—Cookman
Campbell, Joe (E)	6-6	255	22	R	Maryland
Fultz, Mike (T)	6-5	275	22	R	Nebraska

E=end   T=tackle

Dorris, Pollard, Price, Moore, and Baumgartner are the best of the rush liners. They aren't as bad as their rating, but they do lack the big pass rusher who makes the rest of the job look so easy. Moore and DeBernardi each have a chance to unseat somebody. Campbell is an All-America QB sacker and pass blocker. Fultz is as big as they come.

Linebackers	Ht.	Wt.	Age	Exp.	College
Merlo, Jim (O)	6-1	220	26	4	Stanford
Bordelon, Ken (O)	6-4	236	23	2	Louisiana State

Broussard, Bubba (O)	6-2	231	25	2	Houston
Federspiel, Joe (M)	6-1	230	27	6	Kentucky
Kingrea, Rick (M)	6-1	222	28	7	Tulane
Hardin, Junior (M)	6-1	222	24	2	Eastern Kentucky
Westbrooks, Greg (O)	6-2	217	24	3	Colorado
Capone, Warren (O)	6-1	218	26	3	Louisiana State
Hughes, Pat (O)	6-2	225	30	8	Boston University
Watts, Bob (O)	6-3	220	22	R	Boston College

O=outside   M=middle

Here we have "all-everything" Capone, the bust-your-chops guy from
the WFL who had a chance with Dallas and settled for reserve duty
in New Orleans, and not with the Navy. Regulars are Federspiel, a
solid middle backer, and outside men Westbrooks and Merlo. Broussard
has a ghost of a chance. Hughes has experience. Watts was All East in
college.

Cornerbacks	Ht.	Wt.	Age	Exp.	College
Jackson, Ernie	5-10	176	27	6	Duke
Spencer, Maurice	6-0	176	25	4	N.C. Central
Chapman, Clarence	5-10	185	23	2	Eastern Michigan
Johnson, Benny	5-11	178	29	6	Johnson C. Smith

New Orleans tied the Giants with a paltry 12 pass interceptions in
1976. Jackson and Spencer aren't that bad, but they're on the field
too much and get little help from the line. Jackson did intercept two
passes last year, and linebacker Jim Merlo stole four. Johnson and
Chapman may be too small.

Safeties	Ht.	Wt.	Age	Exp.	College
Crist, Chuck	6-2	205	26	6	Penn State
Myers, Tom	5-11	180	27	6	Syracuse
Cassady, Craig	5-10	175	24	2	Ohio State

Crist is improving, but he's failed with the Giants in the past. Myers is
picking up experience, and Cassady needs it.

Note: A complete listing of New Orleans's 1977 college draft selections
can be found on page 255.

DEFENSIVE UNIT

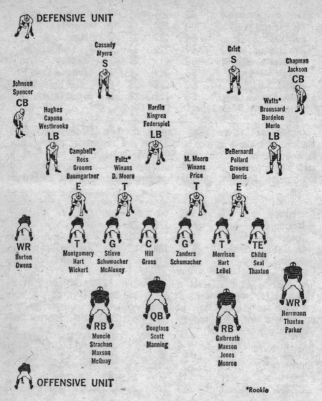

Cassady
Myers
S

Crist
S

Chapman
Jackson
CB

Johnson
Spencer
CB

Hughes
Capone
Westbrooks
LB

Hardin
Kingrea
Federspiel
LB

Watts*
Broussard
Bordelon
Merlo
LB

Campbell*
Ross
Grooms
Baumgartner
E

Fultz*
Winans
D. Moore
T

M. Moore
Winans
Price
T

DeBernardi
Pollard
Grooms
Dorris
E

WR
Burton
Owens

T
Montgomery
Hart
Wickert

G
Stieve
Schumacher
McAleney

C
Hill
Gross

G
Zanders
Schumacher

T
Morrison
Hart
LeBel

TE
Childs
Seal
Thaxton

RB
Muncie
Strachan
Maxson
McQuay

QB
Douglass
Scott
Manning

RB
Galbreath
Maxson
Jones
Monroe

WR
Herrmann
Thaxton
Parker

OFFENSIVE UNIT

*Rookie

1976 SAINTS STATISTICS

	Saints	Opps.
Total Points Scored	253	346
Total First Downs	226	275
Third-Down Efficiency	63—211	81—214
Yards Rushing—First Downs	1766—92	2280—129
Passes Attempted—Completions	402—206	367—200
Yards Passing—First Downs	1984—111	2202—121
QB Sacked—Yards Lost	51—369	39—312
Interceptions—Return Average	12—17.7	14—10.0
Punts—Average Yards	101—39.3	87—39.9
Punt Returns—Return Average	42—8.9	65—11.4
Kickoff Returns—Return Average	60—19.6	55—24.7
Fumbles—Ball Lost	31—18	37—27
Penalties—Yards	103—901	90—883

STATISTICAL LEADERS

Scoring	TDs	Rush.	Pass.	Ret.	PATs	FGs	Total
Szaro	0	0	0	0	25—29	18—23	79
Galbreath	8	7	1	0	0	0	48
Childs	4	1	3	0	0	0	24
Douglass	2	2	0	0	0	0	12
Strachan	2	2	0	0	0	0	12
Muncie	2	2	0	0	0	0	12
Merlo	2	0	0	2	0	0	12
Burton	2	0	2	0	0	0	12

Rushing	Atts.	Yds.	Avg.	Longest	TDs
Muncie	149	659	4.4	51	2
Galbreath	136	570	4.2	74 (TD)	7
Strachan	66	258	3.9	31	2
Maxson	34	120	3.5	16	1
Douglass	21	92	4.4	19	2
Scott	12	48	4.0	13	1

Passing	Atts.	Com.	Yds.	Pct.	Int.	Longest	TDs
Douglass	213	103	1288	48.4	8	74	4
Scott	190	103	1065	54.2	6	60 (TD)	4

Receiving	No.	Yds.	Avg.	Longest	TDs
Galbreath	54	420	7.8	35	1
Herrmann	34	535	15.7	57	0
Muncie	31	272	8.8	33	0
Childs	26	349	13.4	46 (TD)	3
Burton	18	297	16.5	69 (TD)	2
Owens	12	241	20.1	74	1

Interceptions	No.	Yds.	Avg.	Longest	TDs
Merlo	4	142	35.5	83 (TD)	2
Athas	2	22	11.0	22	0
Jackson	2	5	2.5	5	0

Punting	No.	Yds.	Avg.	Longest	Inside 20	Blocked
Blanchard	101	3974	39.3	63	14	0

Punt Returns	No.	FCs	Yds.	Avg.	Longest	TDs
Athas	35	10	332	9.5	67	0

Kickoff Returns	No.	Yds.	Avg.	Longest	TDs
Galbreath	20	399	20.0	32	0
Maxson	11	191	17.4	28	0
McQuay	8	151	18.9	28	0
Thaxton	8	185	23.1	41	0

ATLANTA FALCONS

Head Coach: Leeman Bennett
1st Year

1976 RECORD (4–10) (capital letters indicate home games)		1977 SCHEDULE (capital letters indicate home games)	
14	LOS ANGELES 30	LOS ANGELES	Sept. 18
10	Detroit 24	Washington	Sept. 25
10	Chicago 0	N.Y. GIANTS	Oct. 2
13	PHILADELPHIA 14	San Francisco	Oct. 9
0	New Orleans 30	Buffalo	Oct. 16
17	CLEVELAND 20	Chicago	Oct. 23
0	San Francisco 15	MINNESOTA	Oct. 30
23	NEW ORLEANS 20	SAN FRANCISCO	Nov. 6
13	Seattle 30	DETROIT	Nov. 13
21	SAN FRANCISCO 16	New Orleans	Nov. 20
17	DALLAS 10	Tampa Bay	Nov. 27
14	Houston 20	NEW ENGLAND	Dec. 4
0	Los Angeles 59	Los Angeles	Dec. 11
20	GREEN BAY 24	NEW ORLEANS	Dec. 18

Owner Rankin Smith swept the Falcon nest clean last year and started over completely. He fired Pat Peppler from both his general manager job and his temporary coaching assignments; the final straw was that horrible, embarrassing whomping the Rams administered to Atlanta on national TV in the season's final week. The score was 59–0 and it could have been worse, but not much.

What new coach Leeman Bennett and equally new general manager Eddie LeBaron can do in Year I of the New Falcons remains to be seen. And how LeBaron shapes up for a top NFL job after 14 seasons as a Las Vegas attorney—that remains to be seen, too. Familiarity with playing personnel in both NFL and collegiate circuits is vital to a club general manager's job, and directly determines just who winds up on the playing field. LeBaron, who was one of the great college quarterbacks at the University of the Pacific in the late 1940s and, later, a pro QB with Dallas and Washington, could perhaps "grow" into his post. But will Rankin Smith and the impatient Falcon fans give him the time?

Another problem LeBaron faces is the simple fact that his best defensive lineman, huge Claude Humphrey, wants out of Atlanta's losing syndrome. Back in 1968 Humphrey was NFL rookie of the year, and since then he's seen the Falcons do everything except make the playoffs—although one year they came close. Now, after a decade on the downside, Humphrey wants to see how the other half lives. Maybe he can't be blamed.

Bennett takes over a team that was dead last in NFC total offense last year; the Falcons garnered only 3,103 yards overall. Rushing netted 1,689 yards—so Atlanta did better than Seattle, if that's a comparison, which it isn't. The passing offense was dead last, but here the Seattle Seahawks came in a surprising fourth in the NFC.

Bubba Bean led the rushing in 1976 with a pedestrian 428 yards, while Haskel Stanback ran for 324—hardly enough to cure a coach's headache. Mike Esposito took the ball 60 times for an impressive average of 5.3 yards per carry, and Sonny Collins earned the fullback spot.

John Gilliam, the highly regarded wide receiver, must have wished he was back shivering in the cold northland with his former mates, the Vikings. With Atlanta, he caught only 21 passes for 292 yards and two TDs in 1976. The club's top receiver was Alfred Jenkins, who registered a neat 41 catches for 710 yards and six scores.

Whether quarterback Steve Bartkowski, the man currently in the No. 1 job—and the man with the big potential—can rebound from his knee injury is an Atlanta unknown. He got in 120 throws last season, completing 57 for a 47.5 percent completion average and two TDs. (He was intercepted nine times.) That isn't exactly a world-beating set of stats. In reserve, the Falcons have perennial NFL failure Scott Hunter who, as a rookie, did succeed in leading the vaunted Green Bay Packers to the NFC Central title; that was in 1972. Alas, the lackluster quality of Atlanta's passing game is demonstrated by the 1976 statistics, which show Bartkowski, Hunter, and the third man, Kim McQuilken, all under 505 in their completions.

To be sure, they didn't have the best-quality protection the NFL has to offer, and the Falcon passer usually looked up only to see enemy linemen converging on him one split second after the ball was snapped. This is an area Bennett *must* correct if he is to restore Bartkowski's morale and maintain his playing health. Former quarterback LeBaron may provide some help here.

One strong point is the punting of John James, who put the ball up 101 times in 1976—that's more boots than anyone else in the NFL. His 42.1 average was second only to that of Buffalo's Marv Bateman, the current punting champion. James will help gain some sort of field position or get the ball out of the end zone with his booming kicks.

Placekicker Nick Mike-Mayer connected on ten of 21 FG tries in 1976 and was perfect on points-after—20 for 20. He may find his job in jeopardy, however, if Bennett and LeBaron get on a "change-things-around" kick.

If Claude Humphrey wants out and if the Falcons decide to trade him, perhaps a major package of talent will be forthcoming from another club. What Atlanta needs is enough bodies to fill three or four spots in the lagging lineup. A first-rate running back is one critical need; Atlanta could also use offensive linemen, and, of course, some sort of rush liner to replace big Claude. If they insist on keeping him and he plays without interest, Atlanta may be worse off.

It will be interesting to see if attendance holds up under the new regime. Falcon fans are the same as fans anywhere, and some no longer believe that Atlanta is really in the NFL. In fact, no less an authority than the President's brother, Billy Carter—an Atlanta fan of some standing—told some people in Washington that he didn't think the Falcons were of National Football League caliber. Was he just jesting? Only Billy knows.

OFFENSE

Quarterbacks	Ht.	Wt.	Age	Exp.	College
Hunter, Scott	6-2	205	30	7	Alabama
McQuilken, Kim	6-2	203	26	4	Lehigh
Bartkowski, Steve	6-4	213	24	3	California

A lot depends on whether Bartkowski can become operational again. He was on injured reserve (knee) at last season's close. Hunter and McQuilken haven't demonstrated a flaming ability to move the team— at least not yet.

Running Backs	Ht.	Wt.	Age	Exp.	College
Esposito, Mike	6-0	183	24	2	Boston College
Stanback, Haskel	6-0	210	25	4	Tennessee
Pritchett, Billy Ray	6-3	230	26	3	West Texas State
Collins, Sonny	6-1	196	24	2	Kentucky
Bean, Bubba	5-11	195	23	2	Texas A&M
Thompson, Woody	6-1	228	25	3	Miami (Fla.)
Eley, Monroe	6-2	210	28	3	Arizona State

Bean, a rookie last season, topped Atlanta's rushing unit, which says something about the ground attack. He did it with a meager 428 yards. The others tried, but vital sparks were missing. Thompson and Eley nursed injuries most of the time. Collins ran for 100 yards in one game, thereby becoming only the ninth Falcon running back to accomplish such a feat in the Atlanta franchise's 11-year history. These Falcons don't fly.

Receivers	Ht.	Wt.	Age	Exp.	College
Gilliam, John (W)	6-1	187	32	11	S.C. State
Francis, Wallace (W)	5-11	190	26	5	Arkansas AM&N
Mitchell, Jim (T)	6-1	236	30	9	Prairie View
Farmer, Karl (W)	5-11	165	23	2	Pittsburgh
Adams, Bob (T)	6-2	225	31	9	Pacific (Calif.)
McCrary, Greg (T)	6-3	230	25	3	Clark
Jenkins, Alfred (W)	5-10	172	25	3	Morris Brown
Piper, Scott (W)	6-1	184	23	2	Arizona

W=wide receiver   T=tight end

Gilliam arrived in Atlanta from Minnesota widely heralded as a gift from the Viking good-luck chest. His first Falcon year was something of a disappointment, but after all, his job is to catch passes, not throw 'em. Jenkins, a mite of a receiver physically, was absolutely outstanding for the second straight year. In 1975, his rookie season, Jenkins led the club with 38 catches for 767 yards (a 20.2 yard average). And in his second year he did it again—41 catches for 710 yards and a 17.3 yard average. That's consistency. The other receivers just tagged along behind Jenkins. Farmer sat out his rookie season with injury. McCrary watched the games, too, with a damaged thigh.

Interior Linemen	Ht.	Wt.	Age	Exp.	College
Scott, Dave (T)	6-4	285	24	2	Kansas
Brett, Walt (G)	6-5	241	24	2	Montana
Jackson, Larron (G)	6-3	260	28	7	Missouri
Van Note, Jeff (C)	6-2	252	31	9	Kentucky
Smith, Royce (G)	6-3	250	28	6	Georgia
Ryczek, Paul (C)	6-2	230	25	4	Virginia
Weatherley, Jim (C)	6-3	245	25	2	(none)
Kindle, Gregg (G)	6-4	265	27	4	Tennessee State
Gotshalk, Len (T)	6-4	259	28	7	Humboldt State
McKinnely, Phil (T)	6-4	248	23	2	UCLA
Bryant, Warren (T)	6-6	240	22	R	Kentucky
Thielman, R. C. (G)	6-4	247	22	R	Arkansas
Adams, Brent (T)	6-5	256	25	3	Tennessee—Chattanooga

T=tackle   G=guard   C=center

Van Note is the veteran of this group—and that with only nine NFL years. His credentials include two Pro Bowls as the starting NFC center. He has a bad knee. Atlanta's lowly offensive showing in 1976 has to be blamed, to an appreciable extent, upon the front line. It should be a high-priority action area for Leeman Bennett. Plenty of room for achievement here.

Kickers	Ht.	Wt.	Age	Exp.	College
James, John (P)	6-3	200	28	6	Florida
Mike-Mayer, Nick (Pk)	5-9	187	27	5	Temple

Pk=placekicker   P=punter

James continues to be the Falcons' shining star. His punting, always above the 40-yard average, gives him the same hometown hero status as a baseball home-run king on a cellar-dwelling club. Mike-Mayer did fine on PATs last year but, strangely, his ten for 21 FGs included bull's-eyes on long kicks (five of 'em 40 yards or more) while the short ones usually went astray. Mike-Mayer, despite all, led the club in scoring with a once-over-lightly 50 points.

DEFENSE

Front Linemen	Ht.	Wt.	Age	Exp.	College
Humphrey, Claude (E)	6-5	265	33	10	Tennessee State
George, Steve (T)	6-6	265	26	4	Houston
East, Ron (E)	6-4	250	34	10	Montana State
Tilleman, Mike (T)	6-7	278	33	11	Montana
Lewis, Mike (T)	6-4	261	28	7	Arkansas AM&N
Bailey, Jim (E)	6-6	255	29	8	Kansas
Yeates, Jeff (E)	6-3	248	26	6	Boston College
Merrow, Jeff (E)	6-4	230	24	3	West Virginia
Windauer, Bill (T)	6-4	250	28	5	Iowa
Faumuina, Wilson (T)	6-5	275	23	R	San Jose State
Fields, Edgar (T)	6-3	255	22	R	Texas A&M

E=end   T=tackle

Humphrey, entering his tenth NFL year, yearns for at least one whirl with a winning outfit like the Rams, naturally. (Shades of O.J. and Broadway Joe!) The defensive unit's performance in 1976 wasn't a great deal better than the offensive's, and that says loads. All season long the Falcon defense had an odd hangup, and Atlanta was outscored in the first quarter by a composite seven TDs to one. Little wonder the Falcons were always behind. Faumuina is a native of Samoa, where his father was a chieftain.

Linebackers	Ht.	Wt.	Age	Exp.	College
McClain, Dewey (O)	6-3	236	23	2	East Central State
Roberts, Guy (O)	6-1	220	27	6	Maryland
Brezina, Greg (O)	6-1	221	31	10	Houston
Cope, Jim (M)	6-2	230	24	2	Ohio State
Kuykendall, Fulton (O)	6-5	225	24	3	UCLA
Nobis, Tommy (M)	6-2	243	34	12	Texas
Ortega, Ralph (M)	6-2	220	24	3	Florida
Pennywell, Robert (O)	6-1	222	23	2	Grambling

O=outside   M=middle

Experience—the lack of it—becomes even more of a linebacker problem this time around. A veritable "mountain" of experience is officially retired, and its name is Tommy Nobis. But there's a possibility that he will play again—from his position in the Falcon front office (where he's got a new job), Nobis concedes that he'll stay in condition and not close the door completely on a return to the playing field. "I would never turn my back on the team," says Tommy, and that sounds something like semi-retirement.

Cornerbacks	Ht.	Wt.	Age	Exp.	College
Lawrence, Rolland	5-10	179	26	5	Tabor
Byas, Rick	5-9	180	27	4	Wayne State (Mich.)
Reed, Frank	5-11	193	23	2	Washington
Mabra, Ron	5-10	164	26	3	Howard

Lawrence is a valuable asset. The club leader in interceptions with six in 1976, he was a whirling dervish on both kickoff and punt returns. No tall people here, but there's ability around the corners. Reed showed ability, intercepting three.

Safeties	Ht.	Wt.	Age	Exp.	College
Brown, Ray	6-2	202	28	7	West Texas State
Easterling, Ray	6-0	192	28	6	Richmond
Jones, Bob	6-2	193	26	5	Virginia Union

Would-be wide receivers who venture deep into Atlanta's secondary find themselves surrounded by tall types. Brown and Easterling each intercepted three of those bombs last year and otherwise patrolled their pastures with vigilance.

Note: A complete listing of Atlanta's 1977 college draft selections can be found on page 247.

DEFENSIVE UNIT

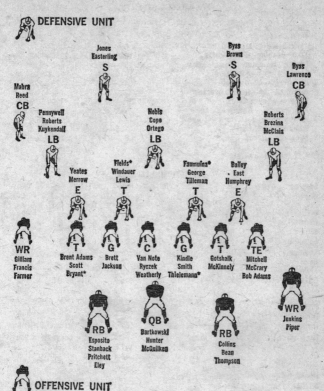

Jones
Easterling
S

Byas
Brown
S

Byas
Lawrence
CB

Mabra
Reed
CB

Pennywell
Roberts
Kuykendall
LB

Nobis
Cope
Ortego
LB

Roberts
Brezina
McClain
LB

Yeates
Merrow
E

Fields*
Windauer
Lewis
T

Faumuina*
George
Tilleman
T

Bailey
East
Humphrey
E

WR
Gilliam
Francis
Farmer

Brent Adams
Scott
Bryant*
T

Brett
Jackson
G

Van Note
Ryczek
Weatherly
C

Kindle
Smith
Thielemann*
G

Gotshalk
McKinnely
T

Mitchell
McCrary
Bob Adams
TE

RB
Esposito
Stanback
Pritchett
Eley

QB
Bartkowski
Hunter
McQuilken

RB
Collins
Bean
Thompson

WR
Jenkins
Piper

OFFENSIVE UNIT

*Rookie

1976 FALCONS STATISTICS

	Falcons	Opps.
Total Points Scored	172*	312
Total First Downs	191	257
Third-Down Efficiency	66—211	87—221
Yards Rushing—First Downs	1689—78	2579—143
Passes Attempted—Completions	354—157	340—184
Yards Passing—First Downs	1414—93	2011—95
QB Sacked—Yards Lost	44—395	35—275
Interceptions—Return Average	18—11.5	24—19.5
Punts—Average Yards	101—42.1	80—38.3
Punt Returns—Return Average	60—6.5	54—6.7
Kickoff Returns—Return Average	60—21.1	39—23.9
Fumbles—Ball Lost	30—21	30—22
Penalties—Yards	84—714	102—868

* Includes one safety

STATISTICAL LEADERS

Scoring	TDs	Rush.	Pass.	Ret.	PATs	FGs	Total
Mike-Mayer	0	0	0	0	20—20	10—21	50
Jenkins	6	0	6	0	0	0	36
Stanback	4	3	1	0	0	0	24
Bean	3	2	1	0	0	0	18
Gilliam	2	0	2	0	0	0	12
Esposito	2	2	0	0	0	0	12

Rushing	Atts.	Yds.	Avg.	Longest	TDs
Bean	124	428	3.5	30	2
Stanback	95	324	3.4	30	3
Esposito	60	317	5.3	36 (TD)	2
Collins	91	319	3.5	47	0
Thompson	42	152	3.6	10	0
Pritchett	14	74	5.3	16	1
Hunter	14	41	2.9	16	1
Hampton	15	32	2.1	10	0

Passing	Atts.	Com.	Yds.	Pct.	Int.	Longest	TDs
Bartkowski	120	57	677	47.5	9	50 (TD)	2
Hunter	110	51	633	46.4	4	34 (TD)	5
McQuilken	121	48	450	39.7	10	39	2

Receiving	No.	Yds.	Avg.	Longest	TDs
Jenkins	41	710	17.3	34 (TD)	6
Gilliam	21	292	13.9	49 (TD)	2
Stanback	21	174	8.3	28	1
Mitchell	17	209	12.3	39	0
Esposito	17	88	5.2	13	0
Bean	16	148	9.3	50 (TD)	1

Interceptions	No.	Yds.	Avg.	Longest	TDs
Lawrence	6	43	7.2	22	0
Brown	3	58	19.3	21	0
Reed	3	48	16.0	42	0
Easterling	3	33	11.0	19	0

Punting	No.	Yds.	Avg.	Longest	Inside 20	Blocked
James	101	4253	42.1	67	28	0

Punt Returns	No.	FCs	Yds.	Avg.	Longest	TDs
Lawrence	54	5	372	6.9	24	0

Kickoff Returns	No.	Yds.	Avg.	Longest	TDs
Lawrence	21	521	24.8	36	0
Byas	12	270	22.5	44	0
Collins	7	141	20.1	24	0

THE 1977 NFL COLLEGE DRAFT

**Team-by-team, round-by-round
lists of each NFL club's 1977
college draft choices**

NATIONAL FOOTBALL LEAGUE
42nd ANNUAL SELECTION MEETING

Hotel Roosevelt, New York City, May 3-4, 1977

NOTE: The number to the left of each player's name designates round in which he was chosen; the number in the fourth column designates the order of selection among 335 players drafted. It will also be noted that some clubs made no choices in certain rounds, or that some had two or more choices in certain rounds. This is because draft choices are often traded off before the selection meeting begins—usually in exchange for experienced NFL players of some merit at their positions.

ATLANTA FALCONS

Round	Player	Pos.	Choice	College
1	BRYANT, Warren	T	6	Kentucky
1	FAUMUINA, Wilson	DT	20	San Jose State
2	THIELEMANN, R. C.	G	36	Arkansas
3	FIELDS, Edgar	DT	63	Texas A&M
4	LEAVITT, Allan	K	89	Georgia
5	DIGGS, Shelton	WR	120	Southern California
6	JENKINS, Keith	DB	161	Cincinnati
8	PACKER, Walter	WR	203	Mississippi State
9	MAXWELL, John	T	230	Boston College
9	SPEER, Robert	DE	242	Arkansas State
10	RYCKMAN, Billy	WR	257	Louisiana Tech
11	FARMER, Dave	RB	287	Southern California
12	PARRISH, Don	DE	314	Pittsburgh

BALTIMORE COLTS

Round	Player	Pos.	Choice	College
1	BURKE, Randy	WR	26	Kentucky
2	OZDOWSKI, Mike	DE	53	Virginia
6	O'NEAL, Calvin	LB	163	Michigan
7	CARTER, Blanchard	T	193	Nevada–Las Vegas
8	HELVIS, Ken	T, C	220	Georgia
9	CAPRIOLA, Glen	RB	247	Boston College
10	BAKER, Ron	G	277	Oklahoma State
11	RUFF, Brian	LB	304	Citadel
12	DEUTSCH, Bill	RB	331	North Dakota

BUFFALO BILLS

Round	Player	Pos.	Choice	College
2	DOKES, Phil	DT	12	Oklahoma State
3	BROWN, Curtis	RB	59	Missouri
3	KIMBROUGH, John	WR	73	St. Cloud
4	DEAN, Jimmy	DT	86	Texas A&M
5	BESANA, Fred	QB	115	California
5	O'DONOGHUE, Neil	K	127	Auburn
6	PRUITT, Ron	DE	157	Nebraska
7	NELMS, Mike	DB	170	Baylor
8	MORTON, Greg	DT	197	Michigan
11	JACKSON, Nate	RB	282	Tennessee State
12	ROMES, Charles	DB	309	North Carolina Central

CHICAGO BEARS

Round	Player	Pos.	Choice	College
1	ALBRECHT, Ted	T	15	California
2	SPIVEY, Mike	DB	43	Colorado
3	EARL, Robin	RB	61	Washington
6	EVANS, Vince	QB	140	Southern California
7	BUTLER, Gerald	WR	182	Nicholls State
9	BUONAMICI, Nick	DT	238	Ohio State
10	BRECKNER, Dennis	DE	266	Miami
11	ZELENCIK, Connie	C	294	Purdue
12	IRVIN, Terry	DB	322	Jackson State

CINCINNATI BENGALS

Round	Player	Pos.	Choice	College
1	EDWARDS, Eddie	DT	3	Miami (Fla.)
1	WHITLEY, Wilson	DT	8	Houston
1	COBB, Mike	TE	22	Michigan State
2	JOHNSON, Pete	RB	49	Ohio State
3	VOIGHT, Mike	RB	76	North Carolina
4	WALKER, Rick	TE	85	UCLA
4	WILSON, Mike	T	103	Georgia
4	ANDERSON, Jerry	DB	105	Oklahoma
5	PHILLIPS, Ray	LB	133	Nebraska
6	DUNIVEN, Tommy	QB	160	Texas Tech
7	BREEDEN, Louis	DB	187	N.C. Central
7	CORBETT, Jim	TE	194	Pittsburgh
8	ST. VICTOR, Jose	G	214	Syracuse
9	ZACHARY, Willie	WR	245	Central State (Ohio)
10	BIALIK, Bob	P	272	Hillsdale
11	PARRISH, Joel	G	292	Georgia
11	ALLEN, Carl	DB	299	Southern Mississippi
12	PERCIVAL, Alex	WR	326	Morehouse

CLEVELAND BROWNS

Round	Player	Pos.	Choice	College
1	JACKSON, Robert	LB	17	Texas A&M
2	SKLADANY, Tom	P, K	46	Ohio State
4	DAVIS, Oliver	DB	102	Tennessee State
4	SIMS, Robert	DT	110	South Carolina State
7	RANDLE, Kenny	WR	173	Southern California
7	SMITH, Blane	TE	184	Purdue
7	LINGENFELTER, Bob	T	188	Nebraska
8	ARMSTRONG, Bill	DB	213	Wake Forest
9	BROWN, Daryl	DB	240	Tufts
10	BURKETT, Tom	T	269	North Carolina
11	NASH, Charles	WR	296	Arizona
12	TIERNEY, Leo	C	325	Georgia Tech

DALLAS COWBOYS

Round	Player	Pos.	Choice	College
1	DORSETT, Tony	RB	2	Pittsburgh
2	CARANO, Glenn	QB	54	Nevada—Las Vegas
3	HILL, Tony	WR	62	Stanford
3	BELCHER, Val	G	81	Houston
4	BROWN, Guy	LB	108	Houston
5	FREDERICK, Andy	DT	137	New Mexico
6	COOPER, Jim	T	164	Temple
7	STALLS, David	DE	191	Northern Colorado
8	CLEVELAND, Al	DE	208	Pacific
8	WILLIAMS, Fred	RB	221	Arizona State
9	CANTRELL, Mark	C	248	North Carolina
10	DE BERG, Steve	QB	275	San Jose State
11	WARDLOW, Don	TE	305	Washington
12	PETERS, Greg	G	332	California

DENVER BRONCOS

Round	Player	Pos.	Choice	College
1	SCHINDLER, Steve	G	18	Boston College
2	LYTLE, Rob	RB	45	Michigan
4	BRYAN, Billy	C	101	Duke
7	SWIDER, Larry	P	185	Pittsburgh
8	CULLIVER, Calvin	RB	212	Alabama
9	JACKSON, Charles	DT	241	Washington
10	MIDDLEBROOK, Orna	WR	268	Arkansas State
11	HECK, Phil	LB	297	California
12	LEVENHAGEN, Scott	TE	324	Western Illinois

DETROIT LIONS

Round	Player	Pos.	Choice	College
2	WILLIAMS, Walt	DB	42	New Mexico State
3	KANE, Rick	RB	69	San Jose State
4	BLUE, Luther	WR	96	Iowa State
5	CROSBY, Ron	LB	114	Penn State
6	PINKNEY, Reggie	DB	166	East Carolina
7	BLACK, Tim	LB	179	Baylor
8	GRIFFIN, Mark	T	209	North Carolina
9	MATHIESON, Steve	QB	236	Florida State
10	ANDERSON, Gary	G	263	Stanford
11	DAYKIN, Tony	LB	293	Georgia Tech
12	GREENWOOD, Dave	G, C	320	Iowa State

GREEN BAY PACKERS

Round	Player	Pos.	Choice	College
1	BUTLER, Mike	DE	9	Kansas
1	JOHNSON, Ezra	DE	28	Morris Brown
2	KOCH, Greg	DT	39	Arkansas
3	SCRIBNER, Rick	G	74	Idaho State
5	SIMPSON, Nathan	RB	122	Tennessee State
6	MORESCO, Tim	DB	149	Syracuse
7	GOFOURTH, Derrel	C	172	Oklahoma State
7	TIPTON, Rell	G	176	Baylor
8	WHITEHURST, David	QB	206	Furman
9	MULLINS, Joel	T	233	Arkansas State
10	CULBREATH, Jimmy	RB	260	Oklahoma
11	RANDOLPH, Terry	DB	290	American International

HOUSTON OILERS

Round	Player	Pos.	Choice	College
1	TOWNS, Morris	T	11	Missouri
2	REIHNER, George	G	38	Penn State
3	WILSON, Tim	RB	66	Maryland
3	GILES, Jimmy	TE	70	Alcorn State
3	CARPENTER, Rob	RB	84	Miami (Ohio)
4	ANDERSON, Warren	WR	98	West Virginia State
6	WOOLFORD, Gary	DB	148	Florida State
6	CARTER, Davis	C	165	Western Kentucky
8	DAVIS, Steve	WR	198	Georgia
8	FOSTER, Eddie	WR	205	Houston
9	CURRIER, Bill	DB	232	South Carolina
10	HULL, Harvey	LB	262	Mississippi State
11	ROMANO, Al	LB	289	Pittsburgh
12	JOHANSSON, Ove	K	316	Abilene Christian

KANSAS CITY CHIEFS

Round	Player	Pos.	Choice	College
1	GREEN, Gary	DB	10	Baylor
2	REED, Tony	RB	37	Colorado
3	HOWARD, Thomas	LB	67	Texas Tech
4	BAILEY, Mark	RB	92	Long Beach State
4	SAMUELS, Andre	TE	94	Bethune—Cookman
4	HELTON, Darius	G	95	N.C. Central
4	HARRIS, Eric	DB	104	Memphis State
6	BURLESON, Rick	DE	150	Texas
6	HERRERA, Andre	RB	167	Southern Illinois
7	GOLUB, Chris	DB	177	Kansas
8	OLSONOSKI, Ron	LB	204	St. Thomas
8	SMITH, Waddell	WR	215	Kansas
9	GLANTON, Derrick	DE	226	Bishop
9	GREEN, Dave	T	235	New Mexico
10	VITALI, Mark	QB	261	Purdue
11	MITCHELL, Maurice	WR	288	Northern Michigan
12	BURKS, Ray	LB	318	UCLA

LOS ANGELES RAMS

Round	Player	Pos.	Choice	College
1	BRUDZINSKI, Bob	LB	23	Ohio State
2	CROMWELL, Nolan	DB	31	Kansas
2	WADDY, Billy	RB, WR	50	Colorado
3	FULTON, Ed	G	68	Maryland
3	TYLER, Wendell	RB	79	UCLA
4	FERRAGAMO, Vince	QB	91	Nebraska
4	JONES, Eary	DE	107	Memphis State
5	HICKMAN, Donnie	G	130	Southern California
5	WILLIAMS, Jeff	G	134	Rhode Island
6	BEST, Art	RB	156	Kent State
8	BOCKWOLDT, Rod	DB	218	Weber State
10	PETERSEN, Don	TE	274	Boston College
11	LONG, Carson	K	302	Pittsburgh
12	CAUDILL, Barry	C	330	Southern Mississippi

MIAMI DOLPHINS

Round	Player	Pos.	Choice	College
1	DUHE, A. J.	DT	13	Louisiana State
2	BAUMHOWER, Bob	DT	40	Alabama
3	WATSON, Mike	T	71	Miami (Ohio)
5	MICHEL, Mike	K	113	Stanford
5	HARRIS, Leroy	RB	123	Arkansas State
7	HERRON, Bruce	LB	180	New Mexico
8	PERKINS, Horace	DB	207	Colorado
9	TURNER, Robert	RB	237	Oklahoma State
10	CARTER, Mark	T	264	Eastern Michigan
11	ALEXANDER, John	DE	291	Rutgers
12	ANDERSON, Terry	WR	321	Bethune—Cookman

MINNESOTA VIKINGS

Round	Player	Pos.	Choice	College
1	KRAMER, Tommy	QB	27	Rice
2	SWILLEY, Dennis	G	55	Texas A&M
3	HANNON, Tom	DB	83	Michigan State
5	MOORE, Ken	TE	138	Northern Illinois
8	STROZIER, Clint	DB	222	Southern California
9	STUDWELL, Scott	LB	250	Illinois
10	BEAVER, Dan	K	278	Illinois
11	HARTWIG, Keith	WR	306	Arizona
12	KELLEHER, Jim	RB	335	Colorado

NEW ENGLAND PATRIOTS

Round	Player	Pos.	Choice	College
1	CLAYBORN, Raymond	DB	16	Texas
1	MORGAN, Stanley	WR	25	Tennessee
2	IVORY, Horace	RB	44	Oklahoma
2	HASSELBECK, Don	TE	52	Colorado
3	BROWN, Sidney	DB	82	Oklahoma
4	SKINNER, Gerald	T	109	Arkansas
7	SMITH, Ken	WR	192	Arkansas—Pine Bluff
8	BENSON, Brad	G	219	Penn State
9	VOGELE, Jerry	LB	249	Michigan
10	RASMUSSEN, John	T	276	Wisconsin
10	ALEXANDER, Giles	DE	279	Tulsa
11	COSTICT, Ray	LB	303	Mississippi State
12	PRESTON, Dave	RB	333	Bowling Green

NEW ORLEANS SAINTS

Round	Player	Pos.	Choice	College
1	CAMPBELL, Joe	DE	7	Maryland
2	FULTZ, Mike	DT	34	Nebraska
3	WATTS, Bob	LB	64	Boston College
5	LAFARY, Dave	T	118	Purdue
5	HUBBARD, Dave	T	136	Brigham Young
6	PARSLEY, Cliff	P	147	Oklahoma State
6	SCHICK, Tom	G	162	Maryland
7	BOYKIN, Greg	RB	174	Northwestern
8	STEWART, Jim	DB	201	Tulsa
9	KNOWLES, Dave	T	231	Indiana
10	SEPTIEN, Rafael	K	258	S.W. Louisiana
11	BLAIN, John	T	285	San Jose State
12	DALTON, Oakley	DE	315	Jackson State

NEW YORK GIANTS

Round	Player	Pos.	Choice	College
1	JETER, Gary	DT	5	Southern California
2	PERKINS, Johnny	WR	32	Abilene Christian
4	VAUGHAN, Mike	T	88	Oklahoma
5	DEAN, Randy	QB	117	Northwestern
6	JORDAN, Bob	T	143	Memphis State
6	MOOREHEAD, Emery	WR, RB	153	Colorado
7	DIXON, Al	TE	178	Iowa State
8	RICE, Bill	DT	199	Brigham Young
8	RODGERS, Otis	LB	211	Iowa State
9	MULLINS, Ken	DE	228	Florida A&M
10	JONES, Mike	WR	255	Minnesota
11	HELMS, Bill	TE	284	San Diego State
12	SIMMONS, Elmo	RB	311	Texas—Arlington

NEW YORK JETS

Round	Player	Pos.	Choice	College
1	POWELL, Marvin	T	4	Southern California
2	WALKER, Wesley	WR	33	California
3	MARSHALL, Tank	DE	72	Texas A&M
4	DIERKING, Scott	RB	90	Purdue
5	GRIGGS, Perry	WR	116	Troy State
5	GREGORY, Gary	T	129	Baylor
6	KLECKO, Joe	DT	144	Temple
7	WHITE, Charlie	RB	168	Bethune—Cookman
7	GRUPP, Bob	DB	171	Duke
7	LONG, Kevin	RB	195	South Carolina
8	ALEXANDER, Dan	DT	200	Louisiana State
8	THOMPSON, Ed	LB	210	Ohio State
9	ROBINSON, Matt	QB	227	Georgia
10	HENNESSY, John	DE	256	Michigan
11	BUTTERFIELD, Dave	DB	307	Nebraska
12	GARGIS, Phil	RB, DB	312	Auburn
12	CONRAD, Dave	T	313	Maryland

OAKLAND RAIDERS

Round	Player	Pos.	Choice	College
2	DAVIS, Mike	DB	35	Colorado
2	McKNIGHT, Ted	RB	57	Minnesota—Duluth
4	MARVIN, Mickey	G	112	Tennessee
5	HAYES, Lester	RB	126	Texas A&M
5	BARNES, Jeff	LB	139	California
7	MARTINI, Rich	WR	190	California—Davis
8	ROBISKIE, Terry	RB	223	Louisiana State
12	MARTIN, Rod	LB	317	Southern California
12	BENIRSHKE, Rolf	K	334	California—Davis

PHILADELPHIA EAGLES

Round	Player	Pos.	Choice	College
5	SHARP, Skip	DB	119	Kansas
6	RUSSELL, Kevin	DB	145	Tennessee State
6	MONTGOMERY, Wilbert	RB	154	Abilene Christian
6	MITCHELL, Martin	DB	158	Tulane
7	JOHNSON, Charles	DT	175	Colorado
8	FRANKLIN, Cleveland	RB	202	Baylor
9	HUMPHREYS, T. J.	G	229	Arkansas State
10	MASTRONARDO, John	WR	259	Villanova
11	MOORE, Rocco	T	283	Western Michigan
11	CORDOVA, Mike	QB	286	Stanford

PITTSBURGH STEELERS

Round	Player	Pos.	Choice	College
1	COLE, Robin	LB	21	New Mexico
2	THORNTON, Sidney	RB	48	N.W. Louisiana
3	BEASLEY, Tom	DT	60	Virginia Tech
3	SMITH, Jim	WR	75	Michigan
4	PETERSEN, Ted	C	93	Eastern Illinois
4	SMITH, Laverne	RB	99	Kansas
4	AUDICK, Dan	G	106	Hawaii
5	STOUDT, Cliff	QB	121	Youngstown State
5	COURSON, Steve	G	125	South Carolina
5	WINSTON, Dennis	LB	132	Arkansas
6	HARRIS, Paul	LB	159	Alabama
7	FRISCH, Randy	DT	186	Missouri
8	AUGUST, Phil	WR	217	Miami
9	KELLY, Roosevelt	TE	244	Eastern Kentucky
10	COWANS, Alvin	DB	253	Florida
10	LA CROSSE, Dave	LB	271	Wake Forest
11	WEST, Lou	DB	298	Cincinnati
12	STEPHENS, Jimmy	TE	310	Florida

ST. LOUIS CARDINALS

Round	Player	Pos.	Choice	College
1	PISARKIEWICZ, Steve	QB	19	Missouri
2	FRANKLIN, George	RB	47	Texas A&I
3	ALLERMAN, Kurt	LB	78	Penn State
3	MIDDLETON, Terdell*	RB	80	Memphis State
5	LEE, Ernest	DT	131	Texas
5	SPIVA, Andy	LB	135	Tennessee
8	WILLIAMS, Eric	LB	216	Southern California
9	JACKSON, Johnny	DT	243	Southern University
10	LE JAY, Jim	WR	270	San Jose State
11	LEE, Greg	DB	301	Western Illinois
12	FENLAW, Rick	LB	328	Texas

* Immediately after being drafted, Middleton was traded to Green Bay.

SAN DIEGO CHARGERS

Round	Player	Pos.	Choice	College
1	RUSH, Bob	C	24	Memphis State
3	KING, Keith	DB	77	Colorado State
5	WILLIAMS, Clarence	RB	124	South Carolina
5	OLANDER, Cliff	QB	128	New Mexico State
6	LINDSTROM, Dave	DE	146	Boston University
6	BARNES, Lawrence	RB	151	Tennessee State
6	SHAW, Pete	DB	152	Northwestern
7	BUSH, Ron	DB	181	Southern California
9	WASHINGTON, Gene	WR	234	Georgia
10	TOWNSEND, Curtis	LB	265	Arkansas
12	STANSIK, Jim	TE	319	Eastern Michigan

SAN FRANCISCO 49ers

Round	Player	Pos.	Choice	College
3	BOYD, Elmo	WR	65	Eastern Kentucky
4	BLACK, Stan	DB	100	Mississippi State
6	BURNS, Mike	DB	141	Southern California
6	HARLAN, Jim	C	155	Howard Payne
7	VAN WAGNER, Jim	RB	183	Michigan Tech
9	POSEY, David	K	239	Florida
11	BILLICK, Brian	TE	295	Brigham Young
12	MARTIN, Scott	G	323	North Dakota

SEATTLE SEAHAWKS

Round	Player	Pos.	Choice	College
1	AUGUST, Steve	G	14	Tulsa
2	LYNCH, Tom	T	30	Boston College
2	BEESON, Terry	LB	41	Kansas
2	CRONAN, Pete	LB	51	Boston College
3	BOYD, Dennis	DE	58	Oregon State
4	YARNO, John	C	87	Idaho
4	SEIVERS, Larry	WR	111	Tennessee
6	BENJAMIN, Tony	RB	142	Duke
7	SIMS, David	RB	169	Georgia
9	ADZICK, George	DB	225	Minnesota
10	ADKINS, Sam	QB	254	Wichita State
11	WESTBELD, Bill	T	281	Dayton
12	WILSON, I. V.	DT	329	Tulsa

TAMPA BAY BUCCANEERS

Round	Player	Pos.	Choice	College
1	BELL, Ricky	RB	1	Southern California
2	LEWIS, Dave	LB	29	Southern California
3	HANNAH, Charles	DE	56	Alabama
8	HEDBERG, Randy	QB	196	Minot State
9	HEMINGWAY, Byron	LB	224	Boston College
9	MUCKER, Larry	WR	251	Arizona State
10	MORGAN, Robert	RB	252	Florida
10	BALL, Aaron	LB	267	Fullerton State
11	RODGERS, Chuck	DB	280	North Dakota State
12	SHEFFIELD, Chip	WR	308	Lenoir Rhyne

WASHINGTON REDSKINS

Round	Player	Pos.	Choice	College
4	McCOLL, Duncan	DE	97	Stanford
7	HAYNES, Reggie	TE	189	Nevada–Las Vegas
9	NORTHINGTON, Mike	RB	246	Purdue
10	SYKES, James	RB	273	Rice
11	HARRIS, Don	DB	300	Rutgers
12	KIRKLAND, Curtis	DE	327	Missouri

WILL ANYTHING
EVER TAKE THE PLACE OF GRASS?

By Jim Hanchett

There's many a slip 'twixt the cup and the Super Bowl, and, while the Giants weren't headed much of anywhere in 1976, they took a bad jolt on the splendid new carpet of their smashing new Meadowlands arena late in November. Larry Csonka, their six-million-dollar man, proved he wasn't indestructible early in the second period when he blasted into the line of the Seattle Seahawks and went down, hard, under a snorting ton of defensive linemen.

It wasn't the first time that expensive first-down machine had been stopped. But this time, it ended his season. He was able to walk off the field, but the next day, three top orthopedic surgeons scrutinized his left knee for five hours.

The following day, he was under the skillful knife of Dr. John Marshall, the team physician, after wishing the doctor "Good luck, and fix her up good, will you?" Csonka was having repairs done on torn ligaments in his right knee right after his teammate, offensive left tackle Tom Mullen, was having a job done on his left knee. (Mullen had torn ligaments in the same Pyrrhic victory [28–16] over the Seahawks.)

Gracious as the Zonker was—and outwardly confident—about the doctor's skill, after his injury he let it be known that artificial turf isn't the favorite kind of grass among some NFL dudes. "I don't think it would have happened on grass," he told *New York Daily News* writer Norm Miller. "I could feel three or four of them on top of me. If I could just have slid my foot out a little, just an inch or two . . . but I couldn't. I've never been a fan of that surface and this doesn't make my heart any warmer toward it."

Medics see "no reason" why Csonka shouldn't be his old self again in 1977. But other physicians claim that no damaged knee ever comes back one-hundred-percent right. And old knee men, returning for homecomings at their college and visiting the team physician after a decade or so, have been seen to blanch as they quote the sawbones over a post-game glass of, say, Dr. Pepper: "So I went into his office and he says, 'Well, here's old Poe Fratt. Poe, shall we drain that knee a little, just for old times' sake?' "

Whether Csonka's knee is actually fit only time will tell, but it's a cinch his feelings about artificial surfaces won't have moderated. And his post-game comments rekindled the old argument: Is the rug more dangerous, more likely to cause injuries, the kind that not only can put you out of a game but can also cripple you for life? Or is it just about as risky as the grass that Mother Nature provides?

Many NFL players agree with Csonka about artificial turf. A few years ago, their contract demands *en masse* included a strong call for an in-depth look at the potential hazards of the big three among rugs—AstroTurf, Poly-Turf, and TartanTurf. They claim it's slippery in hot weather, and that a broiling sun can raise its temperature to about that of burning coals—say 120 degrees or so. And they're not too happy about it in snowy cold weather, either. The Steelers' Rocky Bleier was pointing out late in the season that "It can't absorb snow. The snow can't go anywhere, so it builds up quickly on top. Then the snow sticks to the bottom of your shoes and you have no traction. You have to keep kicking it off." But is it more dangerous to the player than real grass?

Bob Hyland, the Packers' center, acknowledges that "A guy who goes into a game, and plays a game, feels that he's been through a tough ordeal on turf or on grass. . . ." But he points out that turf, which has a solid base under the carpet and under a foam cushion, doesn't give at all. Grass does. Hyland says you will see more stars after a solid ding on the phony field than on Mother Nature's meadowland. "I just feel a little more comfortable hitting the deck on grass than on AstroTurf," he said one cold midwinter evening in a New York *boite*. As a man from the pits, Hyland says the three main turfs are pretty similar. The padding underneath, he repeats, makes a difference to the player.

Consider the artificial turf experience of Ed Marinaro of the Jets. After four years with the Vikings, two trips to the Super Bowl, no significant injuries, and no 100-yard games for Bud Grant, Marinaro played against the Patriots on the ersatz turf at Foxboro in the seventh game of 1976, coming off two 100-yard-plus games for the Jets. He tore up the instep of his left foot and missed the second half of the season. His replacement, Clark Gaines, was voted the Jets' Most Valuable Player by his teammates at the season's end. And Patriot George Webster, the man who hit Marinaro at Foxboro, hit so hard that he went out of the game with a bad back—stretched ligaments and tendons, plus what was gently referred to as "some bone damage."

Shortly after the end of the season, I went to the Patriots' Schaefer Stadium for a look at the turf. (It's springy to the step; walking on it is like walking on sponge rubber, strangely enough.)

I ran my knuckles—hard—across the Poly-Turf. It made red marks that didn't hurt and lasted only four days. But I wasn't skidding ten yards across it on a hot day while running at full speed and being hit by a couple of 250-pound post-collegians who were also moving in high gear. And the turf was wet. It makes a difference. A dry surface would have been a lot more deadly.

The National Football League Players' Association believes the rugs do cause a lot of injuries. One case they cite is the case of Willie McGee, the onetime world-class sprinter who bloomed into a super wide receiver for the San Francisco 49ers in 1976. But his season, and possibly his career, was jolted to a halt on his home surface, the Candlestick Park AstroTurf. Players say Candlestick's is one of the hardest of the hard surfaces around, and they blame it for the broken leg that Willie suffered.

The city fathers of San Francisco gave the players' views some attention—enough to warrant Board of Supervisors hearings in November. But the city also decided to buy a new carpet for the stadium, eschewing the opportunity to revert to natural grass. The players point out that the new surface will cost $1,019,600 to install and $255,000 a year for maintenance. They say that grass costs $470,000 to plant, and then it costs only $164,700 a year to hire men to feed, water, trim, and keep unauthorized people off it.

Candlestick's surface won't win any popularity contests. Visitor Thom Darden of the Browns says playing at Candlestick reminds him of playing in the street, and Bruce Taylor of the 49ers agrees with him. They're defensive backs, out in the open field on every play, and risk a lot of high-speed tumbles.

Robert K. Epstein, a spokesman for the Players'

Association, cites a Stanford Research Institute study that indicates an increasing number of fractures, sprains, abrasions, strains, and injuries to arms, elbows, hands and fingers, abdomens, groins, and ankles and toes on all three forms of artificial turf as compared to natural grass. He says the report reveals that the five stadiums with the highest major-injury rates, and ten of the twelve most dangerous, each have synthetic turf surfaces. On the other hand, the four lowest in major-injury rates—and ten of the eleven least dangerous—all have natural grass.

Quoting the report, Epstein points out that "The significantly higher injury rates consistently obtained in the NFL over the past three years from playing on synthetic surfaces all point to the conclusion that synthetic surfaces for football use cannot be justified on an injury-prevention basis. In general, natural turf fields are safer."

Quoting further from the Stanford report: "The top or surface layer does not react consistently to hot, cold, or ambient air conditions, to different humidity or precipitation, or even to physical wear. Moreover, surface inconsistencies are not only apparent from season to season and from field to field, but, in some cases, within the same field; the hard shock pad or undersurface causes an undue amount of 'punishment' to players when compared to natural turf." Epstein holds up the Stanford report as a call for a movement toward new "natural turf systems."

Foxboro-wise New England Patriots' wide receiver Randy Vataha adds: "Anyone who has to practice and play on it is more susceptible to injury because of leg-muscle fatigue and shin splints. If you don't practice on it, you still have to worry about lack of give, which can tear cartilage and ligaments and cause sprains, and the extremely poor traction in wet weather.

I'm also concerned about the seams and cutting myself because of the danger of staph infection."

Echoing Hyland and others, Vataha says, "Of course, the worst part is hitting the damn stuff because it's so hard. Last year, Julius Adams [a 260-pound defensive lineman] missed the season with a broken leg and this year Tim Fox broke his arm—both just by falling."

Epstein of the Players' Association maintains that Bears quarterback Bob Avellini was so banged up on the Dallas TartanTurf that he came out with a lump the size of a baseball on his throwing arm, even though he finished the game. And the players' spokesman has implied that Cowboys quarterback Roger Staubach had to leave the same game (October 24), when his throwing hand went numb. X rays were to reveal a fracture. In the same game, leading NFL rusher Walter Payton was knocked out of the game and his teammate, Roger Stillwell, made an exit on a stretcher.

Well, can injuries harm a pro team's chances for Super Bowl glory and dollars? Ask anybody from Pittsburgh or environs. Remember how they destroyed Baltimore 40–14 on the Sunday before Christmas? To a casual observer, it was the most impressive victory of the long playoff road. It looked easy. It wasn't.

When the Steelers met the Oakland Raiders on what looked like the next logical step toward their third straight Super Bowl crown, they were a little short after the game in Baltimore. Franco Harris was out because of bruised ribs. His running mate and blocking buddy, Rocky Bleier, had a sprained big toe on his right foot, the one he pushes off on. Even the kicker, Roy Gerela, was put out of business by a pulled calf muscle. Frenchy Fuqua, who played hurt in relief of Bleier against the Colts (and tried to do the same against the Raiders), pulled a calf muscle on the first play in Baltimore. And where did these gentlemen get so severely hurt? On the *natural* grass of Baltimore.

A 1975 study seems to show that "more players continued to be injured during road games than those at home in 1974." Moreover, visiting-team injuries did not seem to be linked with variables such as time-zone changes, playing on Sunday instead of Monday, practicing on a different kind of turf than the one to be played upon, number of days since the previous game, or whether the injured player's team was winning or losing. "However," the study states, "observed was the tendency for a greater percentage of visiting-team injuries to occur on fields with a type of turf different from their usual home turf." The very worst time to be playing, if you didn't want to be hurt, was in a hot pre-season game—on the kickoff platoon.

Most of the artificial surfaces, like the new rug at the Giants' Meadowland complex in Hackensack, N.J., and the second-generation carpet at Candlestick Park, are AstroTurf. So are the Seahawks' Kingdome at Seattle; the Bills' Rich Stadium in Buffalo; the Bengals' Riverfront Stadium in Cincinnati; the Astros' Astrodome in Houston; the Bears' Soldier Field in Chicago; the Lions' Pontiac Stadium, an hour's drive from downtown Detroit; the Saints' Superdome in New Orleans; the Eagles' Veterans Stadium in Philadelphia; and the Cardinals' Busch Memorial Stadium in St. Louis. Notice how many of these are mainly baseball fields.

There's TartanTurf at Arrowhead Stadium, home of the Kansas City Chiefs, at the Texas Stadium home of the Dallas Cowboys, and at Three Rivers Stadium (which is shared by the Pirates and the Steelers) in Pittsburgh. The Patriots, as noted, have Poly-Turf at Foxboro. With some exceptions to be noted below, everybody else plays on real grass. (Plans *are* supposedly afoot to replace the surface at Foxboro—not with grass, but with a different artificial turf.)

Dan Marcott, stadium manager at Foxboro, feels that it would take even more exhaustive studies to show whether artificial turf is really tougher on players than the real sod, but he estimates that it's about fifty-fifty. He does think knees are more vulnerable on the rug and ankles more likely to be injured on grass.

Some people think that an ankle is more likely to give under stress when cleats are deeply imbedded in relatively soft earth, and that knees go when a foot can move laterally a bit on the flat hard artificial surface. This is certainly only conjecture, however.

What is certainly not conjecture is the fact players have been unhappy about artificial surfaces since as far back as 1971, at least. That was the year the Players' Association called for a joint owner-player study of artificial turf surfaces. Epstein says the NFL's commissioner's office rejected the call for a safety study on the grounds (heh heh) that it was a labor problem, one that was in the province of the clubs and the NFL Management Council. Within two months, the Players' Association had called for a moratorium on further installation of artificial turfs and had asked the owners for a study. The Management Council refused to join such a study, Epstein charges, denying that it was subject to collective bargaining and contending that the installation of artificial turf was a "management prerogative." But five players and the Players' Association staff were invited by Representative John Moss (D–Calif.) to meet a House Commerce Subcommittee studying the problem.

A couple of years later, on October 19, 1973, the Consumer Products Safety Commission reported that there was little evidence to support players' contentions that artificial turf causes more serious injuries than real grass. It denied the Players' Association petition to freeze further installations until safety standards had been established for the turf. But it said it would call for development of mandatory standards and hinted at the possibility of public hearings on the game of football itself. Football is the seventh leading cause of injuries throughout the nation.

Meanwhile, the National Labor Relations Board ruled in October, 1972, that the owners are legally *required* to bargain on the issue of whether synthetic turf causes injuries, but in January, 1977, Robert Epstein was charging that the owners have consistently refused to include the turf question in negotiations.

At the same time, Epstein was charging that the league has refused to supply the injury data that the players have requested. In July, 1976, the league lost another decision before the NLRB as Judge Charles Schneider ruled that all injury data must be supplied to the players. The clubs appealed, Epstein points out, and the information was not supplied. But the players were making no fuss over turf when they signed a new agreement with owners in March, 1977.

While the turf seems to be dangerous—and the game itself hazardous—it's obvious that the whole world *doesn't* agree with the proposition that synthetic surfaces cause more injuries than grass. But until somebody provides absolute, immutable proof one way or the other, the players have made some suggestions.

They're looking at a new gimmick with a lot of interest. It's called Prescription Athletic Turf (PAT) and has been in use at Purdue University's stadium for some time. It has been used at RFK Stadium in Washington, D.C., for two years. The players are quick to point out that it was dry the day after a Monday-night deluge when the Redskins played the Cardinals on television. A PAT surface has been installed at Miami, and Denver also has one.

Epstein says PAT is a natural sod on a porous base, allowing for deep roots. It can be irrigated by pumps or sucked dry. Heating cables under the surface—like those in an electric blanket—prevent frozen fields. Epstein of the Players' Association sees this as a viable surface.

In sum, the players and those who think they're right are saying that perhaps one of these days the NFL should decide which is more expensive—lawn-cutting and laundry, or the cost of losing a million-dollar player for a season or a lifetime.

NATIONAL FOOTBALL LEAGUE 1976 STATISTICS

AFC and NFC individual and team leaders for the 1976 regular season, plus final 1976 standings of AFC and NFC teams and the results of championship playoff games

AMERICAN FOOTBALL CONFERENCE

Final 1976 Standings

	W	L	T	Pct.	Pts.	Opps.
Eastern Division						
Baltimore*	11	3	0	.786	417	246
New England†	11	3	0	.786	376	236
Miami	6	8	0	.429	263	264
N.Y. Jets	3	11	0	.214	169	383
Buffalo	2	12	0	.143	245	363
Central Division						
Pittsburgh*	10	4	0	.714	342	138
Cincinnati	10	4	0	.714	335	210
Cleveland	9	5	0	.643	267	287
Houston	5	9	0	.357	222	273
Western Division						
Oakland*	13	1	0	.929	350	237
Denver	9	5	0	.643	315	206
San Diego	6	8	0	.429	248	285
Kansas City	5	9	0	.357	290	376
Tampa Bay	0	14	0	.000	125	412

* Division winner
† Wild card team for playoffs

1976 Playoff Results

AFC divisional playoff: Pittsburgh 40, Baltimore 14 (at Baltimore)
AFC divisional playoff: Oakland 24, New England 21 (at Oakland)
AFC championship game: Oakland 24, Pittsburgh 7 (at Oakland)
Super Bowl XI (at Pasadena): Oakland 32, Minnesota 14

LEADING SCORERS

	TDs	Rush.	Pass.	Ret.	Pts.
Touchdown Leaders					
Harris, Pitt.	14	14	0	0	84
Grogan, N.E.	13	12	0	1	78
Branch, Oak.	12	0	12	0	72

	TDs	Rush.	Pass.	Ret.	Pts.
Carr, Balt.	11	0	11	0	66
McCauley, Balt.	11	9	2	0	66
Casper, Oak.	10	0	10	0	60
Chandler, Buff.	10	0	10	0	60
Johnson, N.E.	10	6	4	0	60
Simpson, Buff.	9	8	1	0	54

Best Performance: 18 pts. on 3 TDs—Reggie Rucker, Cleveland vs. New York Jets, Sept. 12, 1976; Roger Carr, Baltimore vs. Cincinnati, Sept. 19, 1976; Bob Chandler, Buffalo vs. Kansas City, Oct. 3, 1976; Morris Owens, Tampa Bay vs. Miami, Oct. 24, 1976; Rocky Bleier, Pittsburgh vs. Tampa Bay, Dec. 5, 1976; Freddie Solomon, Miami vs. Buffalo, Dec. 5, 1976; Ed Podolak, Kansas City vs. Cleveland, Dec. 12, 1976

	PATs	FGs	Longest	Pts.
Top Kick Scorers				
Linhart, Balt.	49-50	20-27	41	109
Stenerud, K.C.	27-33	21-38	52	90
Smith, N.E.	42-46	15-25	49	87
Gerela, Pitt.	40-43	14-26	47	82
Bahr, Cin.	39-42	14-27	51	81
Turner, Den.	36-39	15-21	47	81
Yepremian, Miami	29-31	16-23	53	77
Butler, Hou.	24-24	16-27	54	72
Cockroft, Cleve.	27-30	15-28	51	72

LEADING PASSERS
(140 Attempts)

	Atts.	Com.	Pct. Com.	Yds.	Avg. Yds.	Had Int.	TDs	Rating
Stabler, Oak.	291	194	66.7	2737	9.41	17	27	103.7
Jones, Balt.	343	207	60.3	3104	9.05	9	24	102.6
Ferguson, Buff.	151	74	49.0	1086	7.19	1	9	90.0
Griese, Miami	272	162	59.6	2097	7.71	12	11	78.9
Livingston, K.C.	338	189	55.9	2682	7.93	13	12	77.9
Sipe, Cleve.	312	178	57.1	2113	6.77	14	17	77.1
Anderson, Cin.	338	179	53.0	2367	7.00	14	19	77.0
Fouts, S.D.	359	208	57.9	2535	7.06	15	14	75.3
Pastorini, Hou.	309	167	54.0	1795	5.81	10	10	68.6
Bradshaw, Pitt.	192	92	47.9	1177	6.13	9	10	65.3
Ramsey, Den.	270	128	47.4	1931	7.15	13	11	65.1

	Atts.	Com.	Pct. Com.	Yds.	Avg. Yds.	Had Int.	TDs	Rating
Grogan, N.E.	302	145	48.0	1903	6.30	20	18	60.8
Spurrier, T.B.	311	156	50.2	1628	5.23	12	7	57.1
Namath, N.Y. Jets	230	114	49.6	1090	4.74	16	4	39.7
Todd, N.Y. Jets	162	65	40.1	870	5.37	12	3	33.4
Marangi, Buff.	232	82	35.3	998	4.30	16	7	30.7

Longest: 88 yards—Ken Stabler to Cliff Branch, Oakland vs. Green Bay, Oct. 24, 1976

Ratings based on percentage completion, average yards gained, TD percentage, interception percentage.

LEADING PASS RECEIVERS

	No.	Yds.	Avg.	Longest	TDs
Lane, K.C. (rb)*	66	686	10.4	44	1
Chandler, Buff.	61	824	13.5	58	10
Mitchell, Balt. (rb)*	60	555	9.3	40	3
Casper, Oak.	53	691	13.0	30	10
Burrough, Hou.	51	932	18.3	69	7
Joiner, S.D.	50	1056	21.1	81	7
Rucker, Cleve.	49	676	13.8	45	8
White, K.C.	47	808	17.2	41	7
B. Johnson, Hou.	47	495	10.5	40	4
Young, S.D. (rb)*	47	441	9.4	33	1
Branch, Oak.	46	1111	24.2	88	12
G. Pruitt, Cleve. (rb)*	45	341	7.6	27	1
Carr, Balt.	43	1112	25.9	79	11
Biletnikoff, Oak.	43	551	12.8	32	7
Curtis, Cin.	41	766	18.7	85	6
Gaines, N.Y. Jets (rb)*	41	400	9.8	27	2
Doughty, Balt.	40	628	15.7	41	5
Coleman, Hou. (rb)*	40	247	6.2	19	3

* rb denotes running back

Best Performance: 12 receptions (136 yards)—Dave Casper, Oakland vs. New England, Oct. 3, 1976; 12 receptions (64 yards)—Lydell Mitchell, Baltimore vs. New York Jets, Nov. 28, 1976

INTERCEPTION LEADERS

	No.	Yds.	Longest	TDs
Riley, Cin.	9	141	53	1
Haynes, N.E.	8	90	28	0
Jackson, Den.	7	136	46	1
Darden, Cleve.	7	73	21	0
Edwards, Pitt.	6	95	55	0
Goode, S.D.	6	82	27	0
Blount, Pitt.	6	75	28	0
McCray, N.E.	5	182	63	2
Greene, Buff.	5	135	101	1
Casanova, Cin.	5	109	33	2
Wallace, Balt.	5	105	41	0
Whittington, Hou.	5	103	50	0
Reardon, K.C.	5	26	22	0

Longest: 101 yards—Tony Greene, Buffalo vs. Kansas City, Oct. 3, 1976 (TD)

LEADING RUSHERS

	Atts.	Yds.	Avg.	Longest	TDs
Simpson, Buff.	290	1503	5.2	75	8
Mitchell, Balt.	289	1200	4.2	43	5
Harris, Pitt.	289	1128	3.9	30	14
Bleier, Pitt.	220	1036	4.7	28	5
van Eeghen, Oak.	233	1012	4.3	21	3
Armstrong, Den.	247	1008	4.1	31	5
G. Pruitt, Cleve.	209	1000	4.8	64	4
Cunningham, N.E.	172	824	4.8	24	3
Young, S.D.	162	802	5.0	46	4
Malone, Miami	186	797	4.3	31	4
Gaines, N.Y. Jets	157	724	4.6	33	3
Calhoun, N.E.	129	721	5.6	54	1
Johnson, N.E.	169	699	4.1	69	6
Coleman, Hou.	171	684	4.0	39	2
Clark, Cin.	151	671	4.4	24	7
Griffin, Cin.	138	625	4.5	77	3
Miller, Cleve.	153	613	4.0	21	4

Best Performance: 273 yards in 29 attempts—O. J. Simpson, Buffalo vs. Detroit, Nov. 25, 1976 (2 TDs)

Longest: 77 yards—Archie Griffin, Cincinnati vs. Houston, Nov. 21, 1976 (TD)

LEADING PUNTERS

	No.	Yds.	Avg.	Longest	Blocked
Bateman, Buff.	86	3678	42.8	78	1
Wilson, K.C.	65	2729	42.0	62	1
Guy, Oak.	67	2785	41.6	66	0
West, S.D.	38	1548	40.7	57	0
Patrick, N.E.	67	2688	40.1	52	0
Carrell, N.Y. Jets	81	3218	39.7	72	0
D. Lee, Balt.	59	2342	39.7	56	0
McInally, Cin.	76	2999	39.5	61	0
Green, T.B.	92	3619	39.3	56	0
Walden, Pitt.	76	2982	39.2	58	0
Cockroft, Cleve.	64	2487	38.9	51	3
Seiple, Miami	62	2366	38.2	56	0
Hoopes, Hou.	49	1849	37.7	57	2
Pastorini, Hou.	70	2571	36.7	74	0
Weese, Den.	52	1852	35.6	55	0

Longest: 78 yards—Marv Bateman, Buffalo vs. Houston, Sept. 19, 1976

PUNT RETURN LEADERS

	No.	Yds.	Avg.	Longest	TDs
Upchurch, Den.	39	536	13.7	92	4
Haynes, N.E.	45	608	13.5	89	2
Fuller, S.D.	33	436	13.2	43	0
Brunson, K.C.	31	387	12.5	48	0
Colzie, Oak.	41	448	10.9	32	0
B. Johnson, Hou.	38	403	10.6	46	0
Moody, Buff.	16	166	10.4	67	1
Bell, Pitt.	39	390	10.0	35	0
Moore, Oak.	20	184	9.2	23	0
Deloplaine, Pitt.	17	150	8.8	36	0
Piccone, N.Y. Jets	21	173	8.2	60	1
Stevens, Balt.	39	315	8.1	44	0
Shelby, Cin.	21	162	7.7	30	0
Reece, T.B.	20	143	7.2	30	0

Longest: 92 yards—Rick Upchurch, Denver vs. San Diego, Oct. 3, 1976 (TD)

KICKOFF RETURN LEADERS

	No.	Yds.	Avg.	Longest	TDs
Harris, Miami	17	559	32.9	69	0
Phillips, N.E.	14	397	28.4	71	0
Perrin, Den.	14	391	27.9	43	0
Williams, K.C.	25	688	27.5	64	0
Jennings, Oak.	16	417	26.1	55	0
Shelby, Cin.	30	761	25.4	97	1
Holden, Cleve.	19	461	24.3	44	0
Davis, Miami	26	617	23.7	47	0
Stevens, Balt.	30	710	23.7	83	0
Upchurch, Den.	22	514	23.4	64	0
Moody, Buff.	26	605	23.3	41	0
Feacher, Cleve.	24	551	23.0	46	0
Giammona, N.Y. Jets	23	527	22.9	34	0
Hooks, Buff.	23	521	22.7	79	0
Deloplaine, Pitt.	17	385	22.7	39	0

Longest: 97 yards—Willie Shelby, Cincinnati vs. Cleveland, Oct. 3, 1976 (TD)

AMERICAN FOOTBALL CONFERENCE
1976 Team Statistics

	Atts.	Yds.	Avg.	Avg. PG
Rushing Offense				
Pittsburgh	653*	2971*	4.5	212.2
New England	589	2957	5.0*	211.2
Buffalo	548	2566	4.7	183.3
Baltimore	565	2303	4.1	164.5
Cleveland	533	2295	4.3	163.9
Oakland	557	2285	4.1	163.2
Miami	491	2118	4.3	151.3
Cincinnati	481	2109	4.4	150.6
San Diego	473	2040	4.3	145.7
Denver	500	1932	3.9	138.0
New York Jets	438	1924	4.4	137.4
Kansas City	498	1873	3.8	133.8
Tampa Bay	433	1503	3.5	107.4
Houston	416	1498	3.6	107.0

* Conference leader

	Atts.	Yds.	Avg.	Avg. PG
Rushing Defense				
Pittsburgh	452	1457*	3.2*	104.1*
Denver	496	1709	3.4	122.1
Cleveland	445	1761	4.0	125.8
New England	462	1847	4.0	131.9
Baltimore	437*	1848	4.2	132.0
Oakland	478	1903	4.0	135.9
Cincinnati	520	1912	3.7	136.6
San Diego	516	2048	4.0	146.3
Houston	540	2072	3.8	148.0
Miami	525	2411	4.6	172.2
Buffalo	532	2470	4.6	176.4
Tampa Bay	588	2560	4.4	182.9
New York Jets	582	2592	4.5	185.1
Kansas City	555	2861	5.2	204.4

* Conference leader

	Atts.	Com.	Pct.	Int.	Avg. PG	QB Sacks
Pass Offense						
Baltimore	361	215	59.6	10*	209.5*	30
Kansas City	419	229	54.7	17	209.2	42
Oakland	361	232*	64.3*	18	207.5	28
San Diego	388	223	57.5	18	172.6	46
Miami	346	193	55.8	15	162.0	37
Cleveland	373	209	56.0	15	160.5	19*
Denver	353	168	47.6	22	157.4	48
Cincinnati	360	187	51.9	15	156.5	37
Houston	423*	227	53.7	19	148.0	39
Buffalo	383	156	40.7	17	131.3	33
New England	309	146	47.2	20	124.1	21
Pittsburgh	277	143	51.6	12	119.0	27
New York Jets	393	180	45.8	28	114.7	45
Tampa Bay	376	181	48.1	20	107.4	50

* Conference leader

	Atts.	Com.	Pct.	Int.	Avg. PG	QB Sacks
Pass Defense						
Cincinnati	364	177	48.6	26*	125.6*	46
Pittsburgh	373	158*	42.4*	22	133.3	41
Houston	345	173	50.1	11	136.7	50
Denver	391	214	54.7	24	144.6	32
Cleveland	392	225	57.4	21	145.1	32
New England	437	229	52.4	23	155.4	47
Tampa Bay	321*	178	55.5	9	160.1	24

	Atts.	Com.	Pct.	Int.	Avg. PG	QB Sacks
Buffalo	337	163	48.4	19	161.4	29
New York Jets	374	204	54.5	11	166.0	16
Baltimore	372	192	51.6	15	167.1	57*
Oakland	389	197	50.6	16	176.9	46
Kansas City	375	215	57.3	23	178.3	22
San Diego	386	219	56.7	20	187.7	23
Miami	347	195	56.2	11	190.7	20

* Conference leader

	Yds.	Rush.	Pass.	Avg. PG
Total Offense				
Baltimore	5236*	2303	2933*	374.0*
Oakland	5190	2285	2905	370.7
Kansas City	4802	1873	2929	343.0
New England	4694	2957	1737	335.3
Pittsburgh	4637	2971*	1666	331.2
Cleveland	4542	2295	2247	324.4
San Diego	4456	2040	2416	318.3
Buffalo	4404	2566	1838	314.6
Miami	4386	2118	2268	313.3
Cincinnati	4300	2109	2191	307.1
Denver	4136	1932	2204	295.4
Houston	3570	1498	2072	255.0
New York Jets	3530	1924	1606	252.1
Tampa Bay	3006	1503	1503	214.7

* Conference leader

	Yds.	Rush.	Pass.	Avg. PG
Total Defense				
Pittsburgh	3323*	1457*	1866	237.4*
Cincinnati	3670	1912	1758*	262.1
Denver	3734	1709	2025	266.7
Cleveland	3793	1761	2032	270.9
Houston	3986	2072	1914	284.7
New England	4022	1847	2175	287.3
Baltimore	4187	1848	2339	299.1
Oakland	4379	1903	2476	312.8
San Diego	4676	2048	2628	334.0
Buffalo	4730	2470	2260	337.9
Tampa Bay	4801	2560	2241	342.9
New York Jets	4916	2592	2324	351.1
Miami	5081	2411	2670	362.9
Kansas City	5357	2861	2496	382.6

* Conference leader

NATIONAL FOOTBALL CONFERENCE

Final 1976 Standings

	W	L	T	Pct.	Pts.	Opps.
Eastern Division						
Dallas*	11	3	0	.786	296	194
Washington†	10	4	0	.714	291	217
St. Louis	10	4	0	.714	309	267
Philadelphia	4	10	0	.286	165	286
N.Y. Giants	3	11	0	.214	170	250
Central Division						
Minnesota*	11	2	1	.821	305	176
Chicago	7	7	0	.500	253	216
Detroit	6	8	0	.429	262	220
Green Bay	5	9	0	.357	218	299
Western Division						
Los Angeles*	10	3	1	.750	351	190
San Francisco	8	6	0	.571	270	190
Atlanta	4	10	0	.286	172	312
New Orleans	4	10	0	.286	253	346
Seattle	2	12	0	.143	229	429

* Division winner
† Wild card team for playoffs

1976 Playoff Results

NFC divisional playoff: Minnesota 35, Washington 20 (at Minnesota)
NFC divisional playoff: Los Angeles 14, Dallas 12 (at Dallas)
NFC championship game: Minnesota 24, Los Angeles 13 (at Minnesota)
Super Bowl XI (at Pasadena): Oakland 32, Minnesota 14

LEADING SCORERS

	TDs	Rush.	Pass.	Ret.	Pts.
Touchdown Leaders					
Foreman, Minn.	14	13	1	0	84
Payton, Chi.	13	13	0	0	78
McCutcheon, L.A.	11	9	2	0	66

	TDs	Rush.	Pass.	Ret.	Pts.
S. White, Minn.	10	0	10	0	60
Jones, St. L.	9	8	1	0	54
Thomas, Wash.	9	5	4	0	54
Williams, S.F.	9	7	2	0	54
Galbreath, N.O.	8	7	1	0	48
Metcalf, St. L.	7	3	4	0	42
D. Pearson, Dall.	7	0	6	1	42

Best Performance: 18 pts. on 3 TDs—Delvin Williams, San Francisco vs. St. Louis, Oct. 31, 1976; also vs. Washington, Nov. 11, 1976; Jean Fugett, Washington vs. San Francisco, Nov. 7, 1976; Walter Payton, Chicago vs. Oakland, Nov. 7, 1976; Lawrence McCutcheon, Los Angeles vs. Atlanta, Dec. 4, 1976; Sammie White, Minnesota vs. Miami, Dec. 11, 1976

	PATs	FGs	Longest	Pts.
Top Kick Scorers				
Moseley, Wash.	31-32	22-34	49	97
Bakken, St. L.	33-35	20-27	43	93
Cox, Minn.	32-36	19-31	49	89
Herrera, Dall.	34-34	18-23	46	88
Dempsey, L.A.	36-44	17-26	49	87
Szaro, N.O.	25-29	18-23	50	79
Mike-Mayer, S.F.	26-30	16-28	45	74
Thomas, Chi.	27-30	12-25	47	63

LEADING PASSERS
(140 Attempts)

	Atts.	Com.	Pct. Com.	Yds.	Avg. Yds.	Had Int.	TDs	Rating
Harris, L.A.	158	91	57.6	1460	9.24	6	8	89.8
Landry, Det.	291	168	57.7	2191	7.53	8	17	89.6
Tarkenton, Minn.	412	255	61.9	2961	7.19	8	17	89.4
Hart, St. L.	388	218	56.2	2946	7.59	13	18	81.7
Staubach, Dall.	369	208	56.4	2715	7.36	11	14	79.9
Kilmer, Wash.	206	108	52.4	1252	6.08	10	12	70.0
Scott, N.O.	190	103	54.2	1064	5.60	6	4	64.3
Plunkett, S.F.	243	126	51.9	1592	6.55	16	13	62.8
Theismann, Wash.	163	79	48.5	1036	6.36	10	8	59.9
Douglass, N.O.	213	103	48.4	1288	6.05	8	4	58.1
Morton, N.Y. Giants	284	153	53.9	1865	6.57	20	9	55.9

	Atts.	Com.	Pct. Com.	Yds.	Avg. Yds.	Had Int.	TDs	Rating
Boryla, Phil.	246	123	50.0	1247	5.07	14	9	53.5
Dickey, G.B.	243	115	47.3	1465	6.03	14	7	52.1
Avellini, Chi.	271	118	43.5	1580	5.83	15	8	49.7
Zorn, Sea.	439	208	47.4	2571	5.86	27	12	49.2

Longest: 85 yards—Jim Plunkett to Delvin Williams, San Francisco vs. Washington, Nov. 7, 1976 (TD)

Ratings based on percentage completion, average yards gained, TD percentage, interception percentage.

LEADING PASS RECEIVERS

	No.	Yds.	Avg.	Longest	TDs
D. Pearson, Dall.	58	806	13.9	40	6
Foreman, Minn. (rb)*	55	567	10.3	41	1
Largent, Sea.	54	705	13.1	45	4
Galbreath, N.O. (rb)*	54	420	7.8	35	1
Rashad, Minn.	53	671	12.7	47	3
Harris, St. L.	52	782	15.0	40	1
S. White, Minn.	51	906	17.8	56	10
Grant, Wash.	50	818	16.4	53	5
DuPree, Dall.	42	680	16.2	38	2
Carmichael, Phil.	42	503	12.0	24	5
Tucker, N.Y. Giants	42	498	11.9	39	1
Jenkins, Atl.	41	710	17.3	34	6
McClanahan, Minn. (rb)*	40	252	6.3	23	1
Jarvis, Det.	39	822	21.1	74	5
H. Jackson, L.A.	39	751	19.3	65	5
Laidlaw, Dall. (rb)*	38	325	8.6	26	1
Howard, Sea.	37	422	11.4	30	0
Gray, St. L.	36	686	19.1	77	5
Smith, Sea.	36	384	10.7	34	1
Kotar, N.Y. Giants (rb)*	36	319	8.9	30	0
C. Sanders, Det.	35	545	15.6	36	5

* rb denotes running back

Best Performance: 11 receptions (132 yards)—Doug Kotar, New York Giants vs. St. Louis, Oct. 3, 1976; 11 receptions (200 yards)—Frank Grant, Washington vs. San Francisco, Nov. 7, 1976

INTERCEPTION LEADERS

	No.	Yds.	Longest	TDs
M. Jackson, L.A.	10	173	46	3
Perry, L.A.	8	79	43	0
Lavender, Wash.	8	77	28	0
Hunter, Det.	7	120	39	1
Brupbacher, Chi.	7	49	25	0
N. Wright, Minn.	7	47	21	0
Johnson, Det.	6	206	76	1
Ellis, Chi.	6	47	22	1
Lawrence, Atl.	6	43	22	0
Fischer, Wash.	5	38	32	0

Longest: 83 yards—Jim Merlo, New Orleans vs. Atlanta, Oct. 10, 1976 (TD)

LEADING RUSHERS

	Atts.	Yds.	Avg.	Longest	TDs
Payton, Chi.	311	1390	4.5	60	13
Williams, S.F.	248	1203	4.9	80	7
McCutcheon, L.A.	291	1168	4.0	40	9
Foreman, Minn.	278	1155	4.2	46	13
Thomas, Wash.	254	1101	4.3	28	5
Otis, St. L.	243	891	3.7	23	2
Bussey, Det.	196	858	4.4	46	3
Jackson, S.F.	200	792	4.0	24	1
Kotar, N.Y. Giants	185	731	4.0	24	3
Cappelletti, L.A.	177	688	3.9	38	1
Muncie, N.O.	149	659	4.4	51	2
Gaines, Det.	155	659	4.3	26	4
Harper, Chi.	147	625	4.3	28	2
Riggins, Wash.	162	572	3.5	15	3
Galbreath, N.O.	136	570	4.2	74	7
Csonka, N.Y. Giants	160	569	3.6	13	4
Hogan, Phil.	123	561	4.6	32	0
Dennison, Dall.	153	542	3.5	14	6
Smith, Sea.	119	537	4.5	53	4
Metcalf, St. L.	134	537	4.0	36	3

Best Performance: 200 yards on 28 attempts—Chuck Foreman, Minnesota vs. Philadelphia, Oct. 24, 1976 (2 TDs)

Longest: 80 yards—Delvin Williams, San Francisco vs. Washington, Nov. 7, 1976 (TD)

LEADING PUNTERS

	No.	Yds.	Avg.	Longest	Blocked
James, Atl.	101	4253	42.1	67	0
Jennings, N.Y. Giants	74	3054	41.3	61	3
Wittum, S.F.	89	3634	40.8	68	2
H. Weaver, Det.	83	3280	39.5	69	1
Blanchard, N.O.	101	3974	39.3	63	0
R. Jackson, L.A.	77	3006	39.0	61	2
Bragg, Wash.	90	3503	38.9	56	0
Clabo, Minn.	69	2678	38.8	55	0
D. White, Dall.	70	2690	38.4	54	2
Engles, Sea.	80	3067	38.3	55	2
Parsons, Chi.	99	3726	37.6	62	1
Beverly, G.B.	83	3071	37.0	60	1
Jones, Phil.	94	3445	36.6	57	3
Joyce, St. L.	64	2331	36.4	54	2

Longest: 69 yards—Herman Weaver, Detroit vs. Chicago, Sept. 12, 1976

PUNT RETURN LEADERS

	No.	Yds.	Avg.	Longest	TDs
E. Brown, Wash.	48	646	13.5	71	1
Bryant, L.A.	29	321	11.1	25	0
Metcalf, St. L.	17	188	11.1	39	0
Johnson, Dall.	45	489	10.9	55	0
Marshall, Phil.	27	290	10.7	29	0
Tilley, St. L.	15	146	9.7	17	0
Athas, N.O.	35	332	9.5	67	0
Rhodes, S.F.	16	142	8.9	22	0
Barney, Det.	23	191	8.3	30	0
Gray, G.B.	37	307	8.3	27	0
Livers, Chi.	28	205	7.3	51	0
Leonard, S.F.	35	253	7.2	60	1
Blackwood, Sea.	19	132	6.9	26	0
Lawrence, Atl.	54	372	6.9	24	0
Willis, Minn.	30	207	6.9	29	0

Longest: 71 yards—Eddie Brown, Washington vs. St. Louis, Oct. 25, 1976 (TD)

KICKOFF RETURN LEADERS

	No.	Yds.	Avg.	Longest	TDs
Bryant, L.A.	16	459	28.7	90	1
Hunter, Det.	14	375	26.8	84	0
Baschnagel, Chi.	29	754	26.0	48	0
M. C. McCoy, G.B.	18	457	25.4	65	0
Lawrence, Atl.	21	521	24.8	36	0
Johnson, Dall.	28	693	24.8	74	0
E. Brown, Wash.	30	738	24.6	67	0
Willis, Minn.	24	552	23.0	57	0
Latin, St. L.	16	357	22.3	39	0
Robinson, N.Y. Giants	20	444	22.2	32	0
Ross, Sea.	30	655	21.8	45	0
Marshall, Phil.	30	651	21.7	41	0

Longest: 90 yards—Cullen Bryant, Los Angeles vs. St. Louis, Nov. 14, 1976 (TD)

NATIONAL FOOTBALL CONFERENCE
1976 Team Statistics

	Atts.	Yds.	Avg.	Avg. PG
Rushing Offense				
Los Angeles	613*	2528*	4.1	180.6*
San Francisco	576	2447	4.2	174.8
Chicago	578	2363	4.1	168.8
St. Louis	580	2301	4.0	164.4
Detroit	516	2213	4.3*	158.1
Dallas	538	2147	4.0	153.4
Washington	548	2111	3.9	150.8
Philadelphia	505	2080	4.1	148.6
Minnesota	540	2003	3.7	143.1
New York Giants	530	1904	3.6	136.0
New Orleans	431	1775	4.1	126.8
Green Bay	485	1722	3.6	123.0
Atlanta	470	1689	3.6	120.6
Seattle	374	1416	3.8	101.1

* Conference leader

	Atts.	Yds.	Avg.	Avg. PG
Rushing Defense				
Los Angeles	429*	1564*	3.6*	111.7*
San Francisco	487	1786	3.7	127.6
Dallas	484	1821	3.8	130.1
Detroit	496	1901	3.8	135.8
St. Louis	491	1979	4.0	141.4
Chicago	522	1984	3.8	141.7
Philadelphia	532	2053	3.9	146.6
Minnesota	487	2096	4.3	149.7
New York Giants	560	2203	3.9	157.4
Washington	555	2205	4.0	157.5
Green Bay	546	2288	4.2	163.4
New Orleans	554	2289	4.1	163.5
Atlanta	574	2577	4.5	184.1
Seattle	614	2876	4.7	205.4

* Conference leader

	Atts.	Com.	Pct.	Int.	Avg. PG	QB Sacks
Pass Offense						
Minnesota	442	270*	61.1*	10*	203.9*	31
St. Louis	392	220	56.1	13	202.5	17*
Dallas	390	222	56.9	13	195.5	30
Seattle	480*	229	47.7	30	189.2	28
Los Angeles	315	171	54.3	15	167.2	32
Detroit	356	201	56.5	12	152.9	67
Washington	370	187	50.5	20	141.8	38
New Orleans	403	206	51.1	14	141.6	51
New York Giants	326	175	53.7	24	128.0	44
Green Bay	357	164	45.9	22	123.6	41
San Francisco	306	155	50.7	21	117.0	34
Philadelphia	369	182	49.3	18	106.6	43
Chicago	278	123	44.2	15	105.7	24
Atlanta	354	157	44.4	24	101.0	44

* Conference leader

	Atts.	Com.	Pct.	Int.	Avg. PG	QB Sacks
Pass Defense						
Minnesota	323	158	48.9	19	112.5*	45
Detroit	313*	137*	43.8	24	120.4	28
San Francisco	374	180	48.1	9	126.9	61*
Green Bay	354	196	55.4	11	131.1	43
Dallas	391	187	47.8	16	136.4	44
Washington	354	146	41.2*	26	136.9	44
New York Giants	330	189	57.3	12	142.0	31

-	Atts.	Com.	Pct.	Int.	Avg. PG	QB Sacks
Atlanta	340	184	54.1	18	142.9	35
Los Angeles	397	199	50.1	32*	149.4	45
St. Louis	342	176	51.5	19	150.7	31
New Orleans	367	200	54.5	12	157.3	39
Chicago	401	200	49.9	24	158.4	49
Seattle	367	223	60.8	15	180.3	27
Philadelphia	404	237	58.7	9	182.1	19

* Conference leader

	Yds.	Rush.	Pass.	Avg. PG
Total Offense				
St. Louis	5136*	2301	2835	366.9*
Dallas	4884	2147	2737	348.9
Los Angeles	4869	2528*	2341	347.8
Minnesota	4858	2003	2855*	347.0
Detroit	4353	2213	2140	310.9
Washington	4096	2111	1985	292.6
San Francisco	4085	2447	1638	291.8
Seattle	4065	1416	2649	290.4
Chicago	3843	2363	1480	274.5
New Orleans	3758	1775	1983	268.4
New York Giants	3696	1904	1792	264.0
Philadelphia	3572	2080	1492	255.1
Green Bay	3452	1722	1730	246.6
Atlanta	3103	1689	1414	221.6

* Conference leader

	Yds.	Rush.	Pass.	Avg. PG
Total Defense				
San Francisco	3562*	1786	1776	254.4*
Detroit	3587	1901	1686	256.2
Los Angeles	3656	1564*	2092	261.1
Minnesota	3671	2096	1575*	262.2
Dallas	3730	1821	1909	266.4
St. Louis	4089	1979	2110	292.1
Washington	4122	2205	1917	294.4
Green Bay	4123	2288	1835	294.5
New York Giants	4191	2203	1988	299.4
Chicago	4201	1984	2217	300.1
New Orleans	4491	2289	2202	320.8
Atlanta	4578	2577	2001	327.0
Philadelphia	4603	2053	2550	328.8
Seattle	5400	2876	2524	385.7

. * Conference leader

LET'S LOOK AT
THE RECORDS

Year-by-year NFL records of . . .

- AFC and NFC individual leaders
- AFC and NFC team leaders
- NFL 1000-yard rushers
- NFL all-time champions
- NFC divisional winners and playoff championship results, 1921–76
- AFC divisional winners and playoff championship results, 1960–76
- Super Bowl results and records, 1967–77
- AFC–NFC Pro Bowl results, 1971–77
- College All-Star Game results, 1934–76

PLUS a selection of NFL all-time individual records and the Professional Football Hall of Fame

FOOTNOTING THE FOOTNOTES

The **Chicago Cardinals,** sometimes listed as "Chi Cards" in the records, existed from 1920 through 1959 and moved to St. Louis beginning with the 1960 season.

The **Cleveland Rams** were in that Ohio city from 1937 through the 1946 season, moving to Los Angeles in 1947.

The **Boston Redskins** were in the Massachusetts capital from 1932 through 1936; they elected to begin the 1937 season in Washington.

Before they traveled to Kansas City to begin the 1963 season, the **Chiefs** were in Dallas for three years; there they were known as the **Texans.**

The **New England Patriots** were the **Boston Patriots** from 1960 through 1970. For those years, they are listed as "Boston" in the records that follow.

The **New York Jets** went by the name of the **Titans** when they first took the field in 1960. They became the Jets beginning with the 1963 season.

The **San Diego Chargers** went by that name in Los Angeles for one season, 1960. That was the first year the old American Football League existed. The AFL eventually evolved into the present American Conference of the National Football League.

The **Detroit Lions** began their history as the **Portsmouth** (Ohio) **Spartans,** playing as same from 1930 through 1933. They moved to Motor City in 1934.

Once upon a time there was an NFL team in Brooklyn, and what else could they have been called except the **Dodgers?**

American Football Conference
INDIVIDUAL LEADERS, YEAR BY YEAR

Scoring

Year	Player	Team	TDs	PATs	FGs	Pts.
1976	Linhart, Toni	Baltimore	0	49	20	109
1975	Simpson, O.J.	Buffalo	23*	0	0	138
1974	Gerela, Roy	Pittsburgh	0	33	20	93
1973	Gerela, Roy	Pittsburgh	0	36	29	123
1972	Howfield, Bobby	New York	0	40	27	121
1971	Yepremian, Garo	Miami	0	33	28	117
1970	Stenerud, Jan	Kansas City	0	26	30	116
1969	Turner, Jim	New York	0	33	32	129
1968	Turner, Jim	New York	0	43	34*	145
1967	Blanda, George	Oakland	0	56	20	116
1966	Cappelletti, Gino	Boston	6	35	16	119
1965	Cappelletti, Gino	Boston	9	27	17	132
1964	Cappelletti, Gino	Boston	7	36	25	155†
1963	Cappelletti, Gino	Boston	2	35	22	113
1962	Mingo, Gene	Denver	4	32	27	137
1961	Cappelletti, Gino	Boston	8	48	17	147
1960	Mingo, Gene	Denver	6	33	18	123

* All-time NFL leader
† Includes safety

Rushing

Year	Player	Team	YG	Atts.	Avg. G per Att.	TDs
1976	Simpson, O.J.	Buffalo	1503	290	5.2	8
1975	Simpson, O.J.	Buffalo	1817	329	5.5	16
1974	Armstrong, Otis	Denver	1407	263	5.3	9
1973	Simpson, O.J.	Buffalo	2003*	332*	6.0	12
1972	Simpson, O.J.	Buffalo	1251	292	4.3	6
1971	Little, Floyd	Denver	1133	284	4.0	6
1970	Little, Floyd	Denver	901	209	4.3	3
1969	Post, Dick	San Diego	873	182	4.8	6
1968	Robinson, Paul	Cincinnati	1023	238	4.3	8
1967	Nance, Jim	Boston	1216	269	4.5	7

* All-time NFL leader

Year	Player	Team	YG	Atts.	Avg. G per Att.	TDs
1966	Nance, Jim	Boston	1458	299	4.9	11
1965	Lowe, Paul	San Diego	1121	222	5.0	7
1964	Gilchrist, Cookie	Buffalo	981	230	4.2	6
1963	Daniels, Clem	Oakland	1099	215	5.1	3
1964	Gilchrist, Cookie	Buffalo	1096	214	5.1	13
1961	Cannon, Billy	Houston	948	200	4.7	6
1960	Haynes, Abner	Dallas Texans	875	156	5.6	9

Pass Receiving

Year	Player	Team	Caught	YG	TDs
1976	Lane, MacArthur	Kansas City	66	686	1
1975	Rucker, Reggie	Cleveland	60	770	3
1975	Mitchell, Lydell	Baltimore	60	544	4
1974	Mitchell, Lydell	Baltimore	72	544	2
1973	Willis, Fred	Houston	57	371	1
1972	Biletnikoff, Fred	Oakland	58	802	7
1971	Biletnikoff, Fred	Oakland	61	929	9
1970	Briscoe, Marlin	Buffalo	57	1036	8
1969	Alworth, Lance	San Diego	64	1003	4
1968	Alworth, Lance	Oakland	68	1312	10
1967	Sauer, George	New York	75	1189	6
1966	Alworth, Lance	San Diego	73	1383	13
1965	Taylor, Lionel	Denver	85	1131	6
1964	Hennigan, Charley	Houston	101*	1546	8
1963	Taylor, Lionel	Denver	78	1101	10
1962	Taylor, Lionel	Denver	77	908	4
1961	Taylor, Lionel	Denver	100	1176	4
1960	Taylor, Lionel	Denver	92	1235	12

* All-time NFL leader

Passing

Year	Player	Team	YG per Att.	Atts.	Com.	Avg. Pct. Com.	YG	TDs
1976	Stabler, Ken	Oak.	9.41	291	194	66.7	2737	27
1975	Anderson, Ken	Cin.	8.41	377	228	60.5	3169	21
1974	Anderson, Ken	Cin.	8.13	328	213	64.9	2667	18

Year	Player	Team	YG per Att.	Atts.	Com.	Avg. Pct. Com.	YG	TDs
1973	Stabler, Ken	Oak.	7.68	260	163	62.7	1997	14
1972	Morrall, Earl	Miami	9.07	150	83	55.3	1360	11
1971	Griese, Bob	Miami	7.94	263	145	55.1	2089	19
1970	Lamonica, Daryle	Oak.	7.07	356	179	50.3	2516	22
1969	Cook, Greg	Cin.	9.4	197	106	53.8	1854	15
1968	Dawson, Len	K.C.	9.4	224	131	58.5	2109	17
1967	Lamonica, Daryle	Oak.	7.6	425	220	51.8	3228	30
1966	Dawson, Len	K.C.	8.9	284	159	56.0	2527	26
1965	Hadl, John	S.D.	8.1	348	174	50.0	2798	20
1964	Dawson, Len	K.C.	8.1	354	199	56.2	2879	30
1963	Rote, Tobin	S.D.	8.7	286	170	59.4	2510	20
1962	Dawson, Len	Dall.†	8.9	310	189	60.9	2759	29
1961	Blanda, George	Hou.	9.2	362	187	51.7	3330	36*
1960	Kemp, Jack	L.A.‡	7.4	406	211	51.9	3018	20

* All-time NFL leader
† Dallas Texans
‡ Los Angeles Chargers
In 1963, Y.A. Tittle of the New York Giants also passed for a record 36 TDs.

Pass Interceptions

Year	Player	Team	No.	Yds.
1976	Riley, Ken	Cincinnati	9	141
1975	Blount, Mel	Pittsburgh	11	121
1974	Thomas, Emmitt	Kansas City	12	214
1973	Anderson, Dick	Miami	8	163
	Wagner, Mike	Pittsburgh	8	134
1972	Sensibaugh, Mike	Kansas City	8	65
1971	Houston, Ken	Houston	9	220
1970	Robinson, Johnny	Kansas City	10	155
1969	Thomas, Emmitt	Kansas City	9	146
1968	Grayson, Dave	Oakland	10	195
	Farr, Miller	Houston	10	264
1967	Janik, Tom	Buffalo	10	222
	Westmoreland, Dick	Miami	10	127
1966	Robinson, Johnny	Kansas City	10	136
	Hunt, Bobby	Kansas City	10	113
1965	Hicks, W.K.	Houston	9	156
1964	Paulson, Dainard	N.Y. Jets	12	157
1963	Glick, Fred	Houston	12	180
1962	Riley, Lee	N.Y. Titans	11	122
1961	Atkins, Billy	Buffalo	10	158
1960	Austin, Gonsoulin	Denver	11	98

Punting

Year	Player	Team	No.	Avg.
1976	Bateman, Marv	Buffalo	86	42.8
1975	Guy, Ray	Oakland	68	43.8
1974	Guy, Ray	Oakland	74	42.2
1973	Wilson, Jerrel	Kansas City	80	45.5
1972	Wilson, Jerrel	Kansas City	66	44.8
1971	Lewis, Dave	Cincinnati	72	44.8
1970	Lewis, Dave	Cincinnati	79	46.2
1969	Partee, Dennis	San Diego	71	44.6
1968	Wilson, Jerrel	Kansas City	63	45.1
1967	Scarpitto, Bob	Denver	105*	44.9
1966	Scarpitto, Bob	Denver	76	45.8
1965	Wilson, Jerrel	Kansas City	69	45.4
1964	Fraser, Jim	Denver	73	44.2
1963	Fraser, Jim	Denver	81	44.4
1962	Fraser, Jim	Denver	55	43.6
1961	Atkins, Billy	Buffalo	85	44.5
1960	Maguire, Paul	L.A. Chargers	43	40.5

* All-time NFL leader

Punt Returns

Year	Player	Team	No.	Yds.	Avg.
1976	Upchurch, Rick	Denver	39	536	13.7
1975	Johnson, Billy	Houston	40	610	15.3
1974	Parrish, Lemar	Cincinnati	18	338	18.8
1973	Smith, Ron	San Diego	27	352	13.0
1972	Farasopoulos, Chris	N.Y. Jets	17	179	10.5
1971	Kelly, Leroy	Cleveland	30	292	9.7
1970	Podolak, Ed	Kansas City	23	311	13.5
1969	Thompson, Bill	Denver	25	288	11.5
1968	Smith, Noland	Kansas City	18	270	15.0
1967	Little, Floyd	Denver	16	270	16.9
1966	Duncan, Les	San Diego	18	238	13.2
1965	Duncan, Les	San Diego	30	464	15.5
1964	Jancik, Bobby	Houston	12	220	18.3
1963	Gibson, Claude	Oakland	26	307	11.8
1962	Christy, Dick	N.Y. Titans	15	250	16.7
1961	Christy, Dick	N.Y. Titans	18	383	21.3
1960	Haynes, Abner	Dallas Texans	14	215	15.4

Kickoff Returns

Year	Player	Team	No.	Yds.	Avg.
1976	Harris, Duriel	Miami	17	559	32.9
1975	Hart, Harold	Oakland	17	518	30.5
1974	Pruitt, Greg	Cleveland	22	606	27.5
1973	Francis, Wallace	Buffalo	23	687	29.9
1972	Laird, Bruce	Baltimore	29	843	29.1
1971	Morris, Eugene	Miami	15	423	28.2
1970	Duncan, Jim	Baltimore	20	707	35.4
1969	Thompson, Bill	Denver	18	513	28.5
1968	Atkinson, George	Oakland	32	802	25.1
1967	Moore, Zeke	Houston	14	405	28.9
1966	Sellers, Goldie	Denver	19	541	28.5
1965	Haynes, Abner	Denver	34	901	26.5
1964	Roberson, Bo	Oakland	36	975	27.1
1963	Jancik, Bobby	Houston	45	1317*	29.3
1962	Jancik, Bobby	Houston	24	726	30.3
1961	Grayson, Dave	Dallas Texans	16	453	28.3
1960	Hall, Ken	Houston	19	594	31.3

* All-time NFL leader

National Football Conference
INDIVIDUAL LEADERS, YEAR BY YEAR

Scoring

Year	Player	Team	TDs	PATs	FGs	Pts.
1976	Moseley, Mark	Wash.	0	31	22	97
1975	Foreman, Chuck	Minn.	22	0	0	132
1974	Marcol, Chester	G.B.	0	19	25	94
1973	Ray, David	L.A.	0	40	30	130
1972	Marcol, Chester	G.B.	0	29	33	128
1971	Knight, Curt	Wash.	0	27	29	114
1970	Cox, Fred	Minn.	0	35	30	125
1969	Cox, Fred	Minn.	0	43	26	121
1968	Kelly, Leroy	Cleve.	20	0	0	120
1967	Bakken, Jim	St. L	0	36	27	117

Year	Player	Team	TDs	PATs	FGs	Pts.
1966	Gossett, Bruce	L.A.	0	29	28	113
1965	Sayers, Gale	Chi.	22	0	0	132
1964	Moore, Lenny	Balt.	20	0	0	120
1963	Chandler, Don	N.Y.	0	52	18	106
1962	Taylor, Jim	G.B.	19	0	0	114
1961	Hornung, Paul	G.B.	10	41	15	146
1960	Hornung, Paul	G.B.	15	41	15	176*
1959	Hornung, Paul	G.B.	7	31	7	94
1958	Brown, Jimmy	Cleve.	18	0	0	108
1957	Baker, Sam	Wash.	1	29	14	77
	Groza, Lou	Cleve.	0	32	15	77
1956	Layne, Bobby	Det.	5	33	12	99
1955	Walker, Doak	Det.	7	27	9	96
1954	Walston, Bobby	Phil.	11	36	4	114
1953	Soltau, Gordie	S.F.	6	48	10	114
1952	Soltau, Gordie	S.F.	7	34	6	94
1951	Hirsch, Elroy	L.A.	17	0	0	102
1950	Walker, Doak	Det.	11	38	8	128
1949	Harder, Pat	Chi.†	8	45	3	102
	Roberts, Gene	N.Y.	17	0	0	102
1948	Harder, Pat	Chi.†	6	53	7	110
1947	Harder, Pat	Chi.†	7	39	7	102
1946	Fritsch, Ted	G.B.	10	13	9	100
1945	Van Buren, Steve	Phil.	18	2	0	110
1944	Hutson, Don	G.B.	9	31	0	85
1943	Hutson, Don	G.B.	12	36	3	117
1942	Hutson, Don	G.B.	17	33	1	138
1941	Hutson, Don	G.B.	12	20	0	95
1940	Hutson, Don	G.B.	7	15	0	57
1939	Farkas, Andy	Wash.	11	2	0	68
1938	Hinkle, Clark	G.B.	7	7	3	58
1937	Manders, Jack	Chi.	5	15	8	69
1936	Clark, Earl	Det.	7	19	4	73
1935	Clark, Earl	Det.	6	16	1	55
1934	Manders, Jack	Chi.	3	28	10	76
1933	Strong, Ken	N.Y.	6	13	5	64
	Pressnell, Glenn	Port.‡	6	10	6	64
1932	Clark, Earl	Port.‡	6	10	3	55

* All-time NFL leader
† Chicago Cardinals
‡ Portsmouth (Ohio) Spartans

Rushing

Year	Player	Team	YG	Atts.	Avg. G per Att.	TDs
1976	Payton, Walter	Chi.	1390	311	4.5	13
1975	Otis, Jim	St. L.	1076	269	4.0	5
1974	McCutcheon, L.	L.A.	1109	236	4.7	3
1973	Brockington, J.	G.B.	1144	265	4.3	3
1972	Brown, Larry	Wash.	1216	285	4.3	8
1971	Brockington, J.	G.B.	1105	216	5.1	4
1970	Brown, Larry	Wash.	1125	237	4.7	5
1969	Sayers, Gale	Chi.	1032	236	4.4	8
1968	Kelly, Leroy	Cleve.	1239	248	5.0	16
1967	Kelly, Leroy	Cleve.	1205	235	5.1	11
1966	Sayers, Gale	Chi.	1231	229	5.4	8
1965	Brown, Jimmy	Cleve.	1544	289	5.3	17
1964	Brown, Jimmy	Cleve.	1446	280	5.2	7
1963	Brown, Jimmy	Cleve.	1863	291	6.4	12
1962	Taylor, Jim	G.B.	1474	272	5.4	19*
1961	Brown, Jimmy	Cleve.	1408	305	4.6	8
1960	Brown, Jimmy	Cleve.	1257	215	5.8	9
1959	Brown, Jimmy	Cleve.	1329	290	4.6	14
1958	Brown, Jimmy	Cleve.	1527	257	5.9	17
1957	Brown, Jimmy	Cleve.	942	202	4.7	9
1956	Casares, Rick	Chi.	1126	234	4.8	12
1955	Ameche, Alan	Balt.	961	213	4.5	9
1954	Perry, Joe	S.F.	1049	173	6.1	8
1953	Perry, Joe	S.F.	1018	192	5.3	10
1952	Towler, Dan	L.A.	894	156	5.7	10
1951	Price, Eddie	N.Y.	971	271	3.2	7
1950	Motley, Marion	Cleve.	810	140	5.8	3
1949	Van Buren, S.	Phil.	1146	263	4.4	11
1948	Van Buren, S.	Phil.	945	201	4.7	10
1947	Van Buren, S.	Phil.	1008	217	4.6	13
1946	Dudley, Bill	Pitt.	604	146	4.1	3
1945	Van Buren, S	Phil.	832	143	5.8	15
1944	Paschal, Bill	N.Y.	737	196	3.8	9
1943	Paschal, Bill	N.Y.	572	147	3.9	10
1942	Dudley, Bill	Pitt.	696	162	4.3	5
1941	Manders, C.	Brook.**	486	111	4.4	5
1940	White, Whizzer	Det.	514	146	3.5	5
1939	Osmanski, Bill	Chi.	699	121	5.8	7
1938	White, Whizzer	Pitt.	567	152	3.7	4
1937	Battles, Cliff	Wash.	874	216	4.1	5
1936	Leemans, Tuffy	N.Y.	830	206	4.1	2
1935	Russell, Doug	Chi.***	499	140	3.6	0

Year	Player	Team	YG	Atts.	Avg. G per Att.	TDs
1934	Feathers, B.	Chi.	1004	101	9.9*	8
1933	Musick, Jim	Bost.†	809	173	4.7	5
1932	Battles, Cliff	Bost.‡	576	148	3.9	3

* All-time NFL leader
** Brooklyn (New York) Dodgers
*** Chicago Cardinals

† Boston Redskins
‡ Boston Braves

Pass Receiving

Year	Player	Team	Caught	YG	TDs
1976	Pearson, Drew	Dall.	58	806	6
1975	Foreman, Chuck	Minn.	73	691	9
1974	Young, Charles	Phil.	63	696	3
1973	Carmichael, Harold	Phil.	67	1116	9
1972	Jackson, Harold	Phil.	62	1048	4
1971	Tucker, Bob	N.Y.	59	791	4
1970	Gordon, Dick	Chi.	71	1026	13
1969	Abramowicz, Dan	N.O.	73	1015	7
1968	McNeil, Clifton	S.F.	71	994	7
1967	Taylor, Charley	Wash.	70	990	9
1966	Taylor, Charley	Wash.	72	1119	12
1965	Parks, Dave	S.F.	80	1344	12
1964	Morris, Johnny	Chi.	93	1200	10
1963	Conrad, Bobby Joe	St. L.	73	967	10
1962	Mitchell, Bobby	Wash.	72	1384	11
1961	Phillips, Jim	L.A.	78	1092	5
1960	Berry, Ray	Balt.	74	1298	10
1959	Berry, Ray	Balt.	66	959	14
1958	Berry, Ray	Balt.	56	794	9
	Retzlaff, Pete	Phil.	56	766	2
1957	Wilson, Billy	S.F.	52	757	6
1956	Wilson, Billy	S.F.	60	889	5
1955	Pihos, Pete	Phil.	62	864	7
1954	Pihos, Pete	Phil.	60	872	10
	Wilson, Billy	S.F.	60	830	5
1953	Pihos, Pete	Phil.	63	1049	10
1952	Speedie, Mac	Cleve.	62	911	5
1951	Hirsch, Elroy	L.A.	66	1495	17*
1950	Fears, Tom	L.A.	84	1116	7
1949	Fears, Tom	L.A.	77	1013	9
1948	Fears, Tom	L.A.	51	698	4
1947	Keane, Jim	Chi.	64	910	10

Year	Player	Team	Caught	YG	TDs
1946	Benton, Jim	L.A.	63	981	6
1945	Hutson, Don	G.B.	47	834	9
1944	Hutson, Don	G.B.	58	866	9
1943	Hutson, Don	G.B.	47	776	11
1942	Hutson, Don	G.B.	74	1211	17*
1941	Hutson, Don	G.B.	58	738	10
1940	Looney, Don	Phil.	58	707	4
1939	Hutson, Don	G.B.	34	846	6
1938	Tinsley, Gaynell	Chi. Cards	41	516	1
1937	Hutson, Don	G.B.	41	552	7
1936	Hutson, Don	G.B.	34	536	8
1935	Goodwin, Tod	N.Y.	26	432	4
1934	Carter, Joe	Phil.	16	238	4
1934	Badgro, Morris	N.Y.	16	206	1
1933	Kelly, John	Brook.†	22	246	3
1932	Flaherty, Ray	N.Y.	21	350	3

* All-time NFL leader
† Brooklyn (New York) Dodgers
In 1961, Bill Groman of the Houston Oilers also had a record 17 TD receptions.

Passing

Year	Player	Team	YG per Att.	Atts.	Com.	Avg. Pct. Com.	YG	TDs
1976	Harris, James	L.A.	9.2	158	91	57.6	1460	8
1975	Tarkenton, Fran	Minn.	7.0	425	273	64.2	2994	25
1974	Jurgensen, Sonny	Wash.	7.1	167	107	64.1	1185	11
1973	Staubach, Roger	Dall.	8.4	286	179	62.6	2428	23
1972	Snead, Norm	N.Y.	7.1	325	196	60.3	2307	17
1971	Staubach, Roger	Dall.	8.9	211	126	59.7	1882	15
1970	Brodie, John	S.F.	7.8	378	223	59.0	2941	24
1969	Jurgensen, Sonny	Wash.	7.0	442	274	62.0	3102	22
1968	Morrall, Earl	Balt.	9.1	317	182	57.4	2909	26
1967	Jurgensen, Sonny	Wash.	7.4	508*	288*	56.7	3747	31
1966	Starr, Bart	G.B.	8.9	251	156	62.2	2257	14
1965	Bukich, Rudy	Chi.	8.5	312	176	56.4	2641	20
1964	Starr, Bart	G.B.	7.8	272	163	59.9	2144	15
1963	Tittle, Y. A.	N.Y.	8.6	367	221	60.2	3145	36*
1962	Starr, Bart	G.B.	8.6	285	178	62.5	2438	12
1961	Plum, Milt	Cleve.	8.0	302	177	58.6	2416	18
1960	Plum, Milt	Cleve.	9.2	250	151	60.4	2297	21
1959	Conerly, Charley	N.Y.	8.8	194	113	58.2	1706	14

Year	Player	Team	YG per Att.	Atts.	Com.	Avg. Pct. Com.	YG	TDs
1958	LeBaron, Eddie	Wash.	9.4	145	79	54.5	1365	11
1957	O'Connell, Tom	Cleve.	12.1	110	63	57.3	1229	9
1956	Brown, Ed	Chi.	9.9	168	96	57.1	1667	11
1955	Graham, Otto	Cleve.	9.3	185	98	52.9	1721	15
1954	Van Brocklin, Norm	L.A.	10.1	260	139	53.5	2637	13
1953	Graham, Otto	Cleve.	10.5	258	167	64.7	2722	11
1952	Van Brocklin, Norm	L.A.	8.5	205	113	55.1	1736	14
1951	Waterfield, Bob	L.A.	8.8	176	88	50.0	1556	13
1950	Van Brocklin, Norm	L.A.	8.8	233	127	54.5	2061	18
1949	Baugh, Sammy	Wash.	7.5	255	145	56.9	1903	18
1948	Thompson, Tommy	Phil.	8.0	246	141	57.3	1965	25
1947	Baugh, Sammy	Wash.	8.4	354	210	59.3	2938	25
1946	Waterfield, Bob	L.A.	7.0	251	127	50.6	1747	18
1945	Baugh, Sammy	Wash.	9.2	182	128	70.3*	1669	11
1945	Luckman, Sid	Chi.	7.9	217	117	53.9	1725	14
1944	Filchock, Frank	Wash.	7.8	147	84	57.1	1139	13
1943	Baugh, Sammy	Wash.	7.3	239	133	55.6	1754	23
1942	Isbell, Cecil	G.B.	7.5	268	146	54.5	2021	24
1941	Isbell, Cecil	G.B.	7.2	206	117	56.8	1479	15
1940	Baugh, Sammy	Wash.	7.7	177	111	62.7	1367	12
1939	Hall, Parker	Cleve.†	5.9	208	106	50.9	1227	9
1938	Danowski, Ed	N.Y.	6.6	129	70	54.3	848	7
1937	Baugh, Sammy	Wash.	6.6	171	81	47.3	1127	8
1936	Herber, Arnie	G.B.	7.2	173	77	44.5	1239	11
1935	Danowski, Ed	N.Y.	7.1	113	57	50.4	795	10
1934	Herber, Arnie	G.B.	6.9	115	42	36.5	799	8
1933	Newman, Harry	N.Y.	7.3	136	53	38.9	973	11
1932	Herber, Arnie	G.B.	6.3	101	37	36.6	639	9

* All-time NFL leader
† Cleveland Rams
In 1961, George Blanda (Houston AFL) also passed for a record 36 TDs.

Pass Interceptions

Year	Player	Team	No.	Yds.
1976	Jackson Monte	Los Angeles	10	173
1975	Krause, Paul	Minnesota	10	201
1974	Brown, Ray	Atlanta	8	164
1973	Bryant, Bobby	Minnesota	7	105

Year	Player	Team	No.	Yds.
1972	Bradley, Bill	Philadelphia	9	73
1971	Bradley, Bill	Philadelphia	11	248
1970	LeBeau, Dick	Detroit	9	96
1969	Renfro, Mel	Dallas	10	118
1968	Williams, Willie	New York	10	103
1967	Barney, Lem	Detroit	10	232
	Whitsell, Dave	New Orleans	10	178
1966	Wilson, Larry	St. Louis	10	180
1965	Boyd, Bobby	Baltimore	9	78
1964	Krause, Paul	Washington	12	140
1963	Lynch, Dick	New York	9	251
	Taylor, Rosie	Chicago	9	172
1962	Wood, Willie	Green Bay	9	132
1961	Lynch, Dick	New York	9	60
1960	Baker, Dave	San Francisco	10	96
	Norton, Jerry	St. Louis	10	96
1959	Derby, Dean	Pittsburgh	7	127
	Davis, Milt	Baltimore	7	119
	Shinnick, Don	Baltimore	7	70
1958	Patton, Jim	New York	11	183
1957	Davis, Milt	Baltimore	10	219
	Christiansen, Jack	Detroit	10	137
	Butler, Jack	Pittsburgh	10	85
1956	Crow, Lindon	Chicago Cards	11	170
1955	Sherman, Will	Los Angeles	11	101
1954	Lane, Dick	Chicago Cards	10	181
1953	Christiansen, Jack	Detroit	12	238
1952	Lane, Dick	Los Angeles	14*	298
1951	Schnellbacher, Otto	New York	11	194
1950	Sanders, Orban	New York Yanks	13	199
1949	Nussbaumer, Bob	Chicago Cards	12	157
1948	Sandifer, Dan	Washington	13	258
1947	Reagan, Frank	New York	10	203
	Seno, Frank	Boston Yanks	10	100
1946	Dudley, Bill	Pittsburgh	10	242
1945	Zimmerman, Roy	Philadelphia	7	90
1944	Livingston, Howard	New York	9	172
1943	Baugh, Sammy	Washington	11	112
1942	Turner, Clyde	Chicago	8	96
1941	Goldberg, M.	Chicago Cards	7	54
	Jones, Arthur	Pittsburgh	7	35
1940	Parker, Ace	Brooklyn	6	146
	Ryan, Kent	Detroit	6	65
	Hutson, Don	Green Bay	6	24

* All-time NFL leader

Punting

Year	Player	Team	No.	Avg.
1976	James, John	Atlanta	101	42.1
1975	Weaver, Herman	Detroit	80	42.0
1974	Blanchard, Tom	New Orleans	88	42.1
1973	Wittum, Tom	San Francisco	79	43.7
1972	Chapple, Dave	Los Angeles	53	44.2
1971	McNeill, Tom	Philadelphia	73	42.0
1970	Fagan, Julian	New Orleans	77	42.5
1969	Lee, David	Baltimore	57	45.3
1968	Lothridge, Billy	Atlanta	75	44.3
1967	Lothridge, Billy	Atlanta	87	43.7
1966	Lee, David	Baltimore	49	45.6
1965	Collins, Gary	Cleveland	65	46.7
1964	Walden, Bobby	Minnesota	72	46.4
1963	Lary, Yale	Detroit	35	48.9
1962	Davis, Tommy	San Francisco	48	45.6
1961	Lary, Yale	Detroit	52	48.4
1960	Norton, Jerry	St. Louis	39	45.6
1959	Lary, Yale	Detroit	45	47.1
1958	Baker, Sam	Washington	48	45.4
1957	Chandler, Don	New York	60	44.6
1956	Van Brocklin, Norm	Los Angeles	48	43.1
1955	Van Brocklin, Norm	Los Angeles	60	44.6
1954	Brady, Pat	Pittsburgh	66	43.2
1953	Brady, Pat	Pittsburgh	80	46.9
1952	Gillom, Horace	Cleveland	61	45.7
1951	Gillom, Horace	Cleveland	73	45.5
1950	Morrison, Fred	Chicago	57	43.3
1949	Boyda, Mike	N.Y. Bulldogs	56	44.2
1948	Muha, Joe	Philadelphia	57	47.3
1947	Jacobs, Jack	Green Bay	57	43.5
1946	McKay, Roy	Green Bay	64	42.7
1945	McKay, Roy	Green Bay	44	41.2
1944	Sinkwich, Frank	Detroit	45	41.0
1943	Baugh, Sammy	Washington	50	45.9
1942	Baugh, Sammy	Washington	37	48.2
1941	Baugh, Sammy	Washington	30	48.7
1940	Baugh, Sammy	Washington	35	51.4*
1939	Hall, Parker	Cleveland Rams	58	40.8

* All-time NFL leader

Punt Returns

Year	Player	Team	No.	Yds.	Avg.
1976	Brown, Eddie	Washington	48	646	13.5
1975	Metcalf, Terry	St. Louis	23	285	12.4
1974	Jauron, Dick	Detroit	17	286	16.8
1973	Taylor, Bruce	S.F.	15	207	13.8
1972	Ellis, Ken	Green Bay	14	215	15.4
1971	Duncan, L.	Washington	22	233	10.6
1970	Taylor, Bruce	S.F.	43	516	12.0
1969	Haymond, Alvin	Los Angeles	33	435	13.2
1968	Hayes, Bob	Dallas	15	312	20.8
1967	Davis, Ben	Cleveland	18	229	12.7
1966	Roland, Johnny	St. Louis	20	221	11.1
1965	Kelly, Leroy	Cleveland	17	265	15.6
1964	Watkins, Tommy	Detroit	16	238	14.9
1963	James, Dick	Washington	16	214	13.4
1962	Studstill, Pat	Detroit	29	457	15.8
1961	Wood, Willie	Green Bay	14	225	16.1
1960	Woodson, Abe	S.F.	13	174	13.4
1959	Morris, Johnny	Chicago	14	171	12.2
1958	Arnett, Jon	Los Angeles	18	223	12.4
1957	Zagers, Bert	Washington	14	217	15.5
1956	Konz, Ken	Cleveland	13	187	14.4
1955	Matson, Ollie	Chi. Cards	13	245	18.8
1954	Switzer, Veryl	Green Bay	24	306	12.8
1953	Trippi, Charlie	Chi. Cards	21	239	11.4
1952	Christiansen, Jack	Detroit	15	322	21.5
1951	Young, Buddy	N.Y. Yanks	12	231	19.3
1950	Rich, Herb	Baltimore	12	276	23.0*
1949	Smith, Vitamin	Los Angeles	27	427	15.8
1948	McAfee, George	Chicago	30	417	13.9
1947	Slater, Walt	Pittsburgh	28	435	15.5
1946	Dudley, Bill	Pittsburgh	27	385	14.2
1945	Ryan, Dave	Detroit	15	220	14.7
1944	Van Buren, Steve	Philadelphia	15	230	15.3
1943	Farkas, Andy	Washington	15	168	11.2
1942	Condit, Merlyn	Brooklyn	21	210	10.0
1941	White, Whizzer	Detroit	19	262	13.8

* All-time NFL leader

Kickoff Returns

Year	Player	Team	No.	Yds.	Avg.
1976	Bryant, Cullen	Los Angeles	16	459	28.7
1975	Payton, Walter	Chicago	14	444	31.7
1974	Metcalf, Terry	St. Louis	20	623	31.2
1973	Garrett, Carl	Chicago	16	486	30.4
1972	Smith, Ron	Chicago	30	924	30.8
1971	Williams, Travis	Los Angeles	25	743	29.7
1970	Turner, Cecil	Chicago	23	752	32.7
1969	Williams, Bobby	Detroit	17	563	33.1
1968	Pearson, P.	Baltimore	15	527	35.1
1967	Williams, Travis	Green Bay	18	739	41.1*
1966	Sayers, Gale	Chicago	23	718	31.2
1965	Watkins, T.	Detroit	17	584	34.4
1964	Childs, C.	New York	34	987	29.0
1963	Woodson, Abe	S.F.	29	935	32.3
1962	Woodson, Abe	S.F.	37	1157	31.3
1961	Bass, Dick	Los Angeles	23	698	30.3
1960	Moore, Tom	Green Bay	12	397	33.1
1959	Woodson, Abe	S.F.	13	382	29.4
1958	Matson, Ollie	Chi. Cards	14	497	35.5
1957	Arnett, Jon	Los Angeles	18	504	28.0
1956	Wilson, Tom	Los Angeles	15	477	31.8
1955	Carmichael, Al	Green Bay	14	418	29.9
1954	Reynolds, Billy	Cleveland	14	413	29.5
1953	Arenas, Joe	S.F.	16	551	34.4
1952	Chandnois, L.	Pittsburgh	17	599	35.2
1951	Chandnois, L.	Pittsburgh	12	390	32.5
1950	Smith, Vitamin	Los Angeles	22	724	33.7
1949	Doll, Don	Detroit	21	536	25.5
1948	Scott, Joe	New York	20	569	28.5
1947	Saenz, Ed	Washington	29	797	27.4
1946	Karnofsky, Abe	Bost. Yanks	21	599	28.5
1945	Van Buren, S.	Philadelphia	13	373	28.7
1944	Thurbon, Bob	Chi. Cards/ Pittsburgh	12	291	24.3
1943	Heineman, Ken	Brooklyn	16	444	27.8
1942	Goldberg, M	Chi. Cards	15	393	26.2
1941	Goldberg, M.	Chi. Cards	12	290	24.2

* All-time NFL leader

American Football Conference
TEAM LEADERS, YEAR BY YEAR

OFFENSE

Total Points Scored

Year	Team	Total	Year	Team	Total
1976	Baltimore	417	1967	Oakland	468
1975	Buffalo	420	1966	Kansas City	448
1974	Oakland	355	1965	San Diego	340
1973	Denver	354	1964	Buffalo	400
1972	Miami	385	1963	San Diego	399
1971	Oakland	344	1962	Dallas Texans	389
1970	Baltimore	321	1961	Houston	513*
1969	Oakland	377	1960	N.Y. Titans	382
1968	Oakland	453			

* All-time NFL leader

Total Yards Gained

Year	Team	Total	Year	Team	Total
1976	Pittsburgh	5236	1967	N.Y. Jets	5152
1975	Buffalo	5467	1966	Kansas City	5114
1974	Oakland	4718	1965	San Diego	5188
1973	Oakland	4773	1964	Buffalo	5206
1972	Miami	5036	1963	San Diego	5153
1971	San Diego	4738	1962	Houston	4971
1970	Oakland	4829	1961	Houston	6288*
1969	Oakland	5036	1960	Houston	4936
1968	Oakland	5696			

* All-time NFL leader

Total Yards Rushing

Year	Team	Total	Year	Team	Total
1976	Pittsburgh	2971	1967	Houston	2122
1975	Buffalo	2974	1966	Kansas City	2274
1974	Pittsburgh	2417	1965	San Diego	2085
1973	Buffalo	3088*	1964	Buffalo	2040
1972	Miami	2960	1963	San Diego	2203
1971	Miami	2429	1962	Buffalo	2480
1970	Miami	2082	1961	Dallas Texans	2189
1969	Kansas City	2220	1960	Oakland	2056
1968	Kansas City	2227			

* All-time NFL leader

Total Yards Passing

Year	Team	Total	Year	Team	Total
1976	Baltimore	2933	1967	N.Y. Jets	3845
1975	Cincinnati	3241	1966	N.Y. Jets	3464
1974	Cincinnati	2804	1965	San Diego	3103
1973	Denver	2519	1964	Houston	3527
1972	N.Y. Jets	2777	1963	Houston	3222
1971	San Diego	3134	1962	Denver	3404
1970	Oakland	2865	1961	Houston	4392*
1969	Oakland	3271	1960	Houston	3203
1968	San Diego	3623			

DEFENSE
Fewest Points Allowed

Year	Team	Points	Year	Team	Points
1976	Pittsburgh	138	1967	Houston	199
1975	Pittsburgh	162	1966	Buffalo	255
1974	Pittsburgh	189	1965	Buffalo	226
1973	Miami	150	1964	Buffalo	242
1972	Miami	171	1963	San Diego	255
1971	Baltimore	140	1962	Dallas Texans	233
1970	Miami	228	1961	San Diego	219
1969	Kansas City	177	1960	Dallas Texans	253
1968	Kansas City	170			

* All-time NFL leader

Fewest Rushing Yards Allowed

Year	Team	Yards	Year	Team	Yards
1976	Pittsburgh	1457	1967	Oakland	1129
1975	Houston	1680	1966	Buffalo	1051
1974	New England	1587	1965	San Diego	1094
1973	Oakland	1470	1964	Buffalo	913
1972	Miami	1548	1963	Boston	1107
1971	Baltimore	1113	1962	Dallas Texans	1250
1970	N.Y. Jets	1283	1961	Boston	1041
1969	Kansas City	1091	1960	Dallas Texans	1338
1968	N.Y. Jets	1195			

Fewest Passing Yards Allowed

Year	Team	Yards	Year	Team	Yards
1976	Cincinnati	1758	1967	Buffalo	1825
1975	Cincinnati	1729	1966	Oakland	2118
1974	Pittsburgh	1466	1965	San Diego	2168
1973	Miami	1290	1964	San Diego	2518
1972	Cleveland	1736	1963	Oakland	2589
1971	Baltimore	1739	1962	Oakland	2306
1970	Kansas City	2010	1961	San Diego	2363
1969	Kansas City	2072	1960	Buffalo	2124
1968	Houston	1671			

Fewest Total Yards Allowed

Year	Team	Yards	Year	Team	Yards
1976	Pittsburgh	3323	1967	Oakland	3294
1975	Oakland	3629	1966	Oakland	3910
1974	Pittsburgh	3074	1965	San Diego	3262
1973	Oakland	3160	1964	Buffalo	3878
1972	Miami	3297	1963	Boston	3834
1971	Baltimore	2852	1962	Dallas Texans	3951
1970	N.Y. Jets	3655	1961	San Diego	3726
1969	Kansas City	3163	1960	Buffalo	3866
1968	N.Y. Jets	3363			

National Football Conference
TEAM LEADERS, YEAR BY YEAR

OFFENSE

Total Points Scored

Year	Team	Total	Year	Team	Total
1976	Los Angeles	351	1953	San Francisco	372
1975	Minnesota	377	1952	Los Angeles	349
1974	Washington	320	1951	Los Angeles	392
1973	Los Angeles	388	1950	Los Angeles	466
1972	San Francisco	353	1949	Philadelphia	364
1971	Dallas	406	1948	Chi. Cards	395
1970	San Francisco	352	1947	Chicago	363
1969	Minnesota	379	1946	Chicago	289
1968	Dallas	431	1945	Philadelphia	272
1967	Los Angeles	398	1944	Philadelphia	267
1966	Dallas	445	1943	Chicago	303
1965	San Francisco	421	1942	Chicago	376
1964	Baltimore	428	1941	Chicago	396
1963	N.Y. Giants	448	1940	Washington	245
1962	Green Bay	415	1939	Chicago	298
1961	Green Bay	391	1938	Green Bay	223
1960	Cleveland	362	1937	Green Bay	220
1959	Baltimore	374	1936	Green Bay	248
1958	Baltimore	381	1935	Chicago	192
1957	Los Angeles	307	1934	Chicago	286
1956	Chicago	363	1933	N.Y. Giants	244
1955	Cleveland	349	1932	Green Bay	152
1954	Detroit	337			

Total Yards Gained

Year	Team	Total	Year	Team	Total
1976	St. Louis	5136	1969	Dallas	5122
1975	Dallas	5025	1968	Dallas	5117
1974	Dallas	4983	1967	Baltimore	5008
1973	Los Angeles	4906	1966	Dallas	5145
1972	N.Y. Giants	4483	1965	San Francisco	5270
1971	Dallas	5035	1964	Baltimore	4779
1970	San Francisco	4503	1963	N.Y. Giants	5024

Year	Team	Total	Year	Team	Total
1962	N.Y. Giants	5005	1946	Los Angeles	3793
1961	Philadelphia	5112	1945	Washington	3549
1960	Baltimore	4245	1944	Chicago	3239
1959	Baltimore	4458	1943	Chicago	4045
1958	Baltimore	4539	1942	Chicago	3900
1957	Los Angeles	4143	1941	Chicago	4265
1956	Chicago	4537	1940	Green Bay	3400
1955	Chicago	4316	1939	Chicago	3988
1954	Los Angeles	5187	1938	Green Bay	3037
1953	Philadelphia	4811	1937	Green Bay	3201
1952	Cleveland	4352	1936	Detroit	3703
1951	Los Angeles	5506	1935	Chicago	3454
1950	Los Angeles	5420	1934	Chicago	3900
1949	Chicago	4873	1933	N.Y. Giants	2973
1948	Chi. Cards	4705	1932	Chicago	2755
1947	Chicago	5053			

Total Yards Rushing

Year	Team	Total	Year	Team	Total
1976	Los Angeles	2528	1953	San Francisco	2230
1975	Dallas	2432	1952	San Francisco	1905
1974	Dallas	2454	1951	Chicago	2408
1973	Los Angeles	2925	1950	N.Y. Giants	2336
1972	Chicago	2360	1949	Philadelphia	2607
1971	Detroit	2376	1948	Chi. Cards	2560
1970	Dallas	2300	1947	Los Angeles	2171
1969	Dallas	2276	1946	Green Bay	1765
1968	Chicago	2377	1945	Cleveland	1714
1967	Cleveland	2139	1944	Philadelphia	1661
1966	Cleveland	2166	1943	Phil.–Pitt.*	1730
1965	Cleveland	2331	1942	Chicago	1881
1964	Green Bay	2276	1941	Chicago	2263
1963	Cleveland	2639	1940	Chicago	1818
1962	Green Bay	2460	1939	Chicago	2043
1961	Green Bay	2350	1938	Detroit	1893
1960	St. Louis	2356	1937	Detroit	2074
1959	Cleveland	2149	1936	Detroit	2885
1958	Cleveland	2526	1935	Chicago	2096
1957	Los Angeles	2142	1934	Chicago	2847
1956	Chicago	2468	1933	Bost. Redskins	2260
1955	Chicago	2388	1932	Chicago	1770
1954	San Francisco	2498			

* In 1943, Philadelphia and Pittsburgh played as a unit.

Total Yards Passing
(Since 1952 based on net yards)

Year	Team	Total	Year	Team	Total
1976	Minnesota	2855	1953	Philadelphia	3089
1975	Washington	2917	1952	Cleveland	2566
1974	Washington	2802	1951	Los Angeles	3296
1973	Philadelphia	2998	1950	Los Angeles	3709
1972	San Francisco	2735	1949	Chicago	3055
1971	Dallas	2786	1948	Washington	2861
1970	San Francisco	2923	1947	Washington	3336
1969	San Francisco	3158	1946	Los Angeles	2080
1968	Dallas	3026	1945	Chicago	1857
1967	Washington	3730	1944	Washington	2021
1966	Dallas	3023	1943	Chicago	2310
1965	San Francisco	3487	1942	Green Bay	2407
1964	Chicago	2841	1941	Chicago	2002
1963	Baltimore	3296	1940	Washington	1887
1962	Philadelphia	3632	1939	Chicago	1965
1961	Philadelphia	3605	1938	Washington	1536
1960	Baltimore	2956	1937	Green Bay	1398
1959	Baltimore	2753	1936	Green Bay	1629
1958	Pittsburgh	2752	1935	Green Bay	1416
1957	Baltimore	2388	1934	Green Bay	1165
1956	Los Angeles	2419	1933	N.Y. Giants	1335
1955	Philadelphia	2472	1932	Chicago	1013
1954	Chicago	3104			

DEFENSE
Fewest Points Allowed

Year	Team	Points	Year	Team	Points
1976	Minnesota	176	1965	Green Bay	224
1975	Los Angeles	135	1964	Baltimore	225
1974	Los Angeles	181	1963	Chicago	144
1973	Minnesota	168	1962	Green Bay	148
1972	Washington	218	1961	N.Y. Giants	220
1971	Minnesota	139	1960	San Francisco	205
1970	Minnesota	143	1959	N.Y. Giants	170
1969	Minnesota	133	1958	N.Y. Giants	183
1968	Baltimore	144	1957	Cleveland	172
1967	Los Angeles	196	1956	Cleveland	177
1966	Green Bay	163	1955	Cleveland	218

Year	Team	Points	Year	Team	Points
1954	Cleveland	162	1942	Chicago	84
1953	Cleveland	162	1941	N.Y. Giants	114
1952	Detroit	192	1940	Brooklyn	120
1951	Cleveland	152	1939	N.Y. Giants	85
1950	Philadelphia	141	1938	N.Y. Giants	79
1949	Philadelphia	134	1937	Chicago	100
1948	Chicago	151	1936	Chicago	94
1947	Green Bay	210	1935	{ Green Bay	96
1946	Pittsburgh	117		{ N.Y. Giants	96
1945	Washington	121	1934	Detroit	59
1944	N.Y. Giants	75	1933	Brooklyn	54
1943	Washington	137	1932	Chicago	44*

* All-time NFL leader

Fewest Rushing Yards Allowed

Year	Team	Yards	Year	Team	Yards
1976	Los Angeles	1564	1954	Cleveland	1050
1975	Minnesota	1532	1953	Philadelphia	1117
1974	Los Angeles	1302	1952	Detroit	1145
1973	Los Angeles	1270	1951	N.Y. Giants	913
1972	Dallas	1515	1950	Detroit	1367
1971	Dallas	1144	1949	Chicago	1196
1970	Detroit	1152	1948	Philadelphia	1209
1969	Dallas	1050	1947	Philadelphia	1329
1968	Dallas	1195	1946	Chicago	1060
1967	Dallas	1081	1945	Philadelphia	817
1966	Dallas	1176	1944	Philadelphia	558
1965	Los Angeles	1409	1943	Phil.–Pitt.†	793
1964	Los Angeles	1501	1942	Chicago	519*
1963	Chicago	1442	1941	Washington	1042
1962	Detroit	1231	1940	N.Y. Giants	977
1961	Pittsburgh	1463	1939	Chicago	812
1960	St. Louis	1212	1938	Detroit	1081
1959	N.Y. Giants	1261	1937	Chicago	933
1958	Baltimore	1291	1936	Bost. Redskins	1148
1957	Baltimore	1174	1935	Bost. Redskins	998
1956	N.Y. Giants	1443	1934	Chi. Cards	954
1955	Cleveland	1189	1933	Brooklyn	964

* All-time NFL leader
† In 1943, Philadelphia and Pittsburgh played as a unit.

Fewest Passing Yards Allowed

Year	Team	Yards	Year	Team	Yards
1976	Minnesota	1575	1954	Cleveland	1608
1975	Los Angeles	1789	1953	Washington	1751
1974	Atlanta	1572	1952	Washington	1580
1973	Atlanta	1430	1951	Pittsburgh	1687
1972	Minnesota	1699	1950	Cleveland	1581
1971	Atlanta	1638	1949	Philadelphia	1607
1970	Minnesota	1438	1948	Green Bay	1626
1969	Minnesota	1631	1947	Green Bay	1790
1968	Green Bay	1796	1946	Pittsburgh	939
1967	Green Bay	1377	1945	Washington	1121
1966	Green Bay	1959	1944	Chicago	1052
1965	Green Bay	1981	1943	Chicago	980
1964	Green Bay	1647	1942	Washington	1093
1963	Chicago	1734	1941	Pittsburgh	1168
1962	Green Bay	1746	1940	Philadelphia	1012
1961	Baltimore	1913	1939	Washington	1116
1960	Chicago	1388	1938	Chicago	897
1959	N.Y. Giants	1582	1937	Detroit	804
1958	Chicago	1769	1936	Philadelphia	853
1957	Cleveland	1300	1935	Chi. Cards	793
1956	Cleveland	1103	1934	Philadelphia	545*
1955	Pittsburgh	1295	1933	Portsmouth	558

* All-time NFL leader

Fewest Total Yards Allowed

Year	Team	Yards	Year	Team	Yards
1976	San Francisco	3562	1963	Chicago	3176
1975	Minnesota	3153	1962	Detroit	3217
1974	Washington	3285	1961	Baltimore	3782
1973	Los Angeles	2951	1960	St. Louis	3029
1972	Green Bay	3474	1959	N.Y. Giants	2843
1971	Minnesota	3406	1958	Chicago	3066
1970	Minnesota	2803	1957	Pittsburgh	2791
1969	Minnesota	2720	1956	N.Y. Giants	3081
1968	Los Angeles	3118	1955	Cleveland	2841
1967	Green Bay	3300	1954	Cleveland	2658
1966	St. Louis	3492	1953	Philadelphia	2998
1965	Detroit	3557	1952	Cleveland	3075
1964	Green Bay	3179	1951	N.Y. Giants	3250

Year	Team	Yards	Year	Team	Yards
1950	Cleveland	3154	1941	N.Y. Giants	2368
1949	Philadelphia	2831	1940	N.Y. Giants	2219
1948	Chicago	2931	1939	Washington	2116
1947	Green Bay	3396	1938	N.Y. Giants	2029
1946	Washington	2451	1937	Washington	2123
1945	Philadelphia	2073	1936	Bost. Redskins	2181
1944	Philadelphia	1943	1935	Bost. Redskins	1996
1943	Chicago	2262	1934	Chi. Cards	1539*
1942	Chicago	1703	1933	Brooklyn	1789

* All-time NFL leader

National Football League
A SELECTION OF
ALL-TIME INDIVIDUAL RECORDS

Most total points in lifetime
George Blanda, 2002; Chicago Bears 1949–58, Baltimore 1959, Houston 1960–66, Oakland 1967–75; 9 TDs, 943 PATs, 335 FGs
Lou Groza, 1349; Cleveland 1950–59, 1961–67; 1 TD, 641 PATs, 234 FGs
Fred Cox, 1316; Minnesota 1963–76; 494 PATs, 274 FGs

Most points in one season
Paul Hornung, 176 (Green Bay 1960); 15 TDs, 41 PATs, 15 FGs
Gino Cappelletti, 155 (Boston 1964); 7 TDs, 38 PATs, 25 FGs
Gino Cappelletti, 147 (Boston 1961); 8 TDs, 49 PATs, 17 FGs

Most points in rookie season
Gale Sayers, 132 (Chicago 1965); 22 TDs
Doak Walker, 128 (Detroit 1950); 11 TDs, 38 PATs, 8 FGs
Cookie Gilchrist, 128 (Buffalo 1962); 15 TDs, 14 PATs, 8 FGs
Chester Marcol, 128 (Green Bay 1972); 29 PATs, 33 FGs
Gene Mingo, 123 (Denver 1960); 6 TDs, 33 PATs, 18 FGs

Most points in one game
Ernie Nevers, 40—Chicago Cardinals vs. Chicago Bears, Nov. 28, 1929 (6 TDs, 4 PATs)
William (Dub) Jones, 36—Cleveland vs. Chicago Bears, Nov. 25, 1941 (6 TDs)
Gale Sayers, 36—Chicago vs. San Francisco, Dec. 12, 1965 (6 TDs)
Paul Hornung, 33—Green Bay vs. Baltimore, Oct. 8, 1961 (4 TDs, 6 PATs, 1 FG)

Most touchdowns in one season
O. J. Simpson, 23 (Buffalo 1975); 16 run, 7 pass
Chuck Foreman, 22 (Minnesota 1975); 13 run, 9 pass
Gale Sayers, 22 (Chicago 1965); 14 run, 6 pass, 1 punt ret., 1 KO ret.
Jim Brown, 21 (Cleveland 1965); 17 run, 4 pass

Most touchdowns in rookie season
Gale Sayers, 22 (Chicago 1965); 14 run, 6 pass, 1 punt ret., 1 KO ret.
Cookie Gilchrist, 15 (Buffalo 1962); 13 run, 2 pass
Billy Howton, 13 (Green Bay 1952); 13 pass
Bob Hayes, 13 (Dallas 1965); 1 run, 12 pass

Most PATs in one season
George Blanda, 64 (Houston 1961)
Danny Villanueva, 56 (Dallas 1966)
George Blanda, 56 (Oakland 1967)

Most FGs in one season
Jim Turner, 34 (N.Y. Jets 1968)
Chester Marcol, 33 (Green Bay 1972)
Jim Turner, 32 (N.Y. Jets 1969)

Most rushing attempts in one season
O. J. Simpson, 332 (Buffalo 1973)
O. J. Simpson, 329 (Buffalo 1975)
Walter Payton, 311 (Chicago 1976)

Most yards rushing in one season
O. J. Simpson, 2003 (Buffalo 1973)
Jim Brown, 1863 (Cleveland 1963)
O. J. Simpson, 1817 (Buffalo 1975)

Best average rushing gain for one season
Beattie Feathers, 9.94 (Chicago Bears 1934); 101 atts., 1004 yds.
Bobby Douglass, 6.87 (Chicago 1972); 141 atts., 968 yds.
Dan Towler, 6.78 (Los Angeles 1951); 126 atts., 854 yds.

Most touchdowns rushing in one season
Jim Taylor, 19 (Green Bay 1962)
Jim Brown, 17 (Cleveland 1958 and 1965)
Lenny Moore, 16 (Baltimore 1964)
Leroy Kelly, 16 (Cleveland 1968)
O. J. Simpson, 16 (Buffalo 1975)

Most passes attempted in one season
Sonny Jurgensen, 508 (Washington 1967)
George Blanda, 505 (Houston 1964)
Joe Namath, 491 (N.Y. Jets 1967)

Most passes completed in one season
Sonny Jurgensen, 288 (Washington 1967)
Sonny Jurgensen, 274 (Washington 1969)
Fran Tarkenton, 273 (Minnesota 1975)
Roman Gabriel, 270 (Philadelphia 1973)

Most passing yards in one season
Joe Namath, 4007 (N.Y. Jets 1967)
Sonny Jurgensen, 3747 (Washington 1967)
Sonny Jurgensen, 3723 (Philadelphia 1961)

Most touchdown passes in one season
George Blanda, 36 (Houston 1961)
Y. A. Tittle, 36 (N.Y. Giants 1963)
Daryle Lamonica, 34 (Oakland 1969)

Fewest passes intercepted in one season
1—Joe Ferguson (Buffalo 1976)
3—Gary Wood (N.Y. Giants 1964); Bart Starr (Green Bay 1966)
4—Sammy Baugh (Washington 1945); Harry Gilmer (Detroit 1955); Charlie Conerly (N.Y. Giants 1959); Bart Starr (Green Bay 1964); Roger Staubach (Dallas 1971); Len Dawson (Kansas City 1975)

Most pass receptions in one season
Charlie Hennigan, 101 (Houston 1964)
Lionel Taylor, 100 (Denver 1961)
Johnny Morris, 93 (Chicago 1964)

Most yards gained receiving in one season
Charlie Hennigan, 1746 (Houston 1961)
Lance Alworth, 1602 (San Diego 1965)
Charlie Hennigan, 1546 (Houston 1964)

Most touchdowns receiving in one season
Don Hutson, 17 (Green Bay 1942)
Elroy Hirsch, 17 (Los Angeles 1951)
Bill Groman, 17 (Houston 1961)
Art Powell, 16 (Oakland 1963)
Cloyce Box, 15 (Detroit 1952)
Ulmo (Sonny) Randle, 15 (St. Louis 1960)

Most interceptions in one season
Richard (Night Train) Lane, 14 (Los Angeles 1952)
Dan Sandifer, 13 (Washington 1948)
Orban (Spec) Sanders, 13 (N.Y. Yanks 1950)

Most interception yards in one season
Charley McNeil, 349 (San Diego 1961)
Don Doll, 301 (Detroit 1949)
Richard (Night Train) Lane, 298 (Los Angeles 1952)

Best punting average for one season
(At least 35 punts to qualify)
Sammy Baugh, 51.4 (Washington 1940)
R. Yale Lary, 48.9 (Detroit 1963)
Sammy Baugh, 48.7 (Washington 1941)

Longest punt
Steve O'Neal, 98 yds.—N.Y. Jets vs. Denver, Sept. 21, 1969
Don Chandler, 90 yds.—Green Bay vs. San Francisco, Oct. 10, 1965
Bob Waterfield, 88 yds.—Los Angeles vs. Green Bay, Oct. 17, 1948

NFL's Exclusive
1000-YARD RUSHERS CLUB

Year	Player	Team	Yards
1934	Beattie Feathers	Chicago	1,004
1947	Steve Van Buren	Philadelphia	1,008
1949	Steve Van Buren	Philadelphia	1,146
	Tony Canadeo	Green Bay	1,052
1953	Joe Perry	San Francisco	1,018
1954	Joe Perry	San Francisco	1,049
1956	Rick Casares	Chicago	1,126
1958	Jim Brown	Cleveland	1,527
1959	Jim Brown	Cleveland	1,329
	J.D. Smith	San Francisco	1,036
1960	Jim Brown	Cleveland	1,257
	Jim Taylor	Green Bay	1,101
	John David Crow	St. Louis	1,071
1961	Jim Brown	Cleveland	1,408
	Jim Taylor	Green Bay	1,307
1962	Jim Taylor	Green Bay	1,474
	John Henry Johnson	Pittsburgh	1,141
	Cookie Gilchrist	Buffalo	1,096
	Abner Haynes	Dallas Texans	1,049
	Dick Bass	Los Angeles	1,033
	Charlie Tolar	Houston	1,012
1963	Jim Brown	Cleveland	1,863
	Clem Daniels	Oakland	1,099
	Jim Taylor	Green Bay	1,018
	Paul Lowe	San Diego	1,010
1964	Jim Brown	Cleveland	1,446
	Jim Taylor	Green Bay	1,169
	John Henry Johnson	Pittsburgh	1,048
1965	Jim Brown	Cleveland	1,544
	Paul Lowe	San Diego	1,121
1966	Jim Nance	Boston	1,458
	Gale Sayers	Chicago	1,231
	Leroy Kelly	Cleveland	1,141
	Dick Bass	Los Angeles	1,090

Year	Player	Team	Yards
1967	Jim Nance	Boston	1,216
	Leroy Kelly	Cleveland	1,205
	Hoyle Granger	Houston	1,194
	Mike Garrett	Kansas City	1,087
1968	Leroy Kelly	Cleveland	1,239
	Paul Robinson	Cincinnati	1,023
1969	Gale Sayers	Chicago	1,032
1970	Larry Brown	Washington	1,125
	Ron Johnson	N.Y. Giants	1,027
1971	Floyd Little	Denver	1,133
	John Brockington	Green Bay	1,105
	Larry Csonka	Miami	1,051
	Steve Owens	Detroit	1,035
	Willie Ellison	Los Angeles	1,000
1972	O.J. Simpson	Buffalo	1,251
	Larry Brown	Washington	1,216
	Ron Johnson	N.Y. Giants	1,182
	Larry Csonka	Miami	1,117
	Marv Hubbard	Oakland	1,100
	Franco Harris	Pittsburgh	1,055
	Calvin Hill	Dallas	1,036
	Mike Garrett	San Diego	1,031
	John Brockington	Green Bay	1,027
	Eugene Morris	Miami	1,000
1973	O.J. Simpson	Buffalo	2,003
	John Brockington	Green Bay	1,144
	Calvin Hill	Dallas	1,142
	Larry McCutcheon	Los Angeles	1,097
	Larry Csonka	Miami	1,003
1974	Otis Armstrong	Denver	1,407
	Don Woods	San Diego	1,162
	O.J. Simpson	Buffalo	1,125
	Lawrence McCutcheon	Los Angeles	1,109
	Franco Harris	Pittsburgh	1,006
1975	O.J. Simpson	Buffalo	1,817
	Franco Harris	Pittsburgh	1,246
	Lydell Mitchell	Baltimore	1,193
	Jim Otis	St. Louis	1,076
	Chuck Foreman	Minnesota	1,070
	Greg Pruitt	Cleveland	1,067
	John Riggins	N.Y. Jets	1,005
	Dave Hampton	Atlanta	1,002
1976	O.J. Simpson	Buffalo	1,503
	Walter Payton	Chicago	1,390
	Delvin Williams	San Francisco	1,203
	Lydell Mitchell	Baltimore	1,200

Year	Player	Team	Yards
1976	Lawrence McCutcheon	Los Angeles	1,168
	Chuck Foreman	Minnesota	1,155
	Franco Harris	Pittsburgh	1,128
	Mike Thomas	Washington	1,101
	Rocky Bleier	Pittsburgh	1,036
	Mark van Eeghen	Oakland	1,012
	Otis Armstrong	Denver	1,008
	Greg Pruitt	Cleveland	1,000

Note: Twelve players rushed a thousand yards in 1976, more than in any single year previously.

The National Football League's
ALL-TIME TOP TEN SCORERS

Player	Seasons	TDs	PATs	FGs	Pts.
George Blanda*	27	9	943	335	2,002
Lou Groza	17	1	641	234	1,349
Fred Cox*	14	0	494	274	1,316
Jim Bakken*	15	0	472	264	1,264
Jim Turner*	13	0	427	267	1,228
Gino Cappelletti†	11	42	350	176	1,130
Bruce Gossett	11	0	374	219	1,031
Jan Stenerud*	10	0	314	239	1,031
Sam Baker	15	2	428	179	977
Lou Michaels‡	13	1	386	187	955

* Active at end of 1976 season
† Includes four 2-point conversions
‡ Includes safety

The National Football League's
ALL-TIME TOP TEN RUSHERS

Player	Seasons	Yds.	Atts.
Jim Brown	9	12,312	2,359
O. J. Simpson*	8	9,626	1,997
Jim Taylor	10	8,597	1,941
Joe Perry	14	8,378	1,737
Leroy Kelly	10	7,274	1,727
John Henry Johnson	13	6,803	1,571
Larry Csonka*	8	6,469	1,446
Floyd Little	9	6,323	1,641
Don Perkins	8	6,217	1,500
Ken Willard	10	6,105	1,622

* Active at end of 1976 season

The National Football League's
ALL-TIME TOP TEN PASS RECEIVERS

Player	Seasons	Caught	Yds.
Charley Taylor*	12	635	8,952
Don Maynard	15	633	11,834
Raymond Berry	13	631	9,275
Lionel Taylor	10	567	7,195
Lance Alworth	11	542	10,266
Fred Biletnikoff*	12	536	8,243
Bobby Mitchell	11	521	7,954
Billy Howton	12	503	8,459
Tommy McDonald	12	495	8,410
Don Hutson	11	488	7,991

* Active at end of 1976 season

The National Football League's
ALL-TIME TOP TEN PASS INTERCEPTORS

Player	Seasons	No.	Yds.
Emlen Tunnell	14	79	1,282
Paul Krause*	13	76	1,111
Dick (Night Train) Lane	14	68	1,207
Dick LeBeau	13	62	762
Bob Boyd	9	57	994
Johnny Robinson	12	57	741
Pat Fischer*	16	56	941
Emmitt Thomas*	11	55	937
Lem Barney*	10	53	1,024
Bob Dillon	8	52	976
Jack Butler	9	52	826
Larry Wilson	13	52	800
Jim Patton	12	52	712

* Active at end of 1976 season

The National Football League's
ALL-TIME TOP TEN PUNTERS
(300 or More Punts)

Player	Seasons	No.	Avg.
Sammy Baugh	16	338	45.1
Tommy Davis	11	511	44.7
Yale Lary	11	503	44.3
Jerrel Wilson*	14	930	43.8
Horace Gillom	7	385	43.8
Jerry Norton	11	358	43.8
Don Chandler	12	660	43.5
Norm Van Brocklin	12	523	42.9
Danny Villanueva	8	488	42.8
Bobby Joe Green	14	970	42.6

* Active at end of 1976 season

The National Football League's
ALL-TIME TOP TEN PUNT RETURNERS
(75 or More Returns)

Player	Seasons	No.	Yds.	Avg.
George McAfee	8	112	1431	12.78
Jack Christiansen	8	85	1084	12.75
Claude Gibson	5	110	1381	12.6
Bill Dudley	9	124	1515	12.2
Mack Herron	3	84	982	11.7
Bill Thompson*	8	156	1811	11.6
Rodger Bird	3	94	1063	11.3
Abisha (Bosh) Pritchard	6	95	1072	11.3
Bob Hayes	11	104	1158	11.1
Floyd Little	9	81	893	11.0

* Active at end of 1976 season

The National Football League's
ALL-TIME TOP TEN KICKOFF RETURNERS
(75 or More Returns)

Player	Seasons	No.	Yds.	Avg.
Gale Sayers	7	91	2781	30.6
Lynn Chandnois	7	92	2720	29.6
Abe Woodson	9	193	5538	28.7
Claude (Buddy) Young	6	90	2514	27.9
Travis Williams	5	102	2801	27.5
Clarence Davis*	6	76	2077	27.3
Joe Arenas	7	139	3798	27.3
Steve Van Buren	8	76	2030	26.7
Lenny Lyles	12	81	2161	26.7
Eugene (Mercury) Morris*	8	111	2947	26.5

* Active at end of 1976 season

The National Football League's
ALL-TIME TOP TWENTY PASSERS

Player	Yrs.	Atts.	Comp.	Yds.	Pct.	Int.	TDs
Ken Anderson*	6	1804	1042	13,326	57.7	58	88
Bart Starr	16	3149	1808	24,718	57.4	138	152
Len Dawson	19	3741	2136	28,711	57.09	183	239
Sonny Jurgenson	18	4262	2433	32,224	57.08	189	255
Roger Staubach*	8	1723	977	13,304	56.7	73	83
Fran Tarkenton*	16	5637	3186	41,801	56.55	220	308
Sammy Baugh	16	2995	1693	21,886	56.52	203	186
Otto Graham	6	1565	872	13,499	55.7	94	88
Y. A. Tittle	15	3817	2118	28,339	55.5	221	212
John Brodie	17	4491	2469	31,548	55.0	224	214
Bob Griese*	10	2477	1361	18,099	54.9	128	139
Johnny Unitas	18	5186	2830	40,239	54.6	253	290
Bill Wade	13	2523	1370	18,530	54.3	134	124
Milt Plum	13	2419	1306	17,536	54.0	127	122
Bill Munson*	13	1901	1023	12,312	53.8	77	79
Norm Van Brocklin	12	2895	1553	23,611	53.6	178	173
Bill Kilmer*	14	2737	1463	18,992	53.4	136	140
Frankie Albert	7	1564	831	10,795	53.1	98	115
Roman Gabriel*	15	4495	2365	29,429	52.7	149	201
Craig Morton*	12	2192	1146	16,013	52.28	122	109
Norm Snead*	16	4353	2276	30,797	52.25	257	196

* Active at end of 1976 season
These standings are based upon best career completion percentages among players with 1,500 or more career attempts.

National Football Conference
DIVISIONAL WINNERS AND
PLAYOFF CHAMPIONSHIP RESULTS, 1921–76

—

NOTE: Wild card qualifiers (WC) are divisional second-place teams with best second-place won-lost percentage in the conference, or teams that qualify otherwise in case of ties.

During the period 1967–69, the National Football League consisted of two conferences, the Eastern and the Western; each had two divisions. In the Eastern Conference they were the Capitol (Ca) and the Century (Cy); in the Western Conference they were the Coastal (Co) and the Central (Ce). Playoffs were between the divisional champions in each conference, and these were followed by the NFL championship game between the conference winners.

During the period 1953–66, the NFL consisted of two conferences, the Eastern and the Western, with no divisions. The NFL championship game was played between the two conference winners.

During the period 1950–52, the NFL consisted of two conferences, the American and the National, with no divisions. The NFL championship game was played between the two conference winners.

During the period 1933–49, the NFL consisted of two divisions, the Eastern and the Western. The NFL championship game was played between the two division winners.

During the period 1921–32, the NFL operated as a single division, with the membership over the years ranging from eight clubs to as many as 22. Therefore, there were no divisional playoffs or championship games. Title winners for those years were the clubs that finished with the best won-lost records.

Year	Winners	Record	Pct.	Coach
1976	Dallas Cowboys (E)	11–3–0	.786	Tom Landry
	Minnesota Vikings (C)	11–2–1	.821	Bud Grant
	Los Angeles Rams (W)	10–3–1	.750	Chuck Knox
	Washington Redskins (WC)	10–4–0	.714	George Allen
	Divisional playoffs: Vikings 35, Redskins 20; Rams 14, Cowboys 12			
	NFC championship game: Vikings 24, Rams 13			
	Super Bowl XI: Raiders (AFC) 32, Vikings (NFC) 14			
1975	St. Louis Cardinals (E)	11–3–0	.786	Don Coryell
	Minnesota Vikings (C)	12–2–0	.857	Bud Grant
	Los Angeles Rams (W)	12–2–0	.857	Chuck Knox
	Dallas Cowboys (WC)	10–4–0	.714	Tom Landry

Year	Winners	Record	Pct.	Coach
	Divisional playoffs: Rams 35, Cardinals 23; Cowboys 17, Vikings 14			
	NFC championship game: Cowboys 37, Rams 7			
	Super Bowl X: Steelers (AFC) 21, Cowboys (NFC) 17			
1974	St. Louis Cardinals (E)	10–4–0	.714	Don Coryell
	Minnesota Vikings (C)	10–4–0	.714	Bud Grant
	Los Angeles Rams (W)	10–4–0	.714	Chuck Knox
	Washington Redskins (WC)	10–4–0	.714	George Allen
	Divisional playoffs: Vikings 30, Cardinals 14; Rams 19, Redskins 10			
	NFC championship game: Vikings 14, Rams 10			
	Super Bowl IX: Steelers (AFC) 16, Vikings (NFC) 6			
1973	Dallas Cowboys (E)	10–4–0	.714	Tom Landry
	Minnesota Vikings (C)	12–2–0	.857	Bud Grant
	Los Angeles Rams (W)	12–2–0	.857	Chuck Knox
	Washington Redskins (WC)	10–4–0	.714	George Allen
	Divisional playoffs: Vikings 27, Redskins 20; Cowboys 27, Rams 16			
	NFC championship game: Vikings 27, Cowboys 10			
	Super Bowl VIII: Dolphins (AFC) 24, Vikings (NFC) 7			
1972	Washington Redskins (E)	11–3–0	.786	George Allen
	Green Bay Packers (C)	10–4–0	.714	Dan Devine
	San Francisco 49ers (W)	8–5–1	.607	Dick Nolan
	Dallas Cowboys (WC)	10–4–0	.714	Tom Landry
	Divisional playoffs: Cowboys 30, 49ers 28; Redskins 16, Packers 3			
	NFC championship game: Redskins 26, Cowboys 3			
	Super Bowl VII: Dolphins (AFC) 14, Redskins (NFC) 7			
1971	Dallas Cowboys (E)	11–3–0	.786	Tom Landry
	Minnesota Vikings (C)	11–3–0	.786	Bud Grant
	San Francisco 49ers (W)	9–5–0	.643	Dick Nolan
	Washington Redskins (WC)	9–4–1	.786	George Allen
	Divisional playoffs: Cowboys 20, Vikings 12; 49ers 24, Redskins 20			
	NFC championship game: Cowboys 14, 49ers 3			
	Super Bowl VI: Cowboys (NFC) 24, Dolphins (AFC) 3			
1970	Dallas Cowboys (E)	10–4–0	.714	Tom Landry
	Minnesota Vikings (C)	12–2–0	.857	Bud Grant
	San Francisco 49ers (W)	10–3–1	.769	Dick Nolan
	Detroit Lions (WC)	10–4–0	.714	Joe Schmidt
	Divisional playoffs: Cowboys 5, Lions 0; 49ers 17, Vikings 14			
	NFC championship game: Cowboys 17, 49ers 10			
	Super Bowl V: Colts (AFC) 16, Cowboys (NFC) 13			
1969	Dallas Cowboys (Ca)	11–2–1	.846	Tom Landry
	Cleveland Browns (Cy)	10–3–1	.769	Blanton Collier
	Los Angeles Rams (Co)	11–3–0	.786	George Allen

Year	Winners	Record	Pct.	Coach
	Minnesota Vikings (Ce)	12–2–0	.857	Bud Grant
	Conference championship games: Browns 38, Cowboys 14; Vikings 23, Rams 20			
	NFL championship game: Vikings 27, Browns 7			
	Super Bowl IV: Chiefs (AFL) 23, Vikings (NFL) 7			
1968	Dallas Cowboys (Ca)	12–2–0	.857	Tom Landry
	Cleveland Browns (Cy)	10–4–0	.714	Blanton Collier
	Baltimore Colts (Co)	13–1–0	.929	Don Shula
	Minnesota Vikings (Ce)	8–6–0	.571	Bud Grant
	Conference championship games: Browns 31, Cowboys 20; Colts 24, Vikings 14			
	NFL championship game: Colts 34, Browns 0			
	Super Bowl III: Jets (AFL) 16, Colts (NFL) 7			
1967	Dallas Cowboys (Ca)	9–5–0	.643	Tom Landry
	Cleveland Browns (Cy)	9–5–0	.643	Blanton Collier
	Los Angeles Rams (Co)	11–1–0	.917	George Allen
	Green Bay Packers (Ce)	9–4–1	.692	Vince Lombardi
	Conference championship games: Cowboys 52, Browns 14; Packers 28, Rams 7			
	NFL championship game: Packers 21, Dallas 17.			
	Super Bowl II: Packers (NFL) 33, Raiders (AFL) 14			
1966	Dallas Cowboys (E)	10–3–1	.769	Tom Landry
	Green Bay Packers (W)	12–2–0	.857	Vince Lombardi
	NFL championship game: Packers 34, Cowboys 27			
	Super Bowl I: Packers (NFL) 35, Chiefs (AFL) 10			
1965	Cleveland Browns (E)	11–3–0	.786	Blanton Collier
	Green Bay Packers (W)	10–3–1	.769	Vince Lombardi
	Baltimore Colts (W)	10–3–1	.769	Don Shula
	Western Conference tie playoff: Packers 13, Colts 10 (14:39 overtime)			
	NFL championship game: Packers 23, Browns 12			
1964	Cleveland Browns (E)	10–3–1	.769	Blanton Collier
	Baltimore Colts (W)	12–2–0	.857	Don Shula
	NFL championship game: Browns 27, Colts 0			
1963	New York Giants (E)	11–3–0	.786	Allie Sherman
	Chicago Bears (W)	11–1–2	.917	George Halas
	NFL championship game: Bears 14, Giants 10			
1962	New York Giants (E)	12–2–0	.857	Allie Sherman
	Green Bay Packers (W)	13–1–0	.929	Vince Lombardi
	NFL championship game: Packers 16, Giants 7			
1961	New York Giants (E)	10–3–1	.769	Allie Sherman
	Green Bay Packers (W)	11–3–0	.786	Vince Lombardi
	NFL championship game: Packers 37, Giants 0			
1960	Philadelphia Eagles (E)	10–2–0	.833	Buck Shaw
	Green Bay Packers (W)	8–4–0	.667	Vince Lombardi
	NFL championship game: Eagles 17, Packers 13			

Year	Winners	Record	Pct.	Coach
1959	New York Giants (E)	10–2–0	.833	Jim Howell
	Baltimore Colts (W)	9–3–0	.750	Weeb Ewbank
	NFL championship game: Colts 31, Giants 16			
1958	New York Giants (E)	9–3–0	.750	Jim Howell
	Cleveland Browns (E)	9–3–0	.750	Paul Brown
	Baltimore Colts (W)	9–3–0	.750	Weeb Ewbank
	Eastern Conference tie playoff: Giants 10, Browns 0			
	NFL championship game: Colts 23, Giants 17 (8:15 overtime)			
1957	Cleveland Browns (E)	9–2–1	.818	Paul Brown
	Detroit Lions (W)	8–4–0	.667	George Wilson
	San Francisco 49ers (W)	8–4–0	.667	Frankie Albert
	Western Conference tie playoff: Lions 31, 49ers 27			
	NFL championship game: Lions 59, Browns 14			
1956	New York Giants (E)	8–3–1	.727	Jim Howell
	Chicago Bears (W)	9–2–1	.818	Paddy Driscoll
	NFL championship game: Giants 57, Bears 7			
1955	Cleveland Browns (E)	9–2–1	.818	Paul Brown
	Los Angeles Rams (W)	8–3–1	.727	Sid Gillman
	NFL championship game: Browns 38, Rams 14			
1954	Cleveland Browns (E)	9–3–0	.750	Paul Brown
	Detroit Lions (W)	9–2–1	.818	Buddy Parker
	NFL championship game: Browns 56, Lions 10			
1953	Cleveland Browns (E)	11–1–0	.917	Paul Brown
	Detroit Lions (W)	10–2–0	.833	Buddy Parker
	NFL championship game: Lions 17, Browns 16			
1952	Cleveland Browns (A)	11–1–0	.917	Paul Brown
	Detroit Lions (N)	9–3–0	.750	Buddy Parker
	Los Angeles Rams (N)	9–3–0	.750	Hamp Pool*
	National Conference tie playoff: Lions 31, Rams 21			
	NFL championship game: Lions 17, Browns 7			
1951	Cleveland Browns (A)	11–1–0	.917	Paul Brown
	Los Angeles Rams (N)	8–4–0	.667	Joe Stydahar
	NFL championship game: Rams 24, Browns 17			
1950	Cleveland Browns (A)	10–2–0	.833	Paul Brown
	New York Giants (A)	10–2–0	.833	Steve Owen
	Los Angeles Rams (N)	9–3–0	.750	Joe Stydahar
	Chicago Bears (N)	9–3–0	.750	George Halas
	American Conference tie playoff: Browns 8, Giants 3			
	National Conference tie playoff: Rams 24, Bears 14			
	NFL championship game: Browns 30, Rams 28			
1949	Philadelphia Eagles (E)	11–1–0	.917	Greasy Neale
	Los Angeles Rams (W)	8–2–2	.800	Clark Shaughnessy
	NFL championship game: Eagles 14, Rams 0			
1948	Philadelphia Eagles (E)	9–2–1	.818	Greasy Neale
	Chicago Cardinals (W)	11–1–0	.917	Jimmy Conzelman

Year	Winners	Record	Pct.	Coach
	NFL championship game: Eagles 7, Cardinals 0			
1947	⎰Philadelphia Eagles (E)	8–4–0	.667	Greasy Neale
	⎱Pittsburgh Steelers (E)	8–4–0	.667	Jock Sutherland
	Chicago Cardinals (W)	9–3–0	.750	Jimmy Conzelman
	Eastern Division tie playoff: Eagles 21, Steelers 0			
	NFL championship game: Cardinals 28, Eagles 21			
1946	New York Giants (E)	7–3–1	.700	Steve Owen
	Chicago Bears (W)	8–2–1	.800	George Halas
	NFL championship game: Bears 24, Giants 14			
1945	Washington Redskins (E)	8–2–0	.800	Dudley De Groot
	Cleveland Rams (W)	9–1–0	.900	Adam Walsh
	NFL championship game: Rams 15, Redskins 14			
1944	New York Giants (E)	8–1–1	.889	Steve Owen
	Green Bay Packers (W)	8–2–0	.800	Curly Lambeau
	NFL championship game: Packers 14, Giants 14			
1943	⎰Washington Redskins (E)	6–3–1	.667	Arthur Bergman
	⎱New York Giants (E)	6–3–1	.667	Steve Owen
	Chicago Bears (W)	8–1–1	.889	George Halas
	Eastern Division tie playoff: Redskins 28, Giants 0			
	NFL championship game: Bears 41, Redskins 21			
1942	Washington Redskins (E)	10–1–0	.909	Ray Flaherty
	Chicago Bears (W)	11–0–0	1.000	George Halas
	NFL championship game: Redskins 14, Bears 6			
1941	New York Giants (E)	8–3–0	.727	Steve Owen
	⎰Chicago Bears (W)	10–1–0	.909	George Halas
	⎱Green Bay Packers (W)	10–1–0	.909	Curly Lambeau
	Western Division tie playoff: Bears 33, Packers 14			
	NFL championship game: Bears 37, Giants 9			
1940	Washington Redskins (E)	9–2–0	.818	Ray Flaherty
	Chicago Bears (W)	8–3–0	.727	George Halas
	NFL championship game: Bears 73, Redskins 0			
1939	New York Giants (E)	9–1–1	.900	Steve Owen
	Green Bay Packers (W)	9–2–0	.818	Curly Lambeau
	NFL championship game: Packers 27, Giants 0			
1938	New York Giants (E)	8–2–1	.800	Steve Owen
	Green Bay Packers (W)	8–3–0	.727	Curly Lambeau
	NFL championship game: Giants 23, Packers 17			
1937	Washington Redskins (E)	8–3–0	.727	Ray Flaherty
	Chicago Bears (W)	9–1–1	.900	George Halas
	NFL championship game: Redskins 28, Bears 21			
1936	Boston Redskins (E)	7–5–0	.583	Ray Flaherty
	Green Bay Packers (W)	10–1–1	.909	Curly Lambeau
	NFL championship game: Packers 21, Redskins 6			

* Joe Stydahar resigned as Rams coach after the first game of 1952.

Year	Winners	Record	Pct.	Coach
1935	New York Giants (E)	9–3–0	.750	Steve Owen
	Detroit Lions (W)	7–3–2	.700	Milo Creighton
	NFL championship game: Lions 26, Giants 7			
1934	New York Giants (E)	8–5–0	.615	Steve Owen
	Chicago Bears (W)	13–0–0	1.000	George Halas
	NFL championship game: Giants 30, Bears 13			
1933	New York Giants (E)	11–3–0	.786	Steve Owen
	Chicago Bears (W)	10–22–1	.833	George Halas
	NFL championship game: Bears 23, Giants 21			
1932	Chicago Bears	7–1–6	.875	Ralph Jones
1931	Green Bay Packers	12–2–0	.857	Curly Lambeau
1930	Green Bay Packers	10–3–1	.769	Curly Lambeau
1929	Green Bay Packers	12–0–1	1.000	Curly Lambeau
1928	Providence Steam-Rollers	8–1–2	.889	Jim Conzelman
1927	New York Giants	11–1–1	.917	Earl Potteiger
1926	Frankford (Pa.) Yellowjackets	14–1–1	.933	Guy Chamberlain
1925	Chicago Cardinals	11–2–1	.846	Norman Barry
1924	Cleveland Bull Dogs	7–1–1	.875	Guy Chamberlain
1923	Canton Bulldogs	11–0–1	1.000	Guy Chamberlain
1922	Canton Bulldogs	10–0–2	1.000	Guy Chamberlain
1921	Chicago Bears	10–1–1	.909	George Halas

The National Football League was organized on Sept. 17, 1920, and was at first called the American Professional Football Association. The name was changed in 1922. During that first season of 1920, there was no organized schedule of games and the number of clubs varied from week to week; at one point there was a total of 13. There's a nostalgic ring to the club nicknames of those original 13, only one of which survives in the modern NFL:

Akron Steels
Buffalo All-Americans
Chicago Cardinals
Chicago Tigers
Canton Bulldogs
Cleveland Panthers
Columbus Panhandles

Dayton Triangles
Decatur Staleys
Detroit Heralds
Hammond Pros
Rochester Jeffersons
Rock Island Independents

American Football Conference
DIVISION WINNERS AND
PLAYOFF CHAMPIONSHIP RESULTS, 1960–76

NOTE: Wild card qualifiers (WC) are divisional second-place teams with best second-place won-lost percentage in the conference, or teams that qualify otherwise in case of ties.

During the period 1960–69, the American Football League consisted of two divisions, the Eastern and Western. The AFL championship games were between winners of the two divisions. (In 1969, divisional playoffs were between the first- and second-place teams in each of the two AFL divisions; the two winners met for the league championship.) The American Football League merged with the National Football League beginning with the 1970 season.

Year	Winners	Record	Pct.	Coach
1976	Baltimore Colts (E)	11–3–0	.786	Ted Marchibroda
	Pittsburgh Steelers (C)	10–4–0	.714	Chuck Noll
	Oakland Raiders (W)	13–1–0	.929	John Madden
	New England Patriots (WC)	11–3–0	.786	Chuck Fairbanks
	Divisional playoffs: Raiders 24, Patriots 21; Steelers 40, Colts 14			
	AFC championship game: Raiders 24, Steelers 7			
	Super Bowl XI: Raiders (AFC) 32, Vikings (NFC) 14			
1975	Baltimore Colts (E)	10–4–0	.714	Ted Marchibroda
	Pittsburgh Steelers (C)	12–2–0	.857	Chuck Noll
	Oakland Raiders (W)	11–3–0	.786	John Madden
	Cincinnati Bengals (WC)	11–3–0	.786	Paul Brown
	Divisional playoffs: Steelers 28, Colts 10; Raiders 31, Bengals 28			
	AFC championship game: Steelers 16, Raiders 10			
	Super Bowl X: Steelers (AFC) 21, Cowboys (NFC) 17			
1974	Miami Dolphins (E)	11–3–0	.786	Don Shula
	Pittsburgh Steelers (C)	10–3–1	.750	Chuck Noll
	Oakland Raiders (W)	12–2–0	.857	John Madden
	Buffalo Bills (WC)	9–5–0	.643	Lou Saban
	Divisional playoffs: Raiders 28, Dolphins 26; Steelers 32, Bills 14			
	AFC championship game: Steelers 24, Raiders 13			
	Super Bowl IX: Steelers (AFC) 16, Vikings (NFC) 6			
1973	Miami Dolphins (E)	12–2–0	.857	Don Shula
	Cincinnati Bengals (C)	10–4–0	.714	Paul Brown

Year	Winners	Record	Pct.	Coach
	Oakland Raiders (W)	9–4–1	.679	John Madden
	Pittsburgh Steelers (WC)	10–4–0	.714	Chuck Noll

Divisional playoffs: Raiders 33, Steelers 14; Dolphins 34, Bengals 16
AFC championship game: Dolphins 27, Raiders 10
Super Bowl VIII: Dolphins (AFC) 24, Vikings (NFC) 7

Year	Winners	Record	Pct.	Coach
1972	Miami Dolphins (E)	14–0–0	1.000	Don Shula
	Pittsburgh Steelers (C)	11–3–0	.786	Chuck Noll
	Oakland Raiders (W)	10–3–1	.750	John Madden
	Cleveland Browns (WC)	10–4–0	.714	Nick Skorich

Divisional playoffs: Steelers 13, Raiders 7; Dolphins 20, Browns 14
AFC championship game: Dolphins 21, Steelers 17
Super Bowl VII: Dolphins (AFC) 14, Redskins (NFC) 7

Year	Winners	Record	Pct.	Coach
1971	Miami Dolphins (E)	10–3–1	.769	Don Shula
	Cleveland Browns (C)	9–5–0	.643	Nick Skorich
	Kansas City Chiefs (W)	10–3–1	.769	Hank Stram
	Baltimore Colts (WC)	10–4–0	.714	Don McCafferty

Divisional playoffs: Dolphins 27, Chiefs 24 (22:40 overtime); Colts 20, Browns 3
AFC championship game: Dolphins 21, Colts 0
Super Bowl VI: Cowboys (NFC) 24, Dolphins (AFC) 3

Year	Winners	Record	Pct.	Coach
1970	Baltimore Colts (E)	11–2–1	.846	Don McCafferty
	Cincinnati Bengals (C)	8–6–0	.571	Paul Brown
	Oakland Raiders (W)	8–4–2	.667	John Madden
	Miami Dolphins (WC)	10–4–0	.714	Don Shula

Divisional playoffs: Colts 17, Bengals 0; Raiders 21, Dolphins 14
AFC championship game: Colts 27, Raiders 17
Super Bowl V: Colts (AFC) 16, Cowboys (NFC) 13

Year	Winners	Record	Pct.	Coach
1969	New York Jets (E)	10–4–0	.714	Weeb Ewbank
	Oakland Raiders (W)	12–1–1	.923	John Madden
	Houston Oilers (E-2d)	6–6–2	.500	Wally Lemm
	Kansas City Chiefs (W-2d)	11–3–0	.786	Hank Stram

Divisional playoffs: Chiefs 13, Jets 6; Raiders 56, Oilers 7
AFL championship game: Chiefs 17, Raiders 7
Super Bowl IV: Chiefs (AFL) 23, Vikings (NFL) 7

Year	Winners	Record	Pct.	Coach
1968	New York Jets (E)	11–3–0	.786	Weeb Ewbank
	⎰ Oakland Raiders (W)	12–2–0	.857	Johnny Rauch
	⎱ Kansas City Chiefs (W)	12–2–0	.857	Hank Stram

Western Division tie playoff: Raiders 41, Chiefs 6
AFL championship game: Jets 27, Raiders 23
Super Bowl III: Jets (AFL) 16, Colts (NFL) 7

Year	Winners	Record	Pct.	Coach
1967	Houston Oilers (E)	9–4–1	.692	Wally Lemm
	Oakland Raiders (W)	13–1–0	.929	Johnny Rauch

AFL championship game: Raiders 40, Oilers 7
Super Bowl II: Packers (NFL) 33, Raiders (AFL) 14

Year	Winners	Record	Pct.	Coach
1966	Buffalo Bills (E)	9–4–1	.692	Joel Collier
	Kansas City Chiefs (W)	11–2–1	.846	Hank Stram
	AFL championship game: Chiefs 31, Bills 7			
	Super Bowl I: Packers (NFL) 35, Chiefs (AFL) 10			
1965	Buffalo Bills (E)	10–3–1	.769	Lou Saban
	San Diego Chargers (W)	9–2–3	.818	Sid Gillman
	AFL championship game: Bills 23, Chargers 0			
1964	Buffalo Bills (E)	12–2–0	.857	Lou Saban
	San Diego Chargers (W)	8–5–1	.615	Sid Gillman
	AFL championship game: Bills 20, Chargers 7			
1963	Boston Patriots (E)	7–6–1	.538	Mike Holovak
	Buffalo Bills (E)	7–6–1	.538	Lou Saban
	San Diego Chargers (W)	11–3–1	.786	Sid Gillman
	Eastern Division tie playoff: Patriots 26, Bills 8			
	AFL championship game: Chargers 51, Patriots 10			
1962	Houston Oilers (E)	11–3–0	.786	Pop Ivy
	Dallas Texans (W)	11–3–0	.786	Hank Stram
	AFL championship game: Texans 20, Oilers 17 (17:54 overtime)			
1961	Houston Oilers (E)	10–3–1	.769	Wally Lemm
	San Diego Chargers (W)	12–2–0	.857	Sid Gillman
	AFL championship game: Oilers 10, Chargers 3			
1960	Houston Oilers (E)	10–4–0	.714	Lou Rykmus
	Los Angeles Chargers (W)	10–4–0	.714	Sid Gillman
	AFL championship game: Oilers 24, Chargers 16			

A Selection of
SUPER BOWL RECORDS AND RESULTS, 1967–77

Results

Super Bowl XI at Pasadena, Jan. 9, 1977
Oakland Raiders (AFC) 32, Minnesota Vikings (NFC) 14
Attendance: 100,421
Super Bowl X at Miami, Jan. 18, 1976
Pittsburgh Steelers (AFC) 21, Dallas Cowboys (NFC) 17
Attendance: 80,187
Super Bowl IX at New Orleans, Jan. 12, 1975
Pittsburgh Steelers (AFC) 16, Minnesota Vikings (NFC) 6
Attendance: 80,997
Super Bowl VIII at Houston, Jan. 13, 1974
Miami Dolphins (AFC) 24, Minnesota Vikings (NFC) 7
Attendance: 71,882
Super Bowl VII at Los Angeles, Jan. 14, 1973
Miami Dolphins (AFC) 14, Washington Redskins (NFC) 7
Attendance: 90,182
Super Bowl VI at New Orleans, Jan. 16, 1972
Dallas Cowboys (NFC) 24, Miami Dolphins (AFC) 3
Attendance: 81,023
Super Bowl V at Miami, Jan. 17, 1971
Baltimore Colts (AFC) 16, Dallas Cowboys (NFC) 13
Attendance: 79,204
Super Bowl IV at New Orleans, Jan. 11, 1970
Kansas City Chiefs (AFL) 23, Minnesota Vikings (NFL) 7
Attendance: 80,562
Super Bowl III at Miami, Jan. 12, 1969
New York Jets (AFL) 16, Baltimore Colts (NFL) 7
Attendance: 75,389
Super Bowl II at Miami, Jan. 14, 1968
Green Bay Packers (NFL) 33, Oakland Raiders (AFL) 14
Attendance: 75,546
Super Bowl I at Los Angeles, Jan. 15, 1967
Green Bay Packers (NFL) 35, Kansas City Chiefs (AFL) 10
Attendance: 61,946

Summary: AFL–AFC teams have won eight Super Bowls and lost three.

Super Bowl
INDIVIDUAL RECORDS

Scoring

Most points scored in one game
Don Chandler, 15—Green Bay vs. Oakland, Jan. 14, 1968 (3 PATs, 4 FGs)

Most touchdowns scored in one game
2—Max McGee, Green Bay vs. Kansas City, Jan. 15, 1967 (2 passes); Elijah Pitts, Green Bay vs. Kansas City, Jan. 15, 1967 (2 runs); Bill Miller, Oakland vs. Green Bay, Jan. 14, 1968 (2 passes); Larry Csonka, Miami vs. Minnesota, Jan. 13, 1974 (2 runs); Pete Banaszak, Oakland vs. Minnesota, Jan. 9, 1977 (2 runs)

Most PATs in one game
Don Chandler, 5—Green Bay vs. Kansas City, Jan. 15, 1967 (5 attempts)

Most FGs in one game
Don Chandler, 4—Green Bay vs. Oakland, Jan. 14, 1968

Longest field goal
Jan Stenerud, 48 yards—Kansas City vs. Minnesota, Jan. 11, 1970

Most safeties in one game
1—Dwight White, Pittsburgh vs. Minnesota, Jan. 12, 1975; Reggie Harrison, Pittsburgh vs. Dallas, Jan. 18, 1976

Rushing

Most attempts in one game
Franco Harris, 34—Pittsburgh vs. Minnesota, Jan. 12, 1975 (158 yards)

Most yards gained in one game
Franco Harris, 158—Pittsburgh vs. Minnesota, Jan. 12, 1968 (34 attempts)

Most touchdowns rushing in one game
2—Elijah Pitts, Green Bay vs. Kansas City, Jan. 15, 1967; Larry Csonka, Miami vs. Minnesota, Jan. 13, 1974; Pete Banaszak, Oakland vs. Minnesota, Jan. 9, 1977

Passing

Most attempts in one game
Fran Tarkenton, 35—Minnesota vs. Oakland, Jan. 9, 1977 (17 completions)

Most completions in one game
Fran Tarkenton, 18—Minnesota vs. Miami, Jan. 13, 1974 (28 attempts)

Highest completion percentage in one game
(At least 10 attempts to qualify)
Bob Griese, 72.7—Miami vs. Washington, Jan. 14, 1973 (8 out of 11)

Most yards passing in one game
Bart Starr, 250—Green Bay vs. Kansas City, Jan. 15, 1967

Most touchdowns passing in one game
2—Bart Starr, Green Bay vs. Kansas City, Jan. 15, 1967; Daryle
   Lamonica, Oakland vs. Green Bay, Jan. 14, 1968; Roger Staubach,
   Dallas vs. Miami, Jan. 16, 1972

Pass Receptions

Most receptions in one game
George Sauer, 8—New York Jets vs. Baltimore, Jan. 12, 1969

Most yards gained in one game
Lynn Swann, 161—Pittsburgh vs. Dallas, Jan. 18, 1976 (4 receptions,
   1 TD)
Max McGee, 138—Green Bay vs. Kansas City, Jan. 15, 1967 (7 receptions, 2 TDs)

Most touchdown receptions in one game
2—Max McGee, Green Bay vs. Kansas City, Jan. 15, 1967; Bill Miller,
   Oakland vs. Green Bay, Jan. 14, 1968

Punting

Most punts in one game
Ron Widby, 9—Dallas vs. Baltimore, Jan. 17, 1971

Highest punting average for one game
(At least 3 punts to qualify)
Jerrel Wilson, 48.5—Kansas City vs. Minnesota, Jan. 11, 1970 (4
   punts)

Longest punt
Jerrel Wilson, 61 yards—Kansas City vs. Green Bay, Jan. 15, 1967

Fumbles

Most fumbles in one game
Roger Staubach, 3—Dallas vs. Pittsburgh, Jan. 18, 1976

Super Bowl
TEAM RECORDS

Scoring

Most points scored in one game
Green Bay, 35—vs. Kansas City, Jan. 15, 1967

Most points scored by both teams in one game
47—Green Bay (33) vs. Oakland (14), Jan. 14, 1968

Fewest points scored by both teams in one game
21—Washington (7) vs. Miami (14), Jan. 14, 1973

Most touchdowns in one game
Green Bay, 5—vs. Kansas City, Jan. 15, 1967

Most PATs in one game
Green Bay, 5—vs. Kansas City, Jan. 15, 1967

Most FGs in one game
Green Bay, 4—vs. Oakland, Jan. 14, 1968

First Downs

Most first downs in one game
Dallas, 23—vs. Miami, Jan. 16, 1972

Fewest first downs in one game
Minnesota, 9—vs. Pittsburgh, Jan. 12, 1975

Most first downs by both teams in one game
41—Oakland (21) vs. Minnesota (20), Jan. 9, 1977

Fewest first downs by both teams in one game
24—Dallas (10) vs. Baltimore (14), Jan. 17, 1971

Total Net Yards Gained

Most yards gained in one game
Oakland, 429—vs. Minnesota, Jan. 9, 1977

Fewest yards gained in one game
Minnesota, 119—vs. Pittsburgh, Jan. 12, 1975

Most yards gained by both teams in one game
782—Oakland (429) vs. Minnesota (353), Jan. 9, 1977

Fewest yards gained by both teams in one game
452—Minnesota (119) vs. Pittsburgh (333), Jan. 12, 1975

Rushing

Most attempts in one game
Pittsburgh, 57—vs. Minnesota, Jan. 12, 1975

Fewest attempts in one game
Kansas City, 19—vs. Green Bay, Jan. 15, 1967
Minnesota, 19—vs. Kansas City, Jan. 11, 1970

Most yards gained in one game
Oakland, 266—vs. Minnesota, Jan. 9, 1977

Fewest yards gained in one game
Minnesota, 17—vs. Pittsburgh, Jan. 12, 1975

Most touchdowns rushing in one game
Green Bay, 3—vs. Kansas City, Jan. 15, 1967
Miami, 3—vs. Minnesota, Jan. 13, 1974

Passing

Most passes attempted in one game
Minnesota, 44—vs. Oakland, Jan. 9, 1977

Fewest passes attempted in one game
Miami, 7—vs. Minnesota, Jan. 13, 1974

Most passes completed in one game
Minnesota, 24—vs. Oakland, Jan. 9, 1977

Fewest passes completed in one game
Miami, 6—vs. Minnesota, Jan. 13, 1974

Most passes attempted by both teams in one game
70—Baltimore (41) vs. New York Jets (29), Jan. 12, 1969

Fewest passes attempted by both teams in one game
35—Miami (7) vs. Minnesota (28), Jan. 13, 1974

Most passes completed by both teams in one game
36—Minnesota (24) vs. Oakland (12), Jan. 9, 1977

Fewest passes completed by both teams in one game
20—Pittsburgh (9) vs. Minnesota (11), Jan. 12, 1975

Most yards gained in one game
Minnesota, 282—vs. Oakland, Jan. 9, 1977

Fewest yards gained in one game
Miami, 63—vs. Minnesota, Jan. 13, 1974

Most yards gained by both teams in one game
445—Minnesota (282) vs. Oakland (163), Jan. 9, 1977

Fewest yards gained by both teams in one game
156—Miami (69) vs. Washington (87), Jan. 14, 1973

Most times tackled attempting passes (QB sacks) in one game
Dallas, 7—vs. Pittsburgh, Jan. 18, 1976

Most touchdown passes in one game
Green Bay, 2—vs. Kansas City, Jan. 15, 1967
Oakland, 2—vs. Green Bay, Jan. 14, 1968
Dallas, 2—vs. Miami, Jan. 16, 1972
Minnesota, 2—vs. Oakland, Jan. 9, 1977

Punting

Most punts in one game
Dallas, 9—vs. Baltimore, Jan. 17, 1971

Fewest punts in one game
Baltimore, 3—vs. New York Jets, Jan. 12, 1969
Minnesota, 3—vs. Kansas City, Jan. 11, 1970
Miami, 3—vs. Minnesota, Jan. 13, 1974

Most punts by both teams in one game
13—Dallas (9) vs. Baltimore (4), Jan. 17, 1971; Pittsburgh (7) vs. Minnesota (6), Jan. 12, 1975

Fewest punts by both teams in one game
7—Baltimore (3) vs. New York Jets (4), Jan. 12, 1969; Minnesota (3) vs. Kansas City (4), Jan. 11, 1970

Highest punting average for one game
Kansas City, 48.5—vs. Minnesota, Jan. 11, 1970 (4 punts)

Lowest punting average for one game
Washington, 31.2—vs. Miami, Jan. 14, 1973 (5 punts)

Penalties

Most penalties in one game
Dallas, 10—vs. Baltimore, Jan. 17, 1971 (133 yards)

Fewest penalties in one game
Miami, 0—vs. Dallas, Jan. 16, 1972
Pittsburgh, 0—vs. Dallas, Jan. 18, 1976

Most penalties, both teams, in one game
14—Dallas (10) vs. Baltimore (4), Jan. 17, 1971

Fewest penalties, both teams, in one game
2—Pittsburgh (0) vs. Dallas (2), Jan. 18, 1976

Most yards penalized in one game
Dallas, 133—vs. Baltimore, Jan. 17, 1971 (10 penalties)

Most yards penalized, both teams, in one game
164—Dallas (133) vs. Baltimore (31), Jan. 17, 1971

Fewest yards penalized, both teams, in one game
15—Miami (0) vs. Dallas (15), Jan. 16, 1972

Fumbles

Most fumbles in one game
Baltimore, 15—vs. Dallas, Jan. 17, 1971

Most fumbles, both teams, in one game
8—Dallas (4) vs. Pittsburgh (4), Jan. 18, 1976

AFC—NFC PRO BOWL
RESULTS, 1971–77

Jan. 17, 1977, at Seattle
AFC 24, NFC 14
Attendance: 65,000
Jan. 26, 1976, at New Orleans
NFC 23, AFC 20
Attendance: 32,108
Jan. 20, 1975, at Miami
NFC 17, AFC 10
Attendance: 26,484
Jan. 20, 1974, at Kansas City
AFC 15, NFC 13
Attendance: 51,482

Jan. 21, 1973, at Dallas
AFC 33, NFC 28
Attendance: 47,879
Jan. 23, 1972, at Los Angeles
AFC 26, NFC 13
Attendance: 53,647
Jan. 24, 1971, at Los Angeles
NFC 27, AFC 6
Attendance: 48,222

SUMMARY: AFC teams have won four and lost three in the seven-game series.

CHICAGO COLLEGE
ALL-STAR GAME
RESULTS, 1934–76

Year	Results	Year	Results
1976	Pittsburgh 24, All-Stars 0*	1954	Detroit 31, All-Stars 6
1975	Pittsburgh 21, All-Stars 14	1953	Detroit 24, All-Stars 10
1974	No game played (strike)	1952	Los Angeles 10, All-Stars 7
1973	Miami 14, All-Stars 3	1951	Cleveland 33, All-Stars 0
1972	Dallas 20, All-Stars 7	1950	All-Stars 17, Philadelphia 7
1971	Baltimore 24, All-Stars 17	1949	Philadelphia 38, All-Stars 0
1970	Kansas City 24, All-Stars 3	1948	Chicago Cards 28, All-Stars 0
1969	N.Y. Jets 26, All-Stars 24	1947	All-Stars 16, Chicago 0
1968	Green Bay 34, All-Stars 17	1946	All-Stars 16, Los Angeles 0
1967	Green Bay 27, All-Stars 0	1945	Green Bay 19, All-Stars 7
1966	Green Bay 38, All-Stars 0	1944	Chicago 24, All-Stars 21
1965	Cleveland 24, All-Stars 16		All-Stars 21
1964	Chicago 28, All-Stars 17	1943	All-Stars 27, Washington 7
1963	All-Stars 20, Green Bay 7	1942	Chicago 21, All-Stars 0
1962	Green Bay 42, All-Stars 20	1941	Chicago 37, All-Stars 13
1961	Philadelphia 28, All-Stars 14	1940	Green Bay 45, All-Stars 28
1960	Baltimore 32, All-Stars 7	1939	N.Y. Giants 9, All-Stars 0
1959	Baltimore 29, All-Stars 0	1938	All-Stars 28, Washington 16
1958	All-Stars 35, Detroit 19	1937	All-Stars 6, Green Bay 0
1957	N.Y. Giants 22, All-Stars 12	1936	Detroit 7, All-Stars 7 (tie)
1956	Cleveland 26, All-Stars 0	1935	Chicago 5, All-Stars 0
1955	All-Stars 30, Cleveland 27	1934	Chicago 0, All-Stars 0 (tie)

SUMMARY: Pro teams have won 31, lost 9, tied 2.

---

* Game was stopped in the third quarter with 13:38 of the period elapsed, because of severe weather conditions. A torrential rain and electrical storm swept Soldier Field in Chicago on the night of the game (July 23, 1976), making playing conditions torturous. Game was terminated by agreement of NFL Commissioner Pete Rozelle and officials of **Chicago Tribune** Charities, sponsors of the contest.

PROFESSIONAL FOOTBALL
HALL OF FAME
Canton, Ohio

The Professional Football Hall of Fame was dedicated on September 7, 1963, at Canton, Ohio, site of the original organizational meeting in 1920 that led to formation of the National Football League. Members are chosen by the Hall of Fame National Board of Selectors, which is made up of media representatives from the various professional football cities. Five new members were elected in 1977, bringing the total roster of members to 93. The new members are Frank Gifford, Bill Willis, Gale Sayers, Forrest Gregg, and Bart Starr.

The first American Football League (AFL) consisted of nine clubs and was organized in 1926. It was disbanded, however, after that one season. The second AFL lasted two seasons, 1936–37, and the third existed from 1940–41. The fourth and much more successful AFL was organized in 1960 and eventually merged with the National Football League in 1970.

The All-American Football Conference (AAFC) was organized in 1946, with eight clubs taking the field. The AAFC was active four seasons before merging with the National Football League effective with the 1950 season.

Roster of Members

Battles, Cliff—West Virginia Wesleyan; halfback, 6′ 1″, 201 lbs.; Boston Braves 1932, Boston Redskins 1933–36, Washington Redskins 1937 . . . Phi Beta Kappa scholar, triple-threat grid star at West Virginia Wesleyan . . . NFL rushing champ, 1933, 1937 . . . All-NFL choice, 1933, 1936, 1937 . . . Six-year career rushing, 3,542 yards . . . First to gain over 200 yards in one game, 1933 . . . Scored three spectacular touchdowns in division-clinching win over Giants, 1937 . . . Retired after 1937 season when salary was frozen at $3,000 . . . Born May 1, 1910, in Akron, Ohio.

Baugh, Sammy—Texas Christian; quarterback, 6' 2", 180 lbs.; Washington Redskins 1937–52 . . . Two-time TCU All-America . . . No. 1 draft choice, 1937 . . . Split career between tailback, T-quarterback . . . Premier passer who influenced great offensive revolution . . . All-NFL six years . . . NFL passing, punting, interception champ, 1943 . . . Six-time NFL passing leader . . . History's top punter . . . Career record: 21,886 yards and 186 touchdowns passing, intercepted only 28 times, punting average 45.1 . . . Born March 17, 1914, in Temple, Texas.

Bednarik, Chuck—Pennsylvania; center-linebacker, 6' 3", 230 lbs.; Philadelphia Eagles 1949–62 . . . Two-time Pennsylvania All-America . . . Eagles' bonus draft choice, 1949 . . . NFL's last "iron man" star . . . Rugged, durable, bulldozing blocker, bone-jarring tackler . . . Missed only three games in 14 years . . . Eight times All-NFL . . . Played in eight Pro Bowls, Most Valuable Player in 1954 game . . . Named NFL's all-time center, 1969 . . . Played 58 minutes, made game-saving tackle in 1960 NFL title game . . . Born May 1, 1925, in Bethlehem, Pa.

Bell, Bert—Pennsylvania; league administrator, owner Philadelphia Eagles 1933–40, owner Pittsburgh Steelers 1941–46 . . . Weathered heavy financial losses as Eagles' owner, 1933–40, Steelers co-owner, 1941–46 . . . Built NFL image to unprecedented heights as commissioner, 1946–1959 . . . Generaled NFL's war with All-American Football Conference . . . Set up farsighted television policies . . . Established strong anti-gambling controls . . . Recognized NFL Players' Association . . . Born Feb. 25, 1895, in Philadelphia, Pa. . . . Died Oct. 11, 1959, at the age of 64.

Berry, Raymond—Southern Methodist; end, 6' 2", 187 lbs.; Baltimore Colts 1955–67 . . . Formed exceptional pass-catch team with Johnny Unitas . . . Caught then-record 631 passes for 9,275 yards, 68 touchdowns . . . All-NFL in 1958, 1959 1960 . . . Played in five Pro Bowl games . . . Fumbled only once in 13-season career . . . Set NFL title game mark with 12 catches for 178 yards in 1958 overtime game . . . Colts' 20th-round future choice in 1954 . . . Born Feb. 27, 1933, in Corpus Christi, Texas.

Bidwell, Charles W.—Loyola of Chicago; owner-administrator, Chicago Cardinals 1933–37 . . . Purchased Cardinals' franchise in 1933 . . . Staunch faith in NFL stood as guiding light during dark Depression years . . . Dealt All-American Football Conference its most stunning blow with $100,000 signing of Charley Trippi in 1947 . . . Built famous "Dream Backfield" but died before it could bring him an NFL championship . . . Financial help saved Bears' ownership for

George Halas in 1932 . . . Born Sept. 16, 1895, in Chicago, Ill. . . .
Died at the age of 51 on April 19, 1947, only months before his
Chicago Cardinals won their first NFL championship in a 28–21
victory over Philadelphia.

Brown, Jim—Syracuse; fullback, 6′ 2″, 228 lbs.; Cleveland Browns
1957–65 . . . Syracuse All-America, 1956 . . . Browns' No. 1 draft
pick, 1957 . . . Most awesome runner in history . . . Led NFL rushers
eight years . . . All-NFL eight of nine years . . . NFL's Most Valuable
Player, 1958, 1965 . . . Rookie of the Year, 1957 . . . Played in nine
straight Pro Bowls . . . Career marks: 12,312 yards rushing, 262
receptions, 15,459 combined net yards, 756 points scored . . . Born
Feb. 17, 1936, in St. Simons, Ga.

Brown, Paul—Miami (Ohio); coach, Cleveland Browns of AAFC 1946–49,
Cleveland Browns of NFL 1950–62, Cincinnati Bengals 1968–75 . . .
Exceptionally successful coach at all levels of football . . . Organized
Browns in All-American Football Conference in 1946 . . . Built great
Cleveland dynasty with 158–48–8 record, four AAFC titles, three NFL
crowns, only one losing season in 17 years . . . A revolutionary inno-
vator with many coaching "firsts" to his credit . . . Born Sept. 7,
1908, in Norwalk, Ohio.

Brown, Roosevelt—Morgan State; offensive tackle, 6′ 3″, 255 lbs.; New
York Giants 1953–65 . . . Black All-America at Morgan State, 1951–
1952 . . . Giants' 27th pick in 1953 draft . . . Joined Giants as a
green 20-year-old . . . Quickly won starting role, held it for 13
seasons . . . Excellent downfield blocker, classic pass protector, fast,
mobile . . . All-NFL eight straight years, 1956–63 . . . Played in nine
Pro Bowl games . . . Named NFL's Lineman of the Year, 1956 . . .
Born Oct. 20, 1932, in Charlottesville, Va.

Canadeo, Tony—Gonzaga; halfback, 5′ 11″ 195 lbs.; Green Bay Packers
1941–44, 1946–52 . . . Gonzaga Little All-America, 1939 . . . Multi-
talented two-way performer . . . Averaged 75 yards all categories in
116 NFL games . . . Led Packers' air game, 1943 . . . Used as
heavy-duty runner on return from service, 1946 . . . Became third
back to pass 1,000-yard mark in one season, 1949 . . . All-NFL 1943,
1949 . . . Career record: 4,197 yards rushing, 1,642 yards passing,
186 points, 69 pass receptions . . . Born May 5, 1919, in Chicago, Ill.

Carr, Joe—no college; league administrator, National Football League
1921–39 . . . Sportswriter, promoter who founded Columbus Panhandles team, 1904 . . . NFL co-organizer, 1920 . . . NFL president,
1921–1939 . . . Gave NFL stability, integrity with rigid enforcement
of rules . . . Introduced standard player's contract . . . Barred use
of collegians in NFL play . . . Worked tirelessly to interest financially
capable new owners . . . Born Oct. 22, 1880, in Columbus, Ohio . . .
Died May 20, 1939, at the age of 58.

Chamberlin, Guy—Nebraska; end, 6′ 2″, 120 lbs.; coach, Canton Bulldogs (pre-NFL) 1919, Decatur Staleys 1920, Chicago Staleys 1921,
Canton Bulldogs 1922–23, Cleveland Bulldogs 1924, Frankford Yellowjackets 1925–26, Chicago Cardinals 1927–28 . . . Legendary grid hero

at Nebraska . . . Became premier end of the NFL in the 1920s . . . Extremely durable two-way performer . . . Player-coach of four NFL championship teams: 1922–1923 Canton Bulldogs, 1924 Cleveland Bulldogs, 1926 Frankford Yellowjackets . . . Six-year coaching record 56–14–5 for a remarkable .780 percentage . . . Born Jan. 16, 1894, at Blue Springs, Neb. . . . Died April 4, 1967, at the age of 73.

Christiansen, Jack—Colorado State University; defensive back, 6′ 1″, 185 lbs.; Detroit Lions 1951–58 . . . Left safety stalwart on three title teams . . . All-NFL six straight years, 1952–57 . . . Played in five Pro Bowls . . . Formidable defender, return specialist . . . Opposition's standard rule: "Don't pass in his area, don't punt to him" . . . NFL interception leader, 1953, 1957 . . . Career marks: 46 steals for 717 yards, three touchdowns; 85 punt returns for 1,084 yards, record eight touchdowns . . . Born Dec. 20, 1928, in Sublette, Kan.

Clark, Earl (Dutch)—Colorado College; quarterback, 6′ 0″, 185 lbs.; Portsmouth Spartans 1931–32, Detroit Lions 1934–38 . . . Colorado College All-America, 1928 . . . Called signals, played tailback, did everything superbly well . . . Quiet, quick-thinking, exceptional team leader . . . NFL's last drop-kicking specialist . . . All-NFL six of seven years . . . NFL scoring champ three years . . . Generaled Lions to 1935 NFL title . . . Scored 368 points on 42 touchdowns, 71 PATs, 15 field goals . . . Player-coach final two seasons . . . Born Oct. 11, 1906, in Fowler, Colo.

Connor, George—Notre Dame; tackle-linebacker, 6′ 3″, 240 lbs.; Chicago Bears 1948–55 . . . All-America at both Holy Cross and Notre Dame . . . Boston Yanks' No. 1 draft pick, 1948 . . . Quickly traded to Bears . . . All-NFL at three positions—offensive tackle, defensive tackle, linebacker . . . All-NFL five years . . . Two-way performer throughout career . . . First of big, fast, agile linebackers . . . Exceptional at diagnosing enemy plays . . . Played in first four Pro Bowl games . . . Born Jan. 21, 1925, in Chicago, Ill.

Conzelman, Jimmy—Washington (Missouri); quarterback, 6′ 0″, 180 lbs.; coach-owner, Decatur Staleys 1920, Rock Island Independents 1921–22, Milwaukee Badgers 1923–24, Detroit Panthers 1925–26, Providence Steamrollers 1927–30, Chicago Cardinals 1940–42, 1946–48 . . . Multi-talented athlete, editor, executive, song-writer, orator . . . Began NFL career with Staleys, 1920 . . . Player-coach of four NFL teams in the 1920s, including 1928 champion Providence . . . Player-coach-owner of Detroit team, 1925–1926 . . . Knee injury ended ten-year playing career, 1929 . . . Coached Cardinals to 1947 NFL, 1948 division crowns . . . Born March 6, 1898, in St. Louis, Mo. . . . Died July 31, 1970, at the age of 72.

Donovan, Art—Boston College; defensive tackle, 6′ 3″, 265 lbs.; Baltimore Colts 1950, New York Yanks 1951, Dallas Texans 1952, Baltimore Colts 1953–61 . . . First Colt to enter Pro Football Hall of Fame . . . Began NFL play as 26-year-old rookie in 1950 . . . Vital part of Baltimore's climb to powerhouse status in the 1950s . . . All-NFL 1954–57 . . . Played in five Pro Bowls . . . Great morale builder on

Colts teams . . . Son of famous boxing referee of same name . . .
Played at Boston College after World War II Marines service . . .
Born June 5, 1925, in the Bronx, N.Y.

Driscoll, John (Paddy)—Northwestern; quarterback, 5' 11", 160 lbs.;
Hammond Pros (pre-NFL) 1919, Decatur Staleys 1920, Chicago Cardinals 1920–25, Chicago Bears 1926–29 . . . Triple-threat on attack,
flawless on defense . . . Drop-kicked record four field goals one game,
1925 . . . Drop-kicked 50-yard field goal, 1924 . . . Scored 27 points
one game, 1923 . . . 23 precision punts stymied Red Grange's NFL
debut, 1925 . . . Sold by Cards to Bears, 1926, to thwart signing with
rival 1926 AFL, which operated for one season . . . Sparked Bears
four years . . . All-NFL six times . . . Born Jan. 11, 1896, in
Evanston, Ill.

Dudley, Bill—Virginia; halfback, 5' 10", 176 lbs.; Pittsburgh Steelers
1942, 1945–46, Detroit Lions 1947-49, Washington Redskins 1950-51,
1953 . . . Virginia's first All-America, 1941 . . . Steelers No. 1 draft
choice, 1942 . . . Small, slow with unorthodox style, but exceptionally
versatile, awesomely efficient . . . Won rare triple crown (NFL rushing,
interception, punt return titles), 1946 . . . All-NFL 1942, 1946 . . .
Most Valuable Player, 1946 . . . Gained 8,147 combined net yards,
scored 484 points, had 23 interceptions in career . . . Born Dec. 24,
1921, in Bluefield, Va.

Edwards, Albert Glen (Turk)—Washington State; tackle, 6' 2½", 260
lbs.; Boston Braves 1932, Boston Redskins 1933–36, Washington Redskins 1937–40 . . . Rose Bowl star, Washington State All-America,
1930 . . . Joined new Boston team for $150 a game, 1932 . . . Giant
of his era . . . Immovable, impregnable 60-minute workhorse . . .
Steamrolling blocker, smothering tackler . . . Official All-NFL 1932,
1933, 1936, 1937 . . . Bizarre knee injury suffered at pre-game coin
toss ended career in 1940 . . . Just before a game that year between
the Washington Redskins and the New York Giants, Edwards, as captain
of the Redskins, met his long-time friend Mel Hein, captain of the
Giants, in mid-field for the customary coin toss to choose goals. The
coin was tossed, they shook hands, then Edwards turned toward the
Washington sidelines and promptly twisted his knee as his foot became caught in the turf. The injury was such that Edwards never
played again . . . Born Sept. 28, 1907, in Mold, Wash.

Fears, Tom—Santa Clara and UCLA; end, 6' 2", 215 lbs.; Los Angeles
Rams 1948–56 . . . Led NFL receivers first three seasons, 1948–50
. . . Top season mark: 84 catches, 1950 . . . Had three touchdown
receptions in 1950 division title game . . . Caught 73-yard pass to
win 1951 NFL title . . . Caught record 18 passes one game, 1950 . . .
All-NFL 1949, 1950 . . . Career mark: 400 catches for 5,397 yards,
38 touchdowns . . . Precise pattern-runner, specialized in the so-called
"button-hook route" in which a receiver runs forward a certain distance, then reverses himself and turns back a few steps to meet the
oncoming pass . . . Born Dec. 3, 1923, in Los Angeles, Calif.

Flaherty, Ray—Gonzaga; coach, Boston Redskins 1936, Washington Redskins 1937–42, New York Yanks (AAFC) 1946–48, Chicago Hornets (AAFC) 1949 . . . Compiled 80–37–5 coaching record . . . Won four Eastern division, two NFL titles with Redskins, two AAFC divisional crowns with Yankees . . . Introduced behind-the-line screen pass in 1937 NFL title game . . . Two-platoon system with one rushing, one passing unit also a Flaherty first . . . Played end with Los Angeles Wildcats (1926 AFL), New York Yankees, New York Giants . . . All-NFL 1928, 1932 . . . Born Sept. 1, 1904, in Spokane, Wash.

Ford, Len—Michigan; defensive end, 6′ 6″, 260 lbs.; Los Angeles Dons (AAFC) 1948–49, Cleveland Browns 1950–57, Green Bay Packers 1958 . . . Caught 67 passes as two-way end with Dons, 1948–1949 . . . After AAFC folded, Browns converted him to full-time defensive end, altered defenses to take advantage of his exceptional pass-rushing skills . . . Overcame serious injuries in 1950 to earn All-NFL honors five times, 1951–55 . . . Played in four Pro Bowls . . . Recovered 20 opposition fumbles in career . . . Born Feb. 18, 1926, in Washington, D.C.

Fortmann, Dan, M.D.—Colgate; guard, 6′ 0″, 210 lbs.; Chicago Bears 1936–43 . . . Bears' No. 9 pick in first NFL draft, 1936 . . . At 19, became youngest starter in NFL . . . 60-minute line leader, battering-ram blocker . . . Deadly tackler, genius at diagnosing enemy plays . . . All-NFL six straight years, 1938–43 . . . Phi Beta Kappa scholar at Colgate . . . Earned medical degree while playing in NFL . . . Born April 11, 1916, in Pearl River, N.Y.

George, Bill—Wake Forest; linebacker, 6′ 2″, 230 lbs.; Chicago Bears 1952–65, Los Angeles Rams 1966 . . . Bears' No. 2 future draft choice, 1951 . . . One of first great middle linebackers . . . Called Bears' defensive signals eight years . . . Exceptionally astute strategist, on-the-field innovator . . . All-NFL eight years . . . Played in eight straight Pro Bowls, 1955-62 . . . Career record: 18 interceptions, 16 opposition fumbles recovered . . . 14 years service longest of any Bear . . . Born Oct. 27, 1930, in Waynesburg, Pa.

Gifford, Frank—Southern California; halfback-flanker, 6′ 1″, 195 lbs.; New York Giants 1952–60, 1962–64 . . . Hailed as a genuine triple-threat in his rookie season with the Giants . . . Likened to an old-time "iron man" . . . Played single tailback and also T-quarterback . . . Punter, defensive back, kickoff returner, you name it, Gifford could do them all . . . All-NFL in 1955, 1956, 1957, 1959 . . . NFL Most Valuable Player, 1956 . . . Born Aug. 16, 1930, in Santa Monica, Calif.

Graham, Otto—Northwestern; quarterback, 6′ 1″, 195 lbs.; Cleveland Browns (AAFC) 1946–49, Cleveland Browns (NFL) 1950–55 . . . College tailback, switched to T-quarterback in pros . . . Guided Browns to ten division or league crowns in ten years . . . Topped AAFC passers four years, NFL two years . . . All-League nine of ten years . . . Four touchdown passes in 1950 NFL title win . . . Had three touchdowns running, three touchdowns passing in 1954 NFL title game . . .

Career passes for 23,584 yards, 174 touchdowns . . . Scored 276 points on 46 touchdowns . . . Born Dec. 6, 1921, in Waukegan, Ill.

Grange, Harold (Red)—Illinois; halfback, 6′ 0″, 185 lbs.; Chicago Bears 1925, New York Yankees (AFL) 1926, New York Yankees (NFL) 1927, Chicago Bears 1929–34 . . . Three-time All-America, 1923–25 . . . Earned "Galloping Ghost" fame as whirling dervish runner at Illinois . . . Joined Bears on Thanksgiving Day, 1925 . . . Magic name produced first huge pro football crowds on 17-game barn-storming tour . . . With manager, founded rival American Football League, 1926 . . . Missed entire 1928 season with injury . . . Excelled on defense in latter years . . . Born June 13, 1903, in Forksville, Pa.

Gregg, Forrest—Southern Methodist; tackle-guard, coach, 6′ 4″, 250 lbs.; Green Bay Packers 1956, 1958–70, Dallas Cowboys 1971, coach Cleveland Browns 1975 to present . . . Member of All-NFL teams eight times . . . Member of three Super Bowl squads—Green Bay 1967 and 1968, Dallas Cowboys 1972 . . . Played in eight Pro Bowls . . . Career 15 seasons, 192 games . . . Born Oct. 18, 1933, in Birthright, Texas.

Groza, Lou—Ohio State; offensive tackle-placekicker, 6′ 3″, 250 lbs.; Cleveland Browns (AAFC) 1946–49, Cleveland Browns (NFL) 1950–59, 1961–67 . . . Last of "original" Browns to retire . . . Regular offensive tackle, 1947–59 . . . Back injury forced layoff, 1960 . . . Kicking specialist only, 1961–67 . . . All-NFL tackle six years . . . NFL Player of the Year, 1954 . . . In nine Pro Bowls . . . Last-second field goal won 1950 NFL title game . . . Scored 1,608 points in 21 years . . . Played in four AAFC, nine NFL title games . . . Born Jan. 25, 1924, in Martin's Ferry, Ohio.

Guyon, Joe—Carlisle and Georgia Tech; halfback, 6′ 1″, 180 lbs.; Canton Bulldogs (pre-NFL) 1919, Canton Bulldogs 1920, Cleveland Indians 1921, Oorang Indians 1922–23, Rock Island Independents 1924, Kansas City Cowboys 1924–25, New York Giants 1927 . . . Thorpe's teammate at Carlisle . . . All-America tackle at Georgia Tech, 1918 . . . Triple-threat halfback in pros . . . Extremely fierce competitor . . . Played with Thorpe on four NFL teams . . . Touchdown pass gave Giants win over Bears for 1927 NFL title . . . Professional baseball injury ended gridiron career, 1928 . . . Born Nov. 26, 1892, on White Earth Indian Reservation in Minnesota.

Halas, George—Illinois; founder, owner, coach, Chicago Bears starting in 1920 . . . Truly "Mr. Everything" of pro football . . . Founded Decatur Staleys, attended league organizational meeting in 1920 . . . Only person associated with NFL throughout first 50 years . . . Coached Bears for 40 seasons, won seven NFL titles . . . 325 coaching wins most by far in pro history . . . Recorded many firsts in pro coaching, administration . . . Also played end for 11 seasons . . . Born Feb. 2, 1895, in Chicago, Ill.

Healey, Ed—Dartmouth; tackle, 6′ 3″, 220 lbs.; Rock Island Independents 1920–22, Chicago Bears 1922–27 . . . Three-year end at Dartmouth . . . Left coaching job to seek tryout with Rock Island in new league,

1920 . . . Converted to tackle as pro . . . Sold to Bears for $100 in 1922—first player sale in NFL . . . Became perennial All-Pro with Bears . . . Rugged, two-way star . . . Called "most versatile tackle ever" by Halas . . . Starred in Bears' long barn-storming tour after 1925 season . . . Born Dec. 28, 1894, in Indian Orchard, Mass.

Hein, Mel—Washington State; center, 6' 2", 225 lbs.; New York Giants 1931–45 . . . Played 25 years in school, college, pros . . . 1930 All-America . . . Wrote to three NFL clubs offering his services . . . Giants bid high at $150 per game . . . 60-minute regular for 15 years . . . Injured only once, never missed a game . . . All-NFL eight straight years, 1933–40 . . . NFL's Most Valuable Player, 1938 . . . Flawless ball-snapper, powerful blocker, superior pass defender . . . Born Aug. 22, 1909, in Reading, Calif.

Henry, Wilbur Pete (Fats)—Washington & Jefferson; tackle, 6' 0", 250 lbs.; Canton Bulldogs 1920–23, 1925–26, New York Giants 1927, Pottsville Maroons 1927–28 . . . Three-year Washington and Jefferson All-America . . . Signed with Bulldogs same day NFL was organized, 1920 . . . Largest player of his time, bulwark of Canton's championship lines, 1922–23 . . . 60-minute performer, also punted, kicked field goals . . . Set NFL marks for longest punt (94 yards), longest drop-kick field goal (50 yards) . . . Born Oct. 31, 1897, at Mansfield, Ohio.

Herber, Arnie—Wisconsin and Regis College; quarterback, 6' 0", 200 lbs.; Green Bay Packers 1930–40, New York Giants 1944–45 . . . Joined Packers as 19-year-old rookie . . . Threw touchdown pass first pro game . . . Exceptional long passer . . . Teamed with Don Hutson for first great pass-catch combo . . . NFL passing leader, 1932, 1934, 1936 . . . Triggered four Packers' title teams . . . Left retirement to lead 1944 Giants to NFL Eastern crown . . . Lifetime passes gained 8,033 yards, 66 touchdowns . . . Born April 2, 1910, in Green Bay, Wis.

Hewitt, Bill—Michigan; end, 5' 11", 191 lbs.; Chicago Bears 1932–36, Philadelphia Eagles 1937–39, Phil-Pitt 1943 (that year Philadelphia and Pittsburgh played as a unit) . . . First to be named All-NFL with two teams—1933, 1934, 1936 Bears; 1937 Eagles . . . Famous for super-quick defensive charge . . . Fast, elusive, innovative on offense . . . Invented many trick plays to fool opposition . . . Middle man on forward-lateral that gave Bears 1933 NFL title . . . Played without helmet until rules change forced use . . . Born Oct. 8, 1909, in Bay City, Mich.

Hinkle, Clarke—Bucknell; fullback, 5' 11", 201 lbs.; Green Bay Packers 1932–41 . . . One of the most versatile stars in NFL annals . . . Fullback on offense, linebacker on defense . . . Famous for head-on duels with Nagurski . . . Did everything well—ran, passed, punted, place-kicked, caught passes . . . Savage blocker, vicious tackler, adept pass defender . . . All-NFL four years . . . Rushed 3,860 yards, scored 373 points, averaged 43.4 yards on punts . . . Top NFL scorer, 1938 . . . Born April 10, 1912, in Toronto, Ohio.

Hirsch, Elroy (Crazylegs)—Wisconsin and Michigan; halfback, end, 6' 2", 190 lbs.; Chicago Rockets (AAFC) 1946–48, Los Angeles Rams 1949–57 . . . Led College All-Stars upset of Rams, 1946 . . . Became key part of Rams' revolutionary "three-end" offense, 1949 . . . Led NFL in receiving, scoring, 1951 . . . Ten of 17 touchdown catches, 1951, were long-distance bombs . . . Mixed sprinter speed with halfback elusiveness . . . Named all-time NFL flanker, 1969 . . . Career record: 387 catches for 7,209 yards, 60 touchdowns; 405 points scored . . . Born June 17, 1923, in Wausau, Wis.

Hubbard, Robert (Cal)—Centenary and Geneva; tackle, 6' 5", 250 lbs.; New York Giants 1927–28, Green Bay Packers 1929–33, 1935, New York Giants 1936, Pittsburgh Pirates 1936 . . . Most feared lineman of his time . . . Rookie star with Giants' great defensive team, 1927 . . . Played end with Giants, switched to tackle with Packers . . . Anchored line for Packers' title teams, 1929–31 . . . Excelled as a blocker, backed up line on defense . . . Extremely fast, strong . . . All-NFL six years, 1928–33 . . . Named NFL's all-time offensive tackle, 1969 . . . Born Oct. 11, 1900, in Keytesville, Mo.

Hunt, Lamar—Southern Methodist; league founder, owner, Dallas Texans 1960–62, Kansas City Chiefs 1963 to present . . . Continually frustrated in attempts to gain NFL franchise . . . Developed idea, became driving force behind organization of rival American Football League, 1959 . . . Founded Dallas Texans, 1960 . . . Moved team to Kansas City in 1963; there solid club, organization provided AFL with stability, strength during AFL-NFL war . . . Spearheaded merger negotiations with NFL . . . Born Aug. 2, 1932, in El Dorado, Ark.

Hutson, Don—Alabama; end, 6' 1", 180 lbs.; Green Bay Packers 1935–45 . . . Alabama All-America, 1934 . . . NFL's first "super end" . . . Also place-kicked, played safety . . . NFL receiving champ eight years . . . Topped scorers five times . . . All-NFL nine years . . . Most Valuable Player, 1941, 1942 . . . Had 488 catches for 7,991 yards, 99 touchdowns . . . Scored 823 points . . . Caught passes in 95 straight games, 1937–45 . . . Named NFL's all-time end, 1969 . . . Born Jan. 31, 1913, in Pine Bluff, Ark.

Kiesling, Walt—St. Thomas (Minnesota); guard, 6' 2", 245 lbs.; coach, Duluth Eskimos 1926–27, Pottsville Maroons 1928, Chicago Cardinals 1929–33, Chicago Bears 1934, Green Bay Packers 1935–36, Pittsburgh Pirates 1937–38, Pittsburgh Steelers 1939–42, 1954–56 . . . 34-year career as pro player, assistant coach, head coach . . . Rugged two-way lineman with six NFL teams . . . All-NFL, 1932 . . . Starred on Bears' unbeaten juggernaut, 1934 . . . Also co-head coach of 1943 Phil–Pitt, 1944 Card–Pitt teams . . . Assistant with Packers, Steelers 14 seasons . . . Led Steelers to first winning season, 1942 . . . Born May 27, 1903, in St. Paul, Minn. . . . Died March 2, 1962, at the age of 58.

Kinard, Frank (Bruiser)—Mississippi; tackle, 6' 1", 210 lbs.; Brooklyn Dodgers 1938–44, New York Yankees (AAFC) 1946–47 . . . Two-time Mississippi All-America . . . Dodgers' second-round draft pick, 1938

. . . Small for tackle position, but tough, aggressive, fast, durable
. . . . Out with injuries only once . . . 60-minute performer . . . Out-
standing blocker, smothering tackler . . . First man to earn both All-
NFL and All-AAFC honors . . . All-NFL 1940, 1941, 1943, 1944 . . .
All-AAFC, 1946 . . . Born Oct. 23, 1914, in Pelahatchie, Miss.

Lambeau, Earl (Curly)—Notre Dame; founder, coach, Green Bay Packers
1919–49, Chicago Cardinals 1950–51, Washington Redskins 1952–53
. . . Founded pre-NFL Packers in 1919 . . . Coach-general manager
for Packers until 1949 . . . Credited with keeping pro football alive
in Green Bay . . . First coach to make forward pass an integral part
of the offense . . . 33-year NFL coaching record: 231–133–23 with six
championships in Green Bay . . . Played halfback for 11 years until
1929 . . . Born April 9, 1898, in Green Bay, Wis. . . . Died June 1,
1965, at the age of 67.

Lane, Dick (Night Train)—Scottsbluff Junior College; defensive back, 6'2"
210 lbs.; Los Angeles Rams 1952–53, Chicago Cardinals 1954–59,
Detroit Lions 1960–65 . . . Joined Rams as free agent after four
years in Army . . . Set NFL interception record (14) as rookie, 1952
. . . All-NFL five years . . . Named to six Pro Bowls . . . Selected all-
time NFL cornerback, 1969 . . . Career interception record: 68 for
1,207 yards, five touchdowns . . . Gambler on field who made spectacular plays . . . Deadly open-field tackler . . . Very fast, agile,
aggressive . . . His colorful nickname, "Night Train," derives from
playing days when he would often spin his favorite recording of the
song by the same name. Later he married singer Dinah Washington,
whose theme song, coincidentally, was "Night Train" . . . Born April
16, 1928, in Austin, Texas.

Lavelli, Dante—Ohio State; end, 6' 0", 199 lbs.; Cleveland Browns
(AAFC) 1946–49, Cleveland Browns (NFL) 1950–56 . . . Played only
three college games, served in U.S. infantry before turning pro . . .
Top AAFC receiver as rookie, scored winning touchdown in title
game, 1946 . . . Caught 11 passes in 1950 NFL championship . . .
All-AAFC, 1946–1947 . . . All-NFL 1951, 1953 . . . In three Pro Bowls
. . . Caught 386 passes for 6,488 yards, 62 touchdowns . . . Had
record 24 catches in six NFL title games . . . Nicknamed "Glue
Fingers" . . . Born Feb. 23, 1923, in Hudson, Ohio.

Layne, Bobby—Texas; quarterback, 6' 2", 190 lbs.; Chicago Bears
1948, New York Bulldogs 1949, Detroit Lions 1950–58, Pittsburgh
Steelers 1958–62 . . . Texas All-America, 1947 . . . Led Lions to
four divisional, three NFL titles in 1950s . . . Exceptional field leader,
at best in clutch . . . Last-second touchdown pass won 1953 NFL
title game . . . Also kicked field goals . . . All-NFL 1952, 1956 . . .
NFL scoring champ, 1956 . . . Career record: 1,814 completions for
26,768 yards, 196 touchdowns; 2,451 yards rushing; 372 points
scored . . . Born Dec. 19, 1926, in Santa Anna, Texas.

Lombardi, Vince—Fordham; coach, Green Bay Packers 1959–67, Washington Redskins 1969 . . . Began head coaching career at age 45 . . .
Transformed Green Bay into winner in two seasons . . . Acclaimed

NFL Man of the Decade in the 1960s . . . Gave Packers 89–29–4 record, five NFL titles, first two Super Bowl crowns in nine years . . . Led 1969 Redskins to first winning record in 14 years . . . Noted taskmaster, never had a losing season . . . Born June 11, 1913, in Brooklyn, N.Y. . . . Died Sept. 3, 1970, at the age of 57.

Luckman, Sid—Columbia; quarterback, 6′ 0″, 195 lbs.; Chicago Bears 1939–50 . . . No. 1 draft pick, 1939 . . . Columbia tailback who became first great T-quarterback as a pro . . . Performance in 73–0 title win, 1940, started mass rush to T-formation . . . Superb signal-caller, ball-handler . . . All-NFL five times, Most Valuable Player, 1943 . . . Threw seven touchdown passes one game, 1943 . . . Had five touchdown passes, 1943 title game . . . Career passing: 14,683 yards, 139 touchdowns . . . Born Nov. 21, 1916, in Brooklyn, N.Y.

Lyman, William Roy (Link)—Nebraska; tackle, 6′ 2″, 252 lbs.; Canton Bulldogs 1922–23, Cleveland Bulldogs 1924, Canton Bulldogs 1925, Frankford Yellowjackets 1925, Chicago Bears 1926–28, 1930–31, 1933–34 . . . Very agile, large for his day . . . Pioneered more sophisticated defensive play with shifting, sliding style . . . Starred on four title teams: 1922–23 Canton, 1924 Cleveland, 1933 Bears . . . Joined Bears for barn-storming tour after 1925 season . . . Played on only one losing team in 16 seasons of college, pro ball . . . Born November 30, 1898, in Table Rock, Neb.

Mara, Tim—no college; founder-administrator, New York Giants 1925–59 . . . Paid $2,500 for Giants' franchise in 1925, thus giving NFL vital showcase in nation's largest city . . . Withstood heavy financial losses until Red Grange's debut in Polo Grounds turned tide . . . Bore brunt of fight against rival AFL in 1926, and against AAFC, 1946–49 . . . Built Giants into perennial powerhouse with three NFL and eight divisional titles . . . Born July 29, 1887, in New York, N.Y. . . . Died Feb. 17, 1959, at the age of 71.

Marchetti, Gino—San Francisco; defensive end, 6′ 4″, 245 lbs.; Dallas Texans 1952, Baltimore Colts 1953–64, 1966 . . . Named top defensive end of NFL's first 50 years . . . New York Yanks' No. 2 draftee, 1952; team moved to Dallas for Gino's rookie season . . . Selected for record 11 straight Pro Bowls but missed one game because of injury suffered in 1958 NFL overtime title game . . . All-NFL seven years, 1957 to 1962, 1964 . . . All-around great defender, best known for vicious pass rushing . . . Born Jan. 2, 1927, in Smithers, W. Va.

Marshall, George Preston—Randolph-Macon; founder-administrator, Boston Braves 1932, Boston Redskins 1933–36, Washington Redskins 1937–69 . . . Acquired Boston franchise, 1932 . . . Moved team to Washington, 1937 . . . Flamboyant, controversial, innovative master showman . . . Pioneered gala halftime pageants, organized first team band . . . Sponsored progressive rules changes, splitting NFL into two divisions with title playoff, 1933 . . . Produced six divisional, two NFL titles in 1936–45 period . . . Born Oct. 11, 1897, in Grafton, W. Va. . . . Died Aug 9, 1969, at the age of 71.

Matson, Ollie—San Francisco; halfback, 6′ 2″, 220 lbs.; Chicago Cardinals

1952, 1954–58, Los Angeles Rams 1959–62, Detroit Lions 1963. Philadelphia Eagles 1964–66 . . . San Francisco U. defensive All-America . . . U.S. Olympic medal winner in track, 1952 . . . No. 1 draft pick, 1952 . . . All-NFL four years, 1954–57 . . . Traded to Rams for nine players, 1959 . . . Career ledger: 12,844 combined net yards, 5,173 yards rushing, 222 receptions, 438 points, record nine touchdowns on punt, kickoff returns . . . Played in five Pro Bowl games . . . Most Valuable Player in 1956 Pro Bowl . . . Born May 1, 1930, in Trinity, Texas.

McAfee, George—Duke; halfback, 6′ 0″, 177 lbs.; Chicago Bears 1940–41, 1945–50 . . . Phenomenal two-way star, a long-distance scoring threat on any play . . . Scored 234 points, gained 5,022 combined net yards, intercepted 21 passes in eight seasons . . . NFL punt-return champ, 1948 . . . Holds career punt-return average record—12.78 yards . . . Left-handed passer, kicker . . . Pioneered use of low-cut shoes . . . All-NFL 1941 . . . Navy service came at peak of career . . . Born March 13, 1918, in Ironton, Ohio.

McElhenny, Hugh—Washington; halfback, 6′ 1″, 198 lbs.; San Francisco 49ers 1952–60, Minnesota Vikings 1961–62, New York Giants 1963, Detroit Lions 1964 . . . Washington U. All-America . . . 49ers' No. 1 draft pick, 1952 . . . Scored 40-yard touchdown on first pro play . . . Had phenomenal first season, winning All-NFL, Rookie-of-Year honors . . . Played in six Pro Bowls . . . Most Valuable Player of 1958 Pro Bowl . . . Gained 11,375 combined net yards in 13 years . . . Record includes 5,281 yards rushing, 264 pass receptions, 360 points . . . Nicknamed "The King" . . . Born Dec. 31, 1928, in Los Angeles, Calif.

McNally, John (Blood)—St. John's (Minnesota); halfback, 6′ 0″, 185 lbs.; Milwaukee Badgers 1925–26, Duluth Eskimos 1926–27, Pottsville Maroons 1928, Green Bay Packers 1929–33, Pittsburgh Pirates 1934, Green Bay Packers 1935–36, Pittsburgh Pirates 1937–38, Pittsburgh Steelers 1939 . . . Famed "vagabond halfback," totally unpredictable fun-maker on and off the field . . . Assumed "Johnny Blood" alias from Valentino movie title, **Blood and Sand** . . . Superb runner with breakaway speed, exceptional pass receiver . . . Scored 37 touchdowns, 224 points in 15 seasons with five NFL teams . . . Official All-NFL 1931 . . . Pittsburgh player-coach, 1937–39 . . . Born Nov. 27, 1904, in New Richmond, Wis.

Michalske, August (Mike)—Penn State; guard, 6′ 0″, 209 lbs.; New York Yankees (AFL) 1926, New York Yankees (NFL) 1927–28, Green Bay Packers 1929–35, 1937 . . . All-America at Penn State . . . Rookie year with 1926 American Football League Yankees . . . Anchored Packers' championship lines, 1929, 1930, 1931 . . . 60-minute workhorse who specialized in blitzing on defense . . . Pioneered idea of using fullbacks at guard to capitalize on size, speed . . . All-NFL 1929, 1930, 1931, 1935 . . . First guard elected to Pro Football Hall of Fame . . . Born April 24, 1903, in Cleveland, Ohio.

Millner, Wayne—Notre Dame; end, 6′ 0″, 191 lbs.; Boston Redskins 1936,

Washington Redskins 1937–41, 1945 . . . Two-time Notre Dame All-America . . . Hero of famous Ohio State upset in 1935 . . . Fierce competitor in crucial games . . . Caught 55-yard, 77-yard touchdown passes in 1937 NFL championship . . . Starred on four Redskins' divisional title teams . . . Top Redskin receiver at retirement with 124 catches . . . Career interrupted by Navy service . . . Player-coach in final 1945 season . . . Born Jan. 31, 1913, in Roxbury, Mass.

Moore, Lenny—Penn State; flanker-running back, 6′ 1″, 198 lbs.; Baltimore Colts 1956–67 . . . No. 1 draft choice, 1956 . . . Rookie of Year, 1956 . . . Started as a flanker, moved to running back in 1961 . . . Amassed 11,213 combined net yards, 5,174 yards rushing, 363 receptions for 6,039 yards . . . Scored 113 touchdowns, 678 points . . . All-NFL five years . . . Played in seven Pro Bowls . . . Comeback Player of the Year, 1964 . . . Scored touchdowns in record 18 straight games, 1963–65 . . . Born Nov. 25, 1933, in Reading, Pa.

Motley, Marion—South Carolina State and Nevada; fullback, 6′ 1″, 238 lbs.; Cleveland Browns (AAFC) 1946–49, Cleveland Browns (NFL) 1950–53, Pittsburgh Steelers 1955 . . . Deadly pass blocker, peerless runner on Browns' famed trap play . . . Also played linebacker early in career . . . All-time AAFC rushing champ . . . Top NFL rusher, 1950 . . . All-AAFC three years, All-NFL in 1950 . . . Lifetime rushing: 828 carries, 4,720 yards . . . 5.7-yard career average all-time record . . . Caught 85 passes, scored 234 points in nine years . . . Played in 1951 Pro Bowl . . . Born June 5, 1920, in Leesburg, Ga.

Nagurski, Bronko—Minnesota; fullback, 6′ 2″, 225 lbs.; Chicago Bears 1930–37, 1943 . . . Joined Bears after legendary college career at Minnesota . . . Became pro football's symbol of power, ruggedness . . . A bulldozing runner on offense, a bone-crushing linebacker on defense . . . Gained 4,031 yards in nine seasons . . . All-NFL 1932, 1933, 1934 . . . His two touchdown passes clinched Bears' 1933 title win . . . Helped 1943 Bears to NFL crown after six-year retirement . . . Born Nov. 3, 1908, in Rainy River, Ontario, Canada.

Neale, Earle (Greasy)—West Virginia Wesleyan; coach, Philadelphia Eagles 1941–50 . . . Extensive college coaching career preceded entry into NFL in 1941 . . . Quickly built second-division Eagles into a contender . . . Produced three straight Eastern division crowns and NFL championships in 1948 and 1949 . . . Both NFL titles came by shutout scores . . . Using an assumed name, played end with the pre-NFL Canton Bulldogs . . . Born Nov. 5, 1891, in Parkersburg, W. Va. . . . Died Nov. 2, 1973, at the age of 81.

Nevers, Ernie—Stanford; fullback, 6′ 1″, 205 lbs.; Duluth Eskimos 1926–27, Chicago Cardinals 1929–31 . . . Stanford All-America, 1925 Rose Bowl hero . . . Lured from pro baseball career by Eskimos . . . Truly a do-everything "iron man," playing 1,714 of 1,740 minutes in 29-game season . . . Missed 1928 with injuries, returned with Cardinals, 1929 . . . Scored record 40 points in one game against Bears, 1929 . . . All-League all five NFL seasons . . . Player-coach two years each in Duluth and Chicago . . . Born June 11, 1903, in Willow River, Minn.

Nomellini, Leo—Minnesota; defensive tackle, 6' 3", 284 lbs.; San Francisco 49ers 1950–63 . . . Two-time Minnesota All-America . . . 49ers' first-ever NFL draft choice, 1950 . . . Played every 49ers game for 14 seasons, 174 regular-season and 266 pro games in all . . . Excellent defensive pass rusher, bulldozing offensive blocker . . . All-NFL six times—two years on offense, four years on defense . . . Named NFL's all-time defensive tackle . . . Played in ten Pro Bowl games . . . Born June 19, 1924, in Lucca, Italy.

Owen, Steve—Phillips University; coach, tackle, 6' 2", 235 lbs.; Kansas City Cowboys 1924–25, New York Giants 1926–53 . . . Great defensive star of the 1920s . . . Captained Giants' 1927 title team, which held foe to record low 20 points . . . Coached Giants 23 years from 1931 to 1953 . . . Coaching record: 150–100–17, eight divisional, two NFL title teams . . . A-formation offense, umbrella defense, two-platoon system among his many coaching innovations . . . Born April 21, 1898, at Cleo Springs, Okla. . . . Died May 17, 1964, at the age of 66.

Parker, Clarence (Ace)—Duke; quarterback, 5' 11", 168 lbs.; Brooklyn Dodgers 1937–41, Boston Yanks 1945, New York Yankees (AAFC) 1946 . . . All-America tailback at Duke . . . Dodgers' No. 1 draftee in 1937, but signed Philadelphia Athletics baseball contract, expecting to play pro football briefly . . . All-NFL 1938, 1940 . . . NFL's Most Valuable Player, 1940 . . . Triple-threat, two-way back who paced Dodgers to their greatest seasons in 1940, 1941 . . . Spearheaded Yankees to AAFC Eastern title in 1946 . . . Born May 17, 1912, in Portsmouth, Va.

Parker, Jim—Ohio State; guard, tackle, 6' 3", 273 lbs.; Baltimore Colts 1957–67 . . . First full-time offensive lineman named to Pro Football Hall of Fame . . . Exceptional blocker, specialized in protecting quarterback . . . All-NFL eight straight years, 1958–65 . . . Played half of 11-year career at tackle, half at guard . . . Played in eight Pro Bowl games . . . No. 1 draft choice in 1957 . . . Two-time All-America, Outland Trophy winner at Ohio State . . . Born April 3, 1934, in Macon, Ga.

Perry, Joe—Compton Junior College; fullback, 6' 0", 200 lbs.; San Francisco 49ers (AAFC) 1948–49, San Francisco 49ers (NFL) 1950–60, Baltimore Colts 1961–62, San Francisco 49ers 1963 . . . Didn't play college football . . . Spotted playing service football by pro scouts . . . Signed as free agent by 49ers . . . Extremely quick runner who earned nickname "The Jet" . . . First to gain over 1,000 yards two straight years, 1953–54 . . . Career record: 12,505 combined net yards, 9,723 yards rushing, 260 receptions, 513 points . . . Played in three Pro Bowls . . . Born Jan. 27, 1927, in Stevens, Ark.

Pihos, Pete—Indiana; end, 6' 1", 210 lbs.; Philadelphia Eagles 1947–55 . . . Indiana All-America, 1943 . . . No. 3 draft pick in 1945 even though he couldn't play until 1947 . . . 60-minute star on Eagles' title teams, 1948–49 . . . Caught winning touchdown pass in 1949 NFL championship . . . All-NFL six times in nine seasons . . . Played in first six Pro Bowls . . . Three-time NFL receiving champ, 1953–55 . . . Career record: 373 catches for 5,619 yards, 378 points . . . Born Oct. 22, 1923, in Orlando, Fla.

Ray, Hugh (Shorty)—Illinois; technical advisor on rules and supervisor of officials . . . Only 5′ 6″ and 136 lbs., but a giant of pro football . . . NFL Supervisor of Officials, 1938–52 . . . Worked tirelessly to improve officiating techniques . . . Streamlined rules to improve tempo of play, increase safety . . . Visited each team annually to educate players, coaches . . . Said to have made 300,000 notations as technical observer . . . Born Sept. 21, 1884, in Highland Park, Ill. . . . Died Sept. 16, 1956, at the age of 71.

Reeves, Dan—Georgetown; owner-administrator, Cleveland Rams 1941–45, Los Angeles Rams 1946–71 . . . One of game's greatest innovators . . . Opened up West Coast to major sports by moving Rams to Los Angeles, 1946 . . . Experiments in game TV paved way for modern NFL policies . . . First postwar NFL owner to sign a black (Kenny Washington), 1946 . . . First to employ full-time scouting staff . . . Born June 30, 1912, in New York, N.Y. . . . Died April 15, 1971, at the age of 58.

Robustelli, Andy—Arnold College; defensive end, 6′ 0″, 230 lbs.; Los Angeles Rams 1951–55, New York Giants 1956–64 . . . Rams' 19th round draft pick, 1951 . . . On winning team 13 of 14 years . . . In eight NFL title games, seven Pro Bowls . . . All-NFL seven years—two with Rams, five with Giants . . . Named NFL's top player by Maxwell Club, 1962 . . . Exceptionally smart, quick, strong . . . Superb pass rusher . . . Recovered 22 opponents' fumbles in career . . . Missed only one game in 14 years . . . Born Dec. 6, 1925, in Stamford, Conn.

Rooney, Arthur J. (Art)—Georgetown; founder-administrator, Pittsburgh Steelers (Pirates), starting in 1933 . . . One of most revered of all sports personalities . . . Bought new Pittsburgh Pirates' franchise for $2,500 in 1933 . . . Renamed team Steelers in 1938 . . . His faith in pro football a guiding light during the dark Depression years . . . Startled NFL with $15,000 signing of fabled Whizzer White in 1938 . . . Organized, operated Western Pennsylvania semipro grid teams before 1933 . . . Born Jan. 27, 1901, in Coulterville, Pa.

Sayers, Gale—Kansas; halfback, 6′ 0″, 200 lbs.; Chicago Bears 1965–71 . . . All-America at Kansas U., where he rushed for 6.5 average yards over three years . . . Brilliant rookie season in 1965 when named All-NFL running back and Rookie of the Year . . . Electrified fans with spectacular runbacks of kickoffs and punts . . . Suffered left knee injury in 1968, then came back in 1969 to rush 1,032 yards for the season, first time on record any NFL running back hit 1,000-plus yards coming off knee surgery . . . Subsequent injury to right knee, and also to one foot, forced his retirement at age 28 . . . He had become an NFL legend in his own time . . . Born May 30, 1943, in Wichita, Kan.

Schmidt, Joe—Pittsburgh; linebacker, 6′ 0″, 222 lbs.; Detroit Lions

1953–65; coach, Detroit Lions 1967–72 . . . Pittsburgh All-America, 1952 . . . Lions' No. 7 draft pick, 1953 . . . Mastered new middle linebacking position which evolved in the 1950s . . . A superb field leader . . . Exceptional at diagnosing foe's plays . . . All-NFL eight years . . . Played in Pro Bowl nine straight years, 1955–63 . . Team captain nine years . . . Lions' Most Valuable Player four times . . . Had 24 career interceptions . . . Born Jan. 18, 1932, in Pittsburgh, Pa.

Starr, Bart—Alabama; quarterback, 6' 1", 195 lbs.; Green Bay Packers 1956–71; coach, Green Bay Packers 1975 to present . . . Finished pro playing career in 1971 with 57.4 pass-completion average, one of NFL's highest career marks . . . Considered prototype of ideal field general . . . Cool, unflappable, calculating in reading enemy defenses . . . Threw 294 consecutive passes at one point in his career without an interception . . . NFL's leading passer, 1962, 1964, 1966 . . . Born Jan. 9, 1934, in Montgomery, Ala.

Stautner, Ernie—Boston College; defensive tackle, 6' 2", 235 lbs.; Pittsburgh Steelers 1950–63 . . . No. 2 draft pick, 1950 . . . Bulwarked strong Pittsburgh defense for 14 years . . . Saw spot service at offensive guard . . . Known for excellent mobility, burning desire, extreme ruggedness, unusual durability . . . All-NFL 1956, 1958 . . . Played in nine Pro Bowls, winning Best Lineman Award, 1957 . . . Recovered 21 opponents' fumbles, scored three safeties in career . . . Born April 20, 1925, in Calm, Bavaria.

Strong, Ken—New York University; halfback, 5' 11", 210 lbs.; Staten Island Stapletons 1929–32, New York Giants 1933–35, New York Yanks (AFL) 1936–37, New York Giants 1939, 1944–47 . . . N.Y.U. All-America, 1928 . . . Excelled in every phase of game—blocking, running, passing, punting, place-kicking, defense . . . Scored 17 points to pace Giants to 1934 title . . . All-NFL 1934 . . . Scored 64 points to top NFL, 1933 . . . Served as place-kicking specialist only, 1944–47 . . . Led NFL in field goals, 1944 . . . Scored 479 points in 14 NFL years . . . Born Aug. 6, 1906, in New Haven, Conn.

Stydahar, Joe—West Virginia; tackle, 6' 4", 230 lbs.; Chicago Bears 1936–42, 1945–46 . . . Bears' No. 1 choice in first-ever NFL draft, 1936 . . . 60-minute performer who bulwarked Bears' line in famous "Monsters of the Midway" era . . . Played on five divisional and three NFL championship teams . . . Named to official All-NFL team four years, 1937–40 . . . Often played without helmet early in career . . . Later coached 1950–52 Rams, 1953–54 Cardinals . . . Born March 3, 1912, in Kaylor, Pa.

Taylor, Jim—Louisiana State; fullback, 6' 0", 216 lbs.; Green Bay Packers 1958–66, New Orleans Saints 1967 . . . L.S.U. All-America, 1957 . . . Packers' No. 2 draft pick, 1958 . . . 1,000-yard rusher five straight years, 1960–64 . . . Rushed for 8,597 yards, caught 225 passes, amassed 10,538 combined net yards, scored 558 points . . . Led NFL rushers, scorers, had record 19 touchdowns rushing in 1962 . . . Excelled in 1962 NFL title game . . . Ferocious runner, rugged blocker, prime disciple of "run to daylight" doctrine . . . Born Sept. 20, 1935, in Baton Rouge, La.

Thorpe, Jim—Carlisle; halfback, 6′ 1″, 190 lbs.; Canton Bulldogs (pre-NFL) 1915–17, 1919, Canton Bulldogs 1920, Cleveland Indians 1921, Oorang Indians 1922–23, Toledo Maroons 1923, Rock Island Independents 1924, New York Giants 1925, Canton Bulldogs 1926, Chicago Cardinals 1928 . . . All-America halfback at Carlisle, 1912 Olympic decathlon champion . . . First big-name athlete to play pro football, signing with pre-NFL Canton Bulldogs in 1915 . . . Named "The Legend" on the all-time NFL team . . . Voted top American athlete of first half of 20th century . . . First president of American Professional Football Association, 1920 . . . Born May 28, 1888, in Prague, Okla.

Tittle, Y. A.—Louisiana State; quarterback, 6′ 0″, 200 lbs.; Baltimore Colts (AAFC) 1948–49, Baltimore Colts (NFL) 1950, San Francisco 49ers 1951–60, New York Giants 1961–64 . . . AAFC Rookie of the Year, 1948 . . . Joined 49ers in 1951 after Colts disbanded . . . Career record: 2,427 completions, 33,070 yards, 242 touchdowns, 13 games over 300 yards passing . . . Paced 1961, 1962, 1963 Giants to division titles . . . Threw 33 touchdown passes in 1962, 36 in 1963 . . . NFL's Most Valuable Player in 1961, 1963 . . . All-NFL 1957, 1962, 1963 . . . Played in six Pro Bowls . . . Born Oct. 24, 1926, in Marshall, Texas.

Trafton, George—Notre Dame; center, 6′ 2″, 235 lbs.; Decatur Staleys 1920, Chicago Staleys 1921, Chicago Bears 1922–32 . . . Turned pro after one year at Notre Dame . . . First center to play for Staleys . . . 60-minute star, excelled on defense . . . First center to rove on defense . . . First to snap ball with one hand . . . Colorful, aggressive, smart . . . Defiantly wore No. 13 . . . Nicknamed "The Brute" . . . Named top NFL center of the 1920s . . . Born Dec. 6, 1896, in Chicago, Ill.

Trippi, Charley—Georgia; halfback, quarterback, 6′ 0″, 185 lbs.; Chicago Cardinals 1944–55 . . . Cards' No. 1 future draft pick, 1945 . . . Georgia All-America, 1946 . . . Played in four Chicago All-Star games as collegian . . . $100,000 signee during AAFC-NFL war, 1947 . . . Final link in Cards' famed "Dream Backfield" . . . Scored two touchdowns in 1947 NFL title win . . . All-NFL 1948 . . . Extremely versatile —played halfback five years, quarterback two years, defense two years . . . Born Dec. 14, 1922, in Pittston, Pa.

Tunnell, Emlen—Toledo University, Iowa; defensive back, 6′ 1″, 200 lbs.; New York Giants 1948–58, Green Bay Packers 1959–61 . . . Signed as free agent, 1948 . . . Known as Giants' "offense on defense," keyed famous "umbrella defense" of 1950s . . . Gained more yards (923) on interceptions, kick returns than NFL rushing leader, 1952 . . . Set career marks in interceptions (79 for 1,282 yards), punt returns (258 for 2,209 yards) . . . All-NFL four years . . . Played in nine Pro Bowls . . . Named NFL's all-time safety, 1969 . . . Born March 29, 1925, in Bryn Mawr, Pa.

Turner, Clyde (Bulldog)—Hardin-Simmons; center, 6′ 2″, 235 lbs.; Chicago Bears 1940–52 . . . Hardin-Simmons Little All-America . . . Bears' No. 1 draft pick, 1940 . . . Rookie starter at age of 20 . . . Terrific blocker, superb pass defender, flawless ball-snapper . . . Had halfback speed . . . Led NFL with eight interceptions in 1942 . . . Stole 16 passes in career . . . All-NFL six times . . . Anchored four NFL championship teams . . . Intercepted four passes in five NFL title games . . . Born Nov. 10, 1919, in Sweetwater, Texas.

Van Brocklin, Norm—Oregon; quarterback, 6′ 1″, 190 lbs.; Los Angeles Rams 1949–57, Philadelphia Eagles 1958–60, coach, Minnesota Vikings 1961–66, coach, Atlanta Falcons 1968–74 . . . Oregon All-America, 1948 . . . Rams' No. 4 draftee, 1949 . . . Led NFL in passing three years, punting twice . . . Career mark: 1,553 completions for 23,611 yards, 173 touchdowns . . . 73-yard pass gave Rams 1951 title . . . Passed for 554 yards in one game, 1951 . . . Led Eagles to 1960 NFL crown . . . NFL's Most Valuable Player, 1960 . . . Threw eight touchdown passes in eight Pro Bowl games . . . Born March 15, 1926, in Eagle Butte, S.D.

Van Buren, Steve—Louisiana State; halfback, 6′ 1″, 200 lbs.; Philadelphia Eagles 1944–51 . . . No. 1 draft pick, 1944 . . . All-NFL four of first five years . . . Provided Eagles a battering-ram punch . . Won NFL rushing title four times . . . 1944 punt-return, 1945 kickoff-return champ . . . Scored only touchdown in 7–0 title win, 1948 . . . Rushed for record 196 yards in 1949 finale . . . Career marks: 5,860 yards rushing, 464 points scored . . . Surpassed 1,000 yards in rushing twice . . . Born Dec. 28, 1920, in La Ceiba, Honduras.

Waterfield, Bob—UCLA; quarterback, 6′ 2″, 200 lbs.; Cleveland Rams 1945, Los Angeles Rams 1946–52 . . . Cleveland Rams' No. 3 future draft pick, 1944 . . . NFL's Most Valuable Player as rookie, 1945 . . . Two touchdown passes keyed Rams' 1945 title win . . . All-NFL three years, NFL passing champ twice . . . Career marks include 11,849 yards, 98 touchdowns passing; 573 points on 13 touchdowns, 315 PATs, 60 field goals, 42.4-yard punting average . . . Also played defense first four years, intercepted 20 passes . . . Born July 26, 1920, in Elmira, N.Y.

Willis, Bill (Deacon)—Ohio State; offensive and defensive guard, 6′ 2½″, 215 lbs.; Cleveland Browns (AAFC) 1946–49, Cleveland Browns (NFL) 1950–53 . . . All-America at tackle for Ohio State . . . Coached at Kentucky State College for three years . . . Joined the Cleveland Browns (AAFC) in 1946, remained with them for four years, and was named All-AAFC three times . . . All-NFL middle guard 1951, 1952, 1953 . . . In defensive line play, he uncoiled out of a crouch, moving at 70 miles per hour and specializing in dumping opposing centers in the quarterback's lap . . . Born Oct. 5, 1921, in Columbus, Ohio.

Wojciechowicz, Alex—Fordham; center-linebacker, 6′ 0″, 235 lbs.; Detroit Lions 1938–46, Philadelphia Eagles 1949–50 . . . Two-time Fordham All-America, center of famed "Seven Blocks of Granite" line . . . Lions' No. 1 draft pick, 1938 . . . Played four games first week as pro . . . Authentic "iron man" for eight and a half years with

Lions . . . Joined Eagles as defensive specialist strictly . . . Known for exceptionally wide center stance . . . Outstanding pass defender with 16 lifetime interceptions . . . Born Aug. 12, 1915, in South River, N.J.

OFFICIATING IN THE NFL

- Let's pity the poor passer—a consideration of the question of whether there should be a roughing-the-passer penalty

- Names and civilian occupations of 1977 NFL officials

LET'S PITY THE POOR PASSER

By Norman MacLean

The most important part of contract negotiations by an NFL quarterback may no longer be the dollar figures on the bottom line. It might be the length of the contract, whether it's guaranteed in case of injury, and the extent of medical benefits provided. Buffalo's O. J. Simpson's impressions are to the point:

"My most vivid memory of the 1976 season wasn't of the great day when I broke the all-time single game rushing record—it was of our quarterback, Joe Ferguson, writhing on the ground with three or four broken bones in his back after being clobbered. I really wondered for a second or two if the whole thing was really worth it," says O. J. "If football is part show business, why isn't something done to protect and help the quarterbacks who are the key to the whole show, the whole offense?"

Simpson has a valid point. Last season went down as the year NFL whistle-tooters blew holding calls at a fantastic pace, in some games entirely disrupting the normal flow of the game and creating complete chaos among offensive linemen, who no longer could defend their passer in the "normal" manner—i.e., with use of their hands in some form or other.

By the eighth week of the season, eight NFL regular quarterbacks had been disabled—and they were still dropping like tenpins after that. As late as the playoffs, the New England Patriots, who lamented that they were robbed by the officials in their loss to the Oakland Raiders, were dead wrong in their complaint that a tipped pass gave "Sugar Bear" Hamilton the right to attempt to dismember Raider quarterback Ken Stabler.

"The rule in the Hamilton-Stabler case is quite clear," says Art McNally, the NFL's Supervisor of Officials. "If you strike the passer with a fist or forearm, it is a penalty, and whether you tip the ball or not has nothing to do with it. When you club a guy in the head, the referee has no choice but to call it."

Hamilton was penalized and the call had a lot to do with the final score in Oakland's 24–21 win over New England. But so often, it seems, just such an infraction isn't called. The roughing-the-kicker situation on fourth-down punts is minutely scrutinized, while almost every other play situation involving the quarterback seems to go unnoticed. At one point last season, no fewer than eight NFL quarterbacks were shelved with injuries.

"Our game is deteriorating as a public spectacle because of the zone defense," says Roger Staubach, the Dallas passer. "We really don't get to connect with the bomb very often any more. Something should be done to give the passer more time—and something should be done to stop the obvious 'get the passer' type of blitz."

Staubach broke a knuckle last season, missed a few games, and didn't play as well as usual when he returned. His under-par work was the main reason the Dallas attack sputtered and finally died in the playoffs —and his injury was the main factor contributing to this.

Ken Stabler played most of the season with a bad knee, Steve Bartkowski was knocked out for more than half the year with a knee, and Ron Jaworksi and

James Harris both were seriously hurt when the Rams' run-oriented line couldn't protect them. That's what gave Rhodes scholar Pat Haden his chance to become L.A.'s number-one player. Archie Manning missed most of the season at New Orleans, and seemingly had become blitz-shy. Terry Bradshaw was out a major portion of the year with a neck injury (leading to the discovery that rookie Mike Kruczek wasn't that bad a quarterback if he followed Chuck Noll's instructions). Mike Phipps tore up his shoulder, the Giants' Craig Morton and backup Norm Snead both were kayoed, Billy Kilmer's availability was almost always in doubt due to injuries—and so it went.

"Why can't a penalty be assessed against a lineman if he hits the passer *after* the ball is released?" asks Snead, a 16-year NFL veteran. "With my knees, that would be a help. And I think it would help a scrambler, like Fran Tarkenton used to be, to give a little head fake and take off. Maybe a guy like Greg Landry, I mean Greg Landry before he got hurt so often, would still be running for big yardage that way. And it certainly would excite the fans."

True, such a rule might create a little hesitation on the part of big linemen who cruise in and ram 270 pounds of hurtling body at the passer, who is usually at least 60 pounds lighter. In order to protect the quarterback, offensive linemen have generally used their hands more forcefully and deliberately in trying to stop the onrushing defensive linemen. Use of the hands in such situations, of course, brings on penalties—the offensive team usually sustains a loss of between 47 and 53 penalty yards a game because of holding.

But last season, during the period between the third and seventh weeks, holding calls almost got completely out of hand. With the blitz against the quarterbacks reaching unprecedented fury, the average number of holding calls jumped nearly 25 percent. And the offensive team was surrendering nearly 70 yards a game for holding penalties, much to the moans and groans of offensive linemen who insisted they were doing nothing different than before.

"I'm still doing the same thing I always did with my hands and arms," roared John Hicks of the Giants following one penalty-laden debacle. "But now it's a penalty!"

Undoubtedly there was a conscious effort to enforce the holding rules more stringently between the third and seventh weeks. The proliferating injuries to quarterbacks were uppermost in the NFL's thinking. But the whole thing boomeranged. The officials all of a sudden began cracking down on offensive linemen who were zealously trying to protect their quarterback by restraining the blitzers. But confusion reigned when the offensive linemen became uncertain of what was accepted and legal and what wasn't. And the quarterback rushers proceeded to have a field day. Then, during the eighth week, the strict interpretations apparently were relaxed, or at least it seemed so to some observers, and things returned to normal—more or less.

If NFL games have been becoming more boring of late, it would speed things up considerably and add lots of interest if penalties for roughing the passer were spelled out and included in the rules. There'd probably be more teams like the St. Louis Cardinals, known to some as the "cardiac Cards," because they still have that old-time "come-from-behind" zest in the fourth quarter.

"I would love a roughing-the-passer penalty," says Cardinal quarterback Jim Hart. "We could put it up long and see what happens. I could stand back there and either dump it off to Terry Metcalf or hang it long in the seams of the zone."

Hart, always thinking attack, suggests that the NFL should outlaw the zone defense entirely. And Moses Levy, general manager of the Montreal Alouettes of the Canadian Football League, attended two New York Giants games late in the 1976 season and came away with almost the same idea. Said he: "I'm appalled at the very little action fans get in some of these games. In the CFL we have the mandatory punt return, and with three downs our game is more wide open and there is a lot more passing. The wider field and deeper end zone also make passing plays easier to complete and open up the entire concept of the attack. In my opinion, the CFL has more action than the NFL."

Thus, the NFL faces trouble on two fronts. The violence level rises to the point where the gunners in the front-line trenches do real damage to the quarterback—the focal point of the attack. And the excitement dies when the quarterback is knocked out. When he's hurt things trail off—straight hand-offs and routine running plays become the norm as the QB backup takes over. That was the way Pittsburgh's backup, Mike Kruczek, did his job: just hand the ball to Franco Harris and get out of the way. Effective, but just about as interesting as Woody Hayes' three-yards-and-a-cloud-of-dust theory.

There's also trouble with the zone defense—which Jim Hart wants done away with altogether. Even with its top attractions healthy and in action, the zone defenders are managing to make the passing game a bit dull. The rule changes that limited the point-making possibilities of field goals did help speed up the game's tempo, but the zone still holds it down.

Is violence hurting the NFL package? Not really, from the fan's standpoint. But it may be from the point of holding down the scores and injuring vital people like quarterbacks and premier ball carriers.

Chicago Bears' general manager Jim Finks notes that "Meshing an attack is much harder than teaching defense. And when one of the key offensive cogs is hurt, the attack often misfires. Look what happens when a center gets banged up and misses a play or two. Frequently the reserve center and the quarterback misconnect, and there's a fumble. Running backs are more interchangeable, but replacing a quarterback almost always means a less adventuresome attack."

After the Oakland-New England playoff game, Raider linebacker Phil Villapiano had his own analysis of what happened. "We gave them a little Raider-style football. We attacked them, held them, grabbed them, smacked them. That's why we won. We did what we wanted—and they got the penalties, or so it seemed."

That's an amazing statement, since the only real blemish on the Raiders' season was the early-season whomping they took in New England (they lost to the tune of 47–17). While the Raider-Patriot playoff game was exciting, many games in which one team physically takes charge become defensive struggles with one team maintaining control.

Setting up a rule whereby the passer is almost forbidden territory would help the attack, which needs help, and would lend itself to more scoring, which fans like. The defense is now ahead of the attack, especially in the lower-level clubs in the league, and the entire NFL is suffering as a result. No one likes the quarterback, usually, and everyone wants to pot-shoot him, but the show grinds to a halt without him.

"With legal problems out of the way, now we need to get to work on the excitement quota in our games," says Al Davis, the majority owner of the Super Bowl Raiders. "A roughing-the-passer penalty might work, and boy, would I love to see Stabler working under that rule. Come to think of it, I shudder to think what would happen to us without Stabler. It would ruin our season—we would have no long striking capabilities."

Taken all in all, the pressure for adoption of a roughing-the-passer rule is very real, and can be expected to increase if quarterbacks continue to turn up on the casualty lists the way they did last year.

1977
NATIONAL FOOTBALL LEAGUE
OFFICIALS

REFEREES

Barth, Gene—No. 14; St. Louis University; oil company president, Florissant, Missouri (7th year)

Cashion, Marion—No. 43; Texas A&M; insurance company board chairman, Bryan, Texas (6th year)

Dreith, Ben—No. 12; Colorado State University; high school teacher, Denver (18th year)

Frederic, Bob—No. 71; University of Colorado; owner of printing and lithography company, Denver (10th year)

Haggerty, Pat—No. 40; Colorado State College; teacher and coach in Denver public schools (13th year)

Heberling, Chuck—No. 46; Washington & Jefferson; sales counselor for consumer products company, Pittsburgh (13th year)

Jorgensen, Dick—No. 60; University of Wisconsin; bank vice-president, Champaign, Illinois (10th year)

Lepore, Cal—No. 72; University of Alabama; youth services officer, Chicago (12th year)

McCarter, Gordon—No. 48; Western Reserve; university registrar, Cleveland (11th year)

Silva, Fred—No. 81; San Jose State; sales manager for consumer sales company, San Jose, California (11th year)

Tunney, Jim—No. 32; Occidental College; superintendent of Los Angeles school district (18th year)

Ulman, Bernie—No. 6; University of Maryland; owner of sporting goods company, Bel Air, Maryland (15th year)

Wedge, Don—No. 28; Ohio Wesleyan; general sales manager, Troy, Ohio (6th year)

Wyant, Fred—No. 75; West Virginia University; insurance and investment broker, Star City, West Virginia (12th year)

UMPIRES

Connell, Joe—No. 57; University of Pittsburgh; district sales manager for steel company, Pittsburgh (26th year)

Conway, Al—No. 27; West Point; assistant vice-president of paint and chemical company, Kansas City (9th year)

Demmas, Art—No. 78; Vanderbilt; insurance company general agent, Nashville (10th year)

Hamilton, Dave—No. 42; University of Utah; assistant to medical director, Atascadero, California (3rd year)

Harder, Pat—No. 88; University of Wisconsin; salesman, Milwaukee, and former NFL player (12th year)

Hart, Gerry—No. 62; Kansas State; general manager of sales for steel company, Birmingham, Michigan (10th year)

Hensley, Tom—No. 19; University of Tennessee; transportation sales representative, Knoxville, Tennessee (11th year)

Keck, John—No. 67; Cornell College; petroleum distributor, Des Moines (6th year)

Kramer, Tony—No. 50; University of Dayton; transportation sales manager, Centerville, Ohio (3rd year)

Morcroft, Ralph—No. 15; Ohio State; general manager, minor league baseball team, Hollywood, Florida (17th year)

Palazzi, Lou—No. 51; Penn State; landscape architect, Scranton, Pennsylvania, and former NFL player (26th year)

Ross, Bill—No. 68; University of Missouri; assistant professor at a college in Kansas City (5th year)

Sinkovitz, Frank—No. 20; Duke; safety specialist, Harrisburg, Pennsylvania, and former NFL player (20th year)

Trepinski, Paul—No. 22; University of Toledo; real estate salesman, Toledo, Ohio (15th year)

Wells, Gordon—No. 89; Occidental College; teacher and track and cross-country coach, Huntington Beach, California (6th year)

HEAD LINESMEN

Bergman, Jerry—No. 17; Duquesne University; product sales manager, Pittsburgh (12th year)

Dodez, Ray—No. 74; Wooster; telephone company executive, Columbus, Ohio (10th year)

Glover, Frank—No. 85; Morris Brown College; personnel specialist, Atlanta (6th year)

Hawk, Dave—No. 66; Southern Methodist; vice-president of manufacturing company, Corsicana, Texas (6th year)

Kragseth, Norm—No. 65; Northwestern; teacher and coach, Minneapolis (4th year)

Mace, Gil—No. 90; Westminster (Pa.); sales manager, Library, Pennsylvania (4th year)

Marion, Ed—No. 26; University of Pennsylvania; vice-president, pension marketing, insurance company, Portland, Maine (18th year)

Miles, Leo—No. 35; University of Virginia; university athletic director, Washington, D.C., and former NFL player (9th year)

Murphy, George—No. 30; Southern California; industrial consultant, Coronado, California (18th year)

Peters, Walt—No. 44; Indiana State; insurance agent, King of Prussia, Pennsylvania (10th year)

Ross, Bill—No. 68; University of Missouri; collegiate assistant professor, Kansas City (5th year)

Sabato, Al—No. 10; University of Cincinnati; director of school district food services, Cincinnati (18th year)

Seeman, Jerry—No. 70; Winona State; public school administrator, Fridley, Minnesota (3rd year)

Sonnenberg, Ray—No. 79; St. Louis University; YMCA executive director, St. Louis (11th year)

Toler, Burl—No. 37; University of San Francisco; associate director of adult and community education, San Francisco Community College District (13th year)

Veteri, Tony—No. 36; special sales representative for distiller's company, Mount Vernon, New York (17th year)

LINE JUDGES

Alford, Bruce—No. 24; Texas Christian; owner of building materials company, Fort Worth, Texas, and former NFL player (18th year)

Beeks, Bob—No. 59; Lincoln University; police community relations officer, St. Louis (10th year)

Cathcart, Royal—No. 16; University of California–Santa Barbara; regional sales manager for medical products company, Irvine, California, and former NFL player (7th year)

Fette, Jack—No. 39; sales division manager for sporting goods company, Kansas City (13th year)

Holst, Art—No. 33; Knox College; professional speaker and president/owner of promotivation company, Peoria, Illinois (14th year)

Jacob, Vince—No. 11; wireman, special apparatus; Verona, Pennsylvania (3rd year)

Johnson, Jack—No. 54; Pacific Lutheran University; athletics and recreation coordinator, Tacoma, Washington (2nd year)

Look, Dean—No. 49; Michigan State; insurance salesman, Lansing, Michigan (6th year)

Markbreit, Jerry—No. 9; University of Illinois; regional sales manager, advertising, Skokie, Illinois (2nd year)

McElwee, Bob—No. 95; construction company president, Haddenfield, New Jersey (2nd year)

Orr, Don—No. 77; Vanderbilt; machine company executive vice-president, Nashville (7th year)

Reynolds, Bill—No. 53; West Chester State; high school teacher and coach, Springfield, Pennsylvania (3rd year)

Swanson, Bill—No. 38; Lake Forest College; bank vice-president in marketing, Libertyville, Illinois (14th year)

Vandenberg, Ralph—No. 47; University of Cincinnati; operations manager for consumer goods company, Cincinnati (18th year)

BACK JUDGES

Douglas, Ray—No. 5; University of Baltimore; supervisor and inventory control manager, Baltimore (10th year)

Fouch, John—No. 45; Southern California; sales manager for distributing company, Redlands, California (12th year)

Hagerty, Ligouri—No. 63; Syracuse University; manager of sporting goods company, Glen Burnie, Maryland (2nd year)

Javie, Stan—No. 29; Georgetown; paint company vice-president, Philadelphia (27th year)

Kelleher, Tom—No. 25; Holy Cross; vice-president, marketing division, Miami (18th year)

Klemmer, Grover—No. 8; University of California; teacher, department chairman, and athletic director, San Francisco Board of Education (15th year)

Knight, Pat—No. 73; Southern Methodist; lumber company general manager, San Antonio, Texas, and former NFL player (5th year)

Marshall, Vern—No. 94; Linfield College; counseling coordinator, Portland (2nd year)

Parry, Dave—No. 64; Wabash College; high school athletic director, Michigan City, Indiana (3rd year)

Poole, James—No. 92; San Diego State; college physical education teacher, Westminster, California (3rd year)

Porter, Don—No. 3; East Los Angeles College; executive director of an amateur softball association, Oklahoma City (2nd year)

Reed, Charles—No. 41; Whittier College; recreation director, Los Angeles (3rd year)

Rice, Bob—No. 80; Denison University; teacher and coach, Cleveland (9th year)

Steffen, John—No. 61; University of Minnesota; airline director of engineering administration, Miami (10th year)

Tompkins, Ben—No. 52; University of Texas; attorney-at-law, Fort Worth, Texas (7th year)

FIELD JUDGES

Cole, Jimmy—No. 86; Memphis State; land developer, Germantown, Tennessee (8th year)

Dolack, Dick—No. 31; Ferris State; pharmacist, Muskegon, Michigan (12th year)

Ferguson, Richard—No. 87; West Virginia University; assistant commissioner of high school athletics, San Jose, California (4th year)

Graf, Fritz—No. 34; Western Reserve; area manager for medical and hospital equipment company, Akron, Ohio (18th year)

Kingzett, Bill—No. 4; Hiram College; athletic coordinator, Lyndhurst, Ohio (3rd year)

Lewis, Bob—No. 18; Air Force base chief of operations, San Antonio, Texas (2nd year)

Mallette, Pat—No. 82; University of Nebraska; vocational director, Blair, Nebraska, Public School System (9th year)

Merrifield, Ed—No. 76; University of Missouri; machinery territorial manager, Leawood, Kansas (3rd year)

Musser, Charley—No. 55; North Carolina State; oil company sales manager, Naperville, Illinois (13th year)

O'Brien, Bill—No. 83; Indiana University; university department chairman and professor, Carbondale, Illinois (11th year)

Stanley, Bill—No. 91; University of Redlands; college athletic director, Whittier, California (4th year)

Swearingen, Fred—No. 21; Ohio University; real estate investment broker, Carlsbad, California (18th year)

Terzian, Armen—No. 23; Southern California; physical education director, San Francisco School District (17th year)

Vaughan, Jack—No. 93; Mississippi State; owner of distributing company, Ponchatonia, Louisiana (2nd year)

Wortman, Bob—No. 84; Findlay College; insurance agency owner, Findlay, Ohio (12th year)

NOTE: As the 1977 season nears its opening kickoffs, changes are still being made in the roster of NFL officials. At least two retirements have been recorded—those of referee Tom Bell (after 15 years) and line judge Bob Baur (after 14 years). New officials announced prior to the season are Don Hakes (No. 96), a graduate of Bradley University who is high school dean of students in South Holland, Illinois; and Nathan Jones (No. 97), a graduate of Lewis & Clark College, a high school principal in Portland, Oregon.